A Fallen Idol Is Still a God

A Fallen Idol
Is Still a God

LERMONTOV AND THE
QUANDARIES OF
CULTURAL TRANSITION

Elizabeth Cheresh Allen

STANFORD UNIVERSITY PRESS
STANFORD, CALIFORNIA
2007

Stanford University Press
Stanford, California

©2007 by the Board of Trustees of the Leland Stanford Junior University. All rights re-
served.

This book has been published with the assistance of a grant from the Madge Miller Research Fund of Bryn Mawr College.

Printed in the United States of America on acid-free, archival-quality paper

Library of Congress Cataloging-in-Publication Data

Allen, Elizabeth Cheresh, 1951-

A fallen idol is still a god : Lermontov and the quandaries of cultural transition / Elizabeth
Cheresh Allen.

p. cm.

Includes bibliographical references and index.

ISBN-13: 978-0-8047-5370-8 (cloth : alk. paper)

ISBN-10: 0-8047-5370-9 (cloth : alk. paper)

1. Lermontov, Mikhail IUr'evich, 1814-1841--Criticism and interpretation. 2. Romanti-
cism--Russia. 3. Lermontov, Mikhail Iur'evich, 1814-1841. Geroi nashego vremeni. I. Title.

PG3337.L47R73 2007

891.71'3--dc22   2006023423

Typeset by Bruce Lundquist in 11/14 Adobe Garamond

To James

Contents

Preface

In 1837, the twenty-three-year-old Russian author Mikhail Lermontov wrote an untitled two-quatrain lyric poem now familiar to most students of Russian literature:

> We have parted, but I treasure
> Your portrait in my heart.
> Like a pale phantom of better times
> It delights my soul.
>
> And though devoted to new passions,
> I could not cease to love it,
> For an abandoned church is still a church,
> A fallen idol is still a god.
>
> Расстались мы; но твой портрет
> Я на груди своей храню:
> Как бледный призрак лучших лет,
> Он душу радует мою.
>
> И новым преданный страстям,
> Я разлюбить его не мог:
> Так храм оставленный – всё храм,
> Кумир поверженный – всё бог! (1: 382)[1]

Although this poem expresses a lover's feelings for his beloved, it contains a metaphor that more generally captures Lermontov's relation to the cultural movement with which he is most often identified: Romanticism. For his works consistently express an attitude toward Romanticism as a "fallen idol" that to Lermontov was nevertheless "still a god." In other words, Romanticism might have lost its authority to command unquestioned allegiance, but it still merited a certain reverence and respect. Those works thus retain many of the trappings of Romanticism, incorporating numerous Romantic images and ideas, but they do not wholly affirm those images and ideas. Lermontov could find inspiration in Romanticism, but he could not find unequivocal conviction. So he was left with ambivalence.

This ambivalence and the metaphor of the fallen idol that mirrors it betoken not just a particular attitude toward Romanticism. They also reflect Lermontov's distinctive place in literary history as an author at the time when Romanticism was on the wane but when nothing had emerged yet to replace it. No one exemplified that transitional time more suggestively, or portrayed the cultural quandaries it posed more provocatively, than Lermontov himself. For whether he knew it or not, Mikhail Lermontov was an artist of the twilight of Romanticism, and he filled his works with the shadows of its passing.

Acknowledgments and Note on the Text

The publication of this book was supported by a grant from the Madge Miller Research Fund of Bryn Mawr College, for which I am grateful.

I also wish to express my gratitude to a number of people who helped bring this book to fruition. Caryl Emerson and Gary Saul Morson gave supremely meticulous readings to different drafts of the manuscript, leading me to clarify key ideas and to enhance rhetorical precision throughout. William Mills Todd, III, responded at length to several drafts, offering characteristically erudite and insightful comments that prompted further research and revision. His writings on the early decades of the nineteenth century in Russia, along with those of Lewis Bagby, Lauren G. Leighton, and John Mersereau, Jr., were instrumental in developing my interpretation of Russian Romanticism and Lermontov's relationship to it. More generally, but no less importantly, I am indebted to my most influential teachers at Yale—Robert Louis Jackson, Victor Erlich, and Riccardo Picchio—whose ideas and works continue to inform my own thinking and writing. Other colleagues, most notably Dan E. Davidson, Linda Gerstein, Robin Feuer Miller, Cathy Popkin, and Stephanie Sandler, thoughtfully suggested valuable ways to strengthen specific aspects of individual chapters. Still other colleagues—Jeanette Owen, Sharon Bain, Billie Jo Stiner, and Brooke Leonard—ensured the completeness and accuracy of the final manuscript. The optimism and encouragement of my father, Sidney Cheresh, and enduringly fond memories of my mother, Theresa D. Christensen, sustained me at every stage of the writing process.

Many thanks to Andrew Frisardi for his exemplary copyediting. I would also like to express special gratitude to Norris Pope at Stanford University Press, who was an epitome of professionalism and civility in arranging for the publication of this book. Other valuable assistance at the press was rendered by Mariana Raykov, who graciously shepherded the book through the production process.

I cannot sufficiently acknowledge the help that my husband, James Sloan Allen, provided as I turned my initial notions about Lermontov into the reality of a book. His intelligence, erudition, and dedication to clarity of thought and expression left their mark on every page of this book. And his surpassing devotion to a humanistic ideal of culture served as a constant source of inspiration. He is *my* idol, never falling, never failing. Thus it is to James, with love, that I dedicate this book.

NOTE ON THE TEXT

Portions of Chapter 3 appeared in "Lermontov's 'Not-Byronism': A Reconsideration," *Romantic Russia* 2 (1998): 9–34; portions of Chapter 5 appeared in "Unmasking Lermontov's *Masquerade*: Romanticism as Ideology," *Slavic and East European Journal* 46, no. 1 (Spring 2002): 75–97.

Unless otherwise noted in the text or Bibliography, all translations are mine; likewise, unless otherwise noted, all ellipses are mine.

A Fallen Idol Is Still a God

Introduction

Cultural Transition and Its Quandaries

LERMONTOV AND HIS GENERATION

"Sadly do I gaze upon our generation!" [Печально я гляжу на наше поколенье!].

With these words, the renowned Russian poet, playwright, and novelist Mikhail Iurevich Lermontov (1814–41) begins one of his most famous—and surely most embittered—poems, "Meditation" ["Дума"] (1838). He goes on from there to describe his generation not only "sadly" but angrily, reproaching its members for being "shamefully indifferent to good and evil," "ignominiously fearful before danger / And before power—contemptible slaves" [К добру и злу постыдно равнодушны/... Перед опасностью позорно-малодушны,/И перед властью—презренные рабы]. A generation without any creative spirit, "its future is either empty or dark" [Его грядущее—иль пусто, иль темно], leading down "a straight path without a goal" [ровный путь без цели] and inducing "some secret cold" that "reigns in the spirit" [царствует в душе какой-то холод тайный]. Devoid of both courage and creativity, his generation, Lermontov declares, will consequently leave no trace behind it, "not having cast to the centuries either a fruitful idea / Or the work begun by a genius" [Не бросивши векам ни мысли плодовитой, / Ни гением начатого труда]. Instead, aimlessly "fruitless" [бесплодное]—a term Lermontov reiterates—he and his generation will simply "hurry toward the grave without happiness and without glory, / Looking back in mockery" [к гробу мы спешим без счастья и без славы / Глядя насмешливо назад]. And so, Lermontov concludes, "he who follows will disdain / Our dust . . . with a scornful verse, / With the bitter laughter of a deluded son / At a dissipated father" [И прах наш . . . /Потомок оскорбит презрительным стихом, / Насмешкой горькою обманутого сына/Над промотавшимся отцом] (1: 400–401).[1]

"Meditation" is both a confession and a critique. And it reveals Lermontov to be an artist who at once identified himself with his generation and rose above it. He shared in that generation's psychological condition—detached from the past, adrift in the present, and purposeless before the future. But he rose above his generation by diagnosing its disorientation and inadequacies as a historical condition, by giving voice to that condition, and by confronting the quandaries that such a condition posed. His ability to rise above his generation in these ways gives Lermontov an unusual, and insufficiently understood, place in literary history. That place, I will argue, is as an emblematic figure of cultural transition.

To be sure, cultural transition is a very large subject, which Lermontov's literary career illuminates in a particular and instructive manner. Before elucidating this particularity and its instructiveness, however, I would first like to look briefly at some versions of cultural change in general—from grand theories of patterns in history (albeit no longer in vogue) to more sharply focused interpretations of transitions in and out of specific historical periods. This brief look will provide my discussion of Lermontov's role in cultural transition with a historiographical context, and it will also provide a theoretical point of departure for my interpretation of Lermontov as both representing his generation and transcending it by leaving his own highly "fruitful" ideas and works of genius for the generations to come.

CULTURAL CHANGE WRIT LARGE

Nothing in history has more causes, complexity, and consequences than cultural change. For cultural change, like culture itself, can encompass everything created by human beings, from the everyday material circumstances of daily life to political systems, social manners, and structures of belief. Cultural change on this scale will necessarily be gradual, accumulating causes as it goes. And it will not be explained simply. Indeed, its theoreticians tend to dismiss all attempts to simplify it. As literary critic and historian Ihab Hassan puts it, "No universal pattern of transformation applies to all human endeavors; some change seems cyclical, some linear, here dialectical, there dramatic, one kind filiative, another affiliative" ("Ideas," 23).[2] Yet aspirations to penetrate the complexity of cultural change have nevertheless exercised many a scholar and thinker who has detected in retrospect a dominant pattern that determines how cultures have changed in the past and that may predict how they will likely change in the future.

Social theorists, for instance, particularly in the nineteenth century, have discerned a pattern of evolution in cultural and social change. Auguste Comte notably saw the human mind progressing through three successive stages in the course of a society's development—the theological, the metaphysical, and the scientific—in a historical sequence he posited as a fundamental law; and Herbert Spencer found a continuous, organic evolution of culture "from an indefinite, incoherent homogeneity to a definite, coherent heterogeneity" (quoted in Becker and Barnes, 667). Karl Marx and Friedrich Engels provided their variation with a dialectical vision of history that explained cultural change through class conflicts that would eventually lead to a classless utopian society.[3] By contrast to these "progressive" nineteenth-century theorists of cultural change, in the twentieth century social theorist Pitirim Sorokin, for one, advanced a theory that accounted for cultural change through a historical cycle of "crisis—catharsis—charisma—resurrection." That is, when cultures descend into creative bankruptcy, they eventually reach a "crisis," which is followed by some form of cultural "catharsis" or purification, after which a process of charismatic healing leads to "resurrection," a new life made possible by the "release of new creative forces" (4: 778).

In their own theoretical vein, some anthropologists have seen cultures evolving through "a symbolic, continuous, cumulative, and progressive process" (White, 140), while others have contended that cultures change by diffusion and acculturation, through direct or indirect interaction with other cultures. According to Bronislaw Malinowski's dialectical version of the latter, cultural change occurs via the "clash and interplay of two cultures" that results not merely in "a mechanical mixture" of objects or traits but in "entirely new products" reflecting "new cultural realities" that entail both "potentialities and dangers" (25, 26, 160). Then there are anthropologists like Clifford Geertz and Mary Douglas, who argue that cultures are intellectually constructed systems of symbols imparting order to local experience, and who therefore imply that cultures change either when significant shifts occur in local experience, or when new systems of symbols are fashioned, or both.[4] In contrast, there are "cultural materialists," such as Marvin Harris, who carry on the Marxist tradition by maintaining that cultures reflect material conditions and will change as those conditions change.[5]

Numerous philosophers of history have, of course, also tried their hand at theories of cultural change.[6] Oswald Spengler gained renown in the early twentieth century for his sweeping and poetic version of such change in *The Decline of the West* (1918–22). Spengler describes "the drama of *a number* of mighty Cultures, each springing with primitive strength from the soil of a mother-region to which it remains firmly bound throughout its whole life-cycle," and each possessing "its own new possibilities of self-expression which arise, ripen, decay, and never return" (21). Some cultural changes, he says, are "willed," while others just "happen" (133), but they all begin in a formative "pre-Culture" period of creative chaos, which subsequently converts to a triumphant period of true "Culture" characterized by clear forms, ideas, and feelings. It is, however, "the inevitable *destiny* of the Culture" eventually to decline into a lesser "civilization."[7] Hence he envisioned "history as a picture of endless formations and transformations, of the marvelous waxing and waning of organic forms" (22). According to this theory, cultures grow and die like plants (and Spengler saw Western culture dying at the beginning of the twentieth century).

Inspired in part by Spengler, Arnold Toynbee poured out a dozen volumes of historical and sociocultural theory in *A Study of History* (1934–61) explaining how all civilizations rise and fall in complex but comprehensible, virtually rhythmic, patterns of challenge and response that first bring an aggregation and then a flagging of spiritual energies among a creative minority or elite that guides a civilization in overcoming the challenges posed to it. When an elite loses its power, the culture disintegrates or petrifies. Thus Toynbee perceived in every civilization a life cycle of birth, growth, breakdown, and final disintegration, which will eventually be succeeded by the birth of some new civilization.

At the end of the twentieth century, another explanation of a culture's rise and decline appeared with the ambitious *From Dawn to Decadence*

(2000), by the eminent cultural historian Jacques Barzun, as he took stock of the whole of Western culture since the Renaissance. But unlike Spengler and Toynbee, Barzun did not invoke an overarching theory of history to account for what he saw. Instead he subtly traced an arc of creative energies and "liberation" that ascended vigorously in the West from about 1500 and then began descending with enervation and a failure of nerve after World War I. To Barzun's critical eye, decline and then decadence set in when Western culture lost respect for authority, standards, discipline, society, sacrifice, and so forth, leaving nothing to believe in by the end of the twentieth century except liberated, self-indulgent, dull-witted individualism. Although Barzun does not offer an explicit theory of cultural change, he suggests that cultures thrive on creative energies and demanding value systems, and that they decline when those energies flag, those value systems wane, and self-indulgence reigns.

Subscription to these or any other "grand theories" of cultural change inevitably entails the belief that some overarching pattern informs the course of human lives and the direction of human societies. I will now add one more interpretation of cultural change to this brief survey of such theories because, while this interpretation denies the validity of affirming any such pattern, it points to a different kind of cultural change and a different perception of that change—the subjects on which this book will focus. This interpretation comes from the celebrated literary historian René Wellek, in his essay "The Concept of Evolution in Literary History" (1956). Wellek initially surveys theories of literary historical change and divides these theories into two groups, both of which he deems falsely deterministic. The first, he claims, comprises "evolutionary" theories that explain the twists and turns of literary history as part of "slow, steady change on the analogy of animal growth" through "germination, expansions, efflorescence, and decay" in "an unfolding of embryonic elements to which nothing can be added and which run their course with iron necessity to their predestined exhaustion" (40, 42). The second group is composed of "revolutionary" theories that find only abrupt "changes, reversals into opposites, annulments, and simultaneously, preservations" within the "dialectical alternation of old into new and back again" (45, 48).[8] However, Wellek then argues, no artist is an agent of either "evolution" or "revolution," because every artist is an autonomous individual for whom creativity is "a free idea, a choice of values which constitutes his own personal hierarchy of values, and will be reflected in the hierarchy of values implied in his works of art." Far from submitting to the forces of history, by freely choosing an autonomous aesthetic "hierarchy of values" the artist "will eventually affect the hierarchy of values of a given period" (51). Wellek thus maintains that cultural changes occur not through impersonal deterministic patterns of history, but through the efficacy of free artistic individuality.[9]

CULTURAL TRANSITION

Wellek might oversimplify allegedly deterministic theories of literary history, and he arguably grants individuals too much freedom from their times. But he brings the issue of cultural change down from grand theories and large-scale historical patterns to the lives of individuals. From this perspective we can see cultural change occurring on a smaller temporal scale, affecting a generation or two along limited lines of thought and behavior. These more limited changes might contribute "causes" to more gradual and broader cultural change, but they might also have lives of their own—and those who experience these changes might lack the grounds to recognize or assert their participation in some larger pattern of change. We see such smaller cultural changes happen most commonly and conspicuously through shifting styles in the arts, and in alterations in values and beliefs that come with the generations at the beginnings and the ends of historical periods. I will refer to these smaller generational cultural changes as *cultural transitions*. The word *transition* itself comes from the Latin verb *ire*, "to go," coupled with the prefix *trans-*, "over or across," and it denotes both the act of passing from one point to another and the time during which this passage takes place. Hence the term *cultural transition* designates at once the process of moving away from the styles, norms, values, and beliefs of one historical period toward those of another, as well as the stretch of time in which that movement takes place. Without presuming to advance a universal theory of cultural transition between periods, I will first explore the conceptual parameters of this idea and then address how it applies to a particular time and how it is especially exemplified by a particular individual, Mikhail Lermontov.

The very existence of historical periods has, of course, long been debated. Those historians and others who believe only in particulars, and therefore dismiss periodization as a blinkered distortion of variegated facts, vigorously dispute those who accept historical periods as at least useful generalizations that synthesize cultural affinities or correspondences. Despite this debate, scholars and critics commonly accept and occupy themselves with historical periods like the Middle Ages, the Renaissance, the Enlightenment, Romanticism, and modernism, even if they date and define them differently. For historical periods are not eras of cultural uniformity but rather times—whether decades or centuries—characterized by, as Wellek puts it, "dominant norms, i.e., conventions, themes, philosophies, styles," and so on, whatever conflicting ideas might also exist (129). Or, as Barzun observes, historical periods are spans of time during which certain attributes "for one reason or another happen to be stressed, valued, cultivated," especially, but not exclusively, by cultural leaders among artists and intellectuals (*Classic*, 9). In other words, not everyone will subscribe to the prevailing norms and other cultural attributes of a particular period, but that prevalence will be evident to leading contemporaries—and will become more distinct in retrospect, sufficient to justify the distinction of a cultural period. As that prevalence weakens, or as a new set of cultural norms and attributes arises, cultural transition is underway.

Thomas Kuhn's well-known, albeit sometimes misused and frequently overworked, description of revolutions in the history of science, *The Structure of Scientific Revolutions* (1962), offers an illuminating analogy to this kind of cultural transition. Kuhn argues that during periods in the history of science a particular "paradigm," or mental model of how the world works, shapes the theoretical categories and practical traditions of scientific research. This paradigm defines the "normal science" of that period. In such periods of "normal science," the paradigm is modified, embellished, and refined, but its fundamental tenets are not challenged. Over time, however, empirical "anomalies," or unanticipated problems, arise in the course of research for which the paradigm offers no solutions. As a result, the old paradigm begins to lose its hold through accumulating inconsistencies, compromises, and doubts in its value. These anomalies accumulate until "normal science" is beset by "a growing sense . . . that an existing paradigm has ceased to function adequately in its explanation of an aspect of nature" (91). "Normal science" then reaches a point of "crisis," which causes "the blurring of a paradigm and the consequent loosening of the rules for normal research" (84). Such a crisis leads to a period of "extraordinary research," characterized by "the proliferation of competing articulations, the willingness to try anything, the expression of explicit discontent, the recourse to philosophy and to debate over fundamentals" (90). Competition among various sets of solutions to the unanswered questions persists until finally a "paradigm shift" occurs, resulting in a new paradigm that is "not only incompatible but often actually incommensurable with the preceding paradigm" (102). That constitutes a "scientific revolution." And it happens only after one prevailing view of the world has lost its hold and given way to another.[10]

Although Kuhn chiefly treats the intellectual and professional character of "normal science" and "scientific revolutions," whereas cultural transitions involve many human endeavors and are more often evolutionary than revolutionary, his theory of how science changes does bear on cultural transition. For I would surmise that, like periods in the history of science, periods in culture likely change through phases of doubt and questioning of the prevailing view of the world ("the perception that something had gone wrong"), followed by phases of radical experimentation and anticipation ("the prelude to a discovery" [57]), until a new vision of the world achieves dominance—the "paradigm shift." The process of change in cultures is more complex and less definitive, but the pattern is probably similar.[11]

The sociologist Ernest Gellner provides some related analogies to cultural change. And because he deals not with revolutionary change into a new period but with the late stage of doubt in the transition out of a period, his ideas have special pertinence to the kind of cultural transition I will be exploring. In a chapter entitled "Metamorphosis" in his study *Thought and Change* (1964), Gellner trenchantly sets forth what he takes to be both the costs and the benefits of social transition. He finds that societies in what he dubs "transitional states" experience "involuntary, dramatic, and largely uncontrolled openness," which undermines "norms and styles of perceiving and valuing" (61, 52, 61). This openness induces "disorientation and bewilderment, a sense of chaos and contradiction, and an attempt to restore some kind of order and direction" (50). But attempts to restore that lost order prove impossible, since "reliance on conventional wisdom named 'tradition' is worthless" when it requires "a stable environment and a repetition more or less of the situations and problems which had formed that tradition—which is precisely what does not obtain during a fundamental transition." In fact, Gellner goes so far as to state that "it is only in transitional situations that it is really true that men learn nothing from history: they cannot" (60).

But this is not all bad, Gellner goes on. He recognizes a potentially salutary effect on individuals from the "openness" of those transitional situations. For "the warm atmosphere of a fixed way of life and being" can "obscure the bleaker ultimate truths" of human existence that must eventually be met. By contrast, "the bleak truths . . . become practical and pressing concerns only in states of transition, when the identity of the believer-agent is uncertain, when the ballasts and dogmas, however unwarranted, that are built into any stable identity have become unavailing" (51). The resulting skepticism, doubt, and hesitancy characteristic of transitional states can therefore help to dispel the illusions of the past and to master the "ultimate realities" of life. Here, he suggests, is the "moral truth" of transitions (60). Consequently, separation from the comforting certainties of the past creates a time of both trial and prospects. As Gellner neatly encapsulates the condition of such a time: "In transition, tomorrow is not *another* day: it is an *other* day altogether" (67; italics Gellner's).

Transitions In

Gellner's depiction of the pure transitional condition is something of an exception among critics and scholars who examine cultural transitions. For unlike Gellner, they incline to concentrate on what we can call *transitions in*, the creative times during which new constellations of styles, values, and beliefs are forming, rather than *transitions out*, the times during which established constellations are in decline—like the late stages of Kuhn's "normal science" prior to the "paradigm shift." One notable exception among historians, Johan Huizinga, remarks this imbalance in his renowned book *The Waning of the Middle Ages* (1949): "History has always been far more engrossed by problems of origins than by those of decline and fall. When studying any period, we are always looking for the promise of what the next is to bring" (4). This preference to seek the seeds of the future rather than to sort through the wilted flowers of the past, especially in the study of specific historical and cultural periods, is unmistakable and understandable. And it is worth pausing to consider some of the reasons for this preference, which stands apart from broad theories of cultural change that delineate cycles of cultural ascent and descent across centuries.

Literary critic and theoretician Gary Saul Morson would likely attribute this preference to a basic historical fallacy, which he labels "backshadowing." In *Narrative and Freedom: The Shadows of Time* (1994), Morson describes "backshadowing" as retrospectively discerning in historical events only "signs pointing to what happened" after those events, leading to the conclusion that "history (or some portion of it) fits a relatively neat pattern" and that "what happened later was either inevitable or highly probable" (235, 236, 237). Such backshadowing can impart an anachronistic orientation toward an as-yet-unknown future to the "portions" of history constituting *transitions out* of a cultural period, when a preceding period's cultural norms and expectations are in decline and nothing has replaced them. Backshadowing effectively reduces those times to *transitions in*, forerunners of the period to come, and obscures what *transitions out* entail in their own right.[12]

In addition, I would argue that the tendency to focus on "the promise" offered by the transition into a coming cultural period, rather than on the residue of the preceding period during the transition out of it, may derive from the influence, whether acknowledged or not, of the rhetorical and logical conception of transition as a means of directly connecting two points. The emphasis on connection inevitably leads to the conclusion that an endpoint *must* be reached. English usage, extrapolating from Greek and Latin, has made this emphasis commonplace. As far back as 1593 in his rhetorical guide *The Garden of Eloquence*, Henry Peacham defines transition, using the Greek term *metabasis*, as "a forme of speech by which the Orator in a few words sheweth what hath bene already said, and also what shal be said next" (quoted in H. Jackson, 223). "What shal be said next" must have been previously determined by the orator—the transition simply paves the way. In the same vein, Isaac Watts, in *Logick; or, The Right Use of Reason in the Enquiry After Truth* (1751), recommends to public speakers, "Keep your main End and Design ever in View" in order to avoid "huge Chasms or Breaks," and "Acquaint yourself with all the proper and decent Forms of Transition from one Part of a Discourse to another, and practice them as Occasion offers" (quoted in H. Jackson, 216).

Similarly, in the eighteenth century Samuel Johnson complained that contemporary poets were feeling free "to neglect the niceties of transition, to start into remote digressions, and to wander without restraint from one scene of imagery to another," whereas "to proceed from one truth to another, and connect distant propositions by regular consequence, is the great prerogative of man" (quoted in Stabler, 307, 325). Later, Samuel Taylor Coleridge would make using transitions the prerogative in particular of "the educated man," who "chiefly seeks to discover and express those *connections* of things, or those relative *bearings* of fact to fact, from which some more or less general law is deducible." By contrast, "the intercourse of uneducated men . . . is distinguished from the diction of their superiors in knowledge and power . . . by the greater *disjunction* and *separation* in the component parts of . . . whatever it is . . . that they wish to communicate. There is a want of that prospectiveness of mind, that *surview*, which enables a man to foresee the whole of what he is to convey" (italics Coleridge's; quoted in H. Jackson, 220, 221).[13]

"Prospectiveness of mind" and the "surview" to "foresee" are virtues indeed. But they can bias the study of cultural transition. The desire to see such transition as part of "the whole" of a subsequent cultural period, just as a phrase or sentence is part of "the whole" of a developing idea or argument, could well be an ingrained habit of thought. And this habit is only reinforced by daily life itself, since, as Alfred North Whitehead remarked, "each moment of experience confesses itself to be a transition between two worlds, the immediate past and the immediate future. This is the persistent delivery of common sense" (405). The impending presence of the future in individual lives can render the presumption of an impending future in cultural history that much easier to make.

In *The Sense of an Ending* (1966), Frank Kermode adds another clue to the tendency to retroject the future into the past. He says that the very idea of historical transition appeared in the West from apocalyptic anticipations of the ultimate destruction of the world. In other words, transition was teleological and eschatological. Kermode calls this idea the "myth of Transition":

> Before the End there is a period which does not properly belong either to the End or to the *saeculum* preceding it. It has its own characteristics. This period of Transition seems not to have been defined until the end of the twelfth century; but the definition then arrived at—by Joachim of Flora—has proved to be remarkably enduring. Its origin is in the three-and-a-half-year reign of the Beast which, in Revelation, precedes the Last Days. Joachim, who died in 1202, divided history into three phases, a division based on the Trinity; the last transition would begin in 1260, a date arrived at by multiplying forty-two by thirty, the number of years in each generation between Abraham and Christ.

"These prophesies had a long life," Kermode asserts, since "not only Dante, at the end of the century, but Hegel and others much later took them seriously." As a result, "the notion of an End-dominated age of transition has passed into our consciousness, and modified our attitudes to historical pattern. As Ruth Kestenberg-Gladstein observes, 'the Joachite triad made it inevitable that the present becomes "a mere transitional stage," and leaves people with a sense of living at a turning-point of time.'" "And so," Kermode sums up, "the paradigms of apocalypse continue to lie under our ways of making sense of the world" (12–13, 13–14, 28).[14]

Whether Kermode is correct that the apocalyptic "myth of Transition" affects how people typically think about historical transitions, scholars and critics do tend to focus on transitions into future periods rather than to explore the transitions out of past periods. Yet this is not to say that scholars and critics have completely ignored or dismissed times of *transition out*. Most of them acknowledge in some fashion that just as cultural periods arise with the ascendancy of new tastes, norms, and expectations, they decline with a certain loss of confidence, or at least a rethinking of—and sometimes a desire to transform and go beyond—those same tastes, norms, and expectations; Jacques Barzun exemplifies this in *From Dawn to Decadence*. Nonetheless, the scholarly inclination toward the ascendancy and arrival of historical periods as a means of comprehending those periods, rather than toward their descent and departure, cannot be denied—the attraction to *transitions in* is hard to resist.[15] And yet such times of departure, the process of transition out of a period, can reveal as much, or more, about that period as can the previous transition into it. *Transitions out* merit more attention than they have received.

Transitions Out

The most conspicuous exception to this lack of attention is Edward Gibbon's *The Decline and Fall of the Roman Empire*. But because Gibbon emphasizes political, social, and religious causes of that decline, Huizinga's magisterial *The Waning of the Middle Ages* represents a more instructive monument to the study of the cultural transition out of a period. Taking as his subject France and the Netherlands during the fourteenth and fifteenth centuries, Huizinga shows how the culture of the Middle Ages waned as honest devotion to the chivalrous conduct of life in this world and to spiritual transcendence in the next lapsed into self-consciously aestheticized, often excessive or manneristic performances, accompanied by spiritual desiccation and malaise. "The mentality of the declining Middle Ages seems to us to display an incredible superficiality and feebleness" (234), Huizinga writes. Rituals were inflated, like the extravagant feasts of Philip the Good that came to appear as "the last manifestations of a dying usage which has become a fantastic ornament after having been a very serious element of earlier civilization" (92). Literature became "enslaved by conventional forms and suffocated under a heap of arid rhetorica" (289). And architecture was encrusted with aimless extravagance: "The flamboyant style of architecture is like the postlude of an organist who cannot conclude. It decomposes all the formal elements endlessly; it interlaces all the details; there is not a line which has not its counter-line. The form develops at the expense of the idea, the ornament grows rank, hiding all the lines and all the surfaces. A *horror vacui* reigns, always a symptom of artistic decline" (248). Across late medieval culture in the north, Huizinga concludes, "what may be called a stagnation of thought prevails, as though the mind, exhausted after building up the spiritual fabric of the Middle Ages, had sunk into inertia" and spiritless disorder (295). Huizinga's observations of the symptoms of cultural decline and the passage out of the Middle Ages have relevance to any transition out of a period, although those symptoms may present themselves somewhat differently.

Taking his cue from Huizinga, another historian, William Bouwsma, trained his sights on a subsequent era of cultural decline—Europe during the sixteenth and early seventeenth centuries. Echoing Huizinga with his title *The Waning of the Renaissance* (2000), Bouwsma also found it "remarkable that historians of early modern Europe have paid so little attention to the problem of the *end* of the Renaissance" (viii–ix). He assigns this particular neglect to "a more or less linear conception of cultural history"—encouraged by Jacob Burckhardt's pioneering and exuberant *The Civilization of the Renaissance in Italy* (1860)—that sees Western culture moving "ineluctably" toward the modern world with no consequential breaks or periods of decline.

To correct this misperception, Bouwsma argues that the culture of the Renaissance did indeed go into decline. This decline occurred when the reigning ideal or value of individuality, which Burckhardt had celebrated, began inducing doubts and discontents. "The dissolution of old boundaries, old categories, old certainties," which is "in the short run liberating," Bouwsma explains, "is in the long run destructive and frightening" (x). As a result, the late Renaissance was characterized by a "pattern of alternation: conflicting impulses were often simultaneously at work, without a clear resolution yet, between the creativity and spontaneity of cultural freedom and a growing tendency toward order and restraint" (260). This made "the age" highly unsettled and "generally ambivalent" (113). Huizinga and Bouwsma thus both describe their respective periods of *transition out* in the generally negative terms of mannerisms and malaise, stagnation and superficiality, ambivalence and doubt. These are attributes, as a recent translation of Huizinga's title phrases it, of a culture in the "autumn" of its years.[16]

Of course, not everyone alive in a time of *transition out* will feel belated and autumnal. As literary critic Jonathan Levin notes in *The Poetics of*

Transition, some artists find "a profound and often liberating sense of uncertainty located . . . at the leading edge of a transitional margin" (15). Levin cites Ralph Waldo Emerson, for instance, as an intellectual who relished transitions without clear conclusions. For Emerson extolled times during which "all that we reckoned settled shakes and rattles; and literatures, cities, climates, religions, leave their foundations, and dance before our eyes" (quoted in Levin, 40). Levin also points to William James, who claimed that "we live, as it were, upon the front edge of an advancing wave-crest," and therefore that "our experience, *inter alia*, is of variations of rate and of direction, and lives in these transitions more than in the journey's end" (quoted in Levin, 56). By experiencing life as an endless series of transitions, James goes on, individuals can discover a sense of "indefinitely radiating subconscious possibilities of increase" that foster "the will to believe" in something that transcends immediate existence (quoted in Levin, 58, 57). In the same vein, Clyde Ryals notes that Robert Browning wrote to Elizabeth Barrett, "The cant is, that 'an age of transition' is a melancholy thing to contemplate and delineate—whereas the worst things of all to look back on are times of comparative standing still, rounded in their impotent completeness" (quoted in Ryals, 2).

These are buoyant responses to the experience of transition. But I would venture that this buoyancy actually comes from a sense of being not at the end of something but at the creative beginning—"at the leading edge," as Levin says, or in James's words, at "the front edge of an advancing wave-crest." These are not really images of *transition out*; they are images of forceful movement forward, closer to the energetic and creative spirit of a *transition in* as it leaves the past behind. For Huizinga and Bouwsma provide strong justification to see *transitions out* of cultural periods as marked less by a feeling of liberation than by a sense of disintegration and disorder, ambivalence and aimlessness, or, as Gellner finds, "disorientation and bewilderment."

W. Jackson Bate finds such a sense of disorientation and bewilderment among English authors and intellectuals in the eighteenth century, which he considers the "essential crossroad" between the Renaissance and the modern era. In *The Burden of the Past and the English Poet* (1970), Bate ascribes these feelings to "the problem of what it means to come *immediately* after a great creative achievement." In quest of originality, poets were "burdened" by the question, "What is there left to do?" which caused a profound "fatigue to the spirit" and a "loss of self-confidence" because "the kind of thing expected" in response to "the challenge of the past" was "so completely beyond one's grasp."[17] Bate emphasizes that this is an age-old problem, quoting an Egyptian scribe in 2000 B.C.E.: "Would I had phrases that are not known, utterances that are strange, in new language that has not been used, free from repetition, not an utterance which has grown stale, which men of old have spoken" (12, 3, 7, 42, 3–4).[18] This aching sense of belatedness belongs to *transitions out*, to those individuals afflicted, like Harry Haller in Hermann Hesse's *Steppenwolf,* with the "sickness of the times themselves" that sets in "when a whole generation is caught . . . between two ages, two modes of life, with the consequence that it loses all power to understand itself and has no standard, no security, no simple acquiescence" (21, 22) to any cultural assumptions.

Novelist Edward Bulwer-Lytton remarked this kind of discomfort in the nineteenth century when he wrote: "We live in an age of visible transition. To me such epochs appear . . . the times of greatest unhappiness to our species." British soldier and memoirist Frederick Roberts echoed the sentiment somewhat later: "It is an awful moment [of transition] . . . when the soul begins . . . to feel the nothingness of many of the traditionary [*sic*] opinions which have been received with implicit confidence, and in that horrible insecurity begins also to doubt whether there be any thing to believe at all" (both quoted in Ryals, 2).

At about the same time, Russian author Alexander Herzen painted a powerful portrait of this autumnal mood of *transitions out* in the essay entitled "Omnia mia mecum porto."[19] There Herzen describes three types of historical periods. The first is characterized by "a whirlpool of events" inspiring energetic struggle in some common cause from which "none retreat because all believe." The second is "peaceful, even sleepy," during which "recognized relations remain unshaken" and "people are absorbed in personal concerns." But the third type of period, Herzen claims, is a sad one, because it is a period

> when the forms of social life, having outlived themselves, slowly and painfully perish. . . . It is divorced in equal measure from the past which it despises and from the future which develops according to other laws. . . . The decrepit world has no longer any belief in itself and defends itself desperately because it is frightened. In its desire for self-preservation it forgets its gods, tramples on rights by which it lives, repudiates culture and honour, becomes bestial, persecutes, kills, but all the while power remains in its hands. It is obeyed not out of cowardice alone, but because on the other side all is

uncertain, nothing decided, nothing ready—above all men are not ready. On this other side, the unknown future looms up on a horizon wrapped in a cloud, a future that confounds all human logic. (130–31)

Herzen cites the ancient Romans as representatives of such a period, and he sees himself and his generation in a similar state after the failed revolutions of 1848. "The old, official Europe," he declares, "is dying," and "the last frail and sickly vestiges of its former life are scarcely sufficient to hold together for a time the disintegrating parts of its body." So, he recalls later on, "life was going out like the last candles in windows before the dawn," and as "the terrible progress of death" proceeded, "the vaster became the desert around us, the vaster grew our loneliness" (123, 135)—the loneliness of an existence seemingly headed nowhere, with nothing to believe in.

CULTURAL INTEGRITY AND CULTURAL ANOMIE

Whether or not *transitions out* of cultural periods exhibit some of this kind of eschatological gloom, one phenomenon common to this type of transition is what I will call a loss of *cultural integration* and *integrity*. That is, during the heyday of a cultural period its dominant norms and attributes are sufficiently integrated to grant that period a high degree of cultural coherence and wholeness, or integrity (befitting the Latin adjectival root of both *integration* and *integrity*, *integer*, denoting complete, entire, or intact). I would also add that at its height a cultural period also has integrity in the more figurative, ethical meaning of the term as moral consistency and authenticity, which it can then impart to the individuals who adhere to its values. When the dominant norms and attributes of a cultural period loosen their hold, therefore, the culture begins to literally *dis-integrate*, losing both the *integration* of its parts and the *integrity* of its wholeness, coherence, consistency, and authenticity. Those norms and attributes then tend to display—as Huizinga, Bouwsma, Bate, Herzen, and others have variously observed and illustrated—symptoms of attenuation and excess, becoming empty conventions or uncertain mannerisms. And while they might continue to elicit ritualistic observance, they lack the power to command honest moral conviction, to lend clear direction, or to inspire fresh and vigorous creativity. As those norms and attributes are increasingly devalued, the culture of a period sinks deeper into decline.

Although the underlying causes of this disintegration and decline are bound to be plentiful, the very loss of cultural integration and integrity themselves will likely surface as a late cause of this cultural change in its own right. This is because perceptive artists and intellectuals who come to maturity during transitions out of cultural periods will tend to be the first to sense this disintegration and loss of cultural integrity, at least vaguely, if not intensely. In any case, they will feel themselves somewhat historically adrift, with "no security, no simple acquiescence" to any cultural assumptions, as Hesse describes it.

This feeling of being historically adrift might usefully be labeled "cultural anomie," akin to the social anomie defined by the pioneering sociologist Emile Durkheim in his study *Suicide* (1897). According to Durkheim, anomie, which literally means "lawlessness" (from the Greek *a-*, without, and *nomos*, law), signifies a lack of the norms and constraints that derive from the "regulative force" of society and lend purpose, direction, and meaning to the lives of individuals. Anomie occurs, Durkheim maintains, "when society is disturbed by some painful crisis or by beneficent but abrupt transitions." During such "transitions," society loses its "regulative force," and so "the limits are unknown between the possible and the impossible, what is just and what is unjust, legitimate claims and hopes and those which are immoderate" (248, 252). At that point,

> reality seems valueless by comparison with the dreams of fevered imaginations; reality is therefore abandoned, but so too is possibility abandoned when it in turn becomes reality. A thirst arises for novelties, unfamiliar pleasures, nameless sensations, all of which lose their savor once known. Henceforth one has no strength to endure the least reverse. The whole fever subsides and the sterility of all the tumult is apparent, and it is seen that all these new sensations in their infinite quantity cannot form a solid foundation of happiness to support one during days of trial. . . . [Then] the man who has always pinned all his hopes on the future, and lived with his eyes fixed upon it, has nothing in the past as a comfort against the present's afflictions. . . . Now he is stopped in his tracks; from now on nothing remains behind or ahead of him to fix his gaze upon. (256)

In this anomic state of mind, equally alienated from the past, the present, and the future, Durkheim concludes, an individual may be primed to commit suicide.

Like Durkheim's social anomie, cultural anomie inspires a sense of alienation and rootlessness in individuals through the loss of some moral authority. I would distinguish cultural anomie from social anomie, however, in several ways. First of all, social anomie, as Durkheim describes it, results from the loss of "force" by the aggregate social system owing primarily to marked shifts in economic and material circumstances. But cultural anomie arises from the erosion of the ideals and norms, the values and beliefs, of a historical period, and this might have little to do with the social system or material conditions. Second, the material and economic ruptures that Durkheim has in mind tend to occur relatively abruptly, and to be visible and short in duration, whereas the cultural transitions I am addressing are more complex and occur more gradually, over a span of years. I will call such a span a "post-period."

Of course, not all cultural periods engender post-periods as I would define them. For by a post-period I mean a stretch of anywhere from a few years to several decades during which a generation or more of artists and intellectuals perceives that the cultural ideals and norms lending structure and constraint to character, under which they grew up and which they had expected to embrace, no longer hold their former authority—and yet no new norms have claimed that authority. Hence I am using the prefix *post-* not simply to signify a chronological sequence but also a historical process of a cultural period's fading away. The members of those post-period generations consequently find themselves suffering from a deepening sense of normlessness. Pervaded by cultural anomie, post-periods are times of *transition out.*

The anomie of post-periods or *transitions out* converts what might be a moment of maximal cultural freedom into an expanse of dispiriting disorientation and uncertainty. These periods are thus more likely to bring to culturally attuned artists and intellectuals living in them not buoyant liberation from stifling standards, or even a comforting feeling of participation in broad cultural patterns or cycles that would be perceptible in retrospect, but a disruptive loss of stabilizing and inspiriting ideals. Instead of seeing unlimited possibilities in the future, those artists and intellectuals tend to feel that they have lost their moorings in the past.

This anomic condition typical of times of *transition out* therefore poses some particular quandaries or predicaments for the artists and intellectuals sensitive to that condition. Paramount among these would be: (1) the artistic quandary of aspiring to originality in the shadow of the preceding period's greatest figures and aesthetic achievements; (2) the ethical quandary of defining good and evil, right and wrong, when the preceding period's values have been eroded; (3) the intellectual quandary of differentiating between genuine ideals of an established cultural period and the self-serving ideology into which a transitional period can convert them; (4) the psychological quandary of living with cultural anomie; and (5) the historical quandary of finding truth without a firm set of cultural values or a clear vision of the future. "Caught between ages," feeling too brief or directionless to seem connected to broad patterns of cultural change, *transitions out* are fraught with quandaries lacking resolutions. And yet gifted artists and intellectuals nonetheless strive to resolve them—or at least to probe the depths of those quandaries and the conditions that give rise to them.

AN AUTHOR OF TRANSITION

This book focuses on one such gifted artist "caught between ages." That author is Mikhail Lermontov, whose literary career unfolded primarily in the 1830s. Notoriously difficult to place historically, the short-lived Lermontov (killed in a duel at the age of twenty-six) was an exceptional artist of a transitional time—to him, that time was the twilight of Romanticism, or what I will call post-Romanticism. For Lermontov's works not only reflect his own particular transitional time, they also more generally illuminate the quandaries of cultural transition out of a period as they show Lermontov uniquely grappling with the loss of Romanticism's cultural integrity. Although confined to his transitional times, he did not succumb to them; instead he plumbed their character and suggested their historical import. And what Lermontov revealed has resonance for our transitional times in the early twenty-first century as well.

My exploration and explanation of Lermontov's transitionality and its implications will proceed as follows. The next chapter, "Romanticism and Its Twilight in Western Europe and Russia," sets the stage for my detailed interpretations of Lermontov's works by surveying aspects of Romanticism and its decline in both Western Europe and Russia and by placing Lermontov in both of these contexts. Succeeding chapters then take up specific works and themes to elucidate Lermontov's distinctive achievements as an artist occupied with the quandaries of the transition out of Romanticism, who was troubled by the loss of Romantic cultural integrity and the malaise of cultural anomie, and who longed for a cure. In each of these chapters I discuss how Lermontov's transitional sensibilities manifest themselves in both the form and content of individual texts, drawing comparisons to works of Western Romanticism that highlight these sensibilities.

Chapter 3, "The Ambivalence of Influence: Lermontov's 'Not-Byronism,'" explores the artistic quandaries of an author admittedly influenced by a preeminent predecessor, the towering Romantic figure Lord Byron, in whose shadow Lermontov and other writers of his generation came to maturity. Chapter 4, "The Attenuation of Romantic Evil: A Demon Undone," addresses the ethical quandaries of identifying evil in transitional times by showing how Lermontov's long and often-revised narrative poem *The Demon* [*Демон*] attenuates the Romantic vision of ethics while drawing on Romantic ideas and images of spiritual transcendence and demonic rebellion. Chapter 5, "Ideals to Ideology: Unmasking *Masquerade*," turns to the intellectual quandaries of guarding against the conversion of a cultural period's authentic ideals into a post-period's derivative ideology as portrayed in Lermontov's most famous play, *Masquerade* [*Маскарад*].

Chapters 6 and 7 demonstrate how Lermontov's transitionality culminates in his most renowned work, the novel *A Hero of Our Time* [*Герой нашего времени*]. For here Lermontov explicitly displays his sense that his times were transitional as he confronts the quandaries posed by what I call post-Romantic cultural anomie. Chapter 6, "Post-Romantic Anomie I: *A Hero of Our Time* and Its Hero*," delves into the psychological quandaries arising from the post-Romantic fragmentation or dis-integration of personality as embodied by the novel's main protagonist, Pechorin. Chapter 7, "Post-Romantic Anomie II: The 'Post-' Scripts of *A Hero of Our Time*," sheds further light on those quandaries by considering how the novel's subordinate characters and multiple narrators in different ways follow post-Romantic "scripts" that generate frustrated expectations and render conclusions inconclusive for characters, narrators, and readers alike.

The final chapter, "Conclusion: Lermontov's Last Words," reveals the historical quandaries of seeking cultural values when none reign as it examines both the author's introduction to *A Hero of Our Time*—added in response to negative criticism after the novel's initial publication—and "Shtoss" ["Штосс"], Lermontov's final, unfinished narrative. In the author's introduction, we see Lermontov openly diagnosing the transitional condition of his times and implying the need to go beyond that condition by establishing a new cultural integrity. In "Shtoss" we find Lermontov unable to achieve that integrity, futilely reverting to Romantic narrative conventions once more, only to abandon the effort. Lermontov's "last words" thus stand as a poignant testimony to the ultimate quandary of post-Romantic transitionality—those who feel the need for integrity most acutely are those most acutely aware of their inability to satisfy that need, or even to envision the shape such integrity would take. This chapter then closes with its own "post-" script, some comments on the affinities between the post-Romanticism of Lermontov's times and the postmodernism of our times. Underscoring the import of the entire book, this conclusion emphasizes that through his struggles with the quandaries of cultural transition, Lermontov not only spoke of his own times, he also speaks to us today.

Romanticism and Its Twilight in Western Europe and Russia

THE INTEGRITY OF EUROPEAN ROMANTICISM

Of all the periods in Western cultural history—except perhaps the Renaissance—none has provoked more academic debate than Romanticism. Romanticism's origins, its duration, its nature, and its very existence have long been disputed, at least since August Wilhelm von Schlegel formally elaborated the "classic-romantic" opposition in his Berlin lectures of 1801–4.[1] And by now everyone who takes up the subject knows A. O. Lovejoy's controversial essay "On the Discrimination of Romanticism," which detects Romanticism throughout Western history and therefore nowhere as a distinct period.[2]

Yet for all the debate, in practice, critics, cultural historians, and literary scholars commonly do recognize Romanticism as a cultural period falling

---

For the purposes of this book, the terms *Romanticism*, *Romanticist*, and *Romantic* will be capitalized when referring to the cultural period, except in quotations by other authors. *Romanticist* will be generally used as a noun referring to people, and *Romantic* will be used as an adjective.

somewhere between 1770 and 1850. Although Romanticism "eludes the classifier, who finds its origins and conclusion dissolve as he tries to pin dates on them and its criteria turn into shapeless generalities as soon as he tries to define them," historian E. J. Hobsbawm remarks, "nobody seriously doubts the existence of Romanticism or our capacity to recognize it" (305). But it is not too much to say that what has made Romanticism so elusive is precisely this: among its dominant characteristics was none other than its embrace of variousness and contradiction in the quest to transcend ordinary life and conventional limitations imposed on human nature, mind and spirit, intellect and imagination. "Whatever its content," Hobsbawm sums up Romanticism, "it is quite evident what it was against: the middle" (306).

Isaiah Berlin nicely captures all of these qualities in *The Roots of Romanticism* by observing that Romanticism is, "in short, unity and multiplicity. It is fidelity to the particular . . . and also mysterious tantalising vagueness of outline. It is beauty and ugliness. It is art for art's sake, and art as an instrument of social salvation. It is strength and weakness, individualism and collectivism, purity and corruption, revolution and reaction, peace and war, love of life and love of death" (18).[3] Again, this embrace of variousness and contradiction does not mean that Romanticism is everything and therefore nothing. Romanticism is rather a summons to the human spirit to embrace the widest possible range of variousness and contradiction (which one historian schematized as "the Romantic syndrome").[4]

Let me begin my exploration of the various and contradictory Romantic spirit by recapitulating an emblematic but little-known story by the German author Ludwig Tieck entitled "The Runenberg" ["Der Runenberg"] (1802). It relates the tale of a young hunter, Christian, who abandons his family, friends, and familiar way of life on a pleasant plain and heads off into the mountains to pursue his dreams of discovering an unknown, exotic world amid nature's sublimity. There he encounters a stranger, to whom he explains that "my father's little, hampered garden, with its trimmed flowerbeds; our narrow dwelling; the wide sky which stretched above us in its dreary vastness, embracing no hill, no lofty mountain, all became more dull and odious to me" (217), until finally he fled. The stranger directs Christian to a ruined mountain castle called the Runenberg, where, the stranger promises, "whoever knows how to seek, whoever feels his heart drawn towards it with a right inward longing, will find friends of former ages there, and glorious things, and all that he wishes most" (219).

Christian evidently "knows how to seek," for after following a dangerous path to the castle, he observes a woman whose extraordinary beauty transfixes and enraptures him. And "within his soul an abyss of forms and harmony, of longing and voluptuousness, was opened; hosts of winged tones, and sad and joyful melodies flew through his spirit, which was moved to its foundations. He saw a world of Pain and Hope arise within him; strong, towering crags of Trust and defiant Confidence, and deep rivers of Sadness flowing by" (221). The woman then presents Christian with a magic tablet, inlaid with dazzling jewels, only to disappear along with the castle, leaving Christian to conclude "that a dream, or sudden madness had come over him that night" (221–22). Disappointed, he decides that "the desires and emotions of the bygone night seemed reckless and wicked; he wished once more, in childlike meekness, helplessly and humbly to unite himself to men as to his brethren, and to fly from his ungodly purposes and feelings" (222). Consequently, he returns to the plain and begins a new life as a farmer, marrying, having children, reconciling with his father, and living in "the most contented and united circle in the world" (226).

Then, over time, Christian grows discontented again, his emotions roiled by a visit from a mysterious traveler who leaves a quantity of gold with him. He begins having strange dreams, sleepwalking, laughing wildly, and claiming that this traveler "was in truth a woman of unearthly beauty" (228). When reproached for his odd behavior by his father, Christian explains, "For long periods of time, for years, I can forget the true form of my inward man, and lead a life that is foreign to me, as it were, with cheerfulness; but then . . . sudden[ly], like a new moon, the ruling star, which I myself am, arises again in my heart, and conquers this other influence" (229). Finally he tells his father, "I have willfully neglected a high, eternal happiness, to win one which is finite and transitory" (230), and he leaves home once more. Returning to the forest, he encounters "an old woman of the utmost hideousness" who informs him that she is called the Woodswoman, but beneath whose exterior Christian recognizes "the golden veil, the lofty gait, the large stately form which he had once beheld of old" (231) in the young beauty at the castle. He also discovers the magic tablet he had lost years earlier, which inspires him to think, "What wonderful, incalculable treasures . . . must there still be in the depths of the Earth! Could one but sound their secret beds and raise them up, and snatch them to oneself! Could one but clasp this Earth like a beloved bride to one's bosom, so that in pain and love she would willingly grant one her costliest riches!" (232). Thus inspired, he runs off with the Woodswoman. Soon thereafter his father dies, and his wife eventually remarries, only to sink into poverty and despair.

Christian returns to visit his wife only once, appearing "all in tatters, barefoot, sunburned to a black brown color in the face, deformed still further by a long matted beard; he wore no covering on his head, but had twisted a garland of green branches through his hair, which made his wild appearance still more strange and haggard" (233). He is carrying what the narrator describes as a heavy sack containing gravel and chunks of stone, but which he describes to his wife as jewels "not ground and polished yet, so they want the glance and the eye; the outward fire, with its glitter, is too deeply buried in their inmost heart" (234). After embracing his wife and eldest child for a final time, he returns to the Woodswoman, after which, the narrator concludes, "the ill-fated creature was never seen again from that day" (235).

Consider what this story says about Romanticism. Here is a character torn between the attractions of the simple life, with the security and affection it offers, and the ecstasies afforded by a life of liberty and adventure, beauty and passion, fantasy and vision—in a word, transcendence. At first ambivalent, Christian finally trades the simple life for transcendence, although it may come at the cost of his very sanity. But does it? Is the story idealistic or ironic, liberating or cautionary?[5] Probably all of these—as is that quintessentially Romantic work of reckless transcendence, Goethe's *Faust*. For "The Runenberg" sets forth a distinctive constellation of values and beliefs that all true Romanticists would, in one way or another, in part or in whole, adopt in their Faustian aspiration to transcend limitations in quest of the unconventional, the unconstrained, the unconditioned.

Even while focusing on disparate aspects of Romanticism, historians and critics tend to agree that this distinctive constellation of values and beliefs gives a certain wholeness or integration and integrity to Romanticism as a cultural period.[6] It is also commonplace among many critics and scholars to assert that this constellation arose as a reaction against the preceding cultural period, identified roughly with classicism or neoclassicism in the arts and even more with the Enlightenment in intellectual life, which prized empirical science, abstract reasoning, and encyclopedic categorization. And no wonder. We need only think, for example, of William Blake's attacks on Sir Joshua Reynolds and on Newton and Locke, Goethe's hostility to Linnaeus, or the famous toast drunk by Keats and his friends at the home of the painter Benjamin Haydon mockingly celebrating "the confusion of mathematics,"[7] to find a certain unmistakable antagonism among some Romanticists toward facets of the Enlightenment.

However, the transition into Romanticism cannot be understood as reaction alone—no transition into a period could happen so mechanistically. For many Romantic artists and thinkers did not reject what the Enlightenment aspired to and substantially achieved, especially the autonomous exercise of intellect as expressed, for instance, in Immanuel Kant's essay "What Is Enlightenment?"[8] The Romanticists just aspired to *more*. They did not reject the free, rational use of intellect, but rather sought to couple it with emotion, imagination, spirit, and new freedoms of all kinds, expanding the range of human nature and activity to reach beyond the limits set by the empiricist rationality of Enlightenment thought. It seems more fruitful to view Romanticists as being inspired by the Enlightenment's emancipation of the mind, and then reacting against the limitations on human nature that the Enlightenment had left in place. The resultant expansiveness helped to create the very constellation of ideas that made Romanticism a period.

High in this constellation of values and beliefs that distinguished Romanticism as a cultural period—contradictions and all—were certain ideals of the self, morality, love, nature, and imagination. And I would emphasize that this constellation also included the values of integrity and its offspring, integration. While integrity can be said to mark any cultural period through the integration of the elements that defined it, integrity proved to be central to Romanticism, in the dual sense that Romanticism embraced not only the psychological integrity of wholeness but also the moral integrity of admitting the variousness and even the contradictions that this wholeness sometimes entailed.[9] Samuel Taylor Coleridge expressed this Romantic devotion to integrity when he wrote of his life-long desire "to behold and know something *great*—something *one & indivisible.*"[10] In the third essay of "On the Principles of Genial Criticism" (1814), he suggested that any such knowledge would arise from an appreciation of "polarities" that naturally occur, separate, and reunite in an evolutionary progression from pure unity to a higher state of integrity, which he famously termed "Multëity in Unity" (*Poetry and Prose*, 345).[11]

In fact, the central Romantic ideals of the self, morality, love, nature, and imagination notably both shape and are shaped by this transcendent ideal of integrity. The changing status of these ideals reveals how the cultural period of Romanticism not only grew out of and reacted against the Enlightenment but—the subject of this book—how that period faded and passed away, leaving behind members of a young generation, including Ler-montov, as they floated in a sea of cultural transition during a time bereft of Romanticism's cultural integrity and integration.

To touch only briefly on how integrity affected those central Romantic ideals—I will explore them more fully in subsequent chapters—I would note first that the Romantic ideal of the self presupposed a psychological core of human identity that always had the potential to become fully in-tegrated and whole, even if divided by conflicting attributes of human na-ture and the complex conditions of contemporary existence.[12] Accordingly, Romanticists eschewed and feared psychological dis-integration, while exalting the union of disparate and even conflicting psychological com-ponents. Søren Kierkegaard baldly, if a tad belatedly, articulated that fear in *Either/Or* (1843): "Can you think of anything more frightful than that it might end up with your nature being resolved into a multiplicity, . . . and you thus would have lost the inmost and holiest thing of all in a man, the unifying power of personality?" (164). Friedrich Schiller worried that, un-like antiquity, when a poet could feel in himself "an undivided sensuous unity and . . . a harmonizing whole," modernity "divides and cuts him in two." This ancient unity could be restored only by seeking anew "the Ideal" of wholeness.[13] Similarly, Samuel Taylor Coleridge, warning of a self "betrayed into the wretchedness of *division*,"[14] looked forward to a time "When [man] by sacred sympathy might make / The one whole Self!" This would be an all-encompassing "Self, that [nothing] alien knows" but "all of all possessing!"[15] And, as the title augurs, in *The Marriage of Heaven and Hell* (1790) William Blake emblematically celebrated the union of all "con-traries" in human nature—"Reason and Energy," "Love and Hate," "Body and Soul" (34).

While striving to unite the divergent parts of the self into a whole, Ro-manticists also often assumed that such a whole self could never exist in mere "sensible people," like those derided by Goethe's Werther for their sober-minded caution and consistency. Individuals possessing an overarch-ing wholeness would be "geniuses" or "heroes" with singular identities and the power and will to take on risks and open up new realms of creativity and experience (see Chapter 5 for further discussion of the Romantic hero). By the same token, they would know and accept themselves, warts and all, in a congruence of self and self-image. Be a criminal if you must, Schiller's Karl Moor or Byron's Corsair would say, but do not be a self-deceiver or a hypocrite, and do not let self-consciousness cripple you. For, as Wordsworth hymned, liberated "consciousness" of one's authentic identity is "the highest bliss that flesh can know" (*The Prelude* [1850 version], 14.113–14). We could therefore say that Tieck's Christian lives out these ideals of the self when he abandons his family and home in order to remain constant to "the true form of my inward man."

Romantic morality follows from the Romantic ideal of the self. Romanticists generally deemed division, alienation, and isolation sources of moral as well as psychological harm. Despite the claim of Irving Babbitt, among others, that "there is no such thing as romantic morality" (217), I would agree with Laurence Lockridge that "the Romantics expressly concern themselves with ethics and affirm its primacy in their own enterprise" (16) time and again.[16] Romantic morality is simply not what many people think morality should be. For Romanticists repeatedly challenged, and in many instances inverted, the traditional hierarchy of values that placed self-restraint near the top and unconstrained self-indulgence near the bottom—Christian's indifference to his family's plight exemplifies this inversion. To many Romanticists, this hierarchy deserved to be upended, so that the liberated and completed self would be recognized as the source of good, despite its dangers, and the constrained and incomplete self would be seen as the source of evil, despite its advantages.

If we can identify one predominant evil in Romanticism, it is any conventional or artificial constraint that denies the energies of human life and thus deprives individuals, and even cultures, of liberty and integrity. Good, by contrast, is the exercise of those energies of life (or what Germaine de Staël would label "enthusiasm"),[17] whatever course that exercise might take—the noted Romantic cults of originality and artistic genius are grounded in this moral stance. As Blake said in *The Marriage of Heaven and Hell*, "Energy is the only life" (34), and he provocatively urged, "Sooner murder an infant in its cradle than nurse unacted desires" (38). We might find exceptions, but they will turn out to prove the rule—any action is superior to no action at all. Goethe's Faust dramatically exemplifies this point, and Goethe's God applauds him for it under the credo: "Man errs as long as he will strive" (87), and humans learn too easily to rest. Errors or not, earnest striving and zealous actions express and enhance the integrity of the self.

Romantic love, and other consuming emotions like sublime awe, became an extension of that same ideal, integrated self, as Tieck's Christian discovers. In fact, for some, only intense Romantic love could complete and

unify the self's capacious wholeness. "Genuine love excludes all oppositions," Hegel remarked in his discourse on love (quoted in Abrams, *Natural
Supernaturalism*, 294), and in his "Essay on Love" Shelley declared, "Love
is the bond and the sanction which connects not only man with man but
with everything which exists" (516–17). That love might take the form of
intimate friendship (e.g., Goethe's deep attachment to Schiller, Byron's to
Scrope Davies),[18] but more often it was expressed as both the physical and
spiritual union of a male and a female who complete each other—sometimes only after death. As a character in Friedrich Schlegel's novel *Lucinde*
(1799) tells his wife, their Romantic love renders their marriage "a timeless
union and conjunction of our spirits" that will last "for our whole eternal
life and being" (48).[19] Of course, it might make a fool of someone experiencing such love, as Stendhal suggests in his discourse on the subject, *On
Love* (1821), when "even the wisest man no longer sees anything *as it really
is*" (60).[20] But this foolishness arises from the abandonment of the self-
constraint that ordinarily keeps individuals from encountering "the magic
of love," as the enamored eponymous narrator of Constant's *Adolphe* extols
it, "that none who has known can ever describe!" (63). This is the magic of
the completed self experiencing complete joy.

Nature also serves the Romantic self in its quest for wholeness, integrity,
and integration. To Romanticists, nature did not merely comprise an inert
set of discrete classifiable elements, as in Linnaeus's system of binomial no-
menclature. It was *alive* (a notion contributing to the coining of the term
biology, the science of life, in 1804).[21] Being alive, nature was composed
of organically connected parts that were born, grew, and decayed while
passing on portions of their identity to their progeny. Just such an organic
vision of the universe (also reflected in many Romanticists' conceptions of
history and nationality as organic entities) led Goethe to pursue the secret
of all plant life through his search for the original life form, the "primal
plant," or *Urpflanze*, from which he believed all others had developed.[22]
This organicism also bespoke the spiritual unity of all things, bridging the
self and nature. Wordsworth, for instance, rhapsodized over how nature
offers those who wander

> A termination, and a last retreat,
> A Centre . . .
> A Whole without dependence or defect
> Made for itself; and happy in itself,
> Perfect Contentment, Unity entire. (*The Recluse* [1800–1806?], ll. 147–51)

Similarly, Novalis described a character immersed in nature blissfully becoming "attentive to the connections that are everywhere" until "he ceased to see anything by itself" and "the perceptions of his senses crowded into great colorful images; he heard, saw, touched and thought at once" in a joyous experience of synesthesia.[23] Nature—particularly in its most awesome or sublime forms, to which Tieck's Christian and so many other Romanticists were drawn—provided a model of organic integrity and facilitated individual transcendence and integration into the universe.

But the all-encompassing Romantic self, with its moral complexities, completed by love and enlarged by nature, could not depend on reason, natural science, or even on love to satisfy its hunger for transcendence, wholeness, and integrity. So Romanticists turned to imagination. As M. H. Abrams has persuasively demonstrated in *The Mirror and the Lamp*, imagination to them was no mere mirror of the world, but a lamp whose light reaches into every corner of existence. Citing Coleridge as the archetypal Romantic theorist of the imagination, Abrams emphasizes the poet's description of this faculty as "a synthetic and magical power" that "blends, and (as it were) *fuses*" into one other "opposite or discordant qualities," and that is "essentially *vital*" in its organic unity.[24] Percy Bysshe Shelley also described the imagination as a synthesizing—and moral—power in his *Defense of Poetry* (1821), attesting that "a man, to be greatly good, must imagine intensely and comprehensively" (540). And in the "Preface to Lyrical Ballads" (1798), Wordsworth depicted imagination as a union of thought and feeling that he later said "shapes and *creates*" by "consolidating numbers into unity" (quoted in Abrams, *Mirror*, 180). At the same time, these synthetic powers of the imagination can give rise to visions, including those of art, that reveal elemental realities and connections among things otherwise hidden from view (such as Christian's perception of jewels within dirty rocks). Romanticists depended on the imagination to uncover what reason or science could not uncover, to discover the living spirit in nature, and to discern the true meaning of experience. "Imagination is a Representation of what Eternally Exists, Really & Unchangeably," proclaimed William Blake ("A Vision of the Last Judgment" [1810], 554). The imagination aided integrity by disclosing truth and revealing wholeness.

Together with the central Romantic ideas of the self, morality, love, nature, and imagination, I might mention two other telling features of Romanticism that also reflect the Romantic quest for wholeness and integrity: the Romanticists' penchant for fragments and their taste for irony. At first glance, a liking for fragments, particularly in literary form, would seem to clash with that quest. In fact, however, it reflects a distinctively Romantic way of looking at things. For instance, the literary fragment—unlike its kindred form the epigram, which presents a polished, witty, compact, complete thought—appealed to Romanticists by virtue of its very incompleteness. For that incompleteness sparked their imaginations to derive from it meaning and wholeness, completion and integrity. In his *Critical Fragments* (an exemplary representative of this genre), Friedrich Schlegel announced that "every whole can be a part and every part really a whole" (144), each one intimating organic interrelationships that an imaginative mind should aspire to perceive. Fragments in various forms—visual vignettes, architectural ruins, aphoristic dicta—gave rise, for numerous Romanticists, not to a sense of disintegration, but to a belief that imagination could create meaning and wholeness out of anything.[25]

Irony played a role related to that of the fragment. But this was a particular kind of irony, known to us as "Romantic irony." By contrast to traditional irony, which offers two conflicting views of some circumstance but implies that one is correct, Romantic irony accepts the validity of both conflicting views of some circumstance, readily accommodating paradoxes and logical oppositions and contradictions. So, to many Romanticists, just as fragments can be wholes when you perceive them (and the world) aright, contradictions and polarities can assume new significance when neither pole excludes the other—each represents an equal truth. As one student of the subject describes it, "irony in its uniquely romantic manifestation" admits "real or potential validity in each component of a dichotomy," and so makes it possible to recognize "complementary contraries, as opposed to adhering doggedly to one position or another" (Fetzer, 21). In other words, the world is too complicated to fit any consistent logical scheme that rules out contradictions (the Romantic idea of history is rooted in the same principle, as Isaiah Berlin contends). Romantic irony requires seeing contradictions as parts of a whole, thereby granting an inherent integration to life, along with an unusual integrity in seeing it for what it is, contradictions and all.

I should also point out that darker strains of melancholy, aimlessness, disillusionment, and despair run throughout Romanticism alongside its more elevating ideals, values, and beliefs. Indeed, some scholars consider a tendency to ennui, passivity, negation, and even imitativeness to be as characteristic of Romanticism as are energy, action, affirmation, and inventiveness.[26] And certainly Romanticists often suffered from these and other negative emotions and experiences when they believed they could not achieve the Romantic ideals of the self, love, imagination, and so on, to which they aspired. But I would argue that even these dark strains of Romanticism reflect its integrity. For true Romanticists undergo negative emotions and experiences in one of two ways: either they integrate those emotions and experiences into their lives as a necessary phase or facet, or they wholly immerse themselves in such emotions and experiences as an act of heroic excess.[27]

Hence many Romantic characters incorporate negativity or darkness—feelings of isolation, melancholy, angst, and so forth—into their lives as a temporary condition preceding a turn to the affirmation of an ideal or the active pursuit of an aspiration. (The critic Morse Peckham explicitly identifies "Negative Romanticism" as a transitory phase of Romantic experience that serves as "the preliminary to Positive Romanticism" [19, 22].)[28] Such miserable feelings become merely a part of a dialectic evolution from a lower, unintegrated state of being to a higher and better-integrated one. In the philosophical treatise *Sartor Resartus* (1836), Thomas Carlyle had his alter ego Teufelsdröch follow just such a course by leaving the "Everlasting No" of spiritual emptiness and despair behind to encounter the "Everlasting Yea" of divine harmony and joy.[29] Teufelsdröch's disorientation and misery become the matrix of his new orientation and jubilation.

Novalis vividly captured this passage from negation and despair to affirmation and exaltation in the third hymn of his *Hymns to the Night* [*Hymnen an die Nacht*] (1800):

Once, when I was shedding bitter tears, when my hopes evaporated into grief, and I stood alone on a bleak hillock that held the focus of my life in its dark confines—more alone than any lone creature had ever been, driven by indescribable anxiety, devoid of strength, conscious of only one great misery,—as I looked round for help, unable to advance or withdraw, clinging with boundless longing to a departing, lost life:—there came from the dim blue distance, from the heights of my former happiness, a tremor of dawn—and all of a sudden . . . earthly splendor vanished and with it my grief—my melancholy flowed over into a new unfathomable world,—you, ecstasy of night, slumber of heaven, came upon me—the countryside rose gently—over it floated my liberated spirit, reborn. . . . I saw the transfigured traits of my beloved. In her eyes was all eternity—I took her hand and my tears became a sparkling, indestructible link. Thousands of years receded into the distance. . . . At her bosom I wept tears of joy at this new life,—It was the first, the only dream—and only since then have I felt an eternal, immutable faith in the heaven of night and its light, my beloved. (Quoted in Furst, *Perspective*, 315; her trans.)

Here bitterness, isolation, and paralysis cede to love, ecstasy, and active faith in a wholeness that brings new life. But even Romantic characters who could not rise from negative emotions and experiences to something higher managed to achieve a form of integrity by utterly steeping themselves in those emotions and experiences, undergoing them intensely, viscerally, titanically. When Byron's Manfred and de Vigny's Satan are afflicted with gloom, it is cosmic gloom; when Goethe's Werther and Chateaubriand's René feel the pang of impossible love, they feel it abysmally; when Schiller's Karl Moor and Hugo's Jean Valjean experience injustice, they experience it excruciatingly. Whatever these characters suffer, they suffer it all-consumingly, almost superhumanly. The very concentration of their emotional intensity exudes Romantic integrity.

In the light of the central elements in the constellation of Romantic ideals, values, and beliefs—the self, love, nature, and imagination, as well as the Romantic affinities for fragments and irony, along with the Romantic sense of integrity and integration that informed them all even while comprising melancholy and misery—we would expect to see the transition out of Romanticism occurring with the declining influence of these elements. And this is precisely what we do see. Just as Romanticism emerged as a period marked by an affirmation of transcendence, wholeness, and the sense of integrity, Romanticism went into decline when this affirmation diminished. From there, the constellation of ideals, values, and beliefs that had brought about the ascendancy of Romanticism as a period disintegrated in one way or another. And, as I will show, no one was more sensitive to this disintegration—with its concomitant loss of cultural integrity—than Lermontov.

ROMANTICISM IN DECLINE

For all of the scholarly and critical writing devoted to the ascendancy of Romanticism,[30] the decline, or transition out, of Romanticism has attracted little concentrated interest. That decline tends to be more or less taken for granted with the emergence of Realism and the political disillusionment that ensued after the revolutions of 1848 buried Romantic hopes for a "great rebirth" and the "harmony of man" in the world (Hobsbawm, 318, 312). Nonetheless, two literary historians who have focused on the ending stages of Romanticism describe and interpret it in contrasting ways—although (in appropriately Romantic fashion) their interpretations ultimately complement each other.

In *The Decline and Fall of the Romantic Ideal*, F. L. Lucas maintains that Romanticism was defeated by its own excesses.[31] Defining Romanticism as "a liberation of the less conscious levels of the mind" (277), he sees Romanticists losing control of themselves, as if drunk on their own ecstasies. "Squeezing 'Joy's grape' against his palate," Lucas declares, early on the Romanticist "grows more eloquent, more magical in the music of phrase and imagery, more impressive in the frank intensity of his feeling and imagination, in the atmosphere that only passion can create" (54). But, "as his intoxication increases, the balance, the proportion, the control, the power to coordinate, of the great masters" fall away, and "the exaggerated ego" grows "as bloated as an ant-queen among her crawling subjects, fertile but grotesque" (54). In this aberrant condition, "the Romantic who drinks too deep, who surrenders too much to the Unconscious, who becomes too completely a child once more" can produce nothing but "Sensationalism, Satanism, Sadism" (277). And so, Lucas concludes, by the middle of the nineteenth century, Romanticism dies of its own self-destructive excesses, its values and beliefs overblown to absurdity.[32]

Virgil Nemoianu shares Lucas's perception that Romanticism was given to powerful intoxicants. But he sees this propensity leading to a different end than self-destructive excesses. It rather led to what Nemoianu terms the "taming" of Romanticism. "The visionary, all-integrating, titanic claims of high romanticism" (by which he means roughly the era of the Napoleonic wars) could not survive for long, he explains, for their "possible-impossible expansion of the self to a seamless identification with the universe" had to be "unstable and explosive" (6, 27). In other words, Nemoianu holds, drawing (like Lucas) on a libational metaphor: "The brew does not age well, not because it is too weak, but because it is too strong" (27). It led many of its devotees to a sense of "a drastically endangered existence" (6).

In consequence of this sense of danger, a fearful reaction spread across Europe during the post-Napoleonic era, as individuals desired "a soothing reform of social and national arrangements" and sought "refuge in the coziness of home and hearth, garden and family" (6). The ideals and joys of Romanticism were not wholly abandoned, but they were "captured and tamed" (28), "compromised" (31), and, in essence, "domesticated" (4) into unthreatening diversions and pallid imitations.[33] This "domestication" meant, among other things, that Romanticism descended from the daring heights of genius and originality to the ordinary plain of the self-satisfied routine life, where "epigonism is placidly accepted and the benefits are enjoyed: pluralism of styles, the reverence for history, the deliberate contrivance of new forms" (7). Indeed, an emblematic novel of the times, Nemoianu notes, is *The Epigones* [*Die Epigonen*] (1836), by Karl Immermann. As Nemoianu describes it, therefore, Romanticism declined gradually, fading into a shadow of itself with a failure of nerve.

Although, like Huizinga and Bouwsma, Lucas and Nemoianu focus on different facets of cultural decline—in this case the decline of Romanticism—they describe what we might consider complementary patterns and consequences in the waning of a cultural period. For whether Romanticism ended through excess, as Lucas says, like Huizinga's Middle Ages, or through diminution, as Nemoianu argues, akin to Bouwsma's Renaissance, the transition out of Romanticism came with a disintegration of the constellation of ideals, values, and beliefs that had defined it, and a concomitant loss of integrity in the cultural life. That is, just as Huizinga saw earnest medieval rituals become aesthetic charades and Bouwsma found Renaissance individuality to provoke an anxious grasping for security, Lucas perceives Romantic ambitions turn into manneristic absurdities while Nemoianu observes those ambitions succumb to comforting epigonal domestication. In each view, cultural integrity disappeared.

In all of these versions of transitions out of a cultural period, those transitions—post-periods, as described in Chapter 1—are times when no integrated constellation of ideals, values, and beliefs clearly inspires and claims allegiance among leading artists and thinkers. Instead of authentic originality and unselfconscious enthusiasm there arises only a manneristic or epigonal devotion displayed through inauthentic imitations and self-indulgent excesses. That kind of transitional condition sets the younger generation adrift in cultural anomie, haunted by a sense of belatedness, lacking a vision of cultural integrity, and so either lapsing into epigonal extravagance and enervation or becoming critical of such lapses while nonetheless remaining uncertain how to avoid them. The post-period centered around the 1830s, when Romantic ideals, values, and beliefs lost their cultural hold, I call post-Romanticism.[34]

In fact, although he does not use the label post-Romanticism, Nemoianu sees just such a loss of integrity when he describes "late Romanticism" as "a long avenue of retreat from the regenerative and totalizing vision of romanticism" into "a separation of the parts . . . a loosening up of the integrative unity (*Auflockerung*)" (31). This "loosening up," he states, results from "a missing central *figura*, the high-romantic paradigmatic human model" (101) that culturally binds the ideal Romantic self and its world together.[35] Without that *figura*, the integral Romantic self dis-integrates; audacious morality becomes ambivalent and ambiguous; ideal love is reduced to affection or derided as delusion; sublime nature loses its thrall; penetrating imaginations cannot find inspiration. Another literary historian labels this time "a centre-less period," one "without power or vitality, where the best was doomed to failure and only the mediocre was destined to success" (Fuerst, 11, 12). In my view, the very loss of a center or core of integrity that distinguished and unified the principal Romantic values signals the shift from Romanticism to post-Romanticism.

Not surprisingly, this shift to post-Romanticism is also signaled by the appearance of distinctive brands of fragments and irony (see especially Chapters 6, 7, and 8 for examples). Whereas Romantic fragments point beyond themselves to their completion in a larger implied whole at some future time, whether sooner or later, post-Romantic fragments point beyond themselves toward nothing. Although they do not convey the utter impossibility of completion in a larger implied whole at some point in the future, they offer no hint of the shape this whole could take. The future is too inscrutable for the post-Romantic imagination, deficient as it is in inspiration, to envision the forms that future might encompass.

Post-Romantic irony works to similar effect. It differs from both traditional irony and Romantic irony (as defined above), by questioning the validity of views in polar opposition to one another, rather than by accepting one, or both. Post-Romantic irony, John Fetzer suggests, reflects "a kind of existential despair, an ontological frustration due to a seemingly 'no-win, no-way-out' situation" in which individuals "find themselves adrift in a rudderless ship . . . floundering in an endless expanse of impossibilities" (22). While evoking the directionless quality of post-Romantic irony, Fetzer goes too far in attributing to it a kind of modernist or postmodernist nihilism. For post-Romantic irony does not fail to acknowledge the *potential* validity of one or more conflicting possibilities, but it does fail to discover the standards or ideals that integrated cultural values provide for judging and choosing among those possibilities. Thus post-Romantic irony betokens the psychological and moral uncertainty and unease pervading the "centre-less" period of post-Romanticism, when insufficient cultural integrity reigned to guide complex judgments and choices.

The post-Romantic loss of cultural integrity appeared in many places during the 1830s and the years shortly preceding and following that decade. In literature, that loss manifested itself in three principal types of authors: (1) those who were themselves epigones and unselfconsciously created epigonal characters; (2) those who criticized the post-Romantic loss of cultural integrity by deliberately creating characters exemplifying post-Romantic fallibilities such as epigonalism, self-deception, and unimaginativeness; and (3) those who criticized that loss of integrity through explicit statements in novels, essays, and poetry.

In post-Romantic times, many authors became Romantic epigones writing novels, stories, plays, and poetry deriving from or overtly imitating Romantic models. Although a number of these epigones chronologically belonged to the generations of mature Romanticism and played a largely epigonal role within Romanticism, that role became more conspicuous as Romanticism declined and they came to typify this prominent aspect of post-Romanticism, showing no particular awareness of their lack of originality, arch imitativeness, or artistic excesses. It is no wonder that, although some were popular in their times, they are for the most part known today chiefly to literary historians. To mention some exemplars: in Germany, there was Franz Grillparzer (1791–1872), whose play *Life Is a Dream* [*Der Traum ein Leben*] (1834) presents an Austrian Faust with a happy ending; Jeremias Gotthelf (1797–1854), whose tales such as "The Black Spider" ["Die schwarze Spinne"] (1842) combine Hoffmanesque fantasy with Gothic medievalism; and Nikolaus Lenau (1802–50), who between 1836 and 1846 wrote fragmentary dramas intended as variations of Goethe's *Faust*. In Britain, there was Mary Russell Mitford (1787–1864), who produced the Byronesque tragedies *Foscari* (1826) and *Rienzi* (1828); John Clare (1793–1864), who wrote the poems of *The Rural Muse* (1835) in imitation of Robert Burns; and Edward Bulwer-Lytton (1803–73), a Walter Scott *manqué* who wrote another version of *Rienzi* in 1835. And in France there was Marceline Desbordes-Valmore (1786–1859), who published the lachrymose collection of nature poetry *Poor Flowers* [*Pauvres Fleurs*] in 1839; Jean-François Casimir Delavigne (1793–1843), whose play *Marino Faliero* (1829) echoed Byron's drama of the same name; and Philothée O'Neddy (1811–75), one of the members of the epigonal group Jeunes France [Young France], whose poetic collection *Fire and Flame* [*Feu et flame*] of 1833, exuded extravagantly Byronic disillusionment and decadence.[36]

But besides such post-Romantic epigonal imitators of preeminent Romantic authors and their works, there were other authors who were aware in varying degrees, to varied effect, of their post-Romantic condition and its consequences for culture and character. Some of these authors reflected that awareness by creating characters who embodied post-Romantic weaknesses and thereby either suffered from them or looked ridiculous. Here I would place Julien Sorel, depicted by Stendhal (1783–1842) in *The Red and the Black* [*Le Rouge et le noir*] (1830) as a torn and frustrated aspirant to Napoleonic triumph when it was too late; the self-inflating, fulsome, and pseudo-idealistic Dr. Folliott, satirized by Thomas Love Peacock (1786–1866) in his novel *Crotchet Castle* (1831); the bored and embittered eponymous artist who cannot fulfill his dreams portrayed by Alfred de Musset (1810–57) in his drama *André del Sarto* (1833)—along with the later treatment of the same character by Robert Browning (1812–89), in *Andrea del Sarto* (1855), as a "faultless" but soulless craftsman utterly lacking in inspiration; and the weak-willed and miserable failure who serves as the title character in the novel *Woyzeck* (1835), by Georg Büchner (1813–37). I would add to this list the title character of Pushkin's *Eugene Onegin* (published serially between 1824 and 1831), which I will address below—and, of course, Lermontov's protagonists. These characters neither surmount negative emotions and experiences in an ultimately affirming existence nor completely immerse themselves in those emotions and experiences with true heroic excess. They remain somehow on the surface of their lives, never able to achieve the psychological or moral integrity of their Romantic forebears.

While epigonal authors and characters dominated the period of post-Romanticism, a few of the authors who created them, and a few other writers, went further, addressing the conditions of post-Romanticism in the 1830s more directly. For example, in Germany, Heinrich Heine (1797–1856), who began his literary career in the 1820s as a thoroughgoing Romantic and who became, according to critic and editor Helen Mustard, "a poet in an age of transition and, as he himself saw clearly, . . . the last of the Romantics" (in Heine, xxii), witnessed the passage of Romanticism with deep regret, plus a witty animosity. In *The Romantic School* [*Die Romantische Schule*], of 1833, written as a response to Germaine de Staël's laudatory description of Romanticism in *On Germany* [*De l'Allemagne*] (1813), Heine mourns the passing of Romanticism as he observes the loss of renowned

Romantic figures either to death or to decline. "The gods are dying," he grieves after the demise of Goethe a year earlier, and then adds cynically, "but we keep the kings" (180). Subsequently he says of August Wilhelm von Schlegel—whom in 1819 he had deemed a "poetic genius" and "the first great man" he had seen besides Napoleon, and whom he had recently seen again—that now "his spirit is dead, and his body still walks the earth like a ghost and in the meantime has become quite fat" (194–95). And he asserts of Ludwig Tieck that lately "a strange disparity between [his] intellect and his imagination" had appeared, so that in Tieck's recent works "a timorous manner, a certain indefiniteness, uncertainty, and weakness are noticeable" (203–4). Overall, Heine inquires of his readers, "Don't you see how sad and wan Germany is? Especially the German youth, who just recently were shouting so joyously and enthusiastically?" (271). Remarking that Germany still "casts a melancholy glance at the past it leaves behind" (268), he urged the young to muster their strength and move forward. For Heine, "the gods" of Romanticism were "dying" in spirit, as well as in body, putting a whole generation at risk of going astray.

Near the same time, in France, Alfred de Musset not only created his André del Sarto, he epochally revealed his sense of his times as an enfeebled aftermath of Romantic grandeur in the *roman à clef* entitled *The Confession of a Child of the Century* [*La Confession d'un enfant du siècle*] (1835). In this novel his alter ego, the main protagonist Octave, laments that after the fall of Napoleon, who had brought "so much joy, so much life . . . such pure sunlight" to the world, and after the deaths of Byron and Goethe, there came a time "between . . . two worlds—like the ocean which separates the old continent from the new America—something vague and floating, a troubled sea filled with wreckage" (2, 7). Then, "instead of having the enthusiasm of evil we had only the renunciation of the good; instead of despair, insensibility" (16). As a result, Musset mournfully reports with a regret equal to Heine's, the youths of that time succumbed to lethargy, disbelief, contempt, and debauchery, incapable of pursuing any ideals, any exaltation. Such was their post-Romantic malaise.

And in England, Robert Browning, saddened at the decline of Romantic idealism and creativity, took out his feelings on Wordsworth for accepting the post of poet laureate in 1843. In one of his poems of that year, "The Lost Leader," Browning excoriates Wordsworth for a venal betrayal: "Just for a handful of silver he left us," Browning snarls, "just for a riband to put in his coat." In so doing, Wordsworth broke faith with the younger generation "that had loved him so, followed him, honoured him," and "made him our pattern to live and to die!" Browning goes on to compare Wordsworth to other sources of Romantic inspiration—"Shakespeare was of us, Milton was for us, / Burns, Shelley, were with us,—they watch from their graves!"—but Wordsworth "alone breaks from the van and the freemen," Browning declares, "He alone sinks to the rear and the slaves!" Wordsworth's act was, deplorably, "One more devils'-triumph and sorrow for the angels, / One wrong more to man, one more insult to God!" So, Browning concludes,

> let him never come back to us!
> There would be doubt, hesitation and pain,
> Forced praise on our part—the glimmer of twilight,
> Never glad confident morning again! (410–11)

Although, like Heine, Browning could envision his culture moving forward, even without a goal clearly in view, he recognized that the culture once represented by a young Wordsworth in the "confident morning" of Romanticism had descended into the twilight.

Heine, Musset, and Browning all lived long enough (Heine to 1856, Musset to 1857, Browning to 1892) to find new norms and values emerging in a new era; they experienced not only a transition out of Romanticism but at least a nascent transition into something else, which would generally become known as Realism. In any case, they largely overcame the "disorientation and bewilderment," as Gellner put it, of transitional times out and no longer faced the quandaries of being "caught between ages," in Hesse's words. Mikhail Lermontov was not so fortunate. He lived his entire short artistic life during that time of transition out of Romanticism, the time of post-Romanticism that stretched from the later 1820s to the early 1840s, so he was unable to elude the quandaries of that transition. That he lived during this post-Romantic time in Russia likely made his transitional quandaries all the more acute—and made his cultural sensibility and his artistic contributions to that time all the more provocative and profound.

RUSSIAN ROMANTICISM AS POST-ROMANTICISM

When we turn to Romanticism in Russia, we are confronted by a complicated historical situation. For European Romanticism was already well underway at the dawn of Russia's modern literary history in the early nineteenth century. Accordingly, the Russian version of Romanticism developed in the shadow cast by the great Romantic artists and thinkers of the West. And Russian artists and thinkers knew it.

The very idea of Russian Romanticism has posed, if anything, more controversy among historians and critics than has European Romanticism. Many Russian critics have questioned whether Romanticism ever took root in Russia at all. Such questioning was standard fare among Soviet literary historians who, for ideological purposes, sought the seeds of Realism in general and Socialist Realism in particular amid the formative years of the Russian literary tradition. These Soviet historians tended virtually to ignore Romanticism altogether, as in their treatments of Nikolai Gogol, or else, when they could not deny its presence, as in Lermontov, they played it down, emphasizing the move away from Romanticism to Realism.[37] As a leading Western historian of Russian Romanticism, Lauren Leighton, observes, during the Soviet era the acceptance of a Romantic movement in Russia was so politically incorrect that "it sometimes became dangerous even to discuss the subject of romanticism" ("Debate," 41).

By contrast to this traditional Soviet view, more recent Russian and Western critics have argued that Russia did experience a Romantic period somewhere between the first decade of the nineteenth century and the 1840s or 1850s.[38] Leighton makes a substantive case for Russian Romanticism as an autonomous movement in his discerning and erudite study, entitled with a nod to Lovejoy, "On a Discrimination of Russian Romanticism" (which Leighton adeptly summarized in his entry on Russian Romanticism in Victor Terras's *Handbook of Russian Literature* and then amplified in the introduction to his collection of translated essays entitled *Russian Romantic Criticism*). Rejecting the "persistent suspicion that Russia did not experience a fully legitimate romantic movement in the European sense" ("Romanticism," 372), Leighton specifies that Russian Romanticism was "a period which is organically related to, as well as distinct from, the Neoclassical age which preceded and the Realist movement which succeeded it" ("Discrimination," 1). "Russianists are now agreed," he maintains, "that the Romantic movement reached Russia at the turn of the century, significantly behind (and greatly influenced by) the movement in England and Germany but well in advance of events in France and America; that the movement had deep roots in pre-Romantic trends of the eighteenth century in both Russian and European literatures; and that the Romantic manner remained viable through at least the 1850s" ("Romantic Criticism," vi).

As evidence for his assertions, Leighton points to the occupation of Russian thinkers and writers in the first half of the century with a wide variety of Romantic philosophical and aesthetic issues. That occupation surfaced especially in abundant literary journals, whose contributors made frequent references to works of the major European Romanticists, and which included whole or partial translations of some of those works—Orest Somov's three-part essay "On Romantic Poetry" ["О романтической поэзии"] (1823), for instance, contains significant portions of Germaine de Staël's *On Germany*. Early debates in Russia over Romantic ideas, Leighton says, led to "the peak of Romanticism in Russia" in the 1820s ("Romantic Criticism," viii) with the assembling of groups of young writers who vigorously claimed the mantle of Romanticism. These groups included both the activist "civic" poets and writers, many of whom became involved in the Decembrist uprising of 1825, and the more contemplative "metaphysical" poets and writers—the two groups that would later evolve into the sociopolitical organizations of liberal Westernizers and conservative Slavophiles, both of which drew further upon European Romantic thought. And although the Romantic movement "almost came to a halt in the very middle" of the 1820s after the suppression of the Decembrist uprising, Leighton continues, it "revived in the 1830s," when "Russia's three greatest Romantics—Pushkin, Gogol, and Lermontov—were all active," and it was sustained into the 1850s, even though "by the mid-1840s Romanticism [was] defunct as a critical concern and by the early 1850s despised as a literary mode of expression" in Russia. At all events, Leighton concludes, "the Russian Romantics were a talented generation, peers of the best men of letters in Germany, France, England, Spain, and Italy," and their literary and critical achievements thoroughly justify terming Russian Romanticism a full-blown "movement" and a legitimate "period" in Russian cultural history ("Romantic Criticism," viii, xi, xii, xiii).

Another leading Western authority on Russian Romanticism, John Mersereau, Jr., defends Russian Romanticism as a discernable "movement" and a distinctive "period" perhaps even more emphatically than Leighton. Mersereau dates Russian Romanticism somewhat more conservatively, placing it between 1815 and 1840, but like Leighton, he identifies it as "a discrete period characterized by prevailing norms" that produced works written "according to the grammar of Romanticism" ("Romanticism," 9). He makes this case most insistently in an essay entitled "Yes, Virginia, There Was a Russian Romantic Movement" (which concludes Christine Rydel's valuable

Ardis Anthology of Russian Romanticism). In this article Mersereau asserts that although "Russian Romanticism owes a debt" to German, English, and French "Romanticisms," Russian Romanticism "as a whole displays as much unity and cohesiveness as any of the others," and so "must still be accorded the courtesy, and prestige, of being considered an individual movement." Hence those who consider themselves Russianists "have the right to speak of a Russian Romantic movement in its own terms" ("Yes, Virginia," 511).

Mersereau stakes his claims on more specific artistic grounds than Leighton does, defining Russian Romanticism as "an esthetic revolution in reaction to conservative literary norms which were no longer productive" and therefore "sought to free itself from the bonds of Neoclassicism." It was truly "national . . . in that it concerned itself with Russian history, folklore, traditions, national types, and it derived its settings from its native landscape"; it was also notably "experimental in that it utilized a new literary language, mixed established genres to form new ones, and engaged in a wide variety of metrical innovations"; and it was markedly "self-conscious, at least to the extent that critics and writers were aware that they were engaged in a common struggle against the literary conservatives, and to the extent that they called themselves 'romantics'" ("Yes, Virginia," 512). While Mersereau acknowledges that many of the best Russian poets of the time do "display some qualities which are more traditionally associated with Classicism than with Romanticism," he stresses that "the presence of non-romantic qualities in the verses of these poets does not make the poets themselves Classicists or Neoclassicists" (514). And, like Leighton, Mersereau names Pushkin, Gogol, and Lermontov "the foremost romantics" (517).

Much as I admire Leighton's and Mersereau's erudite and articulate arguments in favor of a Russian Romantic movement equal in character and stature to those of Germany, England, and France, I must challenge their conclusions for a number of reasons. I offer this challenge *not* because I deny that Romanticism existed in Russia, but because I think that the peculiar form Romanticism took in Russia can best be understood as post-Romanticism.

Let me begin to support my view with a few words on the clever title of Mersereau's essay "Yes, Virginia, There Was a Russian Romantic Movement." At the risk of laboring an unintended irony, I would say that this title inadvertently betrays the "problem" of Russian Romanticism. For by invoking the famous, idealizing editorial in the New York *Sun* in 1897 "Yes, Virginia, There Is a Santa Claus," which reassuringly responded to a child's hopeful question, Mersereau—however unintentionally—suggests that, like Santa Claus, Russian Romanticism as a distinct cultural period equal to the national Romantic movements of Western Europe is something that Russianists *want* to believe in, and *should* believe in, because it is something *valuable* to believe in as an uplifting metaphor, rather than as something that existed on its own.

Playing out this idea, I can conceive of several reasons to *want* a Russian Romantic movement to have occurred. For one thing, it is convenient, both conceptually and terminologically, to subsume the first third or so of nineteenth-century Russian culture under the heading of Romanticism. For another, to do so also carries the gratification of rebutting the Soviet refusal to recognize a true Romantic era in Russia. Furthermore, to affirm the existence of a Russian Romantic era makes it possible to rank the modern Russian literary tradition during its nascence in the early nineteenth century as the equal of the more venerable English, French, and German literary traditions, particularly during their demonstrably great Romantic periods. This is surely an uplifting ideal for a Russianist.

Nonetheless, allusions to Santa Claus aside, and whatever its intent, the effort to confirm a period of full-fledged "Russian Romanticism" fails to succeed on several counts. For one thing, as Leighton concedes, the Russian "Romantic movement" was "more confusing, variegated, and contradictory than other romantic movements," by virtue of the "jumble of alliances, societies, circles, camps, discussion groups, schools, salons, 'evenings,' editorial programs, campaigns, cliques, coteries, and intrigues" that characterized Russian cultural life in the early nineteenth century. Amid this "jumble"— Leighton also describes it as a "porridge" ("Romantic Criticism," vii)—which was often driven by personal, political, and professional rivalries, Leighton rightly observes that "individuals tended to divide and join on specific aesthetic or philosophical questions, to move from one group to another, to belong to several opposing groupings simultaneously," and to "accuse each other of being neoclassicists" ("Romanticism," 373). This ferment of intellectual and artistic activity might have provided vital fuel for the burgeoning Russian literary life. But it also shows that this literary life was still a fledgling reacting to a culture borrowed from abroad and searching for itself, for its own identity, amid the images and ideas of a Western European Romanticism that in some ways was already starting to grow old.

Sarah McLaughlin discerns the same unintegrated Russian cultural "jumble" as Leighton in her informative survey of nineteenth-century Russian uses of the terms signifying "Romantic" and "Romanticism." She demonstrates that the first Russian words referring to Romanticism in Europe, the adjective *romanicheskii* [*романический*] and the noun *romanizm* [*романизм*] (which appeared in the 1790s and are etymologically tied to the Russian word for *novel* borrowed from the French, *roman*), tended to refer to general qualities of spirituality, creativity, unreality, imaginativeness, innovation, and so on.[39] These terms subsequently brought forth the more period-related adjective *romanticheskii* [*романтический*] and the nouns *romantizm* [*романтизм*] and *romantika* [*романтика*], which made their debuts in the 1810s—Pushkin, for one, McLaughlin notes, employed both sets of terms interchangeably, albeit with "growing skepticism" (438), as his own doubts about their precise meaning increased. (He went so far as to declare in a letter of 1825 to a friend that "among us everyone [including you] has only the haziest notion of Romanticism" [quoted in Mersereau, "Pushkin's Conception," 32].) Pushkin's doubts were well-founded, for, as McLaughlin states, a general "amorphousness and muddiness" permeated Russian definitions of terms referring to Romanticism "as a result of the increased influence of Western writings" and the "largely uncritical repetitions of West European definitions." Thus "diverse literary and intellectual phenomena received, often coincidentally, the same designation" (467, 463).[40] This linguistic imprecision reflected the logical and conceptual confusion of Russian authors and literary critics over the values and beliefs, the nature and significance, of Western Romanticism itself. And it is reasonable to conclude that this confusion undermined the potential "integrity" of Russian Romanticism for Russian authors, putting them on uncertain conceptual ground and rendering their relation to authentic Romanticism ambiguous at best.

So it is to be expected that many Russian authors whom Western critics have identified as leading the Romantic movement in Russia—especially poets—displayed, as those critics often concede, at most a divided allegiance to Romanticism. Evgenii Baratynskii, Konstantin Batiushkov, Anton Delvig, Wilhelm Kiukhelbeker, Aleksei Koltsov, and Kondraty Ryleev, to name some of the most prominent, are generally acknowledged to have embraced Romanticism only in part, persistently introducing neoclassical elements, whether of genre, meter, diction, or rhetoric, into their poetry. Although, as noted earlier, Mersereau plausibly points out that "the presence of non-romantic qualities in the verses of these poets does not make the poets themselves Classicists or Neoclassicists" ("Yes, Virginia," 514), by the same token, the presence of Romantic qualities in their poetry—lyricism, emotionality, love of nature, hope of transcendence, admiration of the past, desire for poetic autonomy—does not make them thoroughgoing Romanticists either.

Besides the Russian authors who exhibited such partial allegiance to Romanticism, other authors of the 1820s and 1830s wore their Romanticism as mere epigones. Thus, for example, self-conscious and imitative, the Russian Walter Scottists (e.g., Ivan Kalashnikov, Ivan Lazhechnikov, Konstantin Masalskii, Mikhail Zagoskin), the Russian Byronists (e.g., Nikolai Iazykov, Ivan Kozlov, Aleksandr Odoevskii, Aleksandr Polezhaev), the Russian Schellingists (e.g., Aleksei Khomiakov, Mikhail Pogodin, Stepan Shevyrev, Dmitrii Venevitinov), the Russian Hoffmannists (e.g., Vladimir Odoevskii, Aleksandr Perovskii-Pogorelskii, Nikolai Polevoi, Aleksandr Veltman), and so forth, echoed their European models, adding Russian coloration to pre-established Romantic contents and forms, often with manneristic extravagance. The decade's most popular author, Aleksandr Bestuzhev-Marlinskii, may be the ultimate Romantic epigone, drawing on numerous European authors and works as he indulged in an "ultraromantic style" and "romantic excess" that, according to literary biographer and critic Lewis Bagby, "surpassed all his contemporaries" (5, 45).[41] So pervasive and palpable were these epigonal tendencies in Russia that the poet Wilhelm Kiukhelbeker famously complained in his essay "On the Direction of Our Poetry, Especially Lyric Poetry, in the Past Decade" ["О направлении нашей поэзии, особенно лирической, в последнее десятилетие"], which he published in the journal *Mnemozina* [*Мнемозина*] in 1824:

An imitator does not know inspiration: he does not speak from the depth of his soul, he forces himself to reiterate other people's ideas and feelings. Power?—Where will we discover it in our turgid, vague, effeminate, colorless works? Among us everything is a *dream* and a *vision*, everything is *imagined* and *seems* or *appears to be*, everything is *just as if*, *somehow*, *something or other*, *something*. . . . The tableaux are the same everywhere: the *moon* which, of course, is *dejected* and *pale*, cliffs and oak groves where none ever existed, a forest beyond which the setting sun and dusk have been described a hundred times; sometimes long shadows and ghosts, something invisible, something unknown . . . but especially *fog*—fog over the waters, fog over the pine grove, fog over the fields, fog in the writer's mind. (in Neuhäuser, 182–83)

While granting that Russian authors occasionally produce something new, beautiful, and inspired, Kiukhelbeker goes on to lament that most of them have come to venerate any German or Englishman translated into French, because the French remain the arbiters of taste, and that Russians read works from abroad solely because those works are popular there. These authors, in Kiukhelbeker's view, have not developed the powers of discrimination, much less originality, required to establish an autonomous literary tradition, or even simply to create an independent Romantic movement.

The conceptual vagaries, divided allegiances, and lack of originality and autonomy permeating Russian literary and cultural life in the early nineteenth century have prompted Sarah Pratt to sum up Russia's literary condition in those decades as a "time of troubles" distinguished by "one tangled mass of literary movements," when so many works in the Romantic vein "somehow seemed to bear the indelible stamp 'imported' in spite of the author's efforts to capture the Russian spirit" (217, 1, 3). The same conditions led the eminent Slavic scholar Riccardo Picchio to go further and conclude that Russia could not have mounted a genuine period of Romanticism at that time because Russian literary culture was still in such an eclectic, formative phase. European Romanticism, he explains, arose out of "a traditional discussion," going back to the Italian Renaissance, about poetic principles and practices "within a cultural community to which Russia did not belong up to the XVIII century" (19). Consequently, "Romanticism does not in Russia represent a distinctive mark, but just a poetic ingredient," something of a literary game, "a kind of noble *jeu de société*" (20), since Russian literature in those formative years was assimilating elements of all previous Western literary movements, including not only Romanticism, but sentimentalism, classicism, and neoclassicism. Thus, Picchio maintains, "while there was in Germany a *Romantische Schule*, there were just romantic attitudes in Russia" (22), and so Romanticism "fades and finally gets lost in the European Far East more than elsewhere" (16).[42]

What Picchio generally terms mere "romantic attitudes" I would specify as "post-Romantic attitudes." Cultural confusion, divided allegiances, eclecticism, epigonal imitation—these are all hallmarks of a post-period. Although confused, conflicted, eclectic, and often epigonal artists can certainly be found at the height of any regnant cultural period, they do not define the prevailing norms and values of that period. They can do this only in post-periods—postmodernism is our contemporary proof (see Chapter 8). Mature cultural periods obtain their character and integrity from values and norms that gain ascendancy by means of talented artists and thinkers who create and adhere to them. The period of Romanticism saw such an ascendancy unmistakably across Western Europe. There is hardly a need to name the names of those exceptional individuals whose talents defined Romantic culture, but among the literary artists we can single out Goethe, Schiller, Schlegel, Novalis, Tieck, and Hoffmann in Germany; Blake, Wordsworth, Coleridge, Shelley, Keats, and Byron in England; de Staël, Lamartine, de Vigny, Chateaubriand, Constant, Hugo, and Gautier in France.

Yet when we look for such a cluster of dominant, committed (if not admitted) Romantic artists in Russia during the first three decades of the nineteenth century, we look in vain. In making this assertion I clearly differ from Leighton, Mersereau, and others who regard Pushkin, Lermontov, and Gogol as constituting a constellation of Romantic "stars" in Russia. For I do not think that the artistic achievements of these three authors properly fall under the rubric of Romanticism. To be sure, each of them found inspiration in European Romanticism, like so many of their contemporaries. But in the end each did something with their inspiration that did not belong to Romanticism.

Consider Pushkin (1799–1837). We find in him an early attraction to lyric poetry, a youthful idealization of Byron (expressed especially in Pushkin's narrative "Southern poems" set in the Caucasus), a vigorous admiration of Goethe, a love of Russian history, an insistence on individual creative freedom, and a proclivity for experimentation with literary genres, all of which attest to Pushkin's knowledge and appreciation of European Romanticism—he even dubbed his poetic innovations Romantic.[43] He also labeled his dramatic masterpiece *Boris Godunov* of 1825 a "romantic tragedy" [романтическая трагедия] (Pushkin, 9: 200), for its abandonment of neoclassical conventions, writing in a letter at the time that he feared Russia's "timid taste will not stomach true romanticism" (9: 204), which he identified with Shakespeare.[44] In the same year he wrote an essay entitled "On Classical and Romantic Poetry" ["О поэзии классической и романтической"] to resolve confusion over the nature of "true Romanticism" by explaining formal (rather than substantive) differences between classicism, neoclassicism, and Romanticism, arguing that Romanticism consisted in using forms unknown to classical poetry and, by implication, identifying himself with this movement. Clearly Pushkin was engaged with Romantic ideas and ideals in many ways.

Then there was Lermontov, whose talents rank him alongside Pushkin and Gogol, although the brevity of his life cut short his promise. But unlike Pushkin, fifteen years his senior, Lermontov was not born an insider in the social and cultural swirl of Russia's nascent literary life, nor was he as inclined as Pushkin to consider Romanticism primarily an adventure in literary form or to experiment so extensively with disparate literary styles. And unlike Gogol, he did not veer away from his Romantic origins to become an eccentric author of uncategorizable fiction. Lermontov kept Romanticism flickering in his heart, because for him it was a fallen idol that *was* still a god. And this made Lermontov a Russian Romanticist only in the sense that he became the emblematic author of post-Romanticism. For in the formative decades of modern Russian literary culture, particularly from the early 1820s to the early 1840s—amid Leighton's Romantic "jumble," McLaughlin's conceptual Romantic "muddiness," Kiukhelbeker's complaints about Romantic imitativeness, and Picchio's observation of a *jeu de société* of "romantic attitudes"—Russia did not attain a period of true Romanticism but instead went through an era of post-Romanticism. And Lermontov became its most evocative voice, expressing its historical character and recognizing its historical dilemma. As that emblematic post-Romantic author, Lermontov was at once of his times and above them.

LERMONTOV, ROMANTICISM, AND POST-ROMANTICISM

Lermontov's place in the literary history of both Russia and the West has long stirred debate. Indeed, this debate has persisted for so long that Todd aptly describes it as a *perpetuum mobile* of Russian literary criticism (*Fiction and Society*, 243). This *perpetuum mobile* has in effect created two Lermontovs. The first is honored mainly as a gifted Romantic poet who helped shape the modern Russian literary tradition during its formative phase. The second is hailed as a pioneering author of prose fiction—primarily the novel *A Hero of Our Time* [*Герой нашего времени*]—who spurred that literary tradition on to the maturity it later achieved in the era of Realism. That is to say, some critics contend that Lermontov was essentially a Romanticist and others argue that he left Romanticism behind and became essentially a Realist.

K. N. Grigor'ian, for example, takes the first view, arguing that Lermontov remained a thoroughgoing Romanticist throughout his literary career.

Grigor'ian affirms that Lermontov's works are "surprisingly monolithic and unified" (62–63), all "colored by an acute lyricism" (81) that was "organically typical of Lermontov's personality" (78), and were infused throughout by a "tormented, heroic Romanticism" (299). Lermontov embodied these qualities in protagonists whose isolation, pride, love of freedom, emotional intensity, attraction to nature, and so on, tell us "to love passionately, to strive with all one's soul toward everything noble and exalted" (300), in the most fervent Romantic tradition.[48] Taking a similar tack, Vladimir Golstein holds that Lermontov was virtually the only Russian of his day consistently to portray protagonists who heroically exemplified "the spirit of autonomy, dignity, and self-reliance" that distinguished "the individualistic ethos of Romanticism" (6).[49] And sounding the same theme, Leighton declares that in the decade of the 1830s Lermontov was "all alone" as "Russia's great Romantic" ("Romanticism," 375).[50]

Adopting the opposing view, other critics assert that Lermontov radically altered the course of his literary career by the mid-1830s in turning away from the subjective emotionality and exoticism of his youthful poetry toward the objective observations and exploration of the world around him. Numerous Russian critics from Belinskii to the Soviets (for whom this perception of Lermontov was all but politically obligatory), as well as many critics in the West, have read Lermontov's later works—from the drama *Masquerade* [*Маскарад*] to *A Hero of Our Time* [*Герой нашего времени*]— as the first steps in the development of what would become Russian Realism. Such critics explain that Lermontov essentially abandoned his youthful attachment to Romanticism in favor of the emotional detachment, intellectual skepticism, social criticism, and psychological analysis promoted by the Realist literary enterprise.[51]

The portrait of Lermontov as divided between Romanticism and Realism is somewhat easier to support than the claim that he was a typical Romanticist all along—connecting *A Hero of Our Time* to full-fledged Romanticism is something of a challenge.[52] Still, it is too easy to conclude that Lermontov simply moved from Romanticism to Realism. For to do so leaves unanswered some questions fundamental to Lermontov's literary career and historical significance. Namely: Did Lermontov foresee and deliberately pursue the norms and values that Realists would embrace? And if Lermontov did switch his allegiance from Romanticism to Realism, what were the dynamics of that change? How, for example, did Lermontov move from the subjective lyricism, emotional intensity, and high expectations of Romanticism to the objective scrutiny, emotional caution—even cynicism—and tempered expectations of Realism?

One suggestive answer to these questions comes from the noted Formalist critic Boris Eikhenbaum in his "historico-literary" [историческо-литературное] evaluation of Lermontov's accomplishments. Although Eikhenbaum does not use the period terms Romanticism and Realism, he judges Lermontov to have been an artist whose "main work" in the 1830s was that of "reconciliation and summation," thereby "bringing a literary epoch to a close" in Russia and opening the door to another (*Lermontov*, 88, 13, 46). Lermontov performed that "main work," according to Eikhenbaum, through an "intentional combining of prepared materials," that is, by borrowing "old bits and pieces"—phrases, lines, and even stanzas from a broad range of earlier European and Russian poetic and prose works, including his own—and then binding them together with "a tense lyricism and emotional eloquence" (*Lermontov*, 88, 28). Eikhenbaum concludes that although Lermontov derived many of his literary materials from earlier sources, his gifts enabled him to "remain independent" of these sources, as he rose above the mere epigonal eclecticism that contemporaries such as Kiukhelbeker, Viazemskii, and Gogol attributed to him,[53] and created what Eikhenbaum labels a distinctive art of "fusion" that at once summarized and transcended its context (*Lermontov* 33, 88).

Eikhenbaum's observations and conclusions are erudite and thought-provoking. However, his contention that Lermontov's cultural contributions derived from an art of "fusion" goes somewhat off target. I would argue instead that Lermontov signaled the end of the Romantic era not so much by the "fusion" or "reconciliation and summation" of that era's literary achievements as by reflecting a sense of the disintegration and lost integrity of that era's reigning constellation of values and beliefs. While he yearned for the emergence of a new cultural integration and integrity to unite new values and beliefs, he was unable to envision what forms any of these might take.

And that, as stated in Chapter 1, is the thesis of this book: in their overarching concern with the loss of cultural integration and integrity, Lermontov's works epitomize the condition of living in an epoch of transition. His works reflect neither a lingering, late Romanticism, nor the cultural transition from Romanticism to Realism, but, more precisely, the passage out of Romanticism into a time between cultural periods, in the dimming twilight of one period and before the dawn of another.[54] In their psychological, metaphysical, ethical, and aesthetic ambiguities and ambivalences, Lermontov's works tellingly capture the time of transition out of Romanticism, or what I designate as post-Romanticism.

But this form of post-Romanticism is quite different from those described by Lucas and Nemoianu. For Lermontov's post-Romanticism was characterized by a heightened sensibility to the difficulties, the dilemmas, the quandaries posed by a time of cultural transition that his great contemporaries, Pushkin and Gogol, would leave unresolved as they followed their own creative genius. It is this transitional sensibility, I would suggest, that takes Lermontov's works beyond the realm of Romantic irony, which ultimately denies all dilemmas and quandaries by embracing all contradictions.[55]

Of course, the timing of Lermontov's brief career made his transitional condition likely. Born in Moscow in 1814 and reared in the Russian countryside primarily by his maternal grandmother, Lermontov studied literature in Moscow as an adolescent, when he began to write lyric and narrative poetry. He entered a St. Petersburg military academy in 1832, aspiring to a Byronic life of adventure—at least partly to compensate for a sense of social alienation due to his physical unattractiveness and relative poverty. That year he made his first attempt at prose fiction, starting a Gothic novel he never finished, *Vadim* [*Вадим*]. Two years later, he was commissioned a hussar, but he remained in Petersburg, writing poetry that went unpublished, and working on a novel entitled *Princess Ligovskaia* [*Княгиня Лиговская*], which he also never finished but which foreshadowed *A Hero of Our Time*, while he attempted to publish and stage the play *Masquerade* (1835), which tsarist censors rejected for lacking an uplifting moral.

Lermontov's life significantly changed course in 1837, when he won sudden public acclaim for a clandestinely circulated poem, "The Death of a Poet" ["Смерть поэта"], which angrily blamed envious Petersburg courtiers for Pushkin's fatal duel and prompted Lermontov's arrest and sentencing to military service in the Caucasus. Pardoned the next year, Lermontov returned to St. Petersburg as an esteemed poet—deemed by some the artistic equal of Pushkin—for lyrics that had appeared in several publications, a status granting him entrée to the highest social circles despite his antagonism toward aristocracy. While in Petersburg this time, he wrote his last version of the narrative poem *The Demon* [*Демон*] (1839), on which he had been working for over ten years, as well as some of his most renowned lyric poems, and in 1840 he published his novel *A Hero of Our Time*. But shortly thereafter he was arrested for fighting a duel and sent back to military duty in the Caucasus, where he was killed in 1841 during yet another duel, fought over an affront to his sense of honor, at the age of twenty-six.

Had Lermontov lived as long as Gogol or his younger contemporary Fedor Dostoevsky (1821–81), for instance, Lermontov might have become a Realist, a protomodernist, or something else. But his career, extending only from his first known poem written at the age of fourteen in 1828 to his novel *A Hero of Our Time* in 1840 and the short story "Shtoss" in 1841, largely unfolded in the most transitional decade of his transitional era. Coming to maturity between cultural periods, Lermontov could not wholly hold onto what was passing, but neither could he let it go. This condition might have bred in him an epigonal tendency to either "out-Romanticize" Romanticism (and it could be argued that he made one such attempt in *Vadim*, which he left unfinished, possibly in recognition of its fruitlessness),[56] or merely to recycle and imitate it, as many of his fellow Russian authors did. But Lermontov was exceptional. Thanks to his genius and sensibility, he avoided both fates, expressing his post-Romantic transitional condition in works that showed a keen consciousness of this condition while recognizing both the need to go beyond it to discover a new cultural integrity and the fact that he did not know how to do so.

In emphasizing Lermontov's awareness of his transitional condition and the need for cultural integrity, I should remark that two recent studies of Lermontov also posit integrity as one of his primary values. In *Lermontov's Narratives of Heroism*, Vladimir Golstein asserts that Lermontov was deeply committed to personal and moral integrity and consistently portrayed protagonists who possessed that commitment. And in *Becoming Mikhail Lermontov: The Ironies of Romantic Individualism in Nicholas I's Russia*, David Powelstock likewise maintains that Lermontov prized his own personal integrity, and tried to persuade his readers of that integrity through a variety of literary strategies.[57] My perspective differs from both of these in focusing chiefly not on Lermontov's life and personal moral integrity, but on the ways in which his works bespeak a conception of integrity as the integration of culture through a set of reigning norms and ideals, and a sense that this integrity was dissolving during his transitional times.[58]

Hence, unlike these and most other students of Lermontov, I draw relatively little upon his biography in my reading of his works. I have done this for several reasons. In the first place, my subject is those works themselves and their relation to Russian and Western literary history. In the second place, we have very sketchy information about Lermontov's life and thought outside of his works. He left just some fifty-odd, mostly short, letters that touch lightly on a wide variety of topics in diverse tones disclosing too little of the mind and personality behind them. The testimony of Lermontov's contemporaries to his activities and character is more extensive, but it nonetheless gives us chiefly a picture of the youthful Lermontov through random, anecdotal reports that do not coalesce into a clear portrait.[59] In lieu of more historical evidence regarding his character and literary intentions, many critics have treated the highly Romanticized persona often displayed in his lyric poetry as revealing Lermontov himself. But equating Lermontov's poetry with his personality runs the risk of a fallacious identification of art and life. As Jacques Barzun has observed, when we make this equation for Romantic artists in particular (he mentions Byron and Berlioz as having been especially victimized this way), we are likely to reach exaggerated assessments of both the life and the work—for "we, and not the romantics, do the exaggerating" (*Classic*, 82). In other words, it is all too easy to romanticize the Romanticists.

That said, such biographical evidence as we do have, together with some recurring themes in his works, indicates that Lermontov, like so many of his generation, was not a true Romanticist but wished he were one, particularly one in the Byronic spirit.[60] He arguably tried to live out that aspiration by writing moody poetry and engaging in military derring-do. But for the most part, as an *artist*—unlike his lesser epigonal contemporaries—Lermontov seemed aware that he could not be a genuine Romanticist, because it was too late for that. He could only imitate such Romanticists or, as he increasingly learned, give voice to the condition of living in their shadow during a time that had lost cultural integrity and needed to find it anew.

Granted, Lermontov may have etched a portrait of the Romanticist he wanted to be in many of his lyric poems (the favorite genre of so many Romanticists). But in his major works of narrative poetry, drama, and prose—upon which my study concentrates, with comparative references to European Romantic works of narrative poetry, drama, and prose—he reveals above all his awareness of the post-Romantic culture that he was destined to inhabit as an artist. This awareness was not always as explicit as it became in *A Hero of Our Time*, but it was always there as a transitional cultural sensibility. And it was this sensibility that gave rise to what are best understood as Lermontov's distinctively transitional works, which reflect so provocatively, if often subtly, the aesthetic ambivalence, moral uncertainty, and psychological dis-integration typifying times of *transition out*, when cultural norms and values are in decline.

Lermontov was not alone, of course, in experiencing this post-Romantic transitionality. As indicated earlier, a number of his contemporary European authors felt and, in one way or another, expressed the same condition. These included Søren Kierkegaard (1813–55), who recognized more acutely than most the mentality that this condition engendered. In *The Concept of Irony* (1841), Kierkegaard stated that every "turning point in history" draws forth "the ironic subject" who "has advanced beyond the reach of his age and opened a front against it" because "the given actuality has completely lost its validity," and yet "that which shall come is hidden from him" (277, 278).[61] To Kierkegaard, this transitional role of the "ironist" was one of "absolute negativity" discrediting everything around it. But Lermontov's relation to the passing culture was not as negative as Kierkegaard's transitional "ironist." To Lermontov, Romanticism was a fallen idol that was still a god   in other words, Romanticism might no longer reign, but it could still be revered as a source of lingering ideals in a time that had no clear cultural standards or integrity of its own. This attitude marked Lermontov's works as transitional from the beginning to the end of his brief career, shifting only by degree.

Overall, Lermontov's works therefore reflect not just a loss of the cultural ideals and integrity that came with the decline of Romanticism but an implicit appreciation in principle of cultural ideals and the integrity they entailed, along with a yearning to find new ones. For even while faulting some claims and consequences of Romanticism, Lermontov's works convey a sense that post-Romantic disillusionment was no virtue in itself, since it induced corrosive doubts that could paralyze action, breed cynicism, or pervert thought. His "hero of our time" embodied a host of such failings. True to the Romanticism that Lermontov in many ways did still worship, he remained something of an idealist, even as he saw Romanticism promising too much and then descending into self-deceptive charades—which he seemed to detect sometimes even in himself as, for instance, when he borrowed from Byron and Pushkin while struggling with an ambivalence toward what they represented (see Chapter 3).

Lermontov's relation to Romanticism could in fact be said to have always been marked by a measure of ambivalence for the very reason that his fallen idol was still a god. This is also why I think that Lermontov did not forsake Romanticism for Realism.[62] Although "realistic" tendencies are evident in his later works—such as his turn to prose fiction, his detailed depiction of certain characters, and his occasionally sharp social criticisms—the general orientation of Lermontov's works aesthetically, psychologically, and ethically, looks backward toward Romanticism more than forward toward Realism. These works rely on Romantic structures, themes, ideas, and ideals for their form and substance, even as they question them all and presage an uncertain future.

Thus Lermontov's works truly belong neither to Romanticism, nor to proto-Realism, nor to some combination of the two. Lermontov's literary sensibility was too ambiguous, ambivalent, and self-critical fully to exemplify Romanticism in either the European or the Russian contexts. And his foreshadowings of Realism are actually more the "backshadowings," in Morson's terms (see Chapter 1), of later critics' hindsight. Neither Romanticist nor Realist, the short-lived Lermontov hovers in between, in transition, during the decade of the 1830s. This was a decade when no sensitive young literary artist could have failed to feel he had arrived rather late to the party of Romanticism, if he had not missed it altogether, since so many of its leading lights had already passed from the scene or were soon to go, including Novalis, Schiller, Hoffmann, Schlegel, Goethe, Keats, Shelley, Byron, Blake, Coleridge, de Staël, and Constant. But Lermontov played his transitional role with greatness. For he not only raised questions about Romanticism that Realism would later make its own, he also shed light on Romanticism itself and how it faded. And he illustrated how difficult it is to live in a transitional time devoid of a unifying sense of cultural integration and integrity, suggesting that we may all need such integration and integrity more than we might think.

THREE

The Ambivalence of Influence

Lermontov's "Not-Byronism"

LERMONTOV AND BYRON

In 1832, the young Lermontov opened a now well-known lyric poem with the abrupt denial, "No, I'm not Byron." Lermontov goes on in that poem to offer a few wan comparisons of himself to the renowned British poet, claiming to be "another, / Still unacknowledged chosen one" who, like Byron, is "a wanderer hounded by the world, / Only with a Russian soul." Then with an eerie prescience, as if foreseeing his own premature death just nine years later at the age of twenty-six, Lermontov asserts, "I began earlier, I will finish early." Capped by a final lament, "Who / Will convey my thoughts to the crowd? / I—or God—or no one!" (1: 321),[1] the poem resounds less as a declaration of personal and literary independence than as a plaint of disappointment, as if to say, "No, I'm not Byron—alas!"

Although the adolescent Lermontov might have been speaking here not for himself, but simply in the voice of a poetic persona, his own actual attraction to Byron is one of the few well-documented facts of his biography. First encountering Byron's poems in French and Russian translations as a boy, he had memorized Vasilii Zhukovskii's version of Byron's *The Prisoner of Chillon* by the age of thirteen; at fifteen, having been tutored in English at home, he was translating and adapting Byron's poems (including *The Giaour* and the meditative lyric "Darkness") from the original into Russian on his own; and at sixteen, according to one acquaintance, Ekaterina Sushkova, he was "inseparable" (quoted in Eikhenbaum, *Lermontov*, 28) from Byron, carrying a volume of Byron's works everywhere and proudly identifying himself with the British poet.[2]

Most critics have taken this personal identification with Byron to be at the heart of Lermontov's literary identity, especially during the formative phase of that identity.[3] Biographer John Mersereau, for one, summarily states, "Of all foreign authors, it was Byron who became the particular master of Lermontov" (*Lermontov*, 28–29).[4] The French critic Eugène Duchèsne matches this claim in affirming that Lermontov took the fundamental "point of departure" for his "views on life and people" from Byron (53). More specifically, Russian critic Mikhail Rozanov discerns a "veritable flood of Byronic echoes of every sort" (346)—he itemizes translations, paraphrases, borrowings, and imitations—in Lermontov's early works. Literary historian Nina Diakonova traces a skein of indebtedness to Byron throughout Lermontov's career,[5] and, with Vadim Vatsuro in their overview of Byron's reception in Russia, she maintains that, although the works of many Russian authors exhibit Byron's influence, "Lermontov's art was the culminating point of Russian Byronism" (156). And Sarah Pratt goes so far in her study of Russian Romanticism as to make Byron and Lermontov virtually interchangeable, concluding that "Byronic—or Lermontovian—romanticism . . . nourished Russian literature until the rise of Gogol and the transition to the great age of realism in the middle decades of the century" (3). Even some critics who stress Lermontov's later affinities with Realism rather than his early identification with Byronic Romanticism grant that Lermontov had to "overcome" his early adherence to Byron in order to find his own authentic voice, thereby treating Lermontov's Byronism as a powerful obstacle—almost a disease—or a classic case of Harold Bloom's "anxiety of influence."[6]

To be sure, Lermontov was not a Russian Byron, as numerous differences between the two artists demonstrate: critics comparing them most frequently discern in Lermontov a deeper feeling for nature, broader objectivity, greater historical and psychological concreteness, and simpler language and syntax. But no commentator appears to have much doubt that, at least in his youth, Lermontov did long to be a Byron—not only Byron the artist but Byron the historical figure, so intertwined were the two for Lermontov, as they were for much of Europe's reading public.[7]

This chapter reconsiders the ways in which the young Lermontov both was and was not Byron, so to speak, maintaining that his early works manifested not a Bloomian anxiety that Lermontov was driven to overcome, but a transitional ambivalence toward key components of Byron's psychology and aesthetics. This ambivalence would cause Lermontov openly to adopt Byronic characters and plot lines in admiration of their animating spirit, but then to render them somehow incomplete, their integrity thereby diminished, as if in recognition that those characters and plot lines had lost their spirit. The chapter demonstrates this rendering specifically by exploring relations between the two authors' narrative poetry, since Lermontov's works in this genre afford the most sustained display of Byron's influence.[8] While granting commonalities between Lermontov and Byron—from borrowed lines to shared characters and similar philosophical inclinations—the discussion here will indicate how this ambivalence, appearing from early on, gave Lermontov a distinctive independence from Byron. For his ambivalence toward Byron shifted Lermontov away from the Romanticism that Byron so conspicuously represented, and placed Lermontov amid the post-Romanticism that he would at once inhabit and transcend throughout his brief career. This discussion thus points more broadly to the quandaries of artistic influence in transitional times. Such influence may be desired for its undeniable powers of inspiration, but it also must be doubted for its questionable pertinence to a changing culture.

Before proceeding, we might ask why the youthful Lermontov would have wanted to be Byron at all. But then, what young author of that era would not have wanted to be? George Gordon, Lord Byron, became (with Goethe) the preeminent European literary figure of the first quarter of the nineteenth century, towering over the literary scene much the way Napoleon dominated the European political scene. A titan of inventiveness and feeling, Byron pulsed with the heartbeat of his times; to read his dramas and his lyric and narrative poetry was to feel this heartbeat as a vital force. He enthralled readers with the early narrative poetry above all, in which he portrayed acts of exploration and adventure in a robust, sinewy language of unprecedented emotional intensity—he "heats the materials of his imagination in the furnace of his passions," enthused William Hazlitt (72). So captivated were Byron's readers, in fact, that one contemporary reviewer, John Wilson, asserted in 1817, "Lord Byron has been elected by acclamation to the throne of poetical supremacy" (quoted in Rutherford, 111). And the general European reading populace was not the sole source of Byron's acclaim. A generation of fellow authors famed in their own right, including Balzac, Hugo, Leopardi, Pushkin, Mickiewicz, and Heine, all admired and in some fashion imitated Byron, while Goethe himself—who glowingly reviewed *Manfred* and wrote Byron a moving poem on the eve of Byron's fateful departure for Greece—held the British author in such high esteem that, according to one biographer, Goethe regarded Byron as "his only peer" (Friedenthal, 484).[9]

Byron achieved his exalted status largely by virtue of the emblematic kind of protagonist he invented, a character type that became known as the Byronic hero, depicted primarily in his relatively early works, especially the so-called "Oriental tales" Byron composed between 1813 and 1816: *The Giaour, The Bride of Abydos, The Corsair, Lara, The Siege of Corinth*, and *Parisina*. This character type—with which Byron himself became inevitably, if not altogether correctly, identified—was larger than life,[10] engaging in outsized exploits while experiencing extravagant love, unabating social alienation, cosmic despair, and an all-consuming need for individual freedom at any cost, even crime or death.[11]

Although many critics later turned against this Byronic character type (and against Byron as its putative exemplar), complaining that Byron purveyed a vision of "violence and disorder" (Ridenour, 45), a "massive sense of nothingness" (du Bos, 72), and an abysmal hopelessness in the face of a meaningless universe,[12] a more persuasive view has detected even beneath Byron's gloom and doom an irrepressible vitality. G. K. Chesterton hits the mark when he says: "One of the best tests in the world of what a poet really means is his metre. He may be a hypocrite in his metaphysics, but he cannot be a hypocrite in his prosody. And all the time that Byron's language is of horror and emptiness, his metre is a bounding *pas de quatre*" (40).

Precisely—no matter how grim the subject or how dire the circumstances or how despairing the characters his narrative poetry portrays, Byron infuses that poetry with an exuberant rhythm bespeaking a vigorous embrace of even the darkest aspects of human existence. Indeed, Chesterton's conception of Byron as at the very least an "unconscious optimist" whose elemental being "was spirited and confident"(42) rings far truer to Byron—both the artist and the historical figure—than do images of him as disconsolate, disoriented, and nihilistic. Algernon Swinburne, a decadently inclined poet antagonistic to Byron, was more accurate than he probably knew when he opined, "It pleased [Byron] to seem sadder than he was" (Rutherford, 78).[13] No one so emotionally afflicted as Byron was purported to be would likely have embarked on the bold and high-minded, if quixotic, adventure to fight for Greek independence from the Turks that became Byron's final "Byronic" act.

The Byron whom Lermontov encountered in youth was this poet of fabled daring whose titanic heroes and "bounding *pas de quatre*" he first discovered in translation and then in the original.[14] But what the youthful Lermontov did with this Byron and his influence would characterize the mature Lermontov as well, and would differ significantly, if not wholly, from other so-called Russian Byronists of his time.[15] Lermontov differed from them at least in part because, whereas they tended to be drawn either to the "bright" side of Byron—his spirit of independence, courage, and love of freedom—or to the "dark" side—his expressions of alienation, disillusionment, and despair—Lermontov responded to Byron with a deeper sense of complexity and ambivalence.

Lermontov's response to Byron also differed from that of Pushkin, an early transmitter of Byron's art to Russia. As noted in Chapter 2, Pushkin is traditionally viewed as having gone through a "Byronic phase" during a youthful period of political exile in the Caucasus in the 1820s, when he composed his so-called "Southern poems": *The Prisoner of the Caucasus* [Кавказский пленник], *The Fountain of Bakhchisarai* [Бахчисарайский фонтан], and *The Gypsies* [Цыганы]. These were a group of narrative poems apparently inspired by Byron's "Oriental tales" in their shared portrayal of exotic settings and characters, dramatic plot turns, and tragic denouements. And in letters of that period Pushkin expressed admiration for Byron's love of individual freedom and his advocacy of artistic autonomy. Pushkin nonetheless remained wary of Byron's aesthetic and emotional extremes even in these early poems, and later he firmly denied any strong affinities between his works and Byron's, instead questioning, parodying, or otherwise undermining the lofty image of the Byronic hero in many of his more mature works, most notably *Eugene Onegin*. Indeed, in her analysis of Pushkin's relationship to Byron, Monika Greenleaf argues that Pushkin never went through a phase of true Byronic "apprenticeship," which he subsequently had to outgrow, at all. Instead, she maintains, Pushkin was "less a convert than a gifted impersonator" of

Byron, in that, like Byron, Pushkin deliberately cultivated a public image of himself combining an unconventional public persona with the characters of his rebellious literary protagonists.[16] For Pushkin, this was a way to save himself from "possible oblivion" vis-à-vis the Russian reading public during his exile ("Apprenticeship," 393, 392). Hence, Greenleaf concludes, Pushkin's Byronism—and "the entire Romantic episode in his career"—was for Pushkin actually "a game" played with his readership in order to enhance his own prominence by exploiting Byron's popularity while also excusing any immature infelicities in his youthful works (394).

Greenleaf's provocative denial of Pushkin's early attachment to Byron may be overly influenced by Pushkin's own later dismissal of such an attachment.[17] However, the notion of Pushkin "playing a game" in manipulating Byron's image and "Byronism" to his own ends surely fits with Pushkin's recurring indulgence in pranks, gambling, and play-acting when they suited his purposes (it also calls to mind Picchio's assertion, mentioned in Chapter 2, that Romanticism in Russia overall was more of a *jeu de société* than a sustained cultural movement). Given Pushkin's character and his own peculiar genius, it seems fair to assume that his personal and literary connections to Byron were highly self-conscious, aesthetically calculated, and at least partially self-serving.

Similarities between Pushkin's and Lermontov's "Byronic" works certainly suggest that Pushkin's public behavior and published narrative poems might have triggered or at least encouraged Lermontov's admiration and emulation of Byron—several commentators have asserted Pushkin's intermediary influence in this regard.[18] And it is undeniable that both of these Russian authors would display ambiguous relations to Byron in their early works set in the Caucasus: they would adopt Byron's favorite form, the narrative poem, but relatively restrain its narrative power; they would employ Byronic exotic settings and impassioned plots but somehow deflate them; they would portray seemingly typical Byronic characters and then show them falling short of the typical scale and vitality; and they would manifest a Byronic awareness of the threats to the human spirit posed by self-consciousness, passivity, and dependence, yet stop short of fully endorsing Byron's ideals of self-sacrifice, activity, and transcendence.

But for all of these similarities between Pushkin's and Lermontov's reactions to Byron, as manifested in their "Byronic" narrative poems, pronounced differences appear as well. We might expect this. For Lermontov first came upon Byron in the late 1820s, when Lermontov was in his early teens and Byron had already died, whereas Pushkin first encountered Byron over half a dozen years earlier, when Pushkin was in his early twenties and Byron was still very much alive. Thus to Pushkin, Byron was less of a mythic figure than he was to Lermontov, and Pushkin himself was more mature, more experienced, and more capable of detachment when he chose to incorporate Byronic elements into his poetry, than was Lermontov, the precocious yet inexperienced and enamored adolescent. Moreover, Pushkin wrote his "Byronic" poetry at a time when Romanticism was still entering Russia's cultural atmosphere and its fortunes there had not unfolded. By contrast, Lermontov composed his "Byronic" poetry at a time when Romanticism was starting to fade in the West and had suffered from conflicts, confusion, and inferior imitations in Russia without ever fully taking root (see Chapter 2). Lermontov's early narrative poems therefore reflect more of a post-Romantic ambivalence toward the ideas and ideals informing Byron's narrative poems than do Pushkin's, with their more detached, selective use of those ideas and ideals.

Lermontov revealed his distinctive ambivalence toward Byron, among various ways, by importing more of the aesthetic, psychological, and ethical concepts central to Byron into his own "Southern" narrative poems than Pushkin did, while also conveying a more profound and regretful disillusionment with those concepts as he diffused their impact and cast doubts on their import. And whereas Pushkin turned from an appreciation of Byron to a relative indifference toward him in both life and art, Lermontov remained emotionally and aesthetically engaged with Byron and his works to the end, modeling his behavior on Byron more extensively and grappling more intensely with Byronic images, characters, and themes than Pushkin had. Lermontov thereby embedded a more characteristic, heartfelt, and enduring ambivalence toward Byron in his works than did his brilliant Russian predecessor.[19]

These differences support the conclusion that, notwithstanding any inspiration or influence derived from Pushkin, Lermontov responded to Byron directly and independently, on his own.[20] Hence the discussion that follows will focus on the comparison of Lermontov's narrative poems to Byron's Oriental tales, with only occasional reference to Pushkin's works—after all, it was copies of Byron's poems, not Pushkin's, that Lermontov carried everywhere with him as a youth. This comparison will elucidate the qualities that were to typify Lermontov's Byronism—or rather, his "not-Byronism." For, whether consciously or not, Lermontov increasingly distanced his poems from Byron's, and from the Romanticism that Byron's poems embodied. Byron's influence on the post-Romantic Lermontov could only extend so far.

THE *CORSAIR* AND *KORSAR*

One of Byron's Oriental tales, *The Corsair*, affords an especially instructive opportunity to compare Byron and Lermontov, and to observe the particular use Lermontov made of Byron. There is good reason to think that Lermontov took this poem as the model for his own narrative poem *The Corsair* [*Kopcap*], the only one of Lermontov's works to share a title with one of Byron's. Although there is no direct evidence to show that Lermontov actually knew Byron's poem when he wrote his own (he did cite it in English four years later), the identity of the titles—and the foreignness of the title *Korsar* to Russian—make Lermontov's familiarity with Byron's work almost certain.[21] (It is also worth noting that, according to Diakonova and Vatsuro, the first mention of Byron in the Russian press came in a review of Byron's *Corsair* published in 1815, which emphasized Byron's growing popularity in Russia [144].) Of course, since Lermontov wrote *Korsar* (I will use the transliterated Russian title to identify Lermontov's poem) when he was about fourteen years old, in 1828, it cannot be expected to rival Byron's version, published when Byron was twenty-six (as it happens, in the year Lermontov was born, 1814). Nonetheless, it almost uncannily limns patterns of response to Byron that would stay with Lermontov until his premature death. And even if Lermontov did not then know Byron's *Corsair* at first hand, the comparison of this emblematic Byronic composition to Lermontov's *Korsar* highlights Lermontov's nascent "not-Byronism" and reveals his formative ambivalence toward his most influential predecessor—and toward Romanticism overall.

First, a look at Byron's *Corsair*. Written over the course of a mere ten days, it is a three-part, 696-line narrative poem portraying the adventures of Conrad, leader of a band of pirates, or corsairs, who is an exemplary Byronic hero—proud, reticent, socially alienated, angry, honorable, freedom-loving, fleeing a mysterious past. Although deeply in love with Medora, the beautiful wife with whom he lives in an island hideout, Conrad leaves her behind and heads off to raid the treasure of a Turkish pasha, Seyd. Taken prisoner by Seyd, Conrad is later freed by Seyd's favorite concubine, Gulnare, whom Conrad had saved during the raid and who in return saves

Conrad by murdering Seyd in his sleep. Conrad then returns to his island retreat to discover that Medora has died. Crushed by the loss of his beloved, Conrad mysteriously disappears, never to be heard from again.

Byron's *Corsair* became an instant "best seller"; its publisher, John Murray, excitedly informed the author, "You have no notion of the sensation which the publication has occasioned," and he exulted that the poem "had sold, on the day of publication—a thing perfectly unprecedented—10,000 copies" (Marchand, 433). Francis Jeffrey, an insightful contemporary of Byron, captured the work's extraordinary appeal by observing its "unparalleled rapidity of narrative, and condensation of thoughts and images—a style always vigorous and original . . . expanding only in the eloquent expression of strong and favorite affections, and everywhere else concise, energetic, and impetuous," summing it up: "Nothing diluted in short, or diffused into weakness, but full of life, and nerve, and activity" (quoted in Rutherford, 61),

"Life, and nerve, and activity"—often combined with bouts of heroic gloom—these were the qualities of Byron's Oriental tales (as well as his scandalous life) that seized the public's imagination. And they were for Byron not simply temperamental tendencies that he translated into poetic precepts. They were Romantic ethical values that animated his tales' characters and determined the aesthetic forms through which he presented those characters. To be full of "life" is to embrace the widest possible range of human experience; to be full of "nerve" is to risk any dangers posed by that experience; to be full of "activity" is to engage animatedly and intensively in every experience.

These inspiriting ethical values undoubtedly made for the very qualities that so attracted Lermontov to Byron's works, and to Byron himself, in the first place. Ultimately, however, it was the post-Romantic questioning of these Byronic values—suspecting that life, nerve, and activity were more elusive and illusionary in Lermontov's time than in Byron's—that would separate Lermontov's *Korsar*, and to various extents all of Lermontov's works, from Byron's, despite the similarities that signal Lermontov's continuing attraction to Byron.

The similarities that do exist between Lermontov's *Korsar* and Byron's *Corsair* are broad. Besides the titles, the two poems share the same three-part structure, and largely the same setting—the Turkish-occupied Greek isles. The basic plots also run parallel: both portray exploits of a band of corsairs raiding Turkish ships and strongholds; both focus on the experiences of one corsair in particular; and both hint that an amorous relationship may develop between that corsair and a female captive saved from the Turks. The two corsairs themselves display some similarities as well: both are alienated from the societies of their origins; both are burdened by memories of cruel deception and disillusionment; both resent the Turkish oppression of the Greeks; both evince deep capacities for love and for suffering on love's account. These broad similarities clearly create a framework for considering the two poems as versions of the same thing. But where the similarities end, Lermontov's "not-Byronism" begins. For within Byron's framework, the young Lermontov began to play out the ways in which he was not Byron, the ways in which he would not fully embrace Romanticism.

Consider first some matters of form. Byron casts his *Corsair*, which is nearly twice as long as Lermontov's (almost seven hundred lines compared to four hundred), in taut heroic couplets of traditional iambic pentameter, using all masculine rhymes. By contrast, Lermontov chooses the typically Russian freer four-line groupings in iambic tetrameter, alternating among masculine and feminine rhymes in various patterns within any four-line group. Byron's tighter rhyme scheme and longer rhythmic line impart a driving, consistently dramatic energy to his work duly befitting its rapidly changing plot, whereas Lermontov's shifting rhyme scheme and shorter lines tend to produce a varying narrative tempo suited just as well to the absence of action as to its presence. Byron's poem is also narrated by an impersonal, omniscient, third-person narrator who presents a vividly descriptive account of a few days in the lives of Conrad and his pirate band, occasionally letting the characters speak for themselves and pausing for a few narrative digressions, rarely calling attention to himself. Lermontov instead employs a nameless first-person narrator—his Corsair—who ruefully recounts to an unidentified audience of "friends" [друзья] events of his past, including his stint as a corsair, focusing on himself almost obsessively.

The opening lines of each poem establish their divergent narrative courses. Byron's poem starts with the collective voices of the pirates singing a song of praise to the unfettered joys of the piratical existence:

> O'er the glad waters of the dark blue sea,
> Our thoughts as boundless, and our souls as free,
> Far as the breeze can bear, the billows foam,
> Survey our empire, and behold our home! (278, ll. 1–4)[22]

Conveying the rhythmic surging of the waves along with the pirates' triumphant reveling in their freedom from the conventional limits of life on land, these lines set the energetic pace and tone that drives the narration throughout, even when depicting Conrad's moments of darkest terror and deepest sorrow.

The opening lines of Lermontov's narrative also set the pace and tone of the work, but to radically different effect. The unnamed narrator immediately calls attention to himself—"Friends, look at me!" [Друзья, взгляните на меня!] and then goes on to detail his deteriorated physical and emotional condition:

> I am pale, thin, joy has been extinguished
> In my eyes like a spark of fire;
> My youth has been fading for a long while,
> For a long, long while there have been no clear days,
> For a long while there has been no prospect of hope! . . .
> Everything has disappeared! . . . Only sufferings
> Still burn in my soul.

> Я бледен, худ, потухла радость
> В очах моих, как блеск огня;
> Моя давно увяла младость,
> Давно, давно нет ясных дней,
> Давно нет цели упованья! . . .
> Исчезло всё! . . . одни страданья
> Еще горят в душе моей. (2: 33; ellipses Lermontov's)

His misfortunes, *his* disillusionments, *his* sufferings—these are the subjects of this corsair's narrative, rooted in events long past that he frames within depictions of his current misery. An epitome of enervation, he can muster little animation to infuse into the pace and tone of his narrative.

The two authors' choices of diction further underscore those contrasts in narrative pace and tone. Although Byron draws on an extensive vocabulary in his poem, he allows verbs and verbal forms conveying action, often linked in a series, to dominate the work, generating a rapid pulse of events and intensification of experience. For example, shortly after the battle during which Conrad has been taken prisoner, the narrator reports:

> One hour beheld him since the tide he stemm'd—
> Disguised, discover'd, conquering, ta'en, condemn'd—
> A chief on land, an outlaw on the deep—
> Destroying, saving, prison'd, and asleep! (291, ll. 388–91)

The young Lermontov goes the other way, emphasizing reaction over action, relying on weak, often passive, verbs and favoring, if anything, nouns and adjectives, particularly those referring to emotional or spiritual conditions. Accordingly, his corsair responds to the beloved brother's death with these words: "He has died!—with this terrible cry / I was suddenly overwhelmed with trembling" [Он умер!—страшным восклицаньем / Сражен я вдруг был с содроганьем] (2: 34). Lermontov opts for nouns, even to portray actions—for example, "cry" [восклицаньем] and "trembling" [содроганьем]; Byron prefers verbs, even to depict inaction. Meter and rhyme and diction—these unite to energize Byron's poem; they subdue Lermontov's.

The character of Lermontov's corsair differs as much from Conrad's as do the formal qualities of the works that portray them. Although both protagonists experience the loneliness and sorrow of loss, Conrad is always a heroic figure. A supreme man of action, he does not simply belong to a pirate band, he commands it as *the* corsair, a charismatic leader who rarely speaks but whose powerful mind consistently "moulds another's weakness to its will" (280, l. 184). So imposing is his very presence that even after he is taken prisoner, "Still in his stern and self-collected mien / A conqueror's more than a captive's air is seen" (290, ll. 300–301), as he strives mightily not to betray any sign of weakness to the world. His greatest fear at the prospect of a lingering death is not death itself, therefore, but that he will cry out in pain; and when he sees the terrible sight of his beloved wife's corpse, he weeps bitterly yet briefly in secret, since, as the narrator notes, "if seen, / That useless flood of grief had never been" (302, ll. 652–63). Afterward, he takes his tragic sorrows off to an unknown destination, still possessing enough strength of character to leave an aura of absorbing mystery in his wake.

In striking contrast to Byron's powerfully drawn, larger-than-life Conrad, Lermontov's nameless corsair comes across as rather small, and somewhat pathetic—surprisingly so, since we would more likely expect a teenaged author to invent a swashbuckling, melodramatic derring-doer. And Lermontov's corsair is not only nameless, he is not even the pirate captain, but merely one member of the pirate band—not a leader but a follower (indeed, no leader ever appears or is even mentioned). Byron wrote about *the* corsair, Lermontov about *a* corsair (in fact, the Russian title *Korsar* is probably best translated that way, as *A Corsair*). Indeed, Lermontov's corsair would like *to be* Conrad, or at least to be *like* Conrad, early on declaring himself "dissatisfied with myself, / Wanting to be calm, self-controlled" [Самим собою недоволен, / Желая быть спокоен, волен] (2: 34), qualities that virtually define Conrad but that elude his anonymous descendant.

In further contrast, Conrad leaves his native land to become a corsair in defiance after an act of specific betrayal, whereas Lermontov's corsair explains having left his homeland suffering from broader existential despair, because the ways of "faithless life" [неверной жизни] (2: 35) had deceived him by letting his beloved younger brother die before his eyes. After this death, he begins aimlessly wandering along the shores of the nearby Danube in misery, plagued by the feeling that "the world was alien to me, life was empty" [Мир был чужой мне, жизнь пуста] (2: 37). And although he impulsively decides to forsake his native land—"I suddenly resolved to run away" [Я вдруг решился убежать] (2: 35)—he nonetheless first returns to mourn at his brother's grave again, reporting that

> I stood in silence for a long, long time
> Above the gravestone . . .
> It seemed that my suffering was permeated
> By some dry cold.

> И долго, долго я в молчанье
> Стоял над камнем гробовым . . .
> Казалось, веяло в страданье
> Каким-то холодом сырым. (2: 36; ellipsis Lermontov's)

When he finally does depart, he goes with "uncertain steps" [неверными шагами] (2: 36)—an uncertainty unthinkable for Conrad. Lermontov's corsair suffers from hesitations and doubts that Byron's never knows.

Eventually making his way to Greece in order to fight the Turks, Lermontov's sorrowful protagonist chances upon the hideaway of a corsair band and goes to sea with them not out of any zealous political or social conviction, or even from a youthful desire for adventure, but because, he recalls, "Oh, I thought, / A war, a grave, but not sadness / Perhaps awaits me there" [Ах, думал я, / Война, могила, но не горе / Быть может, встретит там меня] (2: 39). Hence, in contrast to Conrad, who is driven by anger at treachery to lead a life of heroic, violent, criminal action, Lermontov's corsair is motivated by unrelenting misery to seek any escape from heartache—even in death. More self-destructive than Conrad, Lermontov's corsair has no definite goal, no affirmative cause, however rebellious, to pursue. Lacking any ideals, he is not so much disillusioned as psychologically defeated, impervious to the attractions of life and nerve as a result. And so he indifferently lapses into whatever activity comes his way.

Consequently, where Conrad restrains and conceals his sadness, Lermontov's corsair, deprived of purpose in life, wallows in it. "Everything told me that joy / Had been buried forever here" [Всё говорило мне что радость / Навеки здесь погребена] (2: 36), he announces in preparing to leave his homeland. Even after embarking upon the adventurous pirate life, he confesses: "I mourned, languished, and yearned" [Грустил, томился, и желал], acknowledging, "I shed tears" [Я слезы лил], thinking about his idyllic childhood, now forever lost; and he awaits future losses "still more rebelliously / Still more sadly, more hopelessly" [еще мятежней / Еще печальней, безнадежней] (2: 41). And finally, whereas Conrad disappears at the conclusion of Byron's *Corsair* to become an even more mysterious figure, Lermontov's corsair ends up frozen in place, a spiritless, emotionally petrified figure of unfulfillment: "From that time on, I became numb, / Hardened against tender feelings" [С тех же пор я омертвел, / Для нежных чувств окаменел] (2: 44). Hurt so traumatically in his youth, he cannot muster the superhuman psychological strength of a Conrad to rise above his pain—he can only erect an emotional wall against its recurrence.

Not surprisingly, these psychological differences between Byron's and Lermontov's corsairs carry over into the ethics of the two. Conrad is something of an ethical idealist who takes full responsibility for the villainy of his actions while never compromising his own moral code. In fact, although Byron's poem's last words immortalize him as a man "link'd with one virtue, and a thousand crimes" (303, l. 696), he actually displays a wealth of virtues. He clearly values truth and despises hypocrisy. He prizes courage and loyalty in his men, and expects these of himself. He is chivalry incarnate, commanding his men to rescue the women in Seyd's harem trapped by a fire, even though the men will lose their tactical advantage in the battle with Seyd's guards by doing so. And he has an unswerving sense of justice, never complaining about the agonizing form of execution—impalement—Seyd intends for him because, Conrad concedes, he would have decreed a similar end for Seyd. Furthermore, the pasha's cruelty notwithstanding, Conrad refuses to murder a sleeping and defenseless Seyd when offered the chance, even to save his own life, because cold-blooded murder lacks the honor of open battle. A veritable paragon, Conrad personifies an explicit set of moral principles rooted in openness, honor, and constancy, the opposites of which—concealment, hypocrisy, and inconstancy—originally drove him away from conventional society.

Lermontov's corsair personifies none of these principles, nor the openness, honor, and constancy they entail. Self-absorbed and self-pitying, he evinces no moral imagination. Never taking responsibility for his actions or their consequences—his actions are mostly reactions, anyway—he considers himself largely a victim of forces beyond his control: "I was, friends, / The unfortunate debris of daily life, / Seemingly struggling with fate" [Я был, друзья, / Несчастный прах из бытия / Как бы сражаяся с судьбою], a fate he curses for causing him to "destroy / Almost everything I loved" [погубил, / Почти всё то, что я любил] (2: 41; 37). He accepts no blame for their destruction. Nor does he espouse any moral code that consistently guides his actions as he lives out his fate. He can only endure and lament the emptiness of life, without articulating any notion of what experiences could fill it with substance and value. For all his Byronic seafaring and suffering, Lermontov's corsair represents virtually the antithesis of Byron's ethical vision of human existence.

To summarize this comparison of the two *Corsairs*, one might say that Lermontov poured new wine into old bottles; the similar forms hold different contents. The young Lermontov evidently appropriated the external attributes of Byron's poem in structure, subject matter, setting, turns of plot, and dark emotionality. But he proceeded to attenuate and defuse the dynamic potential of those attributes in *Korsar* by turning the story inward, slowing its pace, diminishing its central character, and generally abstaining from the aesthetic exuberance, the psychological exertions, and the unconventional yet unambiguous morality that lent Byron's *Corsair* so much of its appeal. These attenuations thus reflect an ambivalence toward Byron from the very beginning of Lermontov's writing career as a fourteen-year-old youth.

LARA UNFINISHED

It is certainly possible to argue that the hesitancy toward life, the inconstancy of nerve, the doubts about activity, that *Korsar* exhibits merely bespeak the young Lermontov's artistic difficulties in capturing the exhilaration of life, the assurance of nerve, the exaltation of activity that Byron's works convey so powerfully. In other words, Lermontov's *Korsar* may be more a failed attempt to fit the Byronic mold than an early, telling departure from that mold. But I do not think so. For one thing, *Korsar* is unquestionably precocious, displaying a control of poetic form, diction, and rhetoric beyond Lermontov's years. More importantly, other early narrative poems by Lermontov suggest that *Korsar* was in fact a harbinger of the transitional aesthetic and ethical sensibilities that would mark those narratives and distance them from Byron and Byron's Romanticism while disclosing Lermontov's still emerging post-Romanticism.

Examination of one of those narratives, Lermontov's longest and arguably most ambitiously Byronic work, *Izmail-Bei* [Измаил-Бей], further demonstrates that Lermontov's "not-Byronism" was much more than a topos. In this lengthy poem, written in 1832—the same year as the lyric "No, I'm not Byron"—Lermontov plays out, even more by incompletion than by attenuation, the same post-Romantic ambivalence toward Byron that he showed in *Korsar*. Granted, we might view both *Korsar* and *Izmail-Bei* as exemplars of "dark" Romanticism, colored by the melancholic, pessimistic, and despairing moods that appear throughout Romanticism. However, as discussed in Chapter 2, even this strain in Goethe, Byron, Chateaubriand, and other Romanticists had a wrenching emotional vitality and intensity born of a capacious emotionality and a fervent yearning to transcend the darkness, if not in this world, then in the next. As Chesterton metaphorically described this darkness in Byron, it "was only too dense a purple" (40)—rich, impassioned, alluring.

But the darkness clouding Lermontov's narrative poems lacks that vitality and intensity. This darkness is more gray than black, it betrays more a decline of energy and a diminution of yearning than a genuinely wrenching emotional state. Lermontov's narrative poems therefore better belong to the emotionally enervated, morally ambiguous, artistically equivocal atmosphere of post-Romanticism, which had lost the vitality and intensity that made Romanticism so compelling, even at its darkest.

An Oriental tale through and through, *Izmail-Bei* was inspired by stories Lermontov had heard as a youth about Izmail-Bei Atazhukin, a noble Circassian mountain tribesman who distinguished himself fighting against the Turks after being sent by his family to serve in the Russian army.[23] In the poem, Lermontov relates his version of Izmail's return to his tribe as it is being besieged by Russian forces, adding a fictionalized account of a young woman who falls in love with Izmail, and concluding it with Izmail's murder by his brother Roslambek (also based on a historical figure) out of jealousy over Izmail's popularity among the other tribesmen.

Critical assessments of *Izmail-Bei* range from "magnificent" (Kelly, 41) to "feeble" (Maikov, 70). But whatever its overall aesthetic merit, there is no question that in comparison to Lermontov's earlier narrative poems, including *Korsar*, *Izmail-Bei* is far more adept. Although written just four years after *Korsar*, *Izmail-Bei* shows that Lermontov had learned much from the nearly dozen narrative poems he had undertaken to write—albeit leaving most unfinished—in the meantime. Lermontov now had the artistic skill and confidence to make *Izmail-Bei* much more structurally complex, vastly richer in diction, and far more various in characters and events, than any of his previous efforts.

As relatively sophisticated and poetically mature as *Izmail-Bei* may be, however, Lermontov does not hesitate to indicate its indebtedness to Byron, giving it the subtitle *An Eastern Tale* [Восточная повесть], reminiscent of the subtitles of Byron's *The Giaour: Fragment of a Turkish Tale* and *The Bride of Abydos: A Turkish Tale*. An exotic setting in the Caucasus, recurring evocative non-Russian terminology—beginning with the honorific *bei* in the title—an atmosphere of passionate emotions such as love, hate, jealousy, and revenge, periodic rapidity of action and sudden turns of events, and an unhappy outcome all confirm the strong affiliation of *Izmail-Bei* with Byron's Oriental tales. And Lermontov further establishes his Byronic bona fides by attaching epigraphs to parts 1 and 3 of the tripartite *Izmail-Bei* taken respectively from Byron's *Giaour* and from *Lara*.[24] Lermontov also borrows from *Lara* (considered by many a sequel to *The Corsair*) the character and story of Kaled—to whom the epigraph of part 3 refers—which he embodies in Zara, a young woman who becomes utterly devoted to Izmail. All of these facets of *Izmail-Bei* render it a much more deliberate product of Byron's influence than the earlier *Korsar*.

At the same time, Lermontov takes these basic components of Byron's tales, especially *Lara*, and constructs a subtly but distinctly different type of narrative poem, one that both conforms to and also diverges from its Byronic predecessors. For in *Izmail-Bei* Lermontov characteristically diffuses and deflates the Byronic narrative components he incorporates by leaving them somehow incomplete, at once accepting and rejecting the aesthetic, psychological, and moral values they represent.

Lermontov achieves these effects to no small degree through the formal features of *Izmail-Bei*. The first of these is the very length of the poem.

Whereas Lermontov constrained the Byronic spirit of *Korsar* with brevity, he dilutes it in *Izmail-Bei* with length. At 2,289 lines, *Izmail-Bei* is 955 lines longer than Byron's longest Turkish tale, *The Giaour*, and over three times as long as *The Bride of Abydos*, *The Corsair*, or *Lara*. As a result of this length, Lermontov lessens the emotional impact of any single character or moment, instilling a novelistic quality to his narrative by depicting numerous settings, scenes, characters, and actions—many of which in themselves could be considered Byronic, but others of which are quite un-Byronic in their mundanity—by contrast to Byron, whose Turkish tales rather resemble short stories in their tight focus on limited settings, few characters, and concentrated actions that result in high emotional drama. For example, in part 2, stanza 6, of Lermontov's poem, the narrator depicts a typical moment in a Circassian village:

> Here on a summer day, in the midday heat,
> When the steam rises from the stove,
> A crowd of children plays in the grass,
> The tired Circassian man rests;
> Meanwhile his wife sits
> Alone in the hut with her work.

> Здесь в летний день, в полдневный жар,
> Когда с камней восходит пар,
> Толпа детей в траве играет,
> Черкес усталый отдыхает;
> Меж тем сидит его жена
> С работой в сакле одиноко. (2: 158)

Such a quotidian, uneventful moment would have no place in Byron's Oriental tales.[25]

Even more than the length of *Izmail-Bei*, its narrative structure widens the gap between Lermontov's tale and those of Byron. For Byron's tales employ simple structures presenting compelling storytellers—usually an impersonal third-person narrator (except in *The Giaour*)—who lead readers swiftly yet colorfully across exotic geographical and emotional landscapes and who digress or yield to other characters' voices only to heighten the dramatic pitch of events as the narrative advances. In contrast, Lermontov makes *Izmail-Bei* something of a narrative maze by endowing it with a complex narrative structure that diffuses its narratorial point of view and repeatedly disrupts its narrative flow, thereby obscuring and even obstructing the narrative's progress. This structure encompasses a frame introducing a first-person narrator who reports that an "old Chechen man" [Старик-чеченец], whom he happened to encounter, had "told me a tale about olden times" [про старину мне повесть рассказал], which the narrator resolves "to convey to the distant north" [перенесть на север дальный] no matter how strange it may seem there: "As I heard it, thus will I transmit it!" [Как слышал, так его передаю!] (2: 136).

However, neither the language, nor the images, nor the ideas in the subsequent narrative would seem to emanate from the consciousness of such an elderly Islamic former warrior as the "old Chechen." A smattering of Islamic terms notwithstanding,[26] too much relatively sophisticated diction and rhetoric is engaged after a few opening stanzas of the main narrative—for instance, the narrator uses participles including the "newborn day" [день новорождённый], the "awakened wind" [ветер пробуждённый], and the "barely smoking chimney" [едва дымящийся костёр] (2: 138) to describe the scene after the Circassians suddenly abandon their village in fear of the advancing Russian army. These and other linguistic complexities suggest that the insertion of the old Chechen as the ostensible narrator is essentially a ploy to establish the poem's verisimilitude.[27] However, ploy or not, this figure's inclusion permanently leaves ambiguous whose point of view is being expressed, beclouding rather than clarifying the intellectual and emotional perspective being brought to bear on the ensuing events. No such clouds cast their shadows over Byron's Oriental tales.

In addition to obscuring the point of view, the narrative structure of *Izmail-Bei* allows for numerous digressions as well. Some of these easily fit into the narrative flow, but others crop up abruptly, interrupting that flow and hence further confusing the emotional atmosphere. At the pivotal moment of the climactic battle between the Circassians and the Russians, for example, which might be expected to resemble the final, literally explosive, confrontation between the Greeks and the Turks in Byron's *The Siege of Corinth*, Lermontov inserts a full stanza of narrative digression completely at odds in subject and tone with the preceding one describing Izmail being wounded in the heat of that battle. This digression, offering a meditation on the human need for escapist fantasies, begins: "The more rarely happiness indulges us, / The more pleasurably do we give ourselves over to / Imaginings and daydreams" [Чем реже нас балует счастье, / Тем слаще предаваться нам, / Предположеньям и мечтам] (2: 189). This meditation constitutes a set piece that could have been positioned almost anywhere in the poem. But Lermontov places it at the poem's climax, blatantly disrupting his narrative's most dramatic moment.[28] He therefore expressly departs from Byron's narrative lead by using a structure that invites episodes of intense activity but precludes the uninterrupted, crescendoing plot lines Byron employed so effectively.

Besides designing a more complicated structure, Lermontov also deviates from Byron's narrative path, though not at every step, in the persona of the hero he creates for *Izmail-Bei*. On the one hand, Izmail is closer to a Byronic hero than Lermontov's corsair. Izmail is a "prince" [княз] of his mountain tribe who bravely leads the Circassian assault on the Russian enemy like an "angel-destroyer" [ангел-истребитель] (2: 185), and who rejects as ignoble his brother's scheme to organize a nocturnal sneak attack on the Russian camp (a refusal reminiscent of Conrad's rejection of the invitation to murder Seyd in his sleep). Yet, on the other hand, Izmail does not fully rise to the Byronic hero's stature. Although the narrator proclaims that Izmail was "created for great passions" [Он для великих создан был страстей], that he "possessed a fiery spirit" [Он обладал пылающей душою], and that "the storms of the south were reflected in it" [бури юга отразились в ней] (2: 158), he rarely does in fact display this spirit—and almost never in an admirable way. For example, without any warning he kills a Kazakh hunter he comes across in the mountains merely because the hunter laughs at the plight of the Circassians. This killing is hardly virtuous, as Izmail seemingly realizes, hastily riding off like "someone/After whom repentance is chasing" [тот,/За кем раскаяние мчится] (2: 143).

The threat of repentance aside, the emotions Izmail appears truly to experience in actuality are uncertainty, bewilderment, frustration, and self-reproach. He gets lost; he is deceived; he cries. He vows never to rest until he has avenged the Russians' destruction of his native village, but he abandons that quest after being wounded. He becomes violently disturbed upon hearing a song about love and war, but then he evidently forgets all about it. He discovers he loves Zara only when it is too late to consummate that love. These are the experiences of inconsistent, flawed, ordinary men, not consistently extraordinary men—not Byronic heroes.[29] As brave as he is, in many ways the character of Izmail furthers the process begun in Lermontov's *Korsar* of demythologizing that heroic type, winding up closer to Pushkin's Eugene Onegin (who would have been much discussed by 1832) than to Byron's Giaour,[30] to Conrad, or to Alp, the staunch defender of Corinth who gladly fights to the death against an overwhelming enemy. Notably, the narrator explicitly labels Izmail "superfluous" [лишний] (2: 157), a label indicative of his affinities with Onegin and other subsequent Russian literary characters lacking the worldly purpose and psychic satisfactions afforded by a well-defined social role. Byron's heroes may be socially alienated, but they are never superfluous—they carve out heroic roles for themselves.

And this difference in turn points to perhaps the greatest difference of all between Izmail and Byronic heroes—Izmail attributes much of what happens in his life not to himself but to fate. In declining Zara's invitation to stay with her, he declares that he would not share "his turbulent fate" [судьбы мятежной] with her, that "the power was not given" to him "to have mercy" [Щадить . . . власти не дано], and that he is "obligated to sacrifice happiness" [Я в жертву счастье должен принести] (2: 154). His allusion to his fate, coupled with his use of past passive participial forms—"not given" [не дано], "obligated" [должен]—reflects a belief that he lacks free will, that he is a pawn of cosmic forces beyond his control.[31] He exercises such will as he has primarily by refusing to act (abjuring treachery, rebuffing Zara) rather than by relentlessly striving to enact his desires the way the protagonists of Byron's Oriental tales characteristically do—even if they die while striving. The exception is Izmail's willingness to engage in battle, and yet even there he survives not because of his military prowess but because "the prophet [Mohammad] saves him" [его хранит пророк] (2: 186); Ismail dies only when Roslambek fires "the fateful shot" [выстрел роковой] (2: 195). Consequently, unlike his Byronic forebears who ceaselessly exert their wills even in the most hopeless circumstances, Izmail appears as a psychologically crippled victim who yields to circumstances and succumbs to fate rather than persistently endeavoring to overcome either.

However, there is one character in *Izmail-Bei* who does seek to combat circumstances and defy fate—Zara, the most passionate, willful, and in her own way Byronic figure in the entire work. Yet even her story stops short of a Byronic climax, trailing off in anticlimactic ambiguity. Zara falls so deeply in love with Izmail that she disguises herself as a young Circassian warrior named Selim (not incidentally, the name of the main protagonist of Byron's *The Bride of Abydos*) in order to follow Izmail wherever he may go. Pledging undying loyalty to him, she exclaims,

> . . . everywhere,
> In exile, in combat I will be your companion;
> No, I will not forget my oath—
> I will die or live with you!

> . . . Я повсюду,
> В изгнанье, в битве спутник твой;
> Нет, клятвы я не позабуду –
> Угаснуть или жить с тобой!

And she vows,

> The beauty and happiness of youthful years
> My spirit has not treasured;
> I will forsake everything, everything, life and the world,
> But I will not forsake Izmail!

> Красой и счастьем юных лет
> Моя душа не дорожила;
> Всё, всё оставлю, жизнь и свет,
> Но не оставлю Измаила! (2: 181)

After Izmail is wounded in battle and Zara reveals her true identity to him in the final scene of the main narrative, it appears that she will uphold her oath and remain with him until he either dies or recovers. Yet the brief epilogue, set two years later, which discloses that Izmail does recover, also reveals that Zara has disappeared, apparently failing to fulfill her oath after all. Readers are simply left with a series of rhetorical questions speculating on the reasons for her disappearance:

> Where has the gentle Lezghin woman concealed herself?
> What sort of blow hardened that breast,
> Where such a heart once beat for love,
> Which he [Izmail] was unworthy of ruling?
> Was betrayal the cause of their separation?
> Is she alive or does she sleep her final sleep?
> Did kindred hands lay her in her grave?
> Was the final "goodbye" said to her with tears of torment
> Spoken in her native language?
> And if death is having mercy on her now—
> Among which people, in what wilderness?

> Куда лезгинка нежная сокрылась?
> Какой удар ту грудь оледенил,
> Где для любви такое сердце билось,
> Каким владеть он недостоин был?
> Измена ли причина их разлуки?
> Жива ль она иль спит последним сном?

Родные ль в гроб ее сложили руки?
Последнее «прости» с слезами муки
Сказали ль ей на языке родном?
И если смерть щадит ее поныне
Между каких людей, в какой пустыне? (2: 194)

The narrator then implies that Izmail knows the answers to these questions, but observes, "Who would dare to ask Izmail about this?" [Кто б Измаила смел спросить о том?] (2: 194). Hence Zara's story comes to an ambiguous and utterly unanticipated conclusion, one that dramatizes the difference between Zara and her Byronic model, Kaled, in *Lara*. For Kaled follows her beloved, the mysteriously tormented Count Lara, everywhere, even into battle, comforting him when he is wounded, staying with him after he succumbs to his wounds, and absolutely refusing to leave his corpse: "Furious would you tear her from the spot / Where she yet scarce believed that he was not" (319, ll. 604–606). *Lara* subsequently brings Kaled's suffering to a close, concluding with the lines: "This could not last—she lies by him she loved; / Her tale untold, her truth too dearly proved" (319, ll. 626–27). Byron's narrative thereby ends with Kaled's undying love for Lara implicitly consummated in the ultimate Romantic transcendence that is death. The heroic, impassioned, tragic final chapter of this love *has* been told, even if its entire history has not been detailed.

The story of Zara's love, by contrast, remains unfinished, a puzzlement; the questions regarding Zara's fate will go forever unanswered. Lermontov furnishes no transcendent closure for Izmail's story either, since the work's epilogue explains that after Zara's departure, Izmail experienced a prolonged state of "melancholy—but not passions" [тоска,—но нет страстей] (2: 195). He was then suddenly assassinated by his brother and left to "rot ingloriously" [сгниет бесславно] (2: 196). Thus Lermontov's narrative comes to more of an anticlimax than to any gratifying, even if mournful, close.

Indeed, the inconclusive ending of Zara's tale (when Kaled's offered a ready-made alternative), followed by the abrupt ending of Izmail's, suggests that Lermontov chose to conclude his narrative ingloriously, anticlimactically, inconclusively. And this choice, together with Lermontov's other deviations from Byron's narrative course, leaves the impression that at the time he wrote *Izmail-Bei* Lermontov possessed a sense of narrative and its potential that differed in some ways radically from Byron's. It was a sense of narrative less as a rushing stream flowing with a profusion of Byronic life, nerve, and activity than as a twisting path pieced together with fragments taken from Lermontov's "not-Byronic," post-Romantic vision of human experience—the vital alongside the vapid, the energetic next to the enervated, the transcendent amid the trivial. And these are not fragments in the Romantic vein, pointing to wholes greater than themselves; Lermontov's fragments are shards unto themselves, not truly fused but juxtaposed in a style anticipating Lermontov's distinctively transitional, post-Romantic narratives still to come—most notably *A Hero of Our Time*.

TRANSITIONAL AMBIVALENCE

The instructive differences between Lermontov's narrative poems *Korsar* and *Izmail-Bei* and Byron's Oriental tales give new meaning to Lermontov's assertion in the year of *Izmail-Bei*'s composition, "No, I'm not Byron." No mere expression of youthful identification laced with envy, it reflects truths about Lermontov that he himself may not have recognized. He may well have "been" Byron in the sense that he did, from early on, admire the man, profess Byronic idealism and Byronic disillusionment to his acquaintances, articulate these in his lyric poetry, and incorporate key elements of Byron's early narrative poems—settings, plots, characters, and so forth—into his own. But in ways more important for the creation and development of his own literary voice, Lermontov surely was *not* Byron. Notwithstanding Lermontov's admiration for Byron and personal identification with the British poet, and despite Lermontov's profession of certain Byronic ideas and adoption of certain Byronic themes, Lermontov never wrote narrative poems that came as close to Byron's as some critics have assumed—one might even suspect that Lermontov's overt personal identification with Byron has led critics to project into Lermontov's early narrative poetry more Byronism (and Romanticism) than is actually there.[32] For—just as he indicated in "No, I'm not Byron"—Lermontov had not assimilated the Byronic soul.

Harold Bloom might have concluded that Lermontov belonged to the category of "weaker talents" who merely "idealize" their "strong precursors" (5) and try but fail to match the accomplishments of those precursors in new and unique ways. And W. J. Bate might have found that Lermontov suffered so much from the "burden" of Byron's achievements that he simply did not try to emulate them fully. But I would maintain that the core of Lermontov's relation to Byron lies not in any idealized identification or burdened feeling of inadequacy but in his transitional sensibilities, evident in his earliest writings. These sensibilities allowed the young Lermontov to be strongly attracted to Byron's confidently outsized Romantic vision of human experience, and yet they enabled him to embrace that vision ambivalently at most. For however much Lermontov as a poet in his teens was drawn to Byron, he seems also to have sensed that Byron's confident Romanticism did not wholly fit the uncertain times of post-Romanticism. As a result, Lermontov's narrative "not-Byronic" poems can be seen poignantly to exemplify the quandary of aesthetic influence in a period of transition, when an artist at once reveres, doubts, and departs from his most eminent model, along with the ideals of the era he is inexorably leaving behind, as he drifts into the uncharted cultural waters ahead.

FOUR

The Attenuation of Romantic Evil

A Demon Undone

THE DEVIL IN TRANSITION

While ambivalence colored Lermontov's literary relationship to Byron, the Byronic hero, and the Byronic narrative poem, a peculiar ambiguity surfaced in Lermontov's representations of a prominent related aspect of Romanticism—the image of evil. That ambiguity appears most dramatically in Lermontov's best-known narrative poem *The Demon* [Демон], whose eponymous protagonist has haunted readers and critics for generations. Lermontov seems to have been haunted as well, for *The Demon* is the one work that he labored over from almost the beginning of his career to nearly the end.[1] These labors betoken at once the difficulty he encountered in expressing the vision behind this poem and the determination he felt to express that vision. Many plausible explanations have been offered to account for his persistence—*The Demon* has received more critical commentary than any of Lermontov's works except *A Hero of Our Time*. I think we can attribute both this difficulty and this determination to Lermontov's transitional post-Romanticism.

Lermontov started writing *The Demon* in his early teens, in 1829. Over the next ten years he produced no fewer than eight versions of the poem, each sufficiently different from the others to be accepted by critics as a separate redaction—he also wrote variants of several of the redactions. Nonetheless, the basic plot outline remained fairly consistent throughout: a nameless, solitary angel cast out of heaven and called only "the Demon" catches sight of a beautiful young woman, falls in love with her, and decides to seduce her, only to kill her with his kiss. In the early redactions, after she dies, she is simply buried; but in the last two, an angel claims her spirit and escorts it to heaven, leaving the Demon alone. Lermontov retained this basic plot, aside from the alternate endings, for ten years. With one exception, he also preserved the opening line—"The sad Demon, spirit of exile" [Печальный Демон, дух изгнанья] (2: 374)—from the first redaction to the last.[2]

Once that last redaction was completed in 1839, the text of *The Demon* was itself plagued by demons, so to speak. First, government censorship prohibited Lermontov from publishing the work. Then, after a version of it was finally published in 1860, nearly twenty years after Lermontov's death, critics started debating which of the eight redactions was the authoritative one, since Lermontov left no single fair copy for publication. That debate continues. Some critics have favored the sixth redaction, assuming that he wrote the seventh and eighth ones merely as attempts to appease the censors. Others have viewed those latter two as reflections of his still-evolving conception of the poem and have taken the eighth redaction as the finished product.

Critics have also long debated the quality, theme, and import of *The Demon*. Eikhenbaum, for instance, considered it an undistinguished amalgamation of other authors' writings and ideas, whereas Udodov extolled it as one of the great works of world literature. Some commentators have read it primarily as an autobiographical record of Lermontov's private emotional torments; others have understood it mainly as a veiled social portrait of the sufferings Lermontov's generation was undergoing in the struggle to establish individuality and autonomy; still others have interpreted *The Demon* as Lermontov's metaphysical meditation on the relationship of God to humankind—and depending on which redaction these critics accept as the final version, they see it as Lermontov's assertion of either the triumph or the tragedy of evil in the world.[3] Then again, a significant body of critics has tended to treat *The Demon* more as a study in the psychological paradoxes of human nature than as an exploration of moral or philosophical ideas.[4]

But there is one point about *The Demon* on which most Lermontov authorities agree: while writing it, Lermontov drew on the figures of numerous Western Romantic demons and diabolical characters—although which ones, and the extent of their influence, remain in dispute. Below I consider four Romantic works of poetry and prose centering on demonic figures that conspicuously occupied Lermontov's imagination—Alfred de Vigny's *Eloa*, Goethe's *Faust*, Byron's *Cain*, and Maturin's *Melmoth the Wanderer*.[5] This consideration elucidates both the affinities *The Demon* displays with each of these works and, more importantly, its departures from them all as it depicts a distinctive demonic protagonist who embodies a distinguishing conception of evil. For it is through those departures from Lermontov's Romantic forebears that we can best see Lermontov's transitional moral imagination at work. This imagination implicitly questioned earlier ideas of good and evil, along with images of good and evil that reflected clear cultural values or strong judgments, and it set forth cloudier ideas and images that belonged to a time of uncertain cultural values and value judgments.

That time, as I have observed in earlier chapters, was the transitional era of post-Romanticism. Although Lermontov unquestionably took inspiration from Romantic images of demons and from the moral ideas of both good and evil that these demons stood for, he conveyed his own version of the demonic, and of good and evil, in images that were significantly more ambiguous and more equivocal than his models. Thus my contention—in contrast to Joseph T. Shaw, for instance, who claims that *The Demon* is "no doubt the most romantic Russian long poem, by the most romantic Russian poet" (165), and John Mersereau, who asserts even more broadly that *The Demon* is the "quintessence of romanticism" (*Lermontov*, 69)—is that Lermontov's most notable narrative poem moved away from its predecessors and the ethical ideas that underpinned them, while nevertheless retaining a vestigial attachment to those ideas.[6] Lermontov's demon is not so much another Romantic exemplar of opposing moral qualities coexisting in a complex diabolical character, but more a post-Romantic demon wearing diabolical trappings without adhering to a constant moral philosophy or psychology. For this demon is in many ways a more intellectually inconsistent, emotionally elusive, and morally ambiguous figure than his Romantic counterparts—indeed, Lermontov's Demon becomes more, not less, difficult to grasp with every redaction (a fact leading me to judge the eighth redaction, not the sixth, the definitive one).[7]

In essence, Lermontov picked up the widespread Romantic demonic motif but then struggled for ten years with a morally amorphous Demon who ultimately represents no clear idea of evil, who instead attenuates the ideas of evil variously manifested in the Romantic works Lermontov had in his mind's eye during that prolonged struggle. Wrestling with *his* Demon, Lermontov grappled with the quandary of defining evil in a world in transition. Yet I should stress that *The Demon* is not a failed effort at a Romantic tale of evil. It is instead a successful, subtle artistic achievement expressing a view of life to which the exalted Romantic visions of good and evil no longer pertain. According to this post-Romantic view, evil ultimately becomes the inability to tell the difference between good and evil at all.

Before turning to Romantic incarnations of evil and Lermontov's post-Romantic reaction to them, let me first briefly place them, and Lermontov's Demon, in a larger historical context. In creating a work centered on a demonic figure, Lermontov contributed to the age-old discussion of the nature of evil and thereby became a contributor, intentionally or not, to theodicy, the explanation of the presence of evil in a divinely ordered universe.[8] Dictionary definitions tell us that "evil" is anything that causes harm, pain, misery, disaster, and so on, and typically list *bad* as a synonym. But—as Nietzsche explained with such philological zeal and philosophical passion—the term *bad* lacks the weight of moral judgment carried by *evil*. For *evil* implies a severe moral judgment within a hierarchy of values (as Dante vividly delineated in his *Inferno*), usually informed by some theological assumptions. A judgment of "evil" also ordinarily implies choice or will in the doing of evil. In *The City of God* (413–27), for instance, St. Augustine equates evil with the willed choice to descend from the good: "For when the will abandons what is above and turns to what is lower, it becomes evil" (386).[9] In the West, "what is lower," or evil, has traditionally been identified with base appetites, unconstraint, and selfishness, whereas "the higher," or good, is associated with rationality or spirituality, constraint, and social responsibility.

The Christian tradition has, of course, historically found evil incorporated in the figure of the Devil, also called Satan, Lucifer, Beelzebub, and other surrogates, representing the lowest of the low in its hierarchy of moral values. A product of pre-Christian legend, popular superstition, folklore, and subsequent Christian hagiography as much as of scripture, the Christian Devil is often envisioned as an angel who has fallen from the realm of the highest good to a state of the deepest degradation. The Christian image of the Devil as a physically hideous, fearsomely powerful, and eternally hostile spirit, who possesses an obsessive, maniacal, even megalomaniacal determination to oppose God and the order of God's world by corrupting and destroying humanity, reigned throughout the Middle Ages and beyond. Martin Luther thought himself literally besieged by this Devil, who, in the words of the historian of "diabology" Jeffrey Burton Russell, "rattled around behind Luther's stove . . . pelted nuts at the roof and rolled casks down the stairwell . . . grunted audibly, like a pig . . . disputed with Luther like a scholastic . . . emitted stenches . . . [and] sometimes lodged in Luther's bowels" (39). Not long after Luther, Torquato Tasso depicted the baleful appearance of such a Devil in *Jerusalem Delivered* [*Gerusalemme liberate*], written around 1575: "His eyes are red, and their glance, infected with poison, dazzles like an ill-boding comet; his great, shaggy and dense beard covers his chin and descends upon his hairy breast; and his mouth opens like a deep abyss, foul with dark blood" (quoted in Praz, 82). Luther's Devil might have been a shade less gruesome, but the basic idea was the same. Frightful to behold, unappeasable in appetites, and infinitely inventive in pursuit of his diabolical goals, the Christian Devil was the instantiation of supreme evil, the consummate enemy of God and humanity, to be resisted only by the supreme goods of physical self-restraint, spiritual piety, and moral vigilance.

But by the era of Romanticism, thanks to the ascendancy of secularism and to the Enlightenment's emphases on science, rationality, and empiricism, this prevailing Christian image of the Devil as the horrific supernatural incarnation of the lowest of the low, as well as the religious ideas of good and evil entailed by that image, had lost much of their authority.[10] Milton's seventeenth-century revisionist literary rendition of Satan as something of a noble spirit in *Paradise Lost* (1667), of course, both reflected and encouraged this loss. And at the hands of Romanticists, the Devil further metamorphosed into an artistic image signifying various moral ideas. As Russell puts it, there was not "one Romantic Satan or even two, but virtually as many Satans as there were Romantics" (176). (A variation on this theme echoes in Gérard de Nerval's indignant retort upon being accused of being a-religious: "No religion? I have at least seventeen!")

To be sure, this multiplicity of Satanic images and concomitant moral ideas was typical of Romanticism, which prized the originality of divergent visions while celebrating the protean and the unconventional and the unconstrained. Whether fashioned by Blake or Shelley, Nodier or Hugo,

Schiller or E. T. A. Hoffman, along with de Vigny, Goethe, Byron, and Maturin, Romantic diabolical figures possess surprising, often conflicting, attributes that attract as well as repel, that may serve good while doing evil, and that may even be more good than evil. Frequently physically alluring and intellectually engaging, typically endowed with prodigious will, and usually inspired by some philosophical principle, the Romantic Devils and their demonic avatars were far more complex in character and behavior than their Christian predecessors. And, as noted in Chapter 2, they afforded Romanticists a dramatic means of challenging or reordering the traditional Christian hierarchy of values in their endeavor to create a world that was not yet "beyond good and evil," in Nietzsche's phrase, but was a world where, while good and evil clearly remained, they took on radically new and different forms in accordance with widely varying moral visions. As Ruth Anshen points out in *Anatomy of Evil*, "All great historical periods have had their particular relation to the Devil" (142), and Romanticism was no exception.

COMPARATIVE EVIL

Comparing Lermontov's Demon to Romantic incarnations of the Devil sets Lermontov's version and the vision behind it in sharp relief. One of those incarnations appeared in Alfred de Vigny's *Eloa*, which was widely read in its day and was well known to Lermontov, according to his close friend Akim Shan-Girei.[11] Published in 1824, de Vigny's lush and lyrical narrative poem presents a variant of the Christian ideas of evil as physical lust, the corruption of innocence, and estrangement from God. But the unmistakable embodiment of this evil, Satan, is highly "romanticized" both in substance and style. No grotesque monster like Tasso's Devil, de Vigny's Satan is literally a handsome devil, physically dashing, intellectually agile, irresistibly charismatic in speech and manner. He is as entrancing as he is evil. And, aided by these attributes, he readily wins the prey he sets his sights on, the lovely female angel Eloa, who was born from a tear shed by Jesus at the death of Lazarus.

In his evil quest to seduce Eloa, Satan first reveals himself to her regally arrayed in a robe of purple that "enchanted the gaze with its opalescent tints" (33, l. 356) and carrying a scepter of gold "like a king who reviews his army from a mountain" (34, l. 368). His radiant presence strikes Eloa as the very image of beneficence: "Since you are so beautiful," she says to him, "you are no doubt good" (41, l. 619). Every inch a self-assured monarch and an alluring male, he declares himself to be "the secret King of secret loves" (36, l. 434) as he starts spinning his seductive web woven of illusion and yearning, while using "the enchanting force of his eyes" by calculatedly raising "their caressing rays at first only by degrees" (34, ll. 372–73). Proudly affirming, "I give the earth / The voluptuousness of evenings and the blessings of mystery" (36, ll. 443–44), Satan intrigues Eloa by also telling her,

> I am he whom one loves and does not know.
> I have founded my empire . . .
> In the desires of the heart, in the dreams of the spirit,
> In the bonds of bodies . . .
> In the treasures of blood, in the gazes of the eyes. (35, ll. 426–30)

And forswearing the label of "Evildoer," he calls himself "a Consoler" (38, ll. 510, 512), maintaining that it is he, not God, who weeps over the downtrodden and affords them "a bit of delight and occasionally some oblivion" (38, l. 506). Indeed, Satan claims to have been punished as a result of his generosity of spirit: "It is for having loved, it is for having saved, / That I am unhappy, that I have been reproached" (35, ll. 405–6). De Vigny's Satan consequently presents himself as a bit of a martyr, philosophically and morally committed to the indulgence of physical desire not as evil but as good.

In appearance and style, Lermontov's Demon dramatically differs from de Vigny's. Although physically appealing, he is never vividly described or given his own name—he is only referred to by the generic term "the Demon" [демон]. True to this lack of specificity, he remains throughout an amorphous figure of indefinite nature and uncertain intentions. His desired victim, the beautiful young Georgian woman Tamara, first sees him in a daydream, and then only as a "hazy and mute visitor, / Glowing with an unearthly beauty" [Пришлец туманный и немой, / Красой блистая неземной] who looks at her "with such love, / So sadly" [с такой любовью, / Так грустно] that it seems "as though he pitied her" [Как будто он об ней жалел] (2: 384). But she cannot interpret his demeanor with certainty, because his appearance is too indefinite:

> This was no angel-inhabitant of heaven,
> Her divine savior:
> A halo of rainbow rays
> Did not decorate his curls.

Nor was this a horrible spirit of hell,
A depraved torturer—oh no!
He resembled a clear evening:
Neither day nor night—neither dark nor light!

То не был ангел-небожитель,
Ее божественный хранитель;
Венец из радужных лучей
Не украшал его кудрей.
То не был ада дух ужасный,
Порочный мученик – о нет!
Он был похож на вечер ясный:
Ни день, ни ночь, – ни мрак, ни свет! (2: 384)

This fuzzy description, filled with negatively rather than positively phrased attributes, is not just a physical sketch. It is a moral portrait as well—and a highly uncertain one at that. Trying to clarify his moral makeup when the Demon appears in the convent cell to which she has retreated after her fiancé's death, Tamara asks: "Who are you? . . . / Did hell or heaven send you to me? / What do you want? . . . " [Кто ты? . . . /Тебя послал мне ад иль рай? / Чего ты хочешь? . . .] (2: 390). His translucent appearance does not yield a transparently identifiable persona—he might be either good or evil or neither, since he appears to come neither from above nor below the earth. His precise identity and moral nature remain ambiguous, and possibly inscrutable.

The far more explicit evil of de Vigny's Satan, along with his ravishing appearance and enticing speech in making a play for sympathy, brings him a success in corruption that Lermontov's Demon cannot achieve. Satan's confident panache as a seducer renders him thoroughly irresistible to Eloa—he is the ultimate "Tempter," as the poem's narrator labels him. He relentlessly pursues her, except for a brief moral lapse, as it were, when, beguiled by her beauty, the narrator reports, Satan "had forgotten his art and his victim, / And his heart for a moment rested from crime" (43, ll. 686–88). But he swiftly resumes his campaign, promising Eloa that he will make her a queen and that "soon good and evil will be mingled for us" (45, ll. 741–42) if only she will descend to him in order to "unite our spirits" (45, l. 752). And he completely triumphs; Eloa succumbs. "I have carried off my slave," Satan exults, "and I have my victim" (46, ll. 774–75). When, no longer able to see the heavens she has left behind, Eloa cries in dawning despair, "Oh! What have I done?" he informs her coldly that she has committed "a crime"

(46, l. 776). Thus Satan completely vanquishes Eloa, destroying her innocence and depriving her of the chance to return to God. But when, in a
final effort at consolation, she asks, "Are you happier, at least, are you content?" he replies surprisingly that he is "more sad than ever" (46, ll. 777–78).
And this sadness confirms the depravity of his Satanic seduction, since he
does not delight in it and evinces no sympathy for her. He feels only his
Satanic gloom, the rapturous sorrows of his Romantic soul.

De Vigny's Satan, mysterious, irresistible, a touch tragic, wins in his evil
way, even with an angel. But Lermontov's amorphous, almost disembodied
Demon proves to be more resistible, less tragic than pathetic. And he loses
the mortal woman whom he has tried with every power to make his own.
Although the Demon lays claim to supernatural powers equal to those of de
Vigny's Satan—and like Satan, he promises to make his beloved a queen—
the Demon fails to win Tamara or to turn her permanently away from
God. He does manage to attract her "with the elaborate speeches of seduction" [Соблазна полными речами] (2: 397) enough to bestow a fatal kiss,
prompting the narrator to announce that "the evil spirit triumphed!" [злой
дух торжествовал!] (2: 398). But Lermontov leaves utterly ambiguous, if
not downright dubious, both the "evil" and the "triumph." For the text gives
no indication that the Demon intended the kiss to result in Tamara's death,
and that this kiss therefore constitutes a legitimate, intentional triumph.
The narrator merely reports, "The fatal poison of his caress / Instantly penetrated her breast" [Смертельный яд его лобзанья / Мгновенно в грудь
ее проник] (2: 398). This "fatal poison" is apparently the product of his
fateful superhuman nature, not his willed desire. As a result, the narrator's
exclamation, "The evil spirit triumphed!" hangs in the air, punctuated better by a question mark than an exclamation point.

In any event, the triumph is short-lived. For immediately after the fatal
kiss, "one of the heavenly angels" [Один из ангелов святых] comes to carry
off Tamara's "sinful soul" [душу грешную]. Not caring "with what an
evil gaze" the Demon glared or "how full he was of fatal poison" [Каким
смотрел он злобным взглядом, / Как полон был смертельным ядом], the
angel scorns him, snapping, "You have triumphed enough" [Довольно ты
торжествовал] (2: 401). At that point, "the vanquished Demon cursed / His
insane dreams" [проклял Демон побежденный / Мечты безумные свои]
and was left "alone in the universe, as before / Without hope and love! . . . "
[Один, как прежде, во вселенной / Без упованья и любви! . . .] (2: 402;
ellipsis Lermontov's). So in the end, despite his powers, Lermontov's Demon,

unlike de Vigny's Satan, cannot win out against the powers of heaven. The Demon lacks the personal charisma and supernatural strength to achieve any enduring victory. And instead of suffering the heroic sorrows of evil triumphant, he goes off alone to lick his wounds and feel sorry for himself. His appearance, his words, his attractions do not suffice to render his evil, such as it is, triumphant for long.

Comparing de Vigny's Satan to Lermontov's Demon leads to the conclusion that Lermontov's Demon is a diminished devil, his evil seemingly lacking force and conviction. This diminution is further illustrated through a second comparison of the Demon with a Romantic depiction of evil and its diabolical incorporation that Lermontov also undoubtedly had in mind as he created *The Demon*: Goethe's *Faust*. (Lermontov demonstrably knew all of Goethe's major works of narrative poetry and prose quite well, and translated several of Goethe's lyric poems.)[12] Appearing in two parts in 1808 and 1832 respectively, Goethe's *Faust* sets forth moral ideas far less traditional and far more challenging than those of *Eloa*. In fact, Goethe presents in *Faust* what might well be the quintessential Romantic version of good and evil, virtually reversing the traditional Christian views of them. Here it is good to aspire, to act, to strive, whatever the consequences, because these bring freedom, vitality, and the supreme good, creation. As Goethe's God states in the famous line of the Prologue in Heaven, "Man errs as long as he will strive" (87, l. 317)—however hurtful errors may be, they are not evil, because they are the fruits of action.[13] By the same token, not striving, inaction, stasis—these lead to the greatest evil, destruction, which Goethe terms negation.

Hence Goethe has his renowned embodiment of evil in *Faust*, Mephistopheles, seek to end striving, to oppose action, to preclude creation. "I am the spirit that negates," he identifies himself. And he negates, he says, out of his conviction that "all that comes to be / Deserves to perish wretchedly; / 'Twere better nothing would begin" (161, ll. 1338–40). He later adds that, instead of life, "I should prefer Eternal Emptiness" (471, l. 11,603). Negation, emptiness—the eradication of action and creation, the opening of the void of stasis—these are the evils to which the witty, wily Mephistopheles dedicates himself as he proceeds to lead Faust to what he expects will be Faust's own negation, the end of Faust's striving and the consequent forfeiture of Faust's soul.

Mephistopheles plays out his philosophy not languorously, like de Vigny's Satan, but buoyantly. He therefore conceives his plans for Faust with relish:

> Through life I'll drag him at such a rate,
> Through shallow triviality,
> That he shall writhe and suffocate;
> And his insatiability
> With greedy lips, shall see the choicest plate
> And ask in vain for all that he would cherish—

until Faust gives up striving for new experiences and accordingly "must perish" (195, ll. 1860–66). Then Faust will join the rest of Mephistopheles' victims, furthering what Mephistopheles calls his own "planned destruction for the human race" (477, l. 11,690). Assuming different shapes and switching roles at will in his resolute quest to obtain Faust's soul, Mephistopheles consistently sustains his high—or rather, low—hopes of turning Faust against everything that merits affirmation and striving, including the negation of life itself. And at the end, when Mephistopheles loses and Faust's soul is carried off to heaven because God saw that Faust never ceased to strive, Mephistopheles merely curses in irritation, giving no sign that he will abandon his principles or their pursuit. He will find other victims in Goethe's Romantic world, where the force of creative energies (which Goethe dubs the "Eternal Feminine") will inspire new Fausts to strive for new experiences, whatever the risks may be.

In comparison to Goethe's Mephistopheles, Lermontov's Demon is less a resolute spirit of negation than a negated spirit.[14] Mephistopheles has a principled commitment to evil as he—and Goethe's God—envision it; the Demon has no commitment to any principle of evil at all. The Demon does demonic things, or evil, because he has no choice; that is his nature, and he comes to believe that this nature is his curse. When cast out of heaven, he recalls that he went not defiantly or to pursue an evil purpose, but "in fear, waving my wings / I departed—but where? Why? / I don't know . . ." [в страхе я, взмахнув крылами, / Помчался—но куда? зачем? / Не знаю . . .]. He recalls that he then felt like a damaged boat that sails on, "not knowing its destination" [не зная назначенья], or like a storm cloud that is "unable to stop anywhere" [нигде пристать не смея] and then "flies on without a goal or a trace / God knows whence and where!" [Летит без цели и следа, / Бог весть откуда и куда!] (2: 392).

The numerous negative terms in this passage—and elsewhere in the poem—underscore the extent to which the Demon does not go forth to negate but goes forth elementally negated. Aimless, lacking purpose or control, the Demon is not an antagonist of God and humanity and good, like Goethe's amiable, irrepressible evildoer. Rather than an ambitious and dedicated "spirit who negates" others, the Demon is a lost soul, adrift in a universe that affords him no direction—and he cannot find one for himself. Lermontov's Demon is a victim of anomie—not unlike Pechorin in *A Hero of Our Time*, as we shall see.

Even when the Demon discovers his evil superhuman abilities, he takes no particular satisfaction in them and employs them to no particular end, in stark contrast to Mephistopheles, who conspicuously revels in his powers and his malevolent mission. To be sure, the Demon does exercise his diabolical abilities. As he tells Tamara, "I soon taught people sin / I reviled everything noble / And abused everything good," so that "I easily extinguished / Forever the flame of pure belief in them" [Греху недолго их учил, / Всё благородное бесславил / И всё прекрасное худил . . . / Пламень чистой веры / Легко навек я залил в них] (2: 393). Nonetheless, the narrator notes, the Demon "sowed evil without enjoyment" [Он сеял зло без наслажденья] (2: 375), since, as he confesses, "the gloomy games of evil / Did not please me for long!" [здобы мрачные забавы / Недолго нравилися мне!]. For he had begun to wonder, "Were such fools and hypocrites / Worthy of my labors?" [А стоили ль трудов моих / Одни глупцы да лицемеры?] (2: 393). In short, the narrator summarizes, "evil bored him" [зло наскучило ему] (2: 375). Unlike Mephistopheles, who glories in his demonic machinations, the Demon plays *his* demonic part with an indifference bordering on disdain.

The Demon's attenuated or even negated demonism comes through unmistakably toward the end of his tale. Once smitten by love for the beautiful Tamara,[15] he approaches her "with a spirit open to good" [с душой, открытой для добра] (2: 388), and he readily agrees when she asks him to forsake his "evil enterprises" [злых стяжаний] (2: 395). Beyond that, he tells her that he actually longs to renounce evil and return to his original angelic condition, assuring her, "I want to be reconciled with heaven, / I want to love, I want to pray, / I want to believe in good" [Хочу я с небом примириться, / Хочу любить, хочу молиться, / Хочу я веровать добру] (2: 396). He asks Tamara for only one thing in return: "Love me!" [Люби меня!] (2: 397). This is a Demon who believes in nothing and pursues evil almost inadvertently, with one notable exception: he does cause the death of Tamara's fiancé in order to keep her to himself. But having arranged for this murder, he seemingly repents and renounces evil because he wants to "believe in good" and to be "reconciled with heaven." Although we have to consider the possibility that these are just seductive lines, his indifference to evil makes their sincerity plausible. It also renders believable his claim that, after all, what he *really* wants is love. Thus, lacking a psychological or philosophical commitment to evil, once his fatal kiss—another curse of his nature—has deprived him of that love and the angel has carried Tamara off to heaven over his protests, he sinks into an eternity of despair.

If this climactic mood exhibits the pathos of defeat by contrast to the tragic victory of de Vigny's Satan at the end of *Eloa*, it stands in polar opposition to the mentality of Goethe's Mephistopheles at the end of *Faust*. Mephistopheles loses his prey, too, as the angels bear the soul of Faust off to heaven because, despite all the evil he did, Faust never truly stopped striving. But there will be no despairing on Mephistopheles' part over the loss. He is far more resilient than that. In fact, he declares, "In all the world there's nothing more absurd / Than a devil who despairs" (321, ll. 3372–73). Yet Lermontov's Demon has no alternative but to feel despair. For he has no moral principles, no set of beliefs to sustain him. By contrast to Mephistopheles, he does not purvey the evil of negation against the good of striving. He rather suffers from negation in the absence of a philosophy or a vision of evil that should give meaning to a diabolical existence. No wonder this avatar of demonic evil is attenuated—it is obscured by the twilight of post-Romanticism.

A prominent third Romantic treatment of evil and its embodiment that Lermontov knew as he wrote *The Demon* is Byron's poetic drama *Cain*, published in 1821—in an early redaction Lermontov even tried as an epigraph some lines from *Cain* concerning the demonic "master of spirits" but, tellingly, he removed them later.[16] For although Lermontov was unquestionably attracted to Byron's demonic spirit as a type, he rendered that type quite differently—as in so much of his "not-Byronism," the form is there, but not the content (see Chapter 3). In *Cain*, Byron depicts evil in ways akin to Goethe's treatment of it in *Faust*, showing evil to be that which stifles human freedom. But Byron adds a provocative twist by attributing evil not to the character of the devil but to that of God. Byron's God is an oppressive authority figure (utterly unlike Goethe's ultra-tolerant, activity-promoting deity), while Byron's devil, Lucifer, is the consummate rebel fighting for human freedom. Granted, Byron complicates the image of Lucifer by making him arrogant, indifferent to the murderous consequences of the rebelliousness he inspires, and even desirous of worship himself. But Byron's Lucifer also unequivocally values vitality and unconstraint, whatever the costs; he is closer to Goethe's God than to Mephistopheles. And Byron's devil also has a clear moral vision—he serves a cause he believes to be good, even while he is arguably responsible for the introduction into human existence of the worst evil of all, death.

While Lermontov's Demon is an inexplicably discarded angel, Byron's Lucifer is in outright revolt. He has revolted against God precisely because he believes that this God despises human freedom and humanity itself. When he first appears before Cain, Lucifer assails God as an "Omnipotent tyrant" (522; act 1, l. 138). Lucifer is convinced, he tells Cain, that God has created humans solely "to make eternity/Less burthensome to his immense existence" (523; act 1, ll. 149–50), and to entertain himself with their suffering. Lermontov's Demon, by contrast, voices no criticism of God, even when cast out of paradise, unless we count one passing remark to Tamara that God "is occupied with heaven, not earth" [Он занят небом, не землей] (2: 394)—a claim that may be merely part of the Demon's campaign to seduce Tamara. There is no entrenched spirit of rebellion in the Demon, probably because he possesses no specific moral principles that would elicit a defense. He is more concerned with his own condition than with God's.

True to *his* principles, Byron's Lucifer not only rebels against God's rule but avers that humans have completely confused his and God's roles in their lives. Lucifer claims to feel "unbounded sympathy" (523; act 1, l. 160) for the plight of mortals who suffer and die, whereas God is the cause of this plight. Lucifer tells Cain, "I would not have made thee what thou art" (523; act 1, ll. 126–27), for unlike God, he would have given humans immortality—"I would have made ye/Gods" (524; act 1, ll. 199–200), Lucifer proclaims—and thereby protected humans from the pain of death to which God has condemned them. After all, Lucifer provocatively asks Cain,

> Who was the demon? He
> Who would not let ye live, or he who would
> Have made ye live for ever in the joy
> And power of knowledge? (524; act 1, ll. 204–7)

And Lucifer concludes with his own version of theodicy: "If/Evil springs from *him*, do not name it *mine*" (537; act 2, ll. 454–55).

Whatever his motives and moral legitimacy, Lucifer's will and determination to oppose God are unambiguous and uncompromising. He vows to wage an unending battle against this tyrant

> . . . through all eternity,
> And the unfathomable gulfs of Hades,
> And the interminable realms of space,
> And the infinity of endless ages. (537; act 2, ll. 432–35)

And although he concedes that God has authority over the earth, he adamantly denies that God has authority over him, conceding, "I have a victor—true," in the sense that God won the right to create humanity, "but no superior" (537; act 2, l. 429). Willing to fight forever to preserve his independence and display his equality with God, Lucifer urges Cain to do the same, advising him not to allow "tyrannous threats to force you unto faith" but instead to "think and endure—and form an inner world / In your own bosom" (537; act 2, ll. 461–64), in other words, not to worship mindlessly and not to sacrifice his individual autonomy on the altar of conformity. The fact that this advice results in Cain's impulsive murder of his ultra-pious brother, Abel, followed by Cain's intense remorse, might raise questions about the accuracy of Lucifer's claim to be the true friend of humanity. But Lucifer's philosophical commitment to freedom and his will to defend it throughout eternity cannot be doubted. As Goethe's God admitted, in the Romantic cause of striving and freedom, some blood is bound to be spilled.

Lermontov's Demon is a different breed from this devil, just as he differs from the devils of de Vigny and Goethe. He manifests no sweeping conception of himself, much less of God, and he shows only sporadic will or zeal or motive to act. Not only are no reasons given for the Demon's fall— there are no references to any willed act of sin or rebellion by the Demon in the final redaction[17]—but when he thinks back on the "mournful series of fruitless centuries" [Веков бесплодных ряд унылый] that ensued after his fall, he shrinks from remembering: "He did not have the strength to recall" them [припомнить не имел он силы] (2: 374), the narrator observes. This demonic spirit cannot even face the memory of his own experiences, much less justify them.

In contrast to Lucifer, the Demon obviously lacks will and purpose, even in the cause of Tamara's seduction. When he tries to initiate that seduction, he discovers that "he could not find in his mind / words of insidious temptation" [Он слов коварных искушенья / Найти в уме своем не мог]. "Had he forgotten?" the narrator asks rhetorically, adding, "God did not allow forgetting;/ And [the Demon] would not have chosen forgetting anyway!" [Забыть?—забвенья не дал бог;/ Да он и не взял бы забвенья!] (2: 379). If the Demon would not have "chosen" forgetting, then he once again must not have found "the strength to recall" those "words of insidious temptation." Later, when the Demon visits Tamara at the convent to which she has withdrawn, he finds that

> . . . for a long, long time he did not dare
> To disturb the sacred space of the peaceful retreat.
> And there was a minute
> When he seemed ready
> To abandon his cruel plan

> . . . долго, долго он не смел
> Святыню мирного приюта
> Нарушить. И было минута,
> Когда казался он готов
> Оставить умысел жестокой. (2: 387–88)

Lucifer virtually challenges God to a duel, but the Demon is reluctant even to enter God's terrain.

The telling differences between Lermontov's Demon and the devils of de Vigny, Goethe, and Byron show up most dramatically when he tries most to act like them and then tries to escape his evil persona altogether. Bracing himself, he aspires to the very image of an outsized Romantic Devil as he confronts an angel first sent to protect Tamara from his advances. He derisively dismisses this angel, announcing, "She is mine!" [Она моя!] and exulting, "Here it is no longer your sacred place/ Here I rule and love!" [Здесь больше нет твоей святыни,/ Здесь я владею и люблю!] (2: 389). He then boasts to Tamara, "I am the scourge of my earthly slaves,/ I am the tsar of knowledge and freedom,/ I am the enemy of heaven, I am the evil of nature" [Я бич рабов моих земных/ Я цар познанья и свободы,/ Я враг небес, я зло природы] (2: 390). Suddenly, and for the first time, he sounds like a combination of de Vigny's Satan, Goethe's Mephistopheles, *and* Byron's Lucifer. Yet shortly thereafter, he sounds like none of them, as he confesses his love to Tamara, crying, "I am at your feet!" [я у ног твоих!] and then even adding, "I am your slave" [я раб твой] (2: 390). In an instant, he has transmuted from a "scourge" of slaves to a slave himself. Unlike his demonic predecessors, this Demon vacillates between self-assurance and insecurity, self-affirmation and self-abasement.

And at the poem's climax, the Demon actually *betrays* those predecessors when he endeavors to deny his own demonic nature. For after succumbing to Tamara—far more than she succumbs to him—he confesses,

> I secretly suddenly began to hate
> My immortality and my power.
> I unwillingly envied
> The incomplete joys of earth;
> Not to live, like you, became painful for me.

> тайно вдруг возненавидел
> Бессмертие и власть мою.
> Я позавидовал невольно
> Неполной радости земной;
> Не жить, как ты, мне стало больно. (2: 390–91)

He then asks,

> What does this eternity mean to me without you?
> The endlessness of my powers?
> Empty-sounding words
> A vast church—without a divinity!

> Что без тебя мне эта вечность?
> Моих владений бесконечность?
> Пустые звучные слова,
> Обширный храм – без божества! (2: 391)

In complete contrast to de Vigny's Satan, Goethe's Mephistopheles, and Byron's Lucifer, all avowed enemies of the divine on the one hand and of peaceful existence on the other, Lermontov's Demon actually wants both. And he voices his willingness to forsake the ultimate demonic asset, his own eternal life, to obtain them. No true Romantic Devil would ever do that.

And this is exactly the point—Lermontov's Demon is no true Romantic Devil. To be sure, he bears a resemblance. Like Satan in *Eloa*, the Demon is an attractive and articulate seducer; like Mephistopheles in *Faust*, the Demon is more negator than creator; like Lucifer in *Cain*, the Demon is a haughty exile from heaven. Like them all, the Demon has supernatural powers—he flies, he becomes invisible, he crosses physical barriers at will, and, of course, he is immortal. But despite these and other similarities that lead critics regularly to place Lermontov's Demon in the company of various Romantic demonic figures, he does not conform to their mold, as they oppose the reigning order of God and human existence.

Aimless, lacking purpose and control, the Demon in fact fits no mold at all—he is no inveterate seducer, or dedicated "spirit who negates," or rebellious exponent of freedom. As noted earlier, by contrast to the alluringly handsome Satan, the nattily urbane Mephistopheles, and the severely majestic Lucifer, Lermontov's Demon does not even have his own name or distinctive appearance. He is a soul roaming in a universe that affords him no formal identity or shaping goal—and he cannot find these for himself. Thus he comes to an end unlike any of his demonic forebears. Although de Vigny's Satan sinks into gloom after his true triumph over Eloa, it is an abysmal, heroic gloom. Even though Goethe's Mephistopheles fails to win Faust's soul, he remains undaunted. And while Byron's Lucifer does not defeat God, he goes off implacably to continue his battle for freedom. But Lermontov's Demon simply sinks into pathetic despair. Hence he remains in perpetuity an anonymous, amorphous figure of indefinite nature, uncertain intentions, and ambiguous moral makeup, lost in the transition out of Romanticism.

THE EVIL OF UNTOLD STORIES

Lermontov's Demon reveals himself to be no thoroughgoing Romantic Devil animated by an identity, a will, and a moral sensibility to take him beyond ambiguity, respite, and retreat. But he is not just a failed Romantic devil either. Of course, he might be seen as a quasi-human being cursed with supernatural powers that deny him the comforting human love and domestic existence that he desires—virtually an anti-Faust—as some recent critical interpretations have held (see note 4). But I would say that he is more of a post-Romantic devil; or rather, he mirrors Lermontov's intellectually complex, historically ambiguous post-Romantic moral vision. To grasp that vision more fully, we need to look at how Lermontov presents the narrative of evil that tells the Demon's story. In particular, we need to see that not only does *The Demon* offer no clearly diabolical embodiment of evil, it offers no clear *narrative* of evil either. That is, it tells no story occurring over time that explicitly defines and depicts evil. Instead Lermontov authors a narrative poem suggesting that evil can be the uncertainty about what evil really is—the very quality of evil with which Lermontov's transitional moral sensibility contends. This quality particularly stands out when we compare *The Demon* to one more work portraying a devil that Lermontov drew on, *Melmoth the Wanderer.*

Written in 1820 by Charles Maturin, an Irish curate turned playwright-novelist, *Melmoth the Wanderer* was by many accounts one of Lermontov's favorite novels.[18] It comprises a series of tales about individuals who encounter an Irishman named Melmoth born in the late seventeenth century. This Melmoth made a traditionally Faustian bargain enabling him to penetrate the mysteries of the universe while obtaining supernatural powers and enjoying a supernaturally prolonged existence (about 160 years). In return, he consigned his own soul to the devil, with the proviso that he could get out of the arrangement if he could "tempt wretches in their fearful hour of extremity, with the promise of deliverance . . . on condition of their exchanging situations" with him (538). Disenchanted with his part of the bargain after finding prolonged life increasingly tedious, Melmoth tries to make such an exchange, roving the world over, seeking someone to give him release. Yet, although he approaches many individuals in the direst of straits, he nonetheless fails to convince anyone to trade extraordinary powers in this world for damnation in the next. And so, at the novel's conclusion, with his extended term of life finally over, Melmoth apparently dies and goes to hell himself (his death is not explicitly depicted).

There are many striking similarities between Melmoth and the Demon, and between the plots of the works in which they appear as well (for instance, Melmoth falls in love with a beautiful and innocent young girl he happens to encounter during his wanderings). But the differences are more revealing than the similarities. The first difference we can see concerns narrative structure. *Melmoth the Wanderer* is a marvel of narrative complexity—tales within tales within tales are told by multiple narrators, some of whom are named (one is Melmoth himself), while others remain nameless. Maturin has here created a veritable "series of nested boxes," as Robin Feuer Miller has aptly described it (102), at one point going five layers deep: a story about Melmoth is told by one character to another within a story told by Melmoth himself to yet another character; the story Melmoth tells is one of a group of stories about Melmoth included in a manuscript whose contents are reported to a descendent of Melmoth by a Spaniard named Monçada in the course of *his* overarching story regarding his own encounters with Melmoth during the Spanish Inquisition; and this narrative of Monçada's is in turn a major segment of the novel itself, narrated by an impersonal, omniscient, third-person narrator whom it is not unfair to identify with Maturin himself.

By contrast to Melmoth's complex narrative structure, that of *The Demon* is markedly simple and straightforward—there are no tales within tales, no multiple narrators, no layers of mediating consciousnesses.[19] It is true that the prosodic requirements of poetry make such structural complexities more difficult to introduce than in prose fiction. Yet in other narrative poems, such as *Izmail-Bei*, Lermontov does make use of narrative frames, multiple narrators, and other complicating narrative devices. In *The Demon*, however, Lermontov strips the narrative bare, portraying few characters and fewer events over a very brief period of time. His story of demonic evil not only has a highly attenuated devil, it has almost no story at all, besides some short patches of narrated events focusing primarily on Tamara and her family—that is, on the human characters, not on the superhuman one.

A correlative formal difference between *Melmoth the Wanderer* and *The Demon* lies in their narrative points of view. Despite the plethora of narrative voices in *Melmoth the Wanderer*, Maturin nonetheless manages to connect them relatively seamlessly through a single point of view—reminiscent of the way one character metaphorically describes the many different individuals who have encountered Melmoth, "We are all beads strung on the same string" (298). Virtually no variation in style, tone, or judgment complicates the overarching narratorial perspective. Hence, in effect, the many narratives in *Melmoth the Wanderer* appear to have one narrator. And this is a narrator (who sounds like Maturin himself, the fervent anti-Catholic moralist) with a definite point of view and, above all, a firm conception of evil, which he envisions both traditionally—as self-indulgent unconstraint and estrangement from God—and Romantically, as subordination to arbitrary authority and the refusal to exercise individual will. In that narrator's scheme of things, almost all Catholics are evil, some other human beings are evil too, and Melmoth himself is supremely evil. Maturin thus employs both the form and contents of *Melmoth the Wanderer* to convey his moral vision—he spreads out his version of evil across many narratives for all to see. But at the same time he holds this evil in check, as it were, constraining it by a weighty narrative structure and a single point of view.[20]

In comparison to these multiple narrators with a single, coherent moral point of view in *Melmoth the Wanderer*, *The Demon* has only one narrator, and he has no clear moral point of view. Although that single, unnamed narrator's mediating consciousness ostensibly shapes the poem's characters and events, he provides no consistent perspective; indeed, he only sporadically reveals himself as a narratorial persona—and an indefinite one at that. The narrative point of view therefore almost seems to wander: at times it belongs to a detached, omniscient observer; at other times it apparently reflects the narrator's emotional engagement with his narrative; and at still others, it lets the consciousness of one character or another take over the narration by lapsing into *style indirect libre*, almost as though *The Demon* had no controlling narrator at all.

Lermontov's narrator begins in a lyrical and yet distant tone:

> The sad Demon, spirit of exile,
> Flew above the sinful earth,
> And memories of better days
> Beset him in a throng.

> Печальный Демон, дух изгнанья,
> Летал над грешною землей,
> И лучших дней воспоминанья
> Пред ним теснилися толпой. (2: 374)

Shortly thereafter, the narrator steps forward to rhapsodize, first over the beauty of the Georgian mountains, and then over the beauty of Tamara, directly addressing his audience: "I swear that such a beauty / Did not bloom beneath the southern sun" [Клянусь, красавица такая / Под солнцем юга не цвела] (2: 378). Once the narrator begins to introduce characters, however, he allows their points of view to infiltrate his narrative. For example, he represents the reaction of Tamara's fiancé to the attack arranged by the Demon with the immediacy and intensity of the fiancé's own emotional experience: "Suddenly, two men flashed by up ahead / And then more—a shot!—what's that?" [Вдруг впереди мелькнули двое, / больше—выстрел!—что такое?] (2: 380). Likewise, the narrator recreates Tamara's thoughts and emotions as she grows enamored with the Demon, along with her uncertainty as to his motives, by reporting that the Demon "gleamed softly, like a star; / He beckoned and called . . . but—where? . . ." [Сиял он тихо, как звезда; / Манил и звал он . . . но—куда? . . .] (2: 385). The ellipses, the pause, the question—these all belong to Tamara's consciousness. And we see this even more graphically when the narrator reports Tamara's dream about the Demon, in which "she has no strength to breathe, a mist covers her eyes, / Her arms thirstily seek an embrace / Kisses melt on her lips . . . " [Нет сил дышать, туман в очах, / Объятья жадно ищут встречи, / Лобзанья тают на устах . . .] (2: 387), followed by two more lines of ellipses. The shift to the present tense here only further distances the narrator's consciousness from the report of this intense experience.

As we would expect, the Demon's point of view periodically comes to the narrative fore as well. When he hesitates to enter the convent to which Tamara has retreated, for instance, the narrator says that the Demon hears her singing, "and this song was tender, / As if it was composed for the earth / In heaven!" [И эта песнь была нежна, / Как будто для земли она / была на небе сложена!]. The narrator then continues,

Hadn't an angel [who] wanted to meet anew
With a forgotten friend
Secretly flown down here,
And sung about his past,
In order to lessen his torments? . . .

Не ангел ли с забытым другом
Вновь повидаться захотел,
Сюда украдкою слетел
И о былом ему пропел,
Чтоб усладить его мученье? . . . (2: 388; ellipsis Lermontov's)

These are the tentative fantasies, the questioning hopes of the Demon himself.

More tentativeness registers in the narrative voice of *The Demon* through the narrator's recurrent use of the phrase "as if" [как будто]. When the Demon begins his campaign to seduce Tamara, the narrator remarks, "Now it is *as if* she hears / A magical voice above her" [И вот она как будто слышит / Волшебный голос над собой] (2: 382); the narrator reports that the Demon looked at her "*as if* he pitied her" [как будто он об ней жалел] (2: 384); as the Demon approaches Tamara, the narrator observes in him "a vague tremble of expectation, / A fear of mute uncertainty, / As if at their first meeting / There would be an encounter with a proud spirit" [Неясный трепет ожиданья, / Страх неизвестности немой, / Как будто в первое свиданье / Спознались с гордою душой] (2: 388–89); the narrator asks rhetorically whether the graveyard where Tamara is buried on a cliff, "*as if* closer to heaven / Is warmer for the deceased bones? . . . " [Как будто ближе к небесам / Теплей посмертное жилище?] (2: 400–401. All italics in English are mine). While this recurring use of the conditional "as if" may foster the *style indirect libre* by conveying the uncertainty of a given character at a particular moment, it also undermines the narrator's authority—he cannot state with assurance the facts or significance of the experience he is describing.

As a result, it is not surprising when the narrator relinquishes his role as narrator altogether. He does so by presenting a lengthy dialogue between the Demon and Tamara, only resuming that role near the poem's end to report the Demon's fatal kiss, her funeral procession, the Demon's futile attempt to claim her soul, and his resultant condemnation to a life "alone in the universe, as before / Without hope and love!" [Один, как прежде, во вселенной / Без упованья и любви!] (2: 402). And although the narrator occasionally interjects other exclamations betokening a strong reaction to his tale in its final segments,[21] by and large the narrative tone toward the end shifts to one of melancholy resignation, particularly in the rendition of the church on a mountain cliff where Tamara and her father have been buried: "And the eternal restiveness of humanity / Does not disturb their eternal peace" [И вечный ропот человека / Их вечный мир не возмутит] (2: 404).

Even if we attribute the recurring shifts in narrative perspective in *The Demon* to an especially empathetic narrator who identifies with all his characters, that empathy would undermine his moral authority—he too would be succumbing to the sway of his occasionally forceful and yet ultimately impotent protagonist. And either way, whether insufficiently resolute or overly empathetic, by his inconsistency the narrator undermines the moral impact of his most explicit moral assertion, uttered after the Demon fatally kisses Tamara: "Alas! The evil spirit triumphed!" [Увы! злой дух торжествовал!] (2: 398). For by this point we do not really know whose exclamation this is, or what point of view it signifies. Although evil is much in the air of *The Demon* as an abstract idea—the narrator labels the Demon and what he does to Tamara "evil" [зло / злоба; злой] no fewer than fourteen times—no dominant and morally clear narrative voice defines what evil actually is.

At the same time, it must be noted that Lermontov does not provide many evil actions to judge. Unlike Maturin, who makes Melmoth a legend in his own time (and a long time it is) by having characters tell numerous stories about him and his evil deeds, the narrator of *The Demon* reports no legendary stories about the evil his protagonist has wrought. And even when the Demon talks about himself to Tamara, we do not hear about such deeds; he recounts no story of his past or planned future actions. He merely describes his emotional condition: his boredom, his misery, his alienation, his longing for love.

The fact that the Demon defines himself through subjective states rather than through objective actions suggests that he is what Gary Saul Morson has dubbed a "generic fugitive" ("Genre," 356), that is, a character typical of one literary genre who nonetheless inhabits another.[22] That is to say, the Demon's focus on his internal self, rather than on his external behavior, allies him much more closely with the passive, introspective personae of lyric poetry than with the active, assertive protagonists of narrative poetry, especially in the era of Romanticism. In consequence, the Demon evidently has no use for narrative in any form. He even dismisses the narration of world history as insignificant compared to his moods:

What is the story of the burdensome deprivations,
The labors and sufferings of the human mass
Of future and past generations
Before one minute
Of my unacknowledged torments?

Что повесть тягостных лишений,
Трудов и бед толпы людской
Грядущих, прошлых поколений
Перед минутою одной
Моих непризнанных мучений? (2: 393)

In the end, I conclude that the Demon dismisses narratives because he has no story, no narrative, of his *own* in which he roots his identity and with which he identifies himself to others. He has no tale to tell of how or why he fell from the ranks of the angels; he himself reports no specific encounters with individuals he has harmed; he details no fiendish schemes of corruption and betrayal. His evil exists largely as an epithet attached to him by the narrator of *The Demon*. In fact, with one exception, no narratives, including the main one (since Tamara's death may be inadvertent), clearly demonstrate how he elementally *is* evil. And even that exception, the one unequivocally evil act for which the Demon is consciously responsible—the murder of Tamara's fiancé—is nonetheless mitigated by the narrator, as he tells readers only that the Demon distracted the fiancé and thereby rendered him vulnerable to a surprise attack by Muslim highwaymen. It is simply by implication that the Demon caused his rival's death, but he is not shown to have participated in it actively.

This absence of overtly evil action in *The Demon* reminds us why Aristotle made "plot" more important than "character" in drama. For without the portrayal of plot or action, we can never know who a character really is, no matter what that character says. And this would hold particularly true of evil characters—they and their creators need to *prove* how evil their natures are. The Demon's nature, however, remains unproven and thus morally ambiguous. His evil never explicitly manifests itself in his actions; it is left a largely untold story because there is not much of a story to tell about it. It is more of an equivocal, indistinct abstraction—evil as an amorphous idea. Therefore, by contrast to Maturin, Lermontov has no need of a complex narrative structure or a compelling narrator at once to make the Demon's evil clear and to keep it in check.

THE EVIL OF TRANSITION

Yet all of this does not lead to the conclusion that the Demon is not evil at all or, more broadly, that Lermontov had no moral vision of his own. The Demon's moral ambiguity rather signals that Lermontov's moral imagination resists easy categories. Vestiges of both traditional and Romantic ideas of good and evil do appear in *The Demon*, certainly, but they do not add up to any preestablished moral doctrine. In particular, unlike the distinctively embodied, consciously willed, and explicitly principled evil in the Romantic works Lermontov knew so well, evil in *The Demon* comes across as disembodied, not always willed, and not rooted in any explicit principle. For Lermontov's moral vision does not embrace any such explicit moral principles or doctrines. Rather, Lermontov implies that moral judgments are uncertain because they lack firm ground, and so convictions must vacillate and cannot be confidently defined or vigorously defended.

In fact, I would conclude that this is what the narrative poem *The Demon* ultimately identifies as evil—*not knowing what evil is*. When no moral doctrines reign, when no cultural values give clear definition to moral visions— as in times of cultural transition out of a period—evil may be palpable, but it is terribly difficult to grasp. It is too amorphous, too ambiguous, too elusive. As a result, evil is also more insidious and treacherous than when established cultural values and norms are in force, as they are in the heyday of well-defined cultural periods. *The Demon* thus reveals Lermontov's moral vision more accurately than it would seem at first. For while in this poem Lermontov repeatedly observes the presence of evil, he never tells us what it is.

This conception of evil as a kind of ignorance arguably leaves Lermontov on shaky moral ground, by contrast to the Romanticists who had far more emphatic ideas of evil, complicated and contradictory as those ideas could be—hence the confidence with which de Vigny delineates his Satan as an unrelenting seducer, Goethe portrays Mephistopheles as an indefatigable negator, Byron depicts Lucifer as an implacable rebel and God as a selfish tyrant, and Maturin spins manifold stories of Melmoth as a cynical corrupter and enemy of God. These authors' diabolical characters are as clear and strong, if unconventional, as are the categories of good and evil they convey. Morally speaking, Romanticists knew what they stood for, even if they stood all over the map.

Lermontov was not so sure. For he found himself standing as a transitional author on the edge of a cultural era, where he saw the ground of Romantic beliefs eroding and bold Romantic assertions of value fading away. Aptly, Lermontov has an angel label the Demon "the spirit of doubt"— doubt about what is good as well as what is evil—a spirit who consequently ends up doing nothing but what he erratically takes to be good for himself. Such doubts make the Demon the moral and psychological, as well as the immediate chronological, precursor of that most ethically ambiguous of literary characters, Pechorin, in Lermontov's best-known work, *A Hero of Our Time*, which Lermontov commenced writing while he was finishing *The Demon*. Although differing in temperament, both Pechorin and the Demon are emblematic post-Romantic doubters inhabiting the moral limbo of an anomic culture.

Lermontov himself, I suspect, did not relish moral ambiguity and doubt. He depicted these as conditions of his times, when the morally charged images of Romanticism—including its demons—lingered even as their power was draining away, along with the ideals and norms that had engendered them. The quandary he then faced was how to envision good and evil during those times. He could not create a morally strong demonic figure as his Romanticist predecessors had done, even though he would incorporate aspects of their demons into his. Indeed, it is no surprise that Lermontov has his Demon remark of other demonic exiles from heaven after he summons them: "Alas! I myself did not recognize / Their evil words and faces and gazes" [слов и лиц и взоров злобных, / Увы! я сам не узнавал] (2: 392). For fundamentally, Lermontov's Demon is not like them. Caught in a morally inchoate condition, that Demon is truly a "spirit of exile," as he is identified in the poem's very first line. And he is exiled not only within the narrative poem that portrays him but from the Romantic universe of demons as well. He belongs elsewhere. It was Lermontov's genius in *The Demon* to create this unique diabolical character not merely as another avatar of the great Romantic devils, but as a reflection of the ambiguous moral state of his own transitional, post-Romantic times.

Ideals to Ideology

Unmasking Masquerade

THE POST-ROMANTIC IDEOLOGUE

Romanticists worshipped Shakespeare. In their eyes, as historian Jacques Barzun observes, "Shakespeare's art was equal to his genius, his judgment in characterization and dramatic fitness was impeccable; his knowledge of life and human beings was not equaled by any other poet or playwright. . . . Thus was 'the bard' born" (*Dawn*, 516).[1]

Lermontov knelt at the same altar. Both *Othello* and *Hamlet* were staged in Moscow while the young Lermontov was in residence there, and he avidly attended the theater during his stay. He expressed his admiration for *Hamlet* in particular and Shakespeare in general in a letter of 1830 or 1831 to his aunt Maria Shan-Girei, lauding "this immeasurable genius penetrating into the heart of humanity, into the laws of fate, the original, that is, the inimitable Shakespeare" (4: 360–61). Lermontov incorporated direct references or allusions to various Shakespeare plays, especially *Hamlet*, *Macbeth*, and *The Merchant of Venice*, into a number of his own poems, plays, and prose works. And in the last extant letter from him, written in June 1841, less than one month before his death, Lermontov asked his grandmother to send him the complete works of Shakespeare in English, if she could obtain them (4: 429).[2]

Given this admiration, it comes as no surprise that Lermontov would to a conspicuous degree model what became the most prominent of his six plays, *Masquerade* [*Маскарад*] on one of Shakespeare's famed tragedies, *Othello*.[3] Lermontov wrote several versions of this drama between 1834 and 1836, all of which take their skeletal plot from *Othello*. But while Lermontov pays homage to Shakespeare, he transforms Shakespeare's plot into a portrayal of post-Romanticism, and a particularly suggestive portrayal at that, one displaying ideals of Romanticism reduced to post-Romantic ideology. He thereby captures one of the keenest quandaries of post-Romanticism: how clinging to the ideals of Romanticism in its twilight could all too easily become an exercise in ideological self-deception. If a god has become a fallen idol, one must recognize this, or else lapse into misbegotten reverence that can amount to a dangerous ideology.

To see how such an ideology arises, let us first briefly compare these plays of Shakespeare and Lermontov. Like Othello, Lermontov's main protagonist of *Masquerade*, Evgenii Arbenin, falsely believes that his beloved wife, Nina, is being unfaithful to him, and, as a result, he murders her, only to discover his error too late. Also like Othello, Arbenin finds his misguided jealousy fed by someone bent on ruining his life. Further akin to Othello, Arbenin claims that his intense love for his wife, coupled with his intolerance of dishonor and betrayal, leads him to his fatal act.

But there are also notable differences between Shakespeare's Othello and Lermontov's Arbenin that render Arbenin the more psychologically and morally questionable. In the first place, by contrast to the naïve Othello, Arbenin presents himself as worldly-wise and world-weary, and as both intellectually and ethically superior to the society around him, which he views as trafficking in scurrilous gossip and vicious scandal mongering. In the second place, unlike Othello, Arbenin denies responsibility for his own actions in killing his wife, even after acknowledging his error. "It is not I who killed her" [Не я ее убийца] (3: 378), he declares in his final lines, instead casting blame for her death on a vicious society and an implacable fate, as well as on a noble but uncontrollable love. And third, Arbenin does not actively punish himself for his ill-conceived act by honorably committing suicide, as Othello does, but rather collapses in a catatonic stupor, immobilized and speechless.

Notwithstanding Arbenin's denials of responsibility for the murder, critics of the play have made this issue central to every interpretation of *Masquerade* and its variations on *Othello*. And, typical of other areas of Lermontov scholarship, these critics have tended to divide over whether *Masquerade* belongs more to Romanticism or to Realism. Some have treated the play as a Romantic tragedy of a noble Byronesque spirit brought down by a merciless fate and by the force of his own powerful personality, whereas others have deemed the play a sharp satirical portrait in a proto-Realist vein of a pernicious society out to destroy Arbenin for being a superior individual who refuses to conform.[4] Two noteworthy recent commentaries essentially unite these two perspectives (while leaning toward the Romantic side). In one, Amanda Ewington sees Arbenin displaying "gloomy alienation and jealous fury" (101) while striving to achieve demonic heights of evildoing—in effect, demonstrating his Romantically prodigious nature—only to succumb to social and cosmic forces beyond his control.[5] Hence, while granting that "certainly Arbenin bears responsibility for his deadly reaction to Nina's purported betrayal," she concludes that Lermontov "diffuses" this responsibility, in that other characters "relentlessly drive [Arbenin] to despair and must share the burden of culpability," along with inimical circumstances created by a "malevolent fate" (124). However faulty Arbenin may be, in Ewington's view he ends up defeated by both a vice-ridden society and a cruel destiny—just as he wants to believe.

In his analysis of the play, Vladimir Golstein explicitly treats Arbenin as a Romantic hero worthy of Lermontov's "narratives of heroism," as Golstein puts it in the title of his book. He offers this interpretation while pointing out that Arbenin is eventually "led to intellectual bankruptcy, and to madness" (83) by the malevolent scheming of his social acquaintances, as well as by his own "cynical, pessimistic outlook," which is "as much the cause of his fall as are the intrigues of a hostile society" (72). And although attributing this outlook and Arbenin's fatal action to a flawed "philosophy" born of "his own personality and his own 'proud mind'" (63), which cause Arbenin to make an "epistemological and ontological mistake," Golstein insists that Arbenin is so filled with "strength, pride, independence, self-reliance, and nobility" (84) that he remains "a true Byronic hero" (72).

Once again, by contrast to these and other interpretations of Arbenin, I would say that he is neither a proto-Realist victim of society nor a Romantic hero. Arbenin is rather a dramatic protagonist who suffers from a peculiar and tormented relationship to Romanticism not found among true

Romantic heroes. Before making this case, though, I should touch on the concept of the Romantic hero itself.

An early expression of that concept comes from the German Romantic philosopher Hegel, in *The Philosophy of Fine Art* [*Vorlesungen über die Aesthetik*] (1835–38). There Hegel describes heroes as "men who make for themselves a great place in the arena of life through the activity of exceptional volitional power and the inherent greatness and effectiveness of their character" (187). Heroes are therefore "individuals who undertake and accomplish a complete enterprise in consistent reliance upon their personal resources and initiative, and with whom it is consequently a purely arbitrary act of their own when they execute anything" (189). As a result, every hero—Hegel names, among others, Hercules, Oedipus, El Cid, and Goethe's Götz von Berlichengen—feels "bound up wholly in substantial unity" with "the ethical whole to which he belongs" (192), and he accepts full responsibility for "all that he may will, act, and accomplish" (191). This portrait of the hero perfectly exemplifies what I have called the Romantic ideal of the self in its psychological and moral integrity (see Chapter 2).

Romantic historian and critic Thomas Carlyle likewise hailed heroes for their psychological and moral integrity in many of his works, most notably in his lectures of 1840 on "heroes, hero-worship, and the heroic in history." In these lectures Carlyle defined heroes as "Great Men" who have given us "the history of what man has accomplished in this world." Each of these Great Men—Carlyle dwells on historical figures including Mohammad, Dante, Shakespeare, Luther, Johnson, Rousseau, Burns, Cromwell, and Napoleon—merits the epithet of hero because each lived as a "living light-fountain, which it is good and pleasant to be near . . . a flowing light-fountain, as I say, of native original insight, of manhood and heroic nobleness;—in whose radiance all souls feel that it is well with them" (3–4).

Carlyle roots his conception of heroism in what he terms "sincerity." "A deep, genuine sincerity," he says, "is the first characteristic of all men in any way heroes" (39). And although "the Great Man does not boast himself sincere, far from that; perhaps does not ask himself if he is so: I would say rather, his sincerity does not depend on himself; he cannot help being sincere." This sincerity enables a hero to face "the great Fact of Existence" directly, that is, to face "the Reality" of human experience (40), however complex or daunting that experience might be, without fear of dependence or self-deception. Thus "while others walk in formulas and hearsays, contented enough to dwell there, [a hero] could not screen himself in formulas, he was alone with his own soul and the reality of things. . . . Such *sincerity*, as we named it, has in very truth something of [the] divine." And "the word of such a man is a Voice direct from Nature's own Heart" (47), never to be compromised.[6] Carlyle's heroes, like Hegel's, are wholly authentic, fully integrated within themselves, and the highest incarnations of integrity.

These concepts of the hero—along with prominent literary variations on them created by Schiller, Goethe, Shelley, Byron, Chateaubriand, Hugo, and others, as well as what many Romantic contemporaries considered a living example in Napoleon—spawned a tradition of literary scholarship on the subject of the Romantic hero, or the Romantic ideal of the hero. In the twentieth century, some literary critics seeking to define the Romantic hero have taken Hegel's and Carlyle's buoyantly affirmative descriptions as the model. The Romantic idea of the hero, remarks one such critic, was a "composite" of the "great myths of the romantic age" (Bishop, 19) that idealized the likes of Prometheus, Satan, and Napoleon, along with the main characters in MacPherson's Ossian cycle, as superior beings who, whatever their natures, were true to themselves while pursuing transcendent purposes. Or as N. H. Clement exuberantly phrases it, Romantic heroes are

> the titans of thought, feeling, and action, like Faust, [the Spaniard] don Juan, and Napoleon. The sensibility and the imagination of [the Romantic hero] are infinite, they require immense objects on which to exercise themselves, their manifestations must be of an amplitude foreign to mankind. He regards himself as an elemental force of nature that has burst its bonds, and sweeps on in a grand and untrammeled exhibition of energy. Not for him the ordinary rules of life, not for him the usual bounds of action, feeling and conduct; he transcends all, he is above the common run of humanity, beyond its frontiers, he is on his own standard and measure. He likes to fuse himself into nature, to imitate it in its grand displays of power. (429)

But other critics have not been so positive. They have tended to emphasize the dark side of Romantic heroes, such as their acute self-consciousness, melancholy, disillusionment, or despair. As one of these critics puts it, the Romantic hero may be "an exceptional being," but he is given to "an incessant brooding on his state" that leads into "boundless self-idolatry," and can even reach a "point of utter negativity that represents the inversion of the Romantic quest, the bankruptcy of idealism" (Furst, *Contours*, 44, 48, 46–47).[7]

To be sure, a portion of the difference between these divergent twentieth-century views of the Romantic hero comes from the fact that critics choose different characters to support their definitions of this type. Some, for instance, cite Schiller's Karl Moor, Shelley's Prometheus, and Hugo's Jean Valjean to show that Romantic heroes are impassioned rebels and personifications of integrity. Others point to characters like Goethe's Werther, Byron's Childe Harold, and Chateaubriand's René to prove that Romantic heroes are emotional cripples, consumed by melancholy, and deficient in purpose, will, and integrity.

But despite these different temperamental types, I would argue these characters all merit the appellation "Romantic hero." For all true Romantic heroes (as defined by the Romantic ideal of heroism) have some supreme power of personality, some exceptional capacity of will and passion, or some exceptional desire for transcendence that renders them *heroic*, outsized, larger than life, extraordinary, and at least in quest, if not in possession, of some form of exalting integrity that unifies their sometimes troubled beings. (In this light I would differentiate these noble Romantic *heroes* from Romantic *protagonists*, such as Byron's satirically intended Don Juan and Constant's Adolphe, who lack truly heroic qualities.) Even melancholy and misery beset true Romantic heroes on a grand scale, achingly and all-consumingly, plunging them into depths unknown to lesser mortals—or to their literary epigones.[8] It is noteworthy that Clement, who defined the Romantic hero with such élan, selects none other than Chateaubriand's René—deemed by some critics a passive and lugubrious character—as the first exemplar of his definition (429). Whether in action or emotion or both, the Romantic hero greatly exceeds the bounds of mundane experience as he aspires to transcendence and suffers despair—Goethe's Faust arguably sets the standard for both—in hopes of heroically achieving and sustaining an ideal self distinguished by unique psychological and moral integrity.

Against this portrait of the Romantic hero and the Romantic ideal of heroism, Lermontov's Arbenin is no match. As Lermontov repeatedly shows, Arbenin's professions of intellectual and moral superiority, courage, and integrity—defining himself as a Romantic hero—clash with the facts that Arbenin is conformist, cowardly, and self-deceived. Indeed, his failure to live up to the exalted standards he claims to embrace suggests that Arbenin is not an admirable if misguided Romantic hero and idealist, brought low either by an unswerving adherence to those ideals, or by a society that refuses to embrace them, or by cosmic forces that oppose them. He is what I will call a post-Romantic ideologue, someone who has transformed established Romantic ideals into a belated and rigidly systematic set of self-deceiving ideas that blind him to his own folly. Put another way, Arbenin purchases an illusory self-image at the cost of his psychological and moral integrity.

To see Arbenin as an ideologue instead of an idealist and hero is to see *Masquerade* as a cautionary tale against the potential dangers of Romantic ideals as a source of ideology. And yet this does not mean that Lermontov used the play to condemn Romanticism itself as an ideology, but rather that he used it implicitly to condemn the ideological perversion of Romantic ideals *into* an ideology.[9] The play therefore focuses on the transitional quandary of how to guard against the seductions of ideology during a time when existing ideals and the values they represent are fading. Hence *Masquerade* provocatively dramatizes Lermontov's post-Romantic ambivalence toward Romanticism, whose cultural and moral authority and integrity he admired, yet perceived to be aging and vulnerable to distortion.

Before supporting my interpretation by discussing the text itself, I must pause once more in order to explain my use of the term *ideology*. I do not use it in the original, positive (if somewhat condescending) sense intended by Napoleon when he dubbed a group of eighteenth-century French liberal thinkers "ideologues" for their preoccupation with furthering social harmony through ideas and ideals.[10] Nor do I use it in the neutral sociological sense of Talcott Parsons, for example, who defined ideology as an "empirical and evaluative" body of ideas that reflects an individual's relation to a "social system" (23). Here I use *ideology* in the more negative sense adopted by social theorist Karl Mannheim when he described ideologues as those who "falsify to themselves the elemental facts of human existence by deifying, romanticizing, or idealizing them, in short, by resorting to the device of escape from themselves and the world, and thereby conjuring up false interpretations of experience" (96). Mannheim's conception of ideology—basically uniting Marx's theory of ideology as a "false consciousness" born of social class with Nietzsche's idea of self-delusion born of emotional need—in effect shifts ideology from the intellectual to the psychological realm. In this light, ideology is not a philosophy, which analytically explains concepts and experiences and can adjust itself to fit them. Neither is it idealism—even if it entails idealizing—which aspires to high-minded possibilities but may not expect to find them in the real world. Ideology is rather a self-serving system of rigid and absolute ideas about how the real world works, or how it should work, that dictates and justifies virtually everything an ideologue thinks and does.

Lionel Trilling underscored the self-serving psychological character of ideology when he observed in reference to the ideologizing tendency in modern culture that "ideology is not the product of thought; it is the habit or the ritual of showing respect for certain formulas to which, for various reasons having to do with emotional safety, we have very strong ties" ("Meaning," 277). Mannheim and Trilling thus both point to the psychological gratifications of ideology, since ideology provides its adherents with a sense of emotional security in the conviction of complete and infallible comprehension of experience. This security in turn lends adherents a feeling of intellectual and moral superiority to others.[11] These adherents can see what others cannot, since they can penetrate deceptive surfaces to reach the truths beneath. As another prominent student of ideology has observed, ideologues possess an "exalted vision of themselves" as extraordinary individuals who not only "must believe that they know, they must believe that they know better than others" (Sowell, 116, 204). This vision renders them, in their own eyes, "anointed" and everyone else "benighted" (Sowell, 2).[12] Indeed, the emotional appeal of such a vision might even be described as the romance of ideology. For ideologues can virtually fall in love with the image of themselves as possessors of singularly keen insight, pervasive knowledge, and infallible rectitude.

However, ideologues pay a price for their psychological gratifications, and that price is self-deception.[13] Because of the comprehensiveness, rigidity, and self-serving nature of ideologies—which go far beyond the generalizations inherent in any system of thought—they inevitably distort or disguise the complexities of the human mind, individual behavior, and the real world at large, as ideologues represent these to themselves, as well as to others. Although claiming to enable their adherents to pierce the deceptive facades of their surroundings, in fact, ideologies blind those adherents to the authentic nature and significance of their surroundings in the service of "emotional safety." As Mannheim puts it, ideologies function "to conceal the actual meaning of conduct" from adherents, "rather than to reveal it" (95). In other words, an ideology is a masquerade. But it is an unwitting masquerade that, ironically, deceives those who don its masks even while presuming to unmask the false appearances of others.

Hence the "mask" of Lermontov's *Masquerade*—typically considered to be the hypocritical facade of Arbenin's society—may better be understood as an ideology that Arbenin uses to conceal reality from himself. Arbenin certainly fits the negative definition of an ideologue: he adheres to a rigid set of ideas about himself and his circumstances that he uses to rationalize everything he thinks and does, excluding any contradictory facts or ideas. This ideology affords him irresistible psychological gratification, and yet it proves to be profoundly self-deceptive and ultimately self-destructive—it causes not only his wife's death but also his own mental collapse once its protective mask is stripped away. For *Masquerade* unmasks the paradox of ideology itself: a potential fount of insight and inspiration can also be a well of distortion and self-delusion.

Arbenin roots his ideological self-perception in several attributes prized by Romanticists: (1) a vast and rebellious spirit; (2) transcendent emotions; (3) penetrating intellectual insight. Certain that he possesses these attributes, Arbenin is, in his own eyes, a Romantic hero akin to the exceptional characters depicted by the likes of Schiller and Goethe, Shelley and Byron, Chateaubriand and Hugo. And yet, as Lermontov's play reveals, Arbenin is no true Romantic hero with an ideal self. He has a merely Romanticized self-image. That is, he believes that he possesses attributes and ideals incarnated by emblematic Romantic heroes, but his actions prove that he does not. His spirit is not vast and rebellious; it wavers and weakens. His emotions are not transcendent; they are constrained and conventional. His intellect and insight do not penetrate; they misperceive and misjudge. Consequently, Arbenin does not live up to his Romantic role models and ideals by heroically embodying their integrity and acting out their principles. He merely lives out a selfish post-Romantic ideology, which so tightly integrates all his self-deceiving thoughts and emotions that it constitutes a perversion of integrity, and it permits him to justify an exalted self-perception until he can no longer sustain it, at which point he goes mad.

For when Arbenin at last confronts incontrovertible evidence of his fatefully self-serving misperceptions, misjudgments, and misdeeds, his ideologically inflated self-image and his skewed worldview crumble, taking his very sanity along with them. In the end, as a result, Arbenin is more pathetic than tragic, a self-indulgent post-Romantic ideologue rather than a nobly doomed Romantic idealist. If he is a victim at all, Lermontov suggests, he is a victim of his own need for psychological self-aggrandizement, which he satisfies through an ideology that blinds him to himself and to the world around him.

INTEGRATED SELF-DECEPTION

The first ingredient in Arbenin's post-Romantic ideology is his belief in his extraordinary energies and heroic spirit—in short, his strength of will. Critic Michael Cooke labels the will a "prime *topos*" in Romanticism, citing, for example, Goethe's claim that the will is "the god of the modern world," Schiller's avowal that "there is in Man no other power than the Will," and Coleridge's assertion that will is "the law of our [human] nature" (Cooke, *Will*, 51, 9, xii). As distinct from mere "willfulness"—a "lawless, headlong, idiosyncratic, defiant self-assertion" (*Will*, xiv)—will to Romanticists, Cooke affirms, is the active, animating spirit at the core of human existence and human activity, whether exercised consciously or not.[14]

Arbenin equates his own will with an elemental force of nature. "I was born / With a boiling spirit, like lava," he tells Nina. "While it is not heated, it is hard / As stone," but when hot, "it is poor sport / To encounter its flow!" [Я рожден / С душой кипучею, как лава: / Покуда не растопится, тверда / Она, как камень . . . но плоха забава / С ее потоком встретиться!] (3: 294). He also brags about having "a threatening expression and voice" [у меня и вид и голос грозной] and about being a "cruel, / Mad rebel" [я жестокой, / Безумный клеветник] (3: 297, 290) unconstrained by an offensive and corrupt society. "I will prove," he declares before seeking vengeance on his wife's purported lover, "that in our generation / There is at least one spirit in whom an insult, / Having been planted, bears fruit. . . . Oh! I am not [society's] slave" [Я докажу, что в нашем поколенье / Есть хоть одна душа, в которой оскорбленье, / Запав, приносит плод. . . . О! Я не их слуга] (3: 325). And if she has been unfaithful to him, he growls at Nina, "I will not summon the law for my revenge, / But I myself without tears or pity / Will destroy both our lives!" [Закона я на месть свою не призову, / Но сам без слез и сожаленья / Две наши жизни разорву!] (3: 294). Believing himself utterly implacable, Arbenin insists that he cannot be dissuaded or restrained once he sets himself on a course of action. "Do not expect forgiveness" [не ожидай прощенья] (3: 294) for faithlessness, he warns Nina, for he will not be moved. Arbenin thereby aligns himself with the likes of such outsized and unbending Romantic figures as Byron's eponymous Corsair and Giaour, Emily Brontë's Heathcliff, Goethe's Faust, and even Mary Shelley's nameless monstrous creature in *Frankenstein*, by virtue of his fearless willingness to act against all conventions and constraints. He is at once a giant and a rebel (even "an evildoer" [злодеем] [3: 348]), who will burn with vengeance in the face of betrayal and be guided only by his own will. Or so he claims.

However, Arbenin proves to be far less strong-willed, independent, and rebellious than he wants to believe. He does not consistently act with a rebel's disregard for society as he vows to do—he actually reveals himself to be quite conventional, socially self-conscious, and even cowardly. He is tormented, for instance, at the thought that Nina's infidelity has dishonored him in the eyes of society and that those eyes will view him as a laughable buffoon. Fearing society's perception of him as a cuckold, he virtually tortures himself with the notion, "I am pathetic to them, I am comical!" [я жалок им, смешон!] (3: 347). The idea of being deemed by his acquaintances a weakling and a dupe, and therefore inferior, drives him nearly wild. And yet, when he enters the bedroom of the sleeping Prince Zvezdich, the man he suspects of having an affair with Nina and whom he intends to kill in order to redeem his social standing, Arbenin suddenly loses his nerve. He exits a few moments later, looking pale and muttering, "I cannot!" [Не могу!] (3: 325).

Of course, Arbenin's refusal to murder an enemy unawares could be said to display the same sort of honorable conscience that, for example, Byron's noble pirate Conrad evinces in *The Corsair* by refusing to stab his sleeping captor, the Turkish pasha Seyd. But Arbenin's refusal to perform a surreptitious vengeful murder derives not from a deliberate adherence to high-minded moral convictions, it rather results from a breakdown of his will when it is actually tested.[15] As he admits to himself in a momentary and uncharacteristic flash of accurate self-comprehension, "This is beyond my strength and will" [это свыше сил и воли], for "I flew too high" [Я слишком залетел высоко] (3: 325, 326).

But that flash quickly passes and he immediately takes a new tack, plotting a different revenge with the rationalization that "murder is no longer in vogue" [убийство уж не в моде] and so he will follow "a truer path" [верней путь]. That "truer path" is to act not with a hero's will and courage at all but to move with a coward's cunning: he will destroy the prince with his society's tools of "language and gold" [язык и золото]—that is, slander and bribery—as his "dagger and poison" [кинжал и яд] (3: 326). Arbenin thus perversely resorts to a pernicious conformity within a society he believes to be corrupt, proving that he is not who he thinks he is: he not only lacks the Romantic hero's autonomous "strength and will" to act as he desires, but he also succumbs to the lowest forms of conformist malevolence, which he himself has condemned.

Arbenin further exposes the contrivance of his Romanticized self-image when he launches this new strategy of revenge. After he threatens to label the prince a coward, hence ruining him in society, and the prince replies, "Are you a human being or a demon?" [Вы человек иль демон?], Arbenin declares, "I? I am a gambler!" [Я?—игрок!]. Forgetting his previous lapse of will and daring, he persists in thinking of himself as a bold risk taker. This self-deception allies him, as Ian Helfant has suggested, with a gallery of Russian literary gamblers, as well as with a raft of Romantic figures—including the ultimate gambler, Goethe's Faust—willing to risk anything and everything, indifferent to traditional moral constraints, defying both fate and chance, in pursuit of personal exaltation.[16] "The boundary between good and evil has been destroyed" [Преграда рушена между добром и злом] (3: 343) for him, he tells the prince, so no gamble is too great.

Yet Arbenin the ideologue, like most ideologues, does not truly gamble—he wants a sure thing (as Golstein rightly observes, Arbenin is terrified by uncertainty).[17] He had actually forsworn gambling during his marriage, and he returns to the gambling table only after being persuaded of Nina's infidelity. But, ironically, he does not return for the challenge and excitement of the risky unpredictability of gambling. He returns instead to escape from the emotional uncertainties of love and the threatening prospect of losing Nina to another man. As Arbenin responds when the prince asks him if he stopped gambling from fear of losing, "I . . . no! . . . Those blessed days have passed" [Я . . . нет! . . . те дни блаженные прошли] (3: 269; ellipses Lermontov's). For Arbenin, gambling has come to represent, in Golstein's words, "familiar modes of behavior and outlook" (83) that can comfort him in the face of a future rendered radically uncertain by Nina's alleged betrayal. Arbenin's claim to possess a gambler's fearless, risk-taking spirit is therefore yet another self-deceptive component of Arbenin's Romanticized self-image. And so he soon forsakes his plot against the prince.

Even Arbenin's one consummated act of vengeance turns out to be not a courageous act of will but a sly act of cowardice. After abandoning his plotted revenge against the prince, Arbenin decides to get his satisfaction by killing Nina, a less risky target. But then, he does not assault her directly, committing a grand "crime of passion" like Othello or any number of lovers believing themselves wronged. Arbenin rather goes about it like a spider spinning in the shadows. He will not so much as touch Nina. He chooses rather to put poison in her dish of ice cream at a ball—that is, he will kill her with the secret toxins of physical poison in lieu of ruining the prince, as he had vowed to do, with the social poison of slanderous gossip. This way he can get revenge at a safe distance, acting as though ice, not lava, flows in his veins. Arbenin's cold, cowardly vengeance extends to the grim *Schadenfreude*—Karlinsky calls it sadistic pleasure—with which he observes the physical and emotional torments Nina undergoes after she consumes the poison.[18] When she begs him to send for a doctor, he sarcastically replies, "What? Is it impossible for you to die / Without a doctor?" [Что ж? Разве умереть вам невозможно / Без доктора?]. And when she herself acknowledges that she is dying, he coolly remarks, glancing at his watch, "So soon? Not yet. Another half hour remains" [Так скоро? Нет еще. Осталось полчаса] (3: 359, 360). As she dies, Arbenin's physically and emotionally detached revenge on Nina gives him at best the bittersweet pleasure of a coward's resentment fulfilled—seeing an enemy destroyed by subterfuge. And yet Arbenin regards himself as a man of bountiful Romantic energy, will, and daring. That self-regard is an essential element of his post-Romantic ideology, rife with self-deception.

Intertwined with Arbenin's claim to a heroic nature is his claim to possess a transcendent capacity for love, arguably the quintessential Romantic emotion (see Chapter 2). Here again, Romanticism supplies him with an ideal that he converts into ideology. He envisions his love for Nina in ways reminiscent of Romantic love stories from Goethe's *The Sorrows of Young Werther* (1774) to Constant's *Adolphe* (1816) to Emily Brontë's *Wuthering Heights* (1847). But Arbenin's vision of his love is more ideological than genuinely Romantic because it is wholly self-glorifying, confirming to him only his own transcendence as an individual, not his unique union with another individual. His spirit never becomes truly integrated with hers. Indeed, Arbenin's love for Nina is actually self-love.

Arbenin initially describes this love as having transformed him. Before he met Nina, he explains, he had viewed the world "with deep repulsion" [глубоким отвращеньем] (3: 289). And although, he says, "I was often beloved [by women] ardently and passionately," yet "I didn't love even one of them" [Любим был часто пламенно и страстно, / И ни одну из них я не любил] (3: 285). Instead, to his lovers he merely cynically "repeated / Words of love, like a nursemaid's fairy tale" [твердил / Слова любви, как няня сказку]. But upon falling in love with Nina, "the hard crust / Flew off my soul, a beautiful world / Truly opened up before my eyes," so that "I was resurrected for life and goodness" [черствая кора / С моей души слетела, мир прекрасный / Моим глазам открылся не напрасно, / И я воскрес для жизни и добра] (3: 285). The love he claims to feel for her is a Romanticist's dream in its capacity to liberate, elevate, transform, and redeem him. This is the type of love Arbenin clearly believes he *should* have, as an exceptional human being.

And he tries to live it out. "I love you intensely, endlessly" [люблю тебя так сильно, бесконечно], he professes to Nina, acknowledging that he may appear "amusing" [смешон] as a result (3: 293)—evoking Stendhal's image of the Romantic lover driven to ludicrous extremes through the psychological "crystallization" of his beloved.[19] So encompassing does his attachment to Nina become that he says she is his entire world. "All that is left to me of life is you" [Всё, что осталось мне от жизни, это ты], he affirms, adding that, without her love, her smile, her gaze, "I have neither happiness, nor spirit, / Nor feeling, nor existence!" [нет у меня ни счастья, ни души, / Ни чувства, не существованья!] (3: 294). The same exclamation could have come from most Byronic heroes, as well as from Werther, René, Heathcliff, or their many Romantic confrères, in the throes of this passion.

Yet, for all of his professions of this transcendent love, when Arbenin first suspects that his beloved may be a fallible and deceptive woman, he reacts not with the disappointment of a brokenhearted lover but with the cold rejection of an ideologue threatened by a crack in his belief system. He concludes almost immediately that she is as false as everyone else around him, and that his life with her "has been only a dream / And this is the awakening" [то было только сон / А это пробужденье] because she has taken an "ardent lover, a plaything of the masquerade" [Любовник пламенный, игрушка маскарада] (3: 290, 295).

But it is Arbenin who has masked his emotional reality from himself, since his words and actions reveal that he loves himself far more than he loves Nina. Ever the egotist, Arbenin is not merely hurt or angry at the thought of his wife's infidelity, he is offended at the notion that she could have the insolence and audacity to betray *him*. As he declares when he first questions her about his suspicion—prompted by a bracelet that she says she has lost and that he has seen in the prince's possession—"The discussion here is about honor, / About my happiness" [О чести, / О счастии моем тут речь идёт] (3: 291). *His* happiness, *his* honor is at stake—not *their* love or *her* honor. "Is it possible," he later despairs,

> you could sell me out!
> Me, for a fool's kiss? . . . Me, who
> From the first word [we spoke] was happy to hand over my soul?
> To betray me? Me? And so soon [after marriage]!

> Возможно ли! Мне продать! –
> Меня за поцелуй глупца . . . меня, который
> По слову первому был душу рад отдать,
> Мне изменить? мне? И так скоро! (3: 360; ellipsis Lermontov's)

Arbenin's fivefold repetition of the word "me" dramatically conveys his preoccupation with himself and his solicitude solely for his wounded heart.[20]

Arbenin further plays out his self-love by administering the deadly poison to Nina and then lamenting only for himself: "Yes, you will die—and I will remain here / Alone, alone . . . the years will pass, / I will die—and I will always be alone!" [Да, ты умрешь--и я останусь тут / Один, один . . . года пройдут, / Умру—и буду всё один!] (3: 363). He manifests none of the profound, impassioned attachment to his beloved that Romantic lovers display upon the deaths of the women they love—think, by contrast, of Heathcliff's despairing sobs as he beseeches the ghost of his adored Catherine Earnshaw to visit him despite her having chosen in life to marry Edgar Linton: "Cathy, do come. Oh do—*once* more! Oh! my heart's darling!" (70). Nina's death does not likewise mean to Arbenin the loss of the beloved woman for whom he had claimed to live; it rather means the loss of someone who has enabled him to confirm his own self-importance, a mirror in which he sees reflected his superior powers of feeling.

Thus Nina's revealing reaction to his icy pleasure in watching her die rings true to his character: "Oh, you don't love me" [О, ты меня не любишь] (3: 360), she grieves. For Arbenin loves himself too much to have ever truly loved her. His pride, his vanity, and his conviction that he has been wronged blind him to the truth: namely, that Nina honestly loves him and has been faithful to him all along. And so, when Nina dies, still averring her innocence before God, Arbenin approaches her and then, according to Lermontov's stage directions, he "quickly turns away" [быстро отворачивается], uttering his final verdict upon her dying protestations of innocence: "A lie" [Ложь] (3: 364). He clings to his version of the truth rather than believing words of the person he has claimed to love above all else.

Arbenin's ideological blindness is further demonstrated by considering the dramatically different reactions to strikingly similar plot developments displayed by the protagonist Ferdinand in Friedrich Schiller's *Passion and Politics* [*Kabale und Liebe*; literally *Conspiracy and Love*] (1783–84).[21] Like Arbenin, Ferdinand believes that his beloved, Louise, has betrayed him by falling in love with another man despite her pledges of eternal devotion to him. Hence, reviling her as a "devil" and a "serpent" (290, 291), he poisons her in revenge. Yet, in complete contrast to Arbenin, Ferdinand poisons himself at the same time, assuring Louise that "we shall make the journey together" to the next world (293), since he sincerely lacks any desire to go on living without her—he does not merely profess such a lack. Moreover, when Louise, as she dies, tells him that she was forced by Ferdinand's father and her own to declare a false love, Ferdinand instantly believes her and acknowledges, "I have committed a murder" (295), even while also blaming both fathers. As he then dies, he cries out, "Louise, Louise, I am coming to you . . . let me die at this altar" (297)—that is, her corpse. Ferdinand's belief in Louise's veracity, his acceptance of responsibility for her death, and his hope for a spiritual reunion in some afterlife all bespeak a true Romantic love utterly alien to Arbenin. Consequently, Arbenin cannot possibly embrace Nina even as she dies, because he has never embraced her with a transcendent love in life. It is his ideology that he loves.

In fact, Nina herself had hinted at the falseness of Arbenin's love for her in observing to him earlier,

> When eloquently
> You speak to me about your love,
> And your head is aflame,
> And your thought glows keenly in your eyes,
> Then I believe everything without difficulty.
> But often . . .

> Когда красноречиво
> Ты про любовь свою рассказываешь мне,
> И голова твоя в огне,
> И мысль твоя в глазах сияет живо,
> Тогда всему я верю без труда,
> Но часто . . .   (3: 289; ellipsis Lermontov's)

This unfinished qualification, "But often . . . ," suggests that, as devoted to him as Nina is, even she has suspected that his emotions do not match his rhetoric. And she is right. Arbenin's love is much more *rhetorical*, and in essence more ideological, than real; it amounts to a set of phrases expressing ideas that Arbenin has assimilated from the Romanticism of his time describing emotive heights that he thinks he and Nina should rightly attain as lover and beloved.[22] So at the first suspicion that she has slipped from these heights, he condemns her, derisively lumping her together with the other inferior creatures beneath him as he bitterly asserts, "That man is a fool who in one woman / Has dreamed of finding his earthly paradise" [Глупец, кто в женщине одной / Мечтал найти свой рай земной] (3: 321). No, not a fool—rather, a true Romantic lover.

Ironically, if he had seen the truth, Arbenin would have known that he had actually found his paradise on earth in Nina, a woman who loves him above all else, and he could have lived out his life amid it. But as a post-Romantic ideologue rather than a true lover, Arbenin could not sustain that paradise. His ideology masked its presence from his view.

The third component of Arbenin's ideologized Romantic self image is the belief that, besides possessing a heroic nature and transcendent powers of love, he also has superior intellect and insight. Self-important as he is, he cannot fail to believe that he knows what others do not. This belief exhibits what Sowell has called the ideologue's "mindset of omnicompetence," which renders certainties "highly resistant to any facts that threaten" them, and even dismisses such facts "as isolated anomalies or as something tendentiously selected by opponents." That "mindset" gives ideologues a sense of possessing "inherently irrefutable" truths that take on an aura of "inevitability" (110, 250, 2, 94).[23]

Arbenin repeatedly manifests this ideological bent by claiming to know virtually everything, especially in the realm of human behavior—a perversion of the Romantic epistemological ambition of a host of German philosophers and English poets to uncover metaphysical and psychological truths inaccessible to conventional perceptions and ways of thinking. In *Natural Supernaturalism* M. H. Abrams highlights the philosophical calls by German idealists like Fichte, Schelling, and Hegel to apprehend the noumena, or immaterial essence, behind phenomena, and Abrams cites an array of such apprehensions, which he labels "perceptual transvaluations" (391), in British Romantic poetry. Abrams accounts for this array as a Romantic "preoccupation" with "a radical opposition in ways of seeing the world, and the need to turn from . . . 'single vision,' the reliance on the 'bodily,' 'physical,' 'vegetable,' 'corporeal,' or 'outward eye,'" in favor of "the liberated, creative, and resurrected mode of sight 'thro' and not with the eye,' or of sight by means of the 'inward eye,' 'the intellectual eye,' 'the imaginative eye,' or simply 'the imagination.' The shift," Abrams sums up, "is from physical optics to what Carlyle in the title of one of his essays called 'Spiritual Optics,' and what Blake and others often called 'Vision'" (377).

Arbenin insists that he has such insightful vision, and the omniscience that accompanies it. "I have seen everything, / Felt everything, understood everything, found out everything" [я всё видел, / Всё перечувствовал, всё понял, всё узнал] (3: 288), he proclaims to Nina. No event, no emotion, no idea, no information, lies beyond his ken. And what he knows most surely is that deception thrives all around him. "Evil is ubiquitous," he muses at one point to his former gambling comrade Kazarin, "deception is everywhere" [Повсюду зло—везде обман], and later he broadly exclaims, "The whole thing is a deception!" [целое—обман!] (3: 320, 358). In other words, to Arbenin, the social world he inhabits is a masquerade: surface appearances deliberately conceal ugly truths lying beneath those appearances. And Arbenin despises masks. "Masks have neither spirits nor names," he claims, "they have bodies. / And if people's features are hidden by a mask, / Then they can boldly remove the mask from their feelings" [У маски ни души, ни званья нет,—есть тело. / И если маскою черты утаены, / То маску с чувств снимают смело] (3: 270), and act as they secretly desire. But he comforts himself with the assurance that he alone can see through all masks to the truth—his insight has no bounds.

So when a servant reports he could not find the bracelet that Nina says she has lost but that Arbenin believes she has given to a lover, Arbenin snaps, "I knew it" [я это знал]. Moments later, when Nina insists that his suspicions are unfounded, he rebuffs her with the assertion, "I know everything" [я знаю всё] (3: 292; 295). Even when she invokes God as her witness, avowing, "I am innocent . . . may / God punish me, listen . . . " [я невинна . . . пусть / Меня накажет бог, послушай . . .], Arbenin cuts her off, retorting, "By heart / I know everything that you will say" [Наизусть / Я знаю всё, что скажешь ты] (3: 296). And he subsequently announces to the prince, whom he takes to be Nina's lover, "I have understood everything, guessed everything" [Всё понял я, всё отгадал] (3: 338). He believes the two alleged deceivers have failed to carry off their masquerade—that is, to maintain their deception—before him, because his omniscience and insight make it impossible to deceive him for long.

Yet it is worth emphasizing that, for all of his protestations of being deceived, first by Nina and then by those who he says had misled him into mistrusting her, it is Arbenin *alone* who first draws the conclusion that Nina has been unfaithful to him. No one suggests that possibility to him until after he has persuaded himself of her infidelity. Only then does he begin to hear malicious reports that he uses to support his own ready-made conclusion. Insisting on his intellectual infallibility and insight, Arbenin cannot see, until it is too late, that Nina has loved him and has been faithful to him all along.

In order to sustain his claims to infallibility and insight, however, Arbenin must selectively exclude or deliberately distort information that contradicts him, as ideologues are wont to do. He dismisses an acquaintance's assurances of Nina's innocence, for instance, as a cover-up. And he consistently construes Nina's every word upholding her innocence in the most antagonistic fashion possible. When he questions Nina closely about her activities at the masquerade ball, for example, she jocularly dismisses his inquiries, replying, "This is comical, comical, by God! It's shameful, it's a sin, isn't it, / To raise such a fuss over trifles" [Смешно, смешно, ей-богу! Не стыдно ли, не грех / Из пустяков поднять тревогу]. But Arbenin cannot find any real comedy in his suspicions, only confirmation of them, along with validation of his superior love. "I am comical, of course," he sneers, "In that I love you so intensely" [я смешон, конечно, / Тем, что люблю тебя так сильно] (3: 293). However, his misinterpretation of Nina's reply bespeaks not intense love for her but rather his conviction of his own omniscience, along with his obliviousness to the love Nina actually feels for him.

Shortly thereafter, Arbenin again misconstrues Nina's innocent words when she tells him his suspicions are so misguided that "not only I, but all of society will laugh" [Не я одна, но осмеет весь свет] to hear them. Genuinely astonished, she wants to protect him from public embarrassment. But he fails to recognize her benevolent intentions and again twists the import of her words, even as he agrees with them: "Yes! You will laugh at me, all you mundane fools, / You carefree but pathetic husbands / Whom I too once deceived" [Да! Смейтесь надо мной, вы, все глупцы земные, / Беспечные, но жалкие мужья, / Которых некогда обманывал и я] (3: 295). He thinks that Nina imagines him being mocked not because, as she has said, he is unjustly suspicious, but because, as he chooses to believe, his suspicions are justified. Arbenin cannot recognize or appreciate her loving concern for him; he can only envision injury to himself because he "knows" the truth—that she has betrayed him. Thus he continues to misinterpret Nina's protestations of innocence down to her very death, taking them as veiled acknowledgments of her guilt. When she concludes that his accusations have shifted from comedy toward tragedy, Nina insistently denies the "perfidy and deception" [коварство и измену] he accuses her of and sobs, "My bracelet—the prince found it—then / By some sort of slanderer / You were deceived" [Браслет мой—князь нашел,—потом / Каким-нибудь клеветником / Ты был обманут]. But Arbenin hears only further confirmation of her guilt. "So I was deceived!" [Так, я был обманут!] (3: 360, 361), he exclaims in response, focusing solely on the word *deceived*, ignoring her assertion that she herself had not been the deceiver.

To the bitter end, Arbenin keeps trying to bring reality in line with his interpretation of it, rather than adjusting his interpretation to accommodate reality—and he utterly ignores the blatant contradiction residing in his belief that he has been deceived despite his all-knowing insight.[24] Indeed, well after Nina's death he continues to maintain that his judgment of Nina was correct: "Yes, I was a passionate husband," he insists, "but as a judge / I was cold" [Да, я был страстный муж—но был судья / Холодный], for

>   it's impossible
> That I was mistaken—who will prove to me
> Her innocence—it's false, it's false!
> Where are the proofs—I have them!
> I didn't believe her—so whom will I begin to believe?

>   невозможно
> Мне ошибиться – кто докажет мне
> Ее невинность – ложно! ложно!
> Где доказательства – есть у меня оне!
> Я не поверил ей – кому же стану верить? (3: 372, 371–72)

And he asks a final rhetorical question, "Who then will dare / To undeceive me?" [кто же разуверить / Меня осмелится?] (3: 372). No one will dare, since it is *impossible* that he was mistaken. He *must* be right, not only as a matter of objective truth but of ideological vindication—Arbenin's Romanticized self-definition depends on it. Determined to support his ideology, Arbenin winds up sacrificing both his wife and himself on its altar.

ARBENIN'S DIS-INTEGRATION

Given his psychic dependence on his ideologically determined self-image, it should come as no surprise that when Arbenin finally does see the truth of Nina's innocence and his own terrible error, his psyche cannot endure it. Although the occasion of this revelation has something of a facile deus ex machina about it, the consequences are profound. Confronted at last by the prince himself and a mysterious stranger (who claims to have clandestinely observed both Nina and Arbenin throughout) with evidence of Nina's innocence that Arbenin cannot deny—or at least Lermontov does not have him deny it—Arbenin stutters some disjointed phrases and then, as the stage directions dictate, "he falls to the ground and sits, half-reclining, with motionless eyes" [Падает на землю и сидит полулежа с неподвижными глазами].[25] Observing Arbenin descend into this stupor, the stranger simply remarks, "Even this proud mind has collapsed today!" [И этот гордый ум сегодня изнемог!] (3: 380, 379).

Rather than emulating Othello and killing himself in a fit of conscious remorse and self-reproach, or engaging in a flamboyant Romantic suicide like Schiller's Ferdinand, or giving himself over to a manic psychosis like the gambler Germann in Pushkin's "The Queen of Spades," Arbenin instead suffers a complete mental breakdown that leaves him will-less, emotion-less, and mindless, reflecting the demolition of the three mainstays in his exquisitely integrated conceptions of himself and his world—his beliefs in his heroic spirit, his transcendent love, and his superior intellect. Tellingly, in their notes to Lermontov's plays, the editors of Lermontov's collected works similarly distinguish Arbenin from Romantic protagonists in observing that, after his collapse, Arbenin lives on "not in a Romantic frenzy" [романтическим безумием] but in "pure madness" [сумашедствием]. They also argue, however, that this ending is inappropriate because, "according to the logic of his character and established dramatic canon," Arbenin should die (3: 582, 581).

Here I should point out that Boris Eikhenbaum has contended that the entire fourth act of *Masquerade*, along with Arbenin's catatonic collapse, does not in fact belong to the play as originally conceived. Lermontov only added this act, Eikhenbaum argues, as a sop to the censors after they rejected the three-act version of the play that Lermontov had originally submitted for permission to stage, which ended with an unrepentant Arbenin, still ignorant of his fatal error, standing over Nina's corpse and gloating at her demise. In Eikhenbaum's opinion, the three-act version of *Masquerade* also conforms better to Lermontov's moral vision, because it allows Arbenin's evil act of murder, "like all evil in Lermontov," to be a comprehensible "manifestation of rebellion against God" for a "lost heaven," which Arbenin thought he had recovered but which now he finds "had been once again and forever closed to him" (Eikhenbaum, "Пять редакций," 225).

While no one disputes the publication history of *Masquerade* upon which Eikhenbaum bases his interpretation of the play, this interpretation is misguided aesthetically, psychologically, and philosophically. The fourth act depicting Arbenin's collapse into catatonia is the most apt denouement possible, even as it makes a structural departure from the "established dramatic canon" of Romanticism. For it vividly dramatizes how, although Arbenin believed himself to be superior to everyone else by unmasking their falsehoods—especially those of his wife—in the end, it is he who is unmasked as having lacked the integrity to see and acknowledge the truth, especially about himself. Hence he cannot be released into the Romantic transcendence of death.

Thus in *Masquerade* we see Lermontov commending the Romantic ideals of energy and will, transcendent love, and penetrating insight even as he discloses the dangers of converting those ideals into an ideology conceived for the psychological satisfactions it provides. This combination of a tribute to Romantic ideals and a warning against Romanticism as ideology makes *Masquerade* one of the more provocatively transitional works of the 1830s. For it places Arbenin not among the true tragic and Romantic heroes of Goethe, Byron, Chateaubriand, and others but closer to the likes of Stendhal's Julien Sorel in *The Red and the Black* (1830), who self-consciously lives for Romantic heroism and love (as the following chapters show, Pechorin will be closer still).

This interpretation of *Masquerade* and of Lermontov's ambivalent relation to Romanticism receives some additional, if indirect, textual support from the fact that Lermontov did not subtitle *Masquerade* a "Romantic drama" as he did his previous play, *A Strange Man* [*Странный человек*] (1831), which also portrays an alienated character named Arbenin who clashes with an evil society but who dies tragically. Instead Lermontov subtitled *Masquerade* simply *A Drama in Four Acts, in Verse* [*Драма в 4-х действиях, в стихах*] (3: 258). The absence of the adjective "Romantic" from this subtitle is both telling and appropriate, because *Masquerade* is not a "Romantic drama." It is a drama *about* Romanticism—that is, about how Romantic ideals can be perverted into an ideology that deceives and destroys individuals rather than elevating and fulfilling them.

At the same time, the idea that *Masquerade* offers what some critics take to be, as Helfant puts it, a "realistic critique of a 'Romantic' hero" (127), also misses the mark.[26] Certainly Lermontov's criticisms of Romanticism in *Masquerade* have some instructive affinities to those voiced, for example, by figures as disparate as the Underground Man in Dostoevsky's *Notes from Underground* (1864) and the narrator of George Eliot's *Adam Bede* (1859), both of whom oppose the illusions they see promoted by Romantic imagination, idealism, and heroism.

And yet, if we consider in some detail the objections to Romanticism presented by Dostoevsky and Eliot, we can set Lermontov's continuing attachment to Romanticism in further relief. Dostoevsky's Underground Man condemns "the sort of stupid, starry-eyed romantics the Germans and especially the French have—people who would never learn any better even if the ground opened up under their feet or if the whole of France were to perish on its barricades. Even then they wouldn't have the decency to change; they'd sing their starry-eyed songs going to their graves. This is because they are fools" (5: 126) who are completely out of touch with the reality that the Underground Man claims to know so thoroughly. That reality is completely divorced from "the sublime and the beautiful"—qualities highly valued by Romanticism—to which the Underground Man was devoted in his youth, as he confesses: "But how much love, gentlemen, how much love I would experience in my dreams, these escapes to 'the beautiful and the sublime,'" dreams arising from "the beautiful forms of life, already prepared, forcibly stolen from the authors of novels and poems" extolling those qualities (i.e., Romantic literature). In those dreams, he reports, "I inherit millions and immediately sacrifice them to the human race and then at once confess to all the people my ignominy and disgrace which, of course, is not simply disgrace but contains much that is 'beautiful and sublime' in it, something Manfred-like" (5: 137). Investment in Romantic dreams of this sort, the Underground Man argues, has led his contemporary society to become so deluded that "we've all lost touch with life, we're all more or less cripples. We've lost touch to such an extent that now we feel a sort of disgust for 'life as it is lived' and thus we cannot bear to be reminded of it . . . and we have agreed among ourselves that the way it is presented in books is better" (5: 178). By recognizing and condemning his society's psychological investment in the dreams promoted by Romantic literature, the Underground Man stakes his claim to being "more alive" and cognizant of reality than his readers (5: 178).

Although more temperate in tone, Eliot's anonymous narrator in *Adam Bede* similarly suggests that the Romantic cult of the imagination has spawned literature depriving readers of a salutary engagement with reality. Endeavoring "to give a faithful account of men and things as they have mirrored themselves in my mind" (171), the novel's narrator justifies her goal on the grounds that "there are few prophets in the world; few sublimely beautiful women; few heroes. . . . Neither are picturesque lazzaroni or romantic criminals half so frequent as your common laborer, who gets his own bread, and eats it vulgarly but creditably with his own pocket-knife." For "in this world there are so many of these common coarse people, who have no picturesque sentimental wretchedness!" (175). Hence, she says, "I turn, without shrinking, from cloud-borne angels, from prophets, sibyls, and heroic warriors, to an old woman bending over her flower-pot, or eating her solitary dinner, while the noonday light, softened perhaps by a screen of leaves, falls on her mob-cap" (173). These are the individuals who inhabit reality, but whose existence is too readily forgotten. And yet "it is so needful we should remember their existence, else we may happen to leave them quite out of our religion and philosophy, and frame lofty theories which only fit a world of extremes" (177)—the world Romantics loved so dearly, and from which the commonplace was so deliberately excluded.

To be sure, Eliot's narrator is not as utterly antagonistic to the world depicted in Romantic art as the Underground Man is. Conjuring up an artist as auditor, she exhorts: "Paint us an angel, if you can, with a floating violet robe, and a face paled by the celestial light; paint us yet oftener a Madonna, turning her mild face upward and opening her arms to welcome the divine glory." Nonetheless, "do not impose on us any aesthetic rules which shall banish from the region of Art those old women scraping carrots with their world-worn hands, those heavy clowns taking holiday in a dingy pot-house, those rounded backs and stupid weather-beaten faces that have bent over the spade and done the rough work of the world" (174–75). And the narrator advocates the type of art that portrays ordinary human beings in ordinary circumstances not only in the cause of truthfulness to reality, but in the cause of morality, insisting that "these fellow-mortals, every one, must be accepted as they are: you can neither straighten their noses, nor brighten their wit, nor rectify their dispositions; and it is these people—amongst whom your life is passed—that it is needful you should tolerate, pity, and love: it is these more or less ugly, stupid, inconsistent people, whose movements of goodness you should be able to admire—for whom you should cherish all possible hopes, all possible patience" (172–73). Only through the embrace of such people, Eliot indicates, and of the non-Romantic art that represents them, can human beings expand their elemental humanity.

The warnings in *Masquerade* against the post-Romantic reduction of Romantic values to a self-serving and self-deceiving ideology thus implicitly endorse those values, by contrast to the outright condemnation they receive from the Underground Man or the espousal of alternative Realist values endorsed by Eliot's narrator. Moreover, we see Lermontov presenting his warnings within a Romantic rather than a Realist context, since in major works of Realism, actuality is generally complex, ambiguous, and equivocal, whereas *Masquerade* portrays an unequivocally misguided hero in Arbenin and an unambiguously faithful heroine in Nina. In fact, if more fully delineated, Nina could be a model Romantic heroine, true until death to herself and her love, like Schiller's Louise in *Passion and Politics*, Constant's Ellenore in *Adolphe*, and Scott's Lucy Ashton in *The Bride of Lammermoor* (1819), to name but a few—whereas Arbenin, as a post-Romantic ideologue, is true to no one, not even himself.

Masquerade thus offers yet another view of Lermontov's reaction to the quandaries posed by his post-Romantic, transitional time. While conveying his continuing admiration for Romantic ideals, in Arbenin Lermontov embodies one type of response to an underlying sense of the decline of those ideals—a formulaic reduction of a complex, authentically derived worldview and values to a post-period's rigid and self-serving set of ideological concepts.[27] But in the act of portraying Arbenin, Lermontov intimates the possibility of a different response: the acknowledgment, however tacit, that the worldview and values of Romanticism are losing their authority and integrity and that converting them into an ideology will not compensate for the loss. A new worldview, new values, new ideals will have to be found.

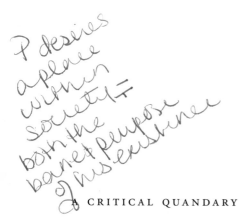

Vice disguised as virtue.

P desires a place within society = both the bane + purpose of his existence

why is he ↔ Vice disguised as virtue?

SIX

Post-Romantic Anomie I

A Hero of Our Time *and Its Hero*

A CRITICAL QUANDARY

In an epochal novel written during the transition out of Romanticism, an attractive, ambitious young man seeks his place in society. Distinctly more intelligent than virtually everyone else he encounters, he identifies himself with great Romantic heroes out of a sense of his own superiority, and he manipulates his inferiors. He excites both the admiration and envy of other men, and he readily seduces women both married and unmarried, driving one to her death. He triumphs in a variety of contests, including a duel. But while he condemns his society for its superficiality and self-deception, he desires a prominent place in it. And he remains unsure of the meaning and purpose of his life down to its end. He is a hero of his time.

Readers of European literature might know him as Julien Sorel, the protagonist of Stendhal's *The Red and the Black* [*Le Rouge et le noir*] (1830), which is subtitled *A Chronicle of the Nineteenth Century*. But they might also know him as Grigorii Pechorin, the protagonist of Lermontov's *A Hero of Our Time*.[1] And the affinities between these two "heroes of their time" do not end with their similarities in personality and experiences. For the two characters appear in novels that can be seen to possess affinities with both Romanticism and Realism, and whose place in literary history has been debated at length as a result. And both characters were created by relatively young men of nearly the same generation. However, Stendhal lived long enough to go on writing and making a reputation,[2] whereas Lermontov was frozen in time by dying almost immediately after completing his novel. Thus *A Hero of Our Time* plays a much more definitive role in determining Lermontov's literary and cultural significance than *The Red and the Black* plays for Stendhal.

A Hero of Our Time [Герой нашего времени] (1840) is Lermontov's best-known work by far, and his only completed novel. In the West, this novel is often the *only* work by Lermontov that readers know. And in both Russia and the West, from the time of its publication to today, critics have judged *A Hero of Our Time* the crowning achievement of Lermontov's brief literary career, the work toward which his creative imagination led him. Hence this novel is commonly taken to exemplify the kind of artist Lermontov was and to define his distinctive contribution to Russian and world literature. However, the agreement about his novel ends there. For critical debates have raged more fiercely over just what *A Hero of Our Time* has to say about the kind of artist Lermontov was and about what constituted his contribution to literature than over the rest of his works combined.[3]

Not surprisingly, these debates have tended to focus on the novel's—and therefore Lermontov's—relationship to Romanticism and Realism.[4] And, as with Lermontov's other major works, critics have differed markedly over the affiliation of *A Hero of Our Time* to these two cultural movements. Anyone familiar with literary history who has read the novel can see why. It unquestionably contains some characteristics that fit Romanticism and others that suggest Realism. Critics who link the novel primarily to Romanticism can point to the presence of several traditional Romantic themes, such as the exaltation of nature and its "sublime" beauties, the quest for transcendent love, and the conflicts between superior individuals and inferior societies. And above all they can point to Pechorin as a Romantic hero towering over the novel's other characters with a force of personality akin to Goethe's Faust, Byron's Manfred, or Chateaubriand's René. This critical perspective has been embraced most recently by Vladimir Golstein, who deems Pechorin heroic in Romantic terms because he "refuses to play the game" (114) of hypocritical posing that his society requires of its members and courageously carves out instead his own admirable "code of honor and chivalry" (118). Golstein declares Pechorin's capture of a homicidal Cossack, for example, to be "a free and heroic action" reflecting Pechorin's "utter nobility" (121, 122).[5]

By contrast, critics who associate *A Hero of Our Time* with Realism point to the detailed observations of facts about nature, society, and characters' physical appearances, the probing of characters' thoughts, emotions, and actions, and the importance attributed to society and social rituals. They also focus above all on the character of Pechorin, albeit from a different point of view than that of critics who see him as a Romantic hero. The critics who connect the novel to Realism consider Pechorin a "realistic" representation of an ignoble, amoral, unheroic hypocrite typical of the Russia of his day. This critical perspective was taken up primarily by Soviet critics who, for largely ideological reasons, viewed *A Hero of Our Time* as a work of realistic social criticism recording and denouncing the depravities of a decaying social order.[6]

A third critical perspective on *A Hero of Our Time*, one that has more or less come down from the seminal Russian literary critic Vissarion Belinskii, is to view the novel as a hybrid of Romanticism and Realism. Belinskii does so when he describes Pechorin as a heroic figure caught up in the banalities of a confining society, whose outsized potential for Romantic heroism had been reduced to the pathetic pursuit of merely selfish gratification amid post-Decembrist Russian society.[7] A. A. Titov follows Belinskii's general lead in claiming that Lermontov, "while not breaking away from Romanticism, took a new decisive step toward Realism" (161). Elena Mikhailova expresses a similar view in broader terms, discerning in Lermontov's novel "the coexistence of realistically objective elements with lyrical-romantic elements" (350); Bagby more succinctly finds in it "a unique combination of romantic and realist elements" ("Double-Voicing," 263). D. E. Maksimov articulates this view in cultural historical terms when he asserts that the novel arises "on the border between the Romantic and Realist periods in the history of Russian art and combines within itself characteristic attributes of both these periods" (98). John Mersereau also shares this perspective, arguing that in his novel Lermontov employed a "special combination of romanticism and realism which successfully exploited the virtues of both manners" that yields "not matter-of-fact realism but what might be expressed as lyrical realism, a realism incorporating the emotion and atmosphere of the romance, yet characterized by fidelity to life" (*Lermontov*, 157).[8] Mersereau elsewhere sums up this hybridizing tendency when he concludes that *A Hero of Our Time* is "a Janus figure standing between Romanticism and Realism" (*Romantic Fiction*, 316).

As remarked above, it is not hard to find features of both Romanticism and Realism in *A Hero of Our Time*—I suspect that, if pressed, few critics would reject the conclusion that *A Hero of Our Time* in some way or another reflects a transition between Romanticism and Realism.[9] Yet it is not enough to say that the novel simply combines Romanticism and Realism. Nor does it suffice to say that the work looks back at Romanticism and forward to Realism—this smacks of what Gary Saul Morson calls "backshadowing," that is, as noted in Chapter 1, attributing to Lermontov a Realism that only hindsight could give, and interpreting its "realistic" touches of local color and psychological insight (which, as Erich Auerbach has famously shown in his magisterial study *Mimesis*, have appeared in Western literature since Homer) as conscious forerunners of the mid-nineteenth-century artistic movement of Realism, which had its own aesthetic and ethical principles. This critical stance thus only leads to the questions: how does Lermontov's novel reflect the transition from Romanticism to Realism, and why? In fact, these questions may be construed as the critical quandary of *A Hero of Our Time*.

One potential resolution to this quandary lies in the peculiar cultural context of Lermontov's career in general and of *A Hero of Our Time* in particular. William Mills Todd III gives us some useful clues to this cultural context and to the novel itself in the erudite and provocative analysis of *A Hero of Our Time* included in his broader study *Fiction and Society in the Age of Pushkin*. There Todd places Lermontov's novel in relation to Russia's emerging modern social and literary institutions at the beginning of the nineteenth century. And he argues that, like the other seminal fictional works of the nascent Russian literary tradition—primarily Pushkin's *Eugene Onegin* (1824–31)and Gogol's *Dead Souls* (1842)—*A Hero of Our Time* offers a critique of the then reigning "ideology of a civilized, secular society" (4). Todd considers Lermontov's novel a far harsher critique than Pushkin's (Gogol's was a "comic subversion" of that society [169]), since Lermontov represents "polite society" as stripped of "all value" (148), lacking any meaningful "aspirations," or animating norms and ideals, and indifferent to the "ideological alternatives that [Lermontov's] contemporaries entertained" (149)—the autocratic (and bureaucratic) government or the Orthodox church. Consequently, Todd sees Lermontov dealing in *A Hero of Our Time* with a "constricted cultural framework" (145) that affords characters only "a relatively narrow set of themes, behavioral patterns, plot movements, and cultural possibilities" upon which to base their actions (151). These limited "cultural possibilities" are also set within the "indefiniteness" of a "historically undefined period"—as Todd points out, the novel contains virtually no references to specific historical dates and concrete historical events (151, 150). In short, he implies, the world of *A Hero of Our Time* is a world in limbo.

I would call this historical limbo the cultural anomie of post-Romanticism. As observed in Chapter 2, "cultural anomie" signifies a lack of sufficient cultural norms—beliefs, values, principles, and ideals—and integrity for individuals to develop a coherent worldview, to give structure to their personalities, and to have clear purposes in life at a given historical moment. Indeed, I would argue that Pechorin suffers from anomie as much as any character in Western literature—he casts about, at times desperately or even violently, for beliefs, values, and ideals, for a coherent worldview and personal identity, because his culture offers him nothing he can believe in. That culture relegates him to a vaunted ego nonetheless devoid of imagination and will, which resultantly cannot independently generate beliefs, values, and ideals to live by. And Pechorin's anomie is only underscored by the subordinate characters he encounters, who themselves may have discovered some beliefs, values, and ideals that do give shape to their personalities and the conduct of their existences but who are typically forced to forsake them after forming a relationship with Pechorin (see Chapter 7). His cultural anomie, colored by a sense of loss of cultural integration and integrity, can justly be deemed the ethos of post-Romanticism.

Reading *A Hero of Our Time* as a post-Romantic novel in this way helps to account for the conflicting and ambiguous critical interpretations it has elicited. Because Lermontov showed his characters often envisioning or longing for Romantic ideals and norms, some critics have found in his novel an affirmation of Romanticism; because he also gave reason to question the validity of those ideals and norms, while portraying Pechorin as significantly flawed, other critics have found in the novel the seeds of Realism. And because Lermontov combined these elements, many critics have not taken sides but rather have discerned both Romanticism and Realism in Lermontov's novel. Granted, each of these lines of interpretation provides valuable insights into this novel. But I would say that, together with interpretations like Todd's, these readings all point to an overarching view of *A Hero of Our Time* as a novel of post-Romanticism, a work in which Lermontov was wrestling with the cultural anomie of his age and coming to grips with the paramount quandaries of cultural transition.

Throughout this study I have endeavored to demonstrate how Lermontov both reflected and transcended post-Romanticism and cultural transition. And in *A Hero of Our Time* we see woven together many of the threads of post-Romantic transitionality that I have discussed in his earlier works—a disenchantment with Byronism alongside an admiration for the heroic Byronic spirit; an attenuation of Romantic moral ideals accompanied by a yearning for such ideals; self-deceived heroics presuming to superiority and a critique of Romanticism as a source of ideology coupled with an appreciation of its genuine ideals of self and love and truth. Here I will suggest that by considering these and other themes in *A Hero of Our Time*, we see post-Romantic cultural anomie in full flower. This chapter and the next will explore this anomie and the quandaries it entails through several related topics: the fragmented structure of the novel; the dis-integrated, often self-deluded hero, Pechorin; Pechorin's detachment from nature, accompanied by lip service to the Romantic ideals of nature's inspiriting power; the failures of Romantic love and friendship experienced by subordinate characters; and the post-Romantic irony and lack of narrative closure that recur throughout the novel, undermining cultural ideals and norms and, in Todd's words, rendering "actions pointless and conclusions inconclusive" (*Fiction and Society*, 150).

This very inconclusiveness nonetheless leads me to suggest that, for all of its post-Romantic anomie, *A Hero of Our Time* should not leave us with the impression that Lermontov saw no way out of that anomie, that he had nothing positive to offer to those living in its midst or coming afterward. He did not find the quandaries of cultural transition ultimately insurmountable. To the contrary. I will contend that, although Lermontov did not spell this out, he had an implicit vision of cultural health, even while representing cultural malaise. This vision recognized that European Romanticism had provided an array of powerful norms and ideals to animate and direct life, and that if those particular norms and ideals had lost their hold, sending culture adrift, the one hope for the future was to reach some other shore and affirm new ideals and norms. What those would be, he could not know. But I will offer a few suggestions at the end.

AN ANOMIC STRUCTURE

The cultural anomie reflected in *A Hero of Our Time* can be said to begin with its structure. This anomie appears in a feature of the work that no reader can fail to notice—the blatant disjointedness of its five main chapters. That disjointedness suggests the absence of a definitive unifying purpose or focused integrated vision, as if Lermontov did not want the pieces of his novel to fit together, or was not sure whether they should.[10]

Nevertheless, critics from Belinskii to today *have* perceived a purpose and a vision of order underlying the novel's disjointed surface. The purpose, many of them maintain, is to reveal Pechorin's character gradually—several of these critics have described the narrative structure of *A Hero of Our Time* as "a nest of Chinese boxes" (Abbott, 64), with Pechorin's true nature at the center.[11] Thus the novel's order emerges in successive chapters that afford deepening insight into this character, first limned by a narrator who talks about Pechorin, next presented in the appearance and actions of Pechorin as seen through another narrator's eyes, and then finally revealed by Pechorin's own words as written in his journal.

In recent decades, Priscilla Meyer and Paul Debreczeny, among others, have provocatively suggested other sources of unity as well. In her article "Lermontov's Reading of Pushkin: *The Tales of Belkin* and *A Hero of Our Time*," Meyer claims that although some chapters of Lermontov's novel were published separately (see note 10), "it is clear from the manuscript" that Lermontov "conceived of the five stories as a united whole" (73–74, n. 20), since he grouped them together under one title. She argues that Lermontov derived his conception of the novel from Pushkin's *Tales of the Late Ivan Petrovich Belkin*, a "story cycle united by themes, motifs, and method," whose achievements Lermontov sought to incorporate "into a novel uniting the five stories and narrator's preface around the figure of Pechorin" (62).[12] Astutely detecting numerous parallels between each of the Belkin tales and a chapter of *A Hero of Our Time*, Meyer concludes that the novel significantly furthers the goal of Pushkin's story cycle, which was to promote "the movement away from dangerous Romantic stereotypes" (72), a movement Meyer identifies with late Romanticism.

Taking another tack, in "Elements of the Lyrical Verse Tale in Lermontov's *A Hero of Our Time*," Paul Debreczeny finds a unifying tendency in the novel to be provided by its affinities in both form and content with lyrical verse tales like S. T. Coleridge's *Rime of the Ancient Mariner* (1798).

These affinities run so deep, Debreczeny maintains, that *A Hero of Our Time* "can be called a narrative poem translated into prose" (94). Declaring that "the undivided nature of the poetic inspiration that informs the book" is embodied in a "unified lyrical personal that stands behind the narrative," he asserts that this persona is expressed equally through the voices of the novel's three narrators—an anonymous traveler, an old army officer, and Pechorin—and that Lermontov's "main concern is to capture" that persona's "static emotional condition, which, by a classical definition of genres, should be the concern of a lyric poet" (106, 100, 99). Debreczeny identifies recurrent character traits, images, and stylistic devices that he says unite not only the novel's narrators but also the subordinate characters, "as though the lyric persona standing behind them could not help conjuring up the same phenomenon time and again" (115).[13] He then concludes by connecting this repetitive circularity with "the lyrical verse tale of the romantic era" (116).

These are illuminating and plausible interpretations of the novel's structure. But I would say that they may be trying a bit too hard to find unity and integration in the disjointed parts of *A Hero of Our Time*, thereby leaving the novel within the compass of Romanticism. I would argue that it is even more illuminating to see the novel as what it appears to be—a loosely bound collection of narrative pieces that are in a sense fragments. For the chapters structurally remain either incomplete in themselves or insufficiently connected to other chapters, their distinct differences ultimately outweighing the measure of unity imparted by the presence of Pechorin or any other recurring elements. And in using the term *fragments* here, I do not have in mind the Romantic idea of fragments as described in Chapter 2, which point to a larger whole or imply an organic wholeness even if incomplete, the way the Schlegels envisioned fragments (which, like Romantic poetry in general, are "still in the state of becoming" and "should forever be becoming and never be perfected" [*Athenaeum Fragments*, in Schlegel, 175]). The fragmented form and contents of *A Hero of Our Time* are what I would call post-Romantic fragments—they never truly evoke anything larger than themselves or become anything greater than themselves. These are the fragments of the condition of cultural anomie. They cannot intimate wholeness because no wholeness exists in a dis-integrated culture, or culture of anomie, largely ruled by a sense of disorientation and disillusion, regret and yearning for guiding norms or ideals. When we see the disjointed structure of *A Hero of Our Time* in this light, we see how remarkable—and post-Romantic—a novel it is.[14]

First let me delineate the manifold ways in which fragmentation pervades the novel's structure from its offhanded start to its ambiguous finish. This fragmentation begins at the very outset of the novel, in its first chapter, "Bela" ["Бэла"], when the anonymous traveler who enters as the narrator announces that he has been making travel notes on a journey through the Caucasus, but that "the greater part" of these "has been lost" (4: 184; 3).[15] So we start with fragments. But the narrator does not even give us many of these fragments of his travel notes. Rather he uses them to frame the bulk of the first chapter, the story (itself broken into two parts) of a failed romance between Pechorin and a native Circassian girl as told to him by an older army officer named Maksim Maksimich, whom the anonymous traveler encounters during his journey. The traveler next presents a different, brief portion of his notes in the second chapter, entitled "Maksim Maksimich" ["Максим Максимыч"], in which he reports an encounter he witnesses between that officer and Pechorin. The remaining three chapters of the novel, "Taman" ["Тамань"], "Princess Mary" ["Княжна Мери"] and "The Fatalist" ["Фаталист"] are then introduced by the traveler as merely a portion of a "fat notebook" or journal in which Pechorin "narrates his entire life." Thus the five narrative chapters of *A Hero of Our Time* are all presented as extracts from larger wholes readers will never see—the traveler's other notes have disappeared, and although the traveler suggests that the remainder of Pechorin's journal will see the light of day "someday" (4: 225; 64), the work gives no reason to think that this day will ever arrive. These fragmentary parts will not be reunited with their sources.

And these are not the only fragmentary "parts" of the novel. In addition to dividing the novel's contents between the traveler's notes and Pechorin's journal, in the table of contents Lermontov also formally divided the novel's chapters into two parts that do not, however, coincide with the division between the traveler's notes and Pechorin's journal. Part 1 [Часть первая] (4: 184) comprises the two chapters "Bela" and "Maksim Maksimich," plus the traveler's "Introduction to Pechorin's Journal" ["Журнал Печорина: Предисловие"], as well as the first section of that journal, "Taman." (Lermontov clearly emphasizes this division by writing "End of Part One" [Конец первой части] [4: 235] at the conclusion of "Taman.") Part 2 [Часть вторая] (4: 236) then consists of "Princess Mary" and "The Fatalist" (at the finale of which Lermontov explicitly wrote "The End" [Конец] (4: 314)—Nabokov omits all these part demarcations in his translation). Although such an odd and unexpected major break between two chapters of Pechorin's journal may help to underscore differences between Pechorin as he appears in "Taman" by contrast to "Princess Mary" and "The Fatalist" (a subject I will address below), it nonetheless strengthens even more an impression of fragmentation, a sense of disunity or disjuncture among narrative segments that are explicitly separated from one another, leaving readers disconcerted at each seemingly arbitrary break. These are not the fragments of a Romantic work that invite an imaginative leap to wholeness or transcendence. These are fragments of a post-Romantic work that, however ingenious, offers no imaginative incentive to envision an encompassing whole.

Lermontov further disconnects the chapters from one another by using three different narrators. The first two chapters and "Introduction to Pechorin's Journal" are technically narrated by the anonymous Russian traveler visiting the Caucasus. But the narrative structure of "Bela" is far more complicated: its narration is begun by the anonymous traveler, is taken over by Maksim Maksimich for a while, reverts to the traveler, and is then resumed by Maksim Maksimich, only to be concluded by the traveler. The traveler then also narrates "Maksim Maksimich" and the subsequent brief "Introduction to Pechorin's Journal," in which he explains that, having learned of Pechorin's death, he has decided to publish portions of Pechorin's journal, which Maksim Maksimich had given to the traveler in a fit of pique after being treated dismissively by Pechorin. The following three chapters, "Taman," "Princess Mary," and "The Fatalist," are then narrated by Pechorin himself as parts of his journal or diary (and "Princess Mary" is further segmented into separately dated diary entries).

These three different narrators not only present events from different points of view, they do so in different narrative styles.[16] While I would grant that the traveler appears to try to emulate Pechorin's emotional detachment when we see him in "Maksim Maksimich," and although all the novel's narrators occasionally echo one another, each of the three is given a distinct voice and personality, typically expressing ideas and employing imagery in characteristic ways that distinguish each from the others. The anonymous traveler reports his experiences in "Bela" and "Maksim Maksimich" in educated language marked by a self-conscious awareness of his role as a narrator, as well as a tendency to emotional coloration, especially at the beginning of "Bela," although this subsides by his "Introduction to Pechorin's Journal." Maksim Maksimich tells his two-part story in "Bela" in a more plain-spoken style bespeaking a lesser education and less sophisticated intellect. And Pechorin writes his journal in not one but two styles and multiple tones. In the first chapter of the journal, "Taman," Pechorin adopts the narrative straightforwardness and naïve tone of an inexperienced adventurer. But in "Princess Mary" and "The Fatalist" he becomes intellectually sophisticated and emotionally convoluted. Hence divisions occur not only among the novel's diverse parts and chapters, but also among the novel's several narrators and even within the same narrative. Certainly all these divisions lend complexity and artistic richness to the novel that readers have long applauded. Yet these divisions also compound the impression that Lermontov's novel lacks an integrated structure.

Lermontov also adds to this impression by setting the five main chapters of *A Hero of Our Time* in different times and places. Although the historical "indefiniteness" perceived in the novel by Todd renders their chronology difficult to establish, Nabokov plausibly calculates that "Taman" is set in 1830, "Princess Mary," part of "Bela," and "The Fatalist" in 1832, the remainder of "Bela" in 1833, and "Maksim Maksimich" in 1837 (viii–ix). The traveler's "Introduction to Pechorin's Journal" would then have been written in 1838 or 1839, after Pechorin's death returning from Persia. This chronology is clearly at odds with the order in which the chapters are presented, and readers have to study the novel closely to work out the chronological relationships among the narrative segments.

This chronological disjuncture goes along with shifts in the geographical setting of each segment, although all the events do take place in the Caucasus. The opening passages of "Bela," which create a narrative frame for Maksim Maksimich's tale, are set in a Caucasian mountain inn; the events of Maksim Maksimich's framed narrative take place in a Chechen fort; the chapter "Maksim Maksimich" occurs in the mountain town of Vladikavkaz; "Taman" is situated on the Crimean coast; "Princess Mary" is placed in the Caucasian spa resort towns of Piatigorsk and Kislovodsk; and "The Fatalist" unfolds in a Cossack settlement. These shifts in setting are, of course, not in themselves a literary oddity, any more than a broken chronology. But along with the disjointed narrative structure of *A Hero of Our Time*, the inconsistencies of time and place make it read all the more like a compilation of fragments.

Besides the narratorial, temporal, and spatial disjunctures of *A Hero of Our Time*, each of its chapters can be said to have affinities with a different literary genre—"Bela" with the sentimental romance, "Maksim Maksimich" with the physiological sketch, "Taman" with the Romantic adventure story, "Princess Mary" with the society tale, and "The Fatalist" with the philosophical *conte*; even the traveler's "Introduction to Pechorin's Journal" can be associated with the confession. To be sure, the literary genre of the novel can include elements of all other literary genres. However, the disparate generic affinities among the chapters of Lermontov's novel are so marked as to have led some critics to question whether the work really constitutes a novel at all, or is rather a collection of short stories.[17] I would not go so far, and I accept Lermontov's decision to publish the parts of *A Hero of Our Time* together as a justification of its consideration as a novel. But I would say it is a novel of structural fragments that do not all ultimately fit together, causing readers to wonder just what this novel is truly about, what its point of view actually is, and why its fragmentation is so pervasive.[18]

One of the few critics to focus on the structural fragmentation of *A Hero of Our Time*, Victor Ripp, links that fragmentation to the era of its composition, although he does not label this era post-Romantic. In his article "*A Hero of Our Time* and the Historicism of the 1830s: The Problem of the Whole and the Parts," Ripp observes that "an acute awareness of discontinuity and chaos was, in fact, widespread in the Russian literature of the 1830s." Although he says he is "less interested in the reasons discontinuity was so significant a concern than in the literary forms the concern took," Ripp locates the source of this awareness in a reaction against "classical orderliness," coupled with the "loss of faith in all public norms following the political debacle of 1825" (970), referring to the failed Decembrist revolt of that year. "One response" to this lack of faith, Ripp finds, "was to write works which were themselves highly discontinuous and chaotic." Although he does not explicitly describe *A Hero of Our Time* itself as "chaotic," he remarks that the novel "proceeds not merely without a symbol of the transcendent order but with a perceptible vacuum where that symbol should be" as it resists the "'architectonic' impulse, the effort at willingly imposing rationality" on a literary composition (979, 978). And this resistance yields "the curious aimlessness of the book, a sense of uncertainty not about how to win the necessary battles but about how to define the battleground in order to fight at all" (979).

Without labeling it as such, Ripp here describes the structure of *A Hero of Our Time* as a manifestation of post-Romantic anomie—a lost confidence in cultural norms to lend wholeness and integrity to the form of artistic works as well as to personal identities.[19] For it was confidence in the elemental integrity of Romanticism that generated its structurally fragmented works of art—they were rooted in the certainty that the imaginations of their audiences could transform fragments into transcendent, organic wholes by performing "acts of inclusion," in Michael Cooke's felicitous phrase.[20] The post-Romantic loss of that confidence can therefore account for the different type of fragmentation with which Lermontov infuses his novel. This is fragmentation that betokens no certainty in cultural norms and values promising ultimate wholeness and integrity; this is fragmentation that betrays the uncertainty that wholeness and integrity are even possible. In essence, then, the aesthetic structure of *A Hero of Our Time* encapsulates the cultural conditions of its time.

As we will see in Chapter 7, the endings of the dis-integrated chapters of the novel bring no closure, as though Lermontov could conjure up no conclusions. Fragmentation, dis-integration, inconclusiveness—these are all formal and structural symptoms of the cultural anomie that pervades *A Hero of Our Time*. But they only set the stage for the chief exemplar of this anomie—the "hero" himself, Pechorin.

PINNING DOWN PECHORIN

We could say that all of what Lermontov tells us about Pechorin's life in *A Hero of Our Time* also amounts to nothing but a fragment. We see Pechorin from different perspectives covering a period of perhaps three years—with a final glimpse of him a few years later—but we learn virtually nothing about him before or after. As Todd points out, "Of [Pechorin's] background we learn only that he came from the best society, and of his subsequent fate we learn only that he died." The lack of information about Pechorin's past, Todd rightly concludes, "renders attempts to create a biography for [him] ultimately fruitless" (*Fiction and Society*, 151). And the absence of any details about his subsequent life and death, except, as the traveler tantalizingly reports in his "Introduction to Pechorin's Journal," that he had died returning from Persia, leaves another curious lacuna—Marie Gilroy has called these blanks bracketing Pechorin's story "the greatest silence" in the novel (60). As it turns out, Lermontov *had* drafted an extended description of Pechorin's death in a duel, but he excised this description prior to the novel's publication. We can only speculate why. Was it to deliberately confine his protagonist to a fragmentary existence between an empty past and an illusory future? Was it to keep readers focused on Pechorin's story as Lermontov chose to tell it and not to obscure it with extraneous information? In any case, if Lermontov had provided the portrayal of Pechorin's death in a duel, this likely would have made Pechorin more of a Romantic figure doomed to a courageous and tragic end than the Pechorin Lermontov chose to give us.[21] Instead, the fragmentary Pechorin he did give us is a hero of a fragmentary time.

In light of what little we know about Pechorin outside the novel's compass—as well as the contradictory ideas, emotions, and behavior exhibited by the Pechorin we do observe within that compass—explaining his nature and motives has proven to be a provocative challenge to literary critics ever since the novel's publication. As C. J. G. Turner puts it, "The question of the origin of Pechorin's diseased character is the basic enigma of the novel" (76). Related questions abound: Is Pechorin unique or typical? Is he a villain or a victim? Is he truly superior and infallibly insightful or somehow inferior and supremely self-deceived?

In a sense, pinning down Pechorin in these ways should not be difficult. Lermontov himself famously declared in his introduction to *A Hero of Our Time* that the novel is "a portrait, but not of a single individual. It is a portrait composed of the vices of our entire generation" (4: 184; 2). However, most critics, especially in the twentieth century, have not chosen to accept this blanket condemnation, that is, they have not catalogued those vices and then conveniently deemed Pechorin a "composite" of them. Instead they have been inclined to locate the source of Pechorin's "problem," however they define it, in an analysis of his character as somehow divided. By doing so, of course, they are tacitly accepting Pechorin's self-assessment that he has been psychologically rent in two: "One half of my soul did not exist," he tells Princess Mary, "it withered away, it evaporated, it died, I cut it off and threw it away" (4: 268; 127). And he later echoes this notion to his close acquaintance Dr. Werner: "Within me there are two individuals: one of them lives in the full sense of this word, the other contemplates and judges him" (4: 292; 163). Thus, in effect following Pechorin's lead, Elena Mikhailova sees Pechorin split between a noble natural self and a corrupt social self (320); Richard Freeborn finds him divided into public and private personas (56); Gary Cox perceives an analytic side opposed to a melodramatic one (168); Herbert Eagle discerns a complex "duality" in Pechorin (312); Marie Gilroy suggests that Pechorin conceives of his own double (68); and so forth. Such conceptions of his personality as divided have led critics to discern widely divergent qualities in Pechorin: they variously label him tragic, Byronic, skeptical, noble, perceptive, dreaming, superfluous, weak, parasitic, blind, cunning, ruthless, cynical, arrogant, egotistical, solipsistic, self-conscious, self-deceived, contradictory, ambiguous, ambivalent, uncertain, elusive, and so on.[22]

In my view, Pechorin's character comprises all the qualities such critics have attributed to him, and more. But these qualities do not meld together into an integrated personality or split neatly into a divided one. They are too disparate to cohere. For the pieces of Pechorin's personality no more fit together into a complete whole than do the pieces of narrative that present his personality. That personality lacks the integrity for Pechorin to establish and sustain a clear, consistent identity. His behavior is too erratic and extreme to bespeak merely a "multifaceted" persona. In essence, the fragmentary narrative structure of the novel refracts Pechorin's elementally fragmented personality.[23]

Here I would differ with Todd, who suggests that the lack of congruence or consistency in Pechorin's identity may be chalked up to the sociopsychological climate in Russia at a time when the culture and its standards of personality were still forming in the Russian literary consciousness.[24] I would suggest instead that Pechorin's enigmatic and inconsistent identity arises not so much from a culture in formation as from one in disintegration. And this disintegration is not so much that of Russian culture as that of Romanticism, which Lermontov knew well, and which conceived of the self in principle as an organic unity integrating disparate qualities, even if divided in practice through the exigencies of life in contemporary society (see Chapter 2). As Lermontov depicted him, Pechorin experiences the psychological dis-integration that engenders an inconsistent identity because the cultural norms of Romanticism were losing their hold, leaving him floundering in post-Romantic anomie, empty ideals, and deepening cynicism. Viewing Pechorin in this context, I part company as well with Andrew Barratt and A. D. P. Briggs, who also find Pechorin "inconsistent," but "ultimately incomprehensible" (124). For I think we can comprehend Pechorin—as well as the difficulties of pinning him down—if we think of him as elementally shaped by post-Romanticism.

However, while depicting Pechorin as a product of post-Romanticism, Lermontov does not reduce him to a blameless victim. Lermontov also makes Pechorin responsible for his misdeeds by portraying him as deficient in two qualities of character especially prized by Romanticists—imagination and will. Granted, Pechorin does have the imagination to envision ways of manipulating other characters, which he does repeatedly and largely for the purpose of demonstrating his superiority to them. But he does not have the imagination to create a true and autonomous identity that he can consistently maintain. When he tries to imagine an identity for himself that he can act upon, he winds up playing roles that he has derived from characters in Romantic literature and culture or from other individuals influenced by that literature and culture. Although Pechorin evidently thinks that he plays these roles merely to further his own schemes, he plays roles so often and becomes so immersed in them that they serve as almost the only identity he has. And this is not a true identity; it is more a series of identifications. Beyond these roles and his vaunted egotism, Pechorin cannot imagine who he truly is or might be—he cannot determine his "own" role in life.

Along with Pechorin's deficient imagination goes his deficient will. Although Pechorin has enough will to adopt various roles and to succeed in manipulating others in order to gratify his pride, he lacks the will to shape a coherent character and to live a satisfying life. As Freeborn remarks, the exercise of such will as Pechorin possesses has led only to the "facsimile of happiness and purpose with which he fills his life" (69). Switching from role to role and congratulating himself for doing so successfully, Pechorin nonetheless experiences recurring dissatisfactions with the roles he plays and the consequences of playing them, despite his success. For he is only an actor, and when the play is over he has nothing left but his pride—and that is not enough.

He concedes these deficiencies of imagination and will in one of his late moments of self-doubt, when he acknowledges:

> My love brought happiness to no one, because I never sacrificed anything for the sake of those whom I loved. I loved for myself, for my own pleasure; I merely satisfied a strange demand of my heart, avidly consuming their emotions, their tenderness, their joys and sufferings—and I could never be sated. Thus a man tormented by hunger and exhaustion goes to sleep and sees before him sumptuous foods and sparkling wines; he devours with delight the airy gifts of imagination and he seems to feel better . . . but as soon as he awakens, the vision vanishes. . . . He is left with redoubled hunger and despair! (4: 290; 159)

But if Pechorin had the imagination to envision a coherent character and satisfying life for himself, as well as the will to live them out, he would not be the peculiar, post-Romantic figure that he is.

Of course, Pechorin usually thinks that he possesses abundant imagination and will. But this only reveals that he recognizes the value of imagination and will as cultural ideals that enable individuals to shape and enact an identity for themselves. His failure to live up to those ideals betrays his fundamental detachment from them. Pechorin admits this, too, in another moment of genuine insight and professed regret:

> In my early youth, I was a dreamer: I liked to fondle images, at times gloomy, at times iridescent, that my restless and avid imagination drew for me. But what of this has remained to me? Only weariness, as after a nocturnal battle with a phantom, and a vague memory full of regrets. In this vain struggle, I exhausted the ardor of soul and the constancy of will required for real life. I entered this life after having already lived through it mentally, and I became bored and disgusted, like someone who reads a bad imitation of a book that he has known long before. (4: 310; 188–89)

Pechorin implies here as elsewhere that this was the condition of his youth, now outgrown. But in truth he does not outgrow it. He only changes its appearance, for he never ceases acting out a "bad imitation" of Romantic ideals, or "images," that he has "long known." And he cannot build an autonomous identity and a satisfying life out of them. So he continues to switch from one performance, and from one failed identity, to another, blown by "phantoms" of Romanticism on a sea of post-Romantic anomie. Unable to grasp Romantic ideals on their own terms, Pechorin finds himself drifting, seeking the identity he wants but cannot will himself to find or imaginatively invent, a flawed hero of a faltering culture. We can see this in detail as we go through his story from its ambiguous beginning to its inconclusive end.

THE LESSONS OF "TAMAN"

Pechorin unintentionally discloses both his flawed self-image and his actual fragmented, anomic self in the first portion of his journal, the chapter "Taman," which depicts the chronologically earliest events of the novel. Through these events, recorded in retrospect,[25] Pechorin reconstructs himself as a young man who has not yet acquired much worldly experience—he is a naïve youth, a relative "innocent abroad," as it were. And he is a youth who has clearly been nurtured on the images, the ideals, and the norms of Romanticism. Hence he envisions himself as a bold adventurer full of curiosity and courage, ready to meet any challenge and vanquish any foe, assuming that this self-image constitutes a coherent Romantic identity. However, his actions during the events he depicts disclose no real Romantic identity but only a vague, Romanticized identification with images and general cultural tendencies of Romanticism, and he ends up losing even that identification. Therefore, instead of an authentically Romantic self that passes the test of reality, the young Pechorin merely acts out a fantasy of a Romanticized self that proves inadequate when confronted with real adventures. Only when he abandons his Romantically inspired imaginings can Pechorin confront the actuality of his unformed identity and his ignorance of himself and the world around him—although he shies away from that confrontation, too, at the very end of "Taman."

yup.

We meet this Romanticized young adventurer as he enters Taman, "the worst little town of all the seacoast towns in Russia" (4: 225; 65)—the periphery of the periphery. He agrees to reside in a particular hut despite being informed that "it's an evil place." His courage in the face of any dangers its "evil" might pose comes from ignorance, however, rather than bold defiance, since, as he acknowledges, "I did not understand the exact sense of that word" (i.e., "evil" [нечисто; literally, "unclean"] [4: 226; 65]). This is the naïve bravado that comes from youthful inexperience rather than the considered courage born of mature experience.

Pechorin's youthful curiosity is soon aroused by two inhabitants of Taman, whom he promptly casts into Romantic roles. The first is a blind boy and the second is a young woman with whom the boy has a midnight rendezvous. The boy has what Pechorin takes to be a mysterious and foreboding appearance, which leads Pechorin to suspect him of some malevolent deception and to dub him a "little devil" (4: 230; 71). "I could not fall asleep," Pechorin reports of his first night in the hut, because "the white-eyed boy kept hovering before me in the darkness" (4: 227; 67). Here Pechorin has converted the boy into a ghostly apparition of the sort seen in Gothic novels and Romantic works from Horace Walpole and Ann Radcliffe to Heinrich Kleist and E. T. A. Hoffmann. And it is precisely this literary imagery that fuels Pechorin's curiosity and inspires him to trail the boy when he heads for the seacoast that very night. Emulating Romantic heroes who find excitement and intrigue in remote lands among exotic peoples, Pechorin elects to follow in their footsteps—playing the first of his many roles—by following the boy.

When Pechorin then sees the boy talking to an intrepid boatman, who lands a small boat on the shore despite the rough waters, and to a young woman evidently acquainted with both, he is baffled, and all the more intrigued. He returns to his hut "disturbed" by these "strange things" (4: 229; 70). The next day he roughly questions the blind boy about his nighttime activities, but to no avail. And he grows determined "to obtain the key to this riddle" (4: 230; 71), since he cannot unlock it with his imagination alone—and he evidently has not encountered precedents in Romantic literature to assist him.

He *has* encountered precedents derived from Romanticism for the behavior of the young woman on the following day, when she signals some amorous interest in him. He labels her "my undine," that is, a female water spirit who can obtain a soul if she marries a man. As Nabokov observes, the image of this "changeling of mermaid origin" would have been well known to Russian readers from Zhukovskii's 1836 adaptation in unrhymed verse of a romance by the German writer La Motte Fouqué, entitled *Undine* (1811) (Lermontov, *Hero*, 204). Once again Pechorin views his experience through the prism of Romantic imagery (in this instance, imagery derived from a post-Romantic version of an authentic Romantic work). He neither sees things as they are, nor exercises an imagination that is truly his own.

Pechorin virtually acknowledges as much in a subsequent description of his "undine": "I imagined I had discovered Goethe's Mignon," he exults, referring to the impassioned, willful Italian girl depicted in *Wilhelm Meister's Apprenticeship* (1795–96). Although he somewhat dismissively refers to Mignon as a "fanciful creation of [Goethe's] German imagination" (and he describes the enticing tilt of the young woman's head as "characteristic only of her"), Pechorin sees the young woman as a copy of the literary original, finding in both "the same rapid transitions from the utmost restlessness to complete immobility, the same enigmatic statements, the same antics and strange songs" (4: 231; 74). Excited by this literary image of the young woman, he zealously responds to a "moist, burning kiss" she suddenly gives him: "I clasped her in my embrace with all the force of youthful passion" (4: 233; 76). The term "youthful passion" may express the energy, excitement, and exuberance of any young man faced with a possible romance. But here it especially captures the young Pechorin's jejune imagination inflamed by Romantic visions of exotic women and impassioned love affairs. He is playing the role of Romantic lover to Romantic heroine, acting on borrowed emotions.

Pechorin underscores the derivative quality of his emotions and actions when he accounts for his attraction to the young woman by remarking on her apparent good "breeding," which he terms "a great thing" in both women and horses, and he observes, "*les Jeunes-France* are responsible for this discovery" (4: 231; 73). An epigonal, dandified social movement of the 1830s that copied a British one of the 1810s, Jeunes-France [Young France], supply the young Pechorin with the attitudes he considers appropriate.[26] Rather than discerning original qualities in the young woman to account for his attraction to her, he relies on literary conventions—both Romantic and post-Romantic. Pechorin appears to have almost no mind of his own, much less an autonomous identity born of his own imagination and enacted according to his own will. He merely indulges in playacting and a self-deceiving identification with ideas and images that have been handed down to him.

Pechorin's naïve identification with Romantic images makes him vulnerable to dangers that a genuine Romantic spirit, nourished by an independent imagination and a strong will, would have enabled him to avoid. These dangers unfold after Pechorin succumbs to the young woman's intimation of a romantic—and Romantic—tryst at the seashore by feigning "deep-seated agitation" and bestowing her kiss (4: 232; 76). He does arm himself with a pistol against the risks that can befall a nighttime adventurer in an isolated place, and he hesitates before agreeing to accompany her onto a rickety boat and out into the water, since, he reports, "I'm not enthusiastic about sentimental outings on the sea"—wisely enough, given that, as it turns out, he cannot swim. And yet, he immediately decides, "This was not the time to retreat" (4: 233; 77). Buoying his courage and certain of his amatory triumph, Pechorin perseveres, braced by his identification with dauntless Romantic heroes.

But his expectations are thwarted. For the young woman steals his pistol and then tries to push him overboard in order to prevent him from revealing to the authorities the smuggling activities in which she, the boatman—with whom, it turns out, she is in love—and the blind boy have been engaging. Now Pechorin discovers the unromantic, nearly mundane actuality to which his Romanticized perceptions had blinded him. He has not commenced a great romantic love affair, or even encountered a noble band of Romantic outlaws à la Byron's *Corsair* (see Chapter 3). He has stumbled into "the peaceful midst of *honest smugglers*" trying to eke out a living. "Like a stone thrown into a smooth pool," he realizes, "I had disturbed their peace, and like a stone, had nearly sunk to the bottom myself!" (4: 235; 79). These "honest smugglers" could readily manipulate

The disappointment of life

and even nearly kill Pechorin because he misconstrued everything as a Romantic literary adventure.

As the realization of his folly sinks into the young Pechorin, the narrative tone of "Taman" distinctly changes. Pechorin begins to scrutinize himself (granted, early on he had offered a few clichéd self-analytical comments about his being subject to prejudices, but his narrative was focused primarily on the unfolding events). Overall, as several critics have rightly noted, the young Pechorin is not self-reflective in "Taman"—until the end.[27] For it is only at the end that he recognizes his own misperceptions and vacuous identity. Until this point, he *had* been merely a small stone making insignificant ripples at best, who had nearly "sunk to the bottom" precisely because he had not possessed a distinctive, authentic persona with which the smugglers needed to reckon—as he finally realizes. Now he has been forced to acknowledge the truth of his "undine's" assessment of him: "You've seen much, but you know little" (4: 232; 75). He may have observed that world, but he has not understood it. Viewing everything in images derived from Romanticism, he had been deluded about that world—and about himself. No diabolical antagonist had arisen for Pechorin to combat and defeat; no swashbuckling adventure had allowed him to demonstrate his mastery of himself and his circumstances; no Mignon had afforded him ineffable bliss. None of his fantasies fed by Romantic images and ideals had been fulfilled.

But instead of digging deep inside himself and striving to form a strong and coherent identity to meet the world on its terms, Pechorin consequently adopts a tone of icy detachment and indifference to the world around him: "What happened to the old woman and the poor blind boy—I don't know. And anyway, what do human joys and sufferings matter to me, me, a traveling military officer, and moreover, one with a road-pass for official obligations! . . . " (4: 235; 80). This is the tone of cynicism and superiority Pechorin will adopt in the future, as he presents a persona that knows the world well enough to become detached from it, or elevated above it.[28] Henceforth he will ostensibly marshal what have proved to be the fragments of Romanticized identifications into a coherent, stable identity as a Romantic hero superior to the petty concerns of everyday life and ordinary individuals. Pechorin thus implies that he leaves Taman with a mature, independent identity—but actually it turns out to be the series of identifications and roles depicted in the remaining chapters of the novel.

Tellingly, those chapters will bear names of individuals (or a type of individual in the case of "The Fatalist") whose identities and actions affect

Pechorin—and, even more, whose identities and actions Pechorin often profoundly affects—unlike "Taman," which refers only to a place where Pechorin embarked on his campaign for psychological significance. In fact, it is noteworthy that in "Taman," with one exception, no characters have identities distinctive enough to merit names. The exception is the boatman, whose name Pechorin reports to be Ianko. Not coincidentally, I think, Ianko displays an autonomous identity far closer to that of a Romantic hero than does Pechorin. For he has the imagination to envision a life he wants to live—and the will to live it. "There's an open road for me wherever the wind blows and the sea sounds!" he exclaims (4: 234; 79). Although Ianko does not play enough of a role to become eponymous, we can see in him precisely what Pechorin has demonstrably lacked—self-knowledge and self-control, insight and understanding, imagination and will. These are qualities Romanticism adopted as ideals and as norms that gave shape to its culture and to the identities of those who embraced this culture.

Accordingly, by contrast to critics who dismiss "Taman" as a slight if artful narrative that reveals little about Pechorin's character,[29] I conclude that it contains a psychological turning point for Pechorin. For the experiences he undergoes there reveal to him, even if subconsciously, that not only does he lack the Romantic identity he thought he possessed, he has no identity at all. From there on he affects an attitude of cynical superiority accompanied by serial identifications with roles he will play. He will think of himself as something of a hero in a fallen world, but he will be more a symptom of that world, with its disintegrating ideals and norms, in ways he cannot understand. Lacking sufficient resources of imagination and will to create and sustain a coherent identity on his own, Pechorin becomes a creature of anomie.

IN QUEST OF IDENTITY

The remaining segments of Pechorin's journal (the chapters "Princess Mary" and "The Fatalist"), along with the two opening chapters of the novel ("Bela" and "Maksim Maksimich"), display the mature Pechorin living out the self-image he devises and the various roles he plays following the events of "Taman." And yet, as Todd remarks, *A Hero of Our Time* is not what he calls "a narrative of becoming," so readers "must question the possibility of character development" (*Fiction and Society*, 149, 150). Indeed, although this mature Pechorin clearly thinks he has developed a cohesive and coherent identity for himself, in fact he has not. He remains as psychologically insubstantial and incoherent, often as self-deceived, as he was in "Taman," albeit less naïve, as he tries to prove to himself that he is who he thinks he is.

The identity Pechorin ascribes to himself is that of a superior individual possessing intellectual and moral superiority to everyone he encounters, a superiority rooted in his sense that, as he writes in his journal, "I was truly intended for a lofty purpose, for I feel boundless strength in my soul" (4: 289; 158).[30] Or, to paraphrase his "undine" in "Taman," Pechorin thinks that he now not only "sees much" but that he "knows everything" about himself and others, and that he can act on his knowledge to pursue his own gratification with supreme insight, bold determination, and "boundless strength."[31]

It is not surprising that Pechorin again here casts himself in the mold of a Romantic hero, the identity he most covets and readily borrows. But he no longer borrows the identity of the heroic adventurer in exotic lands—like Byron's Corsair or Giaour—as he did in "Taman." Now he takes on the persona of the socially alienated hero who stands apart and, in Turner's words, "seeks his lofty destiny, meditates upon his own fate, and impinges fatally on the lives of friends and lovers" (77). He even admits to this act of identification when, in another moment of honest self-doubt, he says that he might, after all, just be one of those individuals who, "beginning his life, thinks he will finish it as Alexander the Great or Lord Byron, and instead, remains a titular counselor for his entire existence" (4: 272; 133). But he soon forgets this admission and denies the doubts—although he will have others—as he goes on to play out his new persona with perverse self-aggrandizement. As he muses, "My principal pleasure—to subjugate to my will everything that surrounds me, and to arouse the emotions of love, devotion, and fear toward me—isn't that the principal sign and greatest triumph of power? To be the cause of someone's sufferings and joys, without having any positive right to it—isn't this the sweetest possible nourishment for our pride?" (4: 265; 123).

And yet, although he repeatedly arouses those emotions and causes those reactions, Pechorin does not find his pride lastingly nourished. He retains no enduring gratification from his triumphs at manipulating others. For he has no true identity of his own to give him genuine and lasting confidence in himself. He even allows himself the sad quasi confession: "If I considered myself to be better and more powerful than anyone else in the world,

I would be happy; if everyone loved me, I would find in myself infinite sources of love" (4: 265; 123). These are the words of someone who yearns for a kind of impossible grandeur as the only condition of happiness. And this yearning is itself a formula for unhappiness. We might see here a variation on the Romantic desire of Goethe's Faust, for example, for the power to transcend constraints, or of Mary Shelley's Frankenstein for the universal gratitude of having conquered death. But Pechorin's yearning for grandeur, by contrast, is laden with the pathos of post-Romantic anomie.

Pechorin's post-Romantic anomie, as both an aimless attitude of mind and a dis-integrated quality of character, manifests itself most notably in three ways: (1) inconsistency; (2) insecurity; and (3) inauthenticity. Inconsistency appears in Pechorin's vacillations and contradictory emotions and actions, betraying the absence of a coherent personality. Insecurity surfaces in Pechorin's recurrent need to test himself, as if seeking affirmation of an identity he does not have or constraints against which to establish an identity. And inauthenticity resides in Pechorin's inclination to play roles, suggesting a fruitless quest for his own "part."

Pechorin's most persistent feature is inconsistency. He repeatedly wavers, backtracks, and contradicts himself in his thoughts, emotions, behavior, and self-perceptions. He even boasts of the fact. "I have an innate passion," he announces, "for contradiction." And, as if to prove the point, in the next breath, the boast becomes a lament as he sighs, "My entire life has been merely a chain of sad and unsuccessful contradictions to heart or reason" (4: 242; 89). And he makes this very kind of contradiction a frequent refrain. As observed earlier, one minute Pechorin claims absolute superiority to others, then in the next he sinks into abject self-doubt and even self-reproach. For instance, he can boldly say, "I love my enemies, though not in a Christian sense: they amuse me, they stir my blood. Always to be on guard, to catch every glance and the meaning of every word, to guess intentions, to thwart plots, to pretend to be deceived, and suddenly, with one push, to overturn the entire enormous and elaborate structure of cunning and scheming—that is what I call life" (4: 274; 136). But he will also plaintively wonder, as he does when he learns that Grushnitskii, an army acquaintance of his, and some other soldiers are plotting to humiliate him, "What do they all hate me for? . . . Have I offended anybody? No" (4: 282; 147)—this notwithstanding the fact that he has sought to humiliate Grushnitskii in Princess Mary's eyes in order to lure away her affections. Then again, two days later he can muse, "Sometimes I despise myself. . . . Isn't that why I also despise other people? . . . I've become incapable of noble impulses" (4: 283; 148). These inconsistent perceptions of himself and his life do not bespeak a personality capacious enough to embrace all contradictions, such as the type extolled by Blake, Goethe, and Coleridge. These are rather the inconsistencies of someone with no coherent personality at all, someone whose every shifting mood and perception reflects the absence of a stable and enduring sense of self.

The same holds for Pechorin's treatment of other characters, especially the women in his life. For example, at one point Pechorin describes himself in his journal as utterly devoted to women: "I, someone who loves nothing in the world except them, I, someone who has always been ready to sacrifice to them tranquility, ambition, life" (142). And yet he brings suffering and despair to every woman he becomes involved with—they are the ones who actually sacrifice "tranquility," "ambition," and even life itself. He promises Vera, a former lover with whom he renews an affair, that he will court the young and beautiful Princess Mary "in order to divert attention" from that affair. But he actually intends to court Princess Mary in order to win her affections away from Grushnitskii, and then to break Mary's heart. "In this way," he gloats, "I will enjoy myself!" (4: 252; 104–5). So Pechorin plans to deceive Vera even while claiming that she is "the only woman on earth whom I could not bear to deceive" (4: 253; 106). In the same vein, he sets out, as he acknowledges, "to gain the love of a quiet young woman [Princess Mary] whom I do not wish to seduce and whom I will never marry" (4: 264; 122). Professing to be devoted to women, Pechorin nonetheless treats them like mere toys in the wayward game of his life (see Chapter 7). For just as he has no secure identity, he is devoid of the psychological and moral integrity that true devotion and loyalty to other individuals require.

Pechorin exhibits kindred inconsistencies—although not all malign—in an array of his actions toward others. He can be ruthless, as when he engineers innocent Bela's kidnapping, and violent, as when he shoots Grushnitskii in their duel. But he can also act with decency and honor. After all, Pechorin does help to nurse the wounded Bela, he twice rescues Princess Mary from distressing social situations, and he single-handedly captures a murderous Cossack, thereby preventing the Cossack's potential harming of soldiers who must attempt to arrest him. It is beneficial acts such as these that, as noted earlier, have led some critics, most recently Golstein, to conclude that Pechorin is genuinely heroic. But within the pattern of his behavior as a whole, Pechorin's noble acts clash with the rest, punctuating the inconsistency that pervades his fragmentary character. And if we look at the motives for his noble acts, we find contradictions there, too—Pechorin does decent things for various reasons, but always to make himself feel good about a self that is not there. And although he asserts that his contrariness is deliberate, a conscious form of rebellion, the mature Pechorin repeatedly reveals contradictions without any indication whatsoever that he is conscious of doing so. This sort of contradiction bespeaks not a well-defined identity rooted in rebellion but an ill-defined psyche restlessly moving from one psychological stance to another in search of an enduring foundation on which to base a lasting sense of self.

Pechorin makes these kinds of contradictory claims not only about his relationships with women, but also about himself and his life. First he represents himself as a victim of unjustified animosity, then as a despicable wrongdoer. Likewise, at several times he claims to be "an axe in the hands of fate," as a result of which, "I would fall upon the head of doomed victims, often without malice, always without regret" (4: 290; 159), but at other times he avows his complete control over his own harmful actions. At those times he makes no reference whatsoever to fate—Pechorin gleefully attributes the disruption he causes to his own intentions alone.

Recognizing Pechorin's inconsistent nature, Todd argues that *A Hero of Our Time* offers readers "explicit invitations to contradictory understandings of Pechorin" and leads them "to infer contradictory conclusions" about him while waiting for "a resolution which never satisfactorily presents itself" (*Fiction and Society*, 162, 163). Likewise observing Pechorin's inconsistencies, Victor Ripp determines that Pechorin is "a character anxiously seeking to become a type" in order to find "a meaning that will fit the randomness of his life to a pattern" (972), precisely because Pechorin has no elemental character to rely upon. And I would contend further that no "resolution" of Pechorin's "randomness" is forthcoming or even possible. He is simply a collection of fragments held together by the shifting patterns of a fragile ego searching for a character and for meaning. But he has neither the Romantic imagination nor the will nor the integrity to find either. That is a curse of his post-Romantic anomie.

It is no surprise that underlying Pechorin's inconsistencies runs a thread of insecurity. This insecurity manifests itself in many of those inconsistencies we have seen. But it also propels many of the dramatic incidents in the novel. In each of these, Pechorin perceives some psychological or moral limit, which he regards as an obstacle to be heroically overcome. I would say, in fact, that he needs these obstacles, which he then strives to overcome, in order to escape from his anomie through acts that give limits, structure, and purpose to his life and thereby impart substance and coherence to his character—that is, a satisfying identity. However, even though he always overcomes the obstacles he perceives, Pechorin never attains the satisfactions he seeks. For the obstacles are too ephemeral and their purpose is too narcissistic. Identity continues to elude him, and his anomie persists.

For example, when Pechorin sees the lovely Bela at a wedding, he determines to make a sexual conquest of her, overcoming the resistance of her family, her local suitor, and Bela herself. He begins by persuading Bela's brother to bring her to him in exchange for a powerful horse that the brother covets. After her brother delivers Bela, Pechorin dismisses the concerns of Maksim Maksimich, who complains that this is a "bad" deal, defending his actions on the grounds that "a wild Circasssian girl would be lucky to have such a nice husband as [Pechorin] would be, because according to their way of thinking, he was, after all, her husband" (4: 196; 20–21), and that if he returned Bela to her family upon their demand, her father would "either slit her throat or sell her off" (4: 198; 24). Having obtained Bela, Pechorin then has to win her over. He first assures her that she should not resist on religious grounds: "Allah is the same for all races, and if he allows me to love you, why should he forbid you to return my love?" (4: 199; 25). When she continues to reject his amorous advances, he strengthens his resolve, declaring to Maksim Maksimich, "I give you my word of honor that she will be mine" (4: 200; 26). And he prevails.

But soon he becomes dissatisfied and bored with her. Despite once imagining, he tells Maksim Maksimich, that "she was an angel sent to me by a compassionate fate" to fill his emotional void, he subsequently finds that "the love of a wild girl was little better than that of a noblewoman; the ignorance and the naiveté of the one become as tiresome as the coquetry of the other" (4: 210; 40). Although his will has proven stronger than Bela's, the triumph is an empty one, as Pechorin's triumphs always are. The task was too easy, the resistance too feeble, the success too shallow, to make Pechorin feel that he has truly proven himself to be who he wants to be—a Romantic lover with an exotic paramour. He does not have enough identity to establish a foundation upon which to build one by means of such feats. His insecurity will always demand more victims.

Actually, the same insecurity had manifested itself over a year earlier, when Pechorin challenges himself to win the affections of Princess Mary, the daughter of a wealthy family visiting the Caucasus, notwithstanding his admission in his journal that he does not want to seduce or to marry her, merely to enamor her and then to disappoint her hopes. Hatching his plot, he calculatedly ignores her, provoking her irritation, then he plays upon her emotions in affecting an attachment, and finally he wins her heart by stirring her compassion with descriptions of his unjust rejection by society. As it happens, Mary, like Bela, affords Pechorin no significant challenge at all. In consequence, he quickly loses interest in his own scheme, remarking after one of her predictable reactions to his manipulations, "I already know all this by heart—that's what's boring" (4: 269; 129). Although he carries out his plan to the end, breaking her heart by announcing that he will not marry her, it does not turn out quite as he had intended. Mary's suffering is so palpable that he actually pities her and goes so far as to ease her sorrow by getting her to hate him. He even winds up wondering why he did not love her, so sincere and strong was her love. But he cannot love, any more than he can gain lasting satisfaction over his female conquests by enjoying their love. He is too empty. He always needs more of these conquests to try to fill the bottomless pit of his being.[32]

Pechorin sets up another of his arbitrary obstacles by thwarting the hopes of Grushnitskii to win the love of Princess Mary for himself. Pechorin does this by playing the two of them off against each other. He perversely encourages Grushnitskii's hopes with assurances that Mary is in love with him, and at the same time Pechorin ridicules Grushnitskii to Mary for Grushnitskii's false Romantic poses—while he confides to his journal that Grushnitskii "has not deserved this at all" (4: 265; 122). He then advises Grushnitskii as to the most effective methods of pursuing the princess, although smugly warning him that she will become bored with him. When the smitten Grushnitskii later expresses his tormented affections by passionately pounding a table and pacing around the room, Pechorin reports, "I laughed inwardly," and decides, "I want him to choose me for a confidant himself—then I'll enjoy myself!" (4: 250; 102). Grushnitskii's conceit and naiveté are putty in Pechorin's hands. And Pechorin does gain temporary pleasure here in gulling the gullible.

But after Grushnitskii learns of Mary's preference for Pechorin over him, the drama takes a more malignant turn. Grushnitskii challenges Pechorin to a duel in which he knows that Pechorin's gun will not be loaded. At the last minute Grushnitskii has a change of heart and lets the gun be loaded, foreseeing the result. Pechorin then calmly and cold-bloodedly shoots him dead. Another triumph, and this time not only over a contrived obstacle but a real challenge. And *still* Pechorin feels no gratification. He reports that at the duel's end he merely remarks, "*Finita la commedia!*" as though Grushnitskii's death were a staged performance, after which he says, "I shrugged my shoulders and bowed to Grushnitskii's seconds" (4: 298; 171). Then, averting his eyes from Grushnitskii's body, he mounts his horse and rides off alone, wandering aimlessly to "a spot that was completely unknown to me" (4: 299; 171). There, in an "unknown spot" emotionally as well as geographically, we can only guess what he feels. But we hear nothing of the pride of victory or of his vaunted sense of superiority. He is alone with himself, which is to say with only an uncertain ego lacking the psychological assurance to condone his actions, much less to derive satisfaction from them.

The final obstacle Pechorin sets himself is a challenge to fate itself. Learning that a homicidal Cossack had locked himself in an empty hut and was about to be shot by soldiers for fear of being hurt themselves during an attempt to take him prisoner, Pechorin records that "it occurred to me to test my fate" by making that attempt himself. Hurling himself through the hut's window and literally dodging a bullet before grasping the Cossack, then handing him over to the other soldiers, Pechorin succeeds again. He has once more risked his life in an indisputable act of will.[33] Perhaps he even triumphs over fate itself. Yet his only further comment about the incident is that "the officers kept congratulating me—and in truth, there was good reason to do so" (4: 313; 193). He certainly does not glory in his success, nor does he conclude that he has actually conquered fate, since afterward he says he is unsure whether fate even exists. His very test of fate was a mere performance. He continues to be an emotional cipher, acquiring no satisfying sense of accomplishment from this potentially heroic deed.

Pechorin cannot get satisfaction from any of the tests he passes so successfully because, for one thing, he wants too much from them—a complete and transcendent identity of Romantically outsized proportions to overcome his inveterate insecurities. For another thing, he may sense that his tests are too arbitrary and meretricious. After all, he has chosen or "written" these tests himself (by contrast to traditional fictional protagonists), and so they are not authentic tests at all. He has not been truly challenged by the world and triumphed over its adversities. In truth, we might say that these are post-Romantic tests, comprising feeble imitations and faint echoes of authentic Romantic quests, transforming potentially "harmonizing rituals into disjunctive contests" (Todd, *Fiction and Society*, 156). Hence throughout these tests Pechorin's identity remains incoherent and uncertain, his dis-integrated ego always dissatisfied.

The third way that Pechorin's lack of an integrated identity comes through is in his propensity to play roles, to act.[34] At different times he performs the part of desperate lover, lifelong friend, Byronic loner, chivalrous rescuer, fatalist, and devotee of free will. Although he claims to play these roles strictly for his own amusement, or to advance his interests, his performances more tellingly bespeak a post-Romantic inability to find his own "part" or to establish an autonomous, integrated identity, even while considering himself a superior individual after leaving Taman. As R. L. Kesler insightfully observes, for Pechorin, "those conditions favoring the appearance of 'unique individuality' [have] passed, leaving the paradoxical possibility of 'individuality' only through increasingly exaggerated imitation" (501).

Pechorin may not exaggerate, but he engages in performances with both self-consciousness and a perverse delight. Often he reports, for instance, donning a particular "air" [вид] in order to convey a particular impression. "I assumed a serious air," he says more than once (4: 250; 101; 4: 264; 121), or "a humble air" (4: 264; 121), or "a most submissive air" (4: 258; 113), or "a deeply touched air" (4: 268; 126). And he clearly revels in the effects he achieves with these "airs," plus a range of feigned emotions. To take but one example, after representing himself to Princess Mary as a socially misunderstood and unjustly outcast youth, he records: "I met her eyes: tears swam in them; her arm, leaning on mine, trembled, her cheeks glowed; she felt sorry for me! Compassion—an emotion to which all women so easily submit—had sunk its claws into her inexperienced heart" (4: 268; 128). Pechorin has clearly calculated in advance the effect he wants to achieve—for the malevolent purpose of first winning and then spurning Mary's love—and he has achieved it. He has played the role of an abused and injured youth to perfection, just as he plays his other roles.

But unlike those actors who have such distinctive personalities that those personalities overwhelm any part they play—as a result of which, such actors always seem to be playing the same part—Pechorin often completely merges into the parts he plays. One might therefore conclude that he is simply an exceptionally talented actor capable of expertly pretending. But Pechorin does more than pretend. He repeatedly finds himself actually thinking and feeling what he had begun simply pretending to think and feel. And this is more than Stanislavskian "method acting." Pechorin periodically appears to *become* the characters he pretends to be. For example, after he has threatened to throw his life away if Bela will not give herself to him, we are told by Maksim Maksimich that at this moment Pechorin "was capable of actually carrying out what he had said in jest" (4: 201; 27). Pechorin has identified here with the role of the Byronic lover so thoroughly that he is willing to die for it. And when Pechorin misses seeing Mary one evening, he wonders, "I couldn't really have fallen in love, could I?" instead of merely pretending. Although he dismissively answers the question by exclaiming, "What nonsense!" (4: 275; 137), Pechorin apparently senses that he has started living out the role he had thought he was only playing.

Moments such as these demonstrate that Pechorin instinctively tends to embrace the parts he plays as an identity. But he never finds one to call his own, and so he switches from role to role, from identity to identity, or rather from identification to identification. In fact, the frequency with which Pechorin performs roles has led Helena Goscilo to conclude that Pechorin is arguably "addicted to role-playing" (276). If so, it is an addiction he cannot live without, because he has no life, no identity of his own, outside his roles.

And when none of the social and emotional roles Pechorin plays grants him an enduring identity as the superior individual he claims to be, another one still holds out that promise. For it transcends all of his others: the role he plays as an author of his own story. Pechorin takes on this role after his unsettling experiences in Taman. Although he once wonders whether fate had destined him "to become the author of bourgeois tragedies and family novels" (4: 272; 133), he chooses another genre—the personal journal. As the author of this journal, Pechorin has the power to define himself and his circumstances any way he chooses. If society will not proclaim him a hero in life, he will proclaim himself one in literature.[35] But as it turns out, the self-portrait he provides in his journal is a peculiar one. It is not that of a Romantic hero in the Byronic style with which he so identifies himself; it is closer to those of Rousseau and a range of Romanticists who wrote "confessions."[36] But Pechorin's self-portrait differs from those as well, since Rousseau and subsequent Romantic "confessors" demonstrate very clear identities amid their discomfiting self-revelations. Pechorin's self-portrait is that of a post-Romantic "hero" for a post-Romantic time, a hero without an identity—even as he tries to create one for himself by writing the journal.

In a sense, on the basis of his journal, we could call Pechorin an anti-hero. Over two decades before Dostoevsky would coin this term for his Underground Man as "one of the characters of a time recently passed" (5: 99), Lermontov gives Pechorin the attributes of an antihero as an individual who has no clear ideals or identity but has the virtue of thoroughly revealing himself (Diderot's *Rameau's Nephew* [*Le Neveu de Rameau*] [1761] set the psychological model of the type, but in an eighteenth-century context). That virtue gained vogue by the twentieth century as "authenticity." Authenticity in this context entailed a new kind of integrity: an unflinching, often searing, exposure of psychological and moral contradictions of all sorts, with weaknesses alongside strengths, fears as well as courage, self-disgust accompanied by self-exaltation.[37]

It is as a kind of antihero, albeit without the appellation, that Pechorin writes his journal, in which he avers the authenticity of his self-revelation: "I am used to admitting everything to myself," Pechorin declares (4: 242; 90). And he proceeds to many unflattering admissions. He acknowledges, for instance, when "an unpleasant but familiar sensation skimmed over my heart," that he recognizes it as "envy" (4: 242; 90). On another occasion, as he relishes the "boundless delight" he feels at causing Princess Mary to suffer, he confesses: "There are moments when I understand the vampire" (4: 280; 145). Again and again he describes his pleasure in manipulating people, consuming their emotions, and destroying their plans. And, as noted earlier, he concedes, "I have become incapable of noble impulses" and, "Sometimes I despise myself. . . . Isn't that why I also despise other people?" (4: 283; 148). The traveler who ostensibly publishes Pechorin's journal even lauds Pechorin in the introduction to it as someone "who so mercilessly exhibited his own weaknesses and vices," and who wrote it "without the conceited desire to provoke sympathy or surprise" (4: 225; 63, 64). Nonetheless, the traveler implies that Pechorin's candor *has* won his sympathy when he comments further that "we almost always forgive what we understand" (4: 225; 64). Pechorin has succeeded in his role as an author to the extent that he has convinced the traveler of his "authenticity." For to be "authentic" he does not need to demonstrate any consistency between intellect and emotion, between appearance and reality; he does not have to espouse, much less adhere to, any ideals. He merely has to have the integrity to reveal himself as he actually is.

However, to be true to authenticity, an antihero must be wholly self-aware. Self-deception compromises authenticity and precludes its elemental integrity. Here is where Pechorin, as a post-Romantic type of antihero, falls short. Lacking a coherent identity, he repeatedly plays roles born of Romantic ideals or models with the aim of demonstrating his superiority, and yet he does not truly grasp what he is doing, and often seems quite blind to himself. We see this in his relations with the women whom he claims to control, but finds himself growing attached to. And at least in the case of Vera, he is driven to "tears and sobs," "anxiety," and "despair" when he loses her after the duel with Grushnitskii, only later to attribute these feelings dismissively "to upset nerves, to a sleepless night, to a couple of minutes spent facing the muzzle of a pistol, and to an empty stomach" (4: 302; 176). Instances like this, filled with patent rationalization and denial of attachment and vulnerability, undermine the authenticity and integrity of the self-portrait Pechorin paints in his journal. That authenticity becomes simply another role—the role Pechorin chooses to play as author of his own life story. It is a role that produces at most a post-Romantic antihero at a time when authenticity and integrity are notably difficult to envision, much less to achieve.

In his monograph exploring Pechorin's character, Turner remarks that "one may legitimately doubt whether one ever sees the 'real' Pechorin, as opposed to a role that he is acting out." Quite so. But in addition to doing this "for his own amusement" (45), as Turner concludes, or because of an "addiction" to role-playing, as Goscilo maintains, or for his own self-perception by an "internal spectator," as Todd indicates (*Fiction and Society*, 161), these performances betray Pechorin's continual search for a role that fits. Todd points out that Pechorin finds only a limited number of roles to choose from (*Fiction and Society*, 157), because the times did not supply more, and for related reasons R. L. Kesler finds Pechorin's "story already written" (493). These limitations betoken Pechorin's affiliation with post-Romantic culture. In addition, I would emphasize that Pechorin belongs to this culture not only by playing limited or empty roles but also because he lacks the imagination and will to go beyond his Romantic predecessors and create a role of his own that satisfies him. The role of post-Romantic antihero that Pechorin does create, however unintentionally—or rather, that Lermontov creates for him—as the author of his journal does not suffice. For it is primarily, as Lermontov says in the end, a symptom of a cultural malaise (see Chapter 8).

As I have sought to demonstrate, that malaise is post-Romantic anomie. While Goscilo does not use the term *anomie*, she describes this very cultural condition when she asserts, "Pechorin cannot commit himself wholeheartedly because he is trapped in a world devoid of final meaning, with no ultimate sanctions for any beliefs or code of behavior" (283–84). However, she suggests that Pechorin successfully acquires a sense of self by acting "as though he had convictions" (293). By contrast, I would argue that without cultural "sanctions," or clear purposes and limits and restraints, Pechorin lacks the psychological integration and coherence ever to shape the convictions born of a consistent sense of self or a full-blown identity, much less a heroic one—setting him far from Romantic heroes with their fully integrated personas (see Chapter 5). I do agree that he suffers not so much from any oppressive constraints engendered by reigning beliefs and norms as from the absence of beliefs and norms that can give purpose and direction to life—no one and nothing ever stop him. That is anomie.

Pechorin conveys his awareness of this condition subtly, yet tellingly, when, after declaring, "I may set my life upon a card twenty times, and even my honor—but I will not sell my freedom," he then asks rhetorically, "Why do I treasure it so? What good is it to me? What am I preparing myself for? What do I expect from the future? . . . Indeed, absolutely nothing" (4: 283; 149). He idealizes freedom, but he can see no clear use for it, he has no hopes for the future (albeit in a journal entry two days later, he allows that "one keeps expecting something new"—but he swiftly dismisses that expectation as "comical and irritating!" [4: 290; 159]). Pechorin literally has nothing to look forward to. This is anomie incarnate, and it is both his fault and a fault of his times.

His anomie here is quintessentially post-Romantic anomie because while Pechorin yearns for the Romantic raptures bestowed by freedom, love, new experiences, and hopes for the future, he cannot partake of those raptures. So, as always, he is left adrift—"coming," as Kesler puts it, "'after the fact'— after the paradigm and syntax of romanticism and the romantic hero had been established elsewhere" (502)—agitated by Romantic ideals that do not hold in a transitional culture that is aimlessly moving beyond ideals toward an unforeseen future. Incessantly trying to prove himself and never succeeding, Pechorin is at most a post-Romantic hero of post-Romantic times.

NATURAL DETACHMENT

Pechorin's post-Romantic anomie is perfectly encapsulated in his relationship to nature. For Pechorin distinctively differs from Romanticists who thrilled to nature's awe-inspiring grandeur and sublimity, rhapsodized over its organic wholeness, and experienced the "sentiment of being," in Wordsworth's phrase, a life-affirming bond of communion with it. Granted, Pechorin does periodically express admiration of nature, especially for its Romantically awe-inspiring scenes, and he occasionally finds in nature a means of escape from what he judges oppressive social constraints. And many critics have taken these expressions and moments of escape to reflect Pechorin's own genuinely Romantic inclinations.[38] Yet the truth is that Pechorin does not sustain his admiration for nature or draw spiritual sustenance from being in its midst. He rather uses nature to give himself a certain Romantic aura, an identification with a prominent strain in Romanticism that bestows on him what he takes to be a desirable sensibility.

In short, Pechorin uses nature to play another role. For he displays none of the profound and lasting affinity for nature or the need to commune with it spiritually that betokens a genuine Romantic temperament. Instead, most often Pechorin merely pauses to note the natural surroundings, often without any emotional reaction to them, and at times he ignores natural phenomena altogether. Overall, despite some Romanticized observations of nature, Pechorin is actually remarkably indifferent to it. His post-Romantic character gives him a derivative Romantic attraction to nature without a truly Romantic devotion to it. Nature can thus no more serve as an ideal and guide for Pechorin's life than can anything else.

We see Pechorin's peculiarly detached relation to nature from the chronological beginning, in the first section of Pechorin's diary, "Taman." Here the natural features of the rural seacoast setting of Taman rarely receive more than a matter-of-fact mention. The sky, the cliffs, the sea—these are not even scenery, but merely background details of the setting that evoke virtually no emotional response from Pechorin. He sets this dispassionate tone when he arrives in Taman, announcing simply, without further comment, "The weather was cold" (4: 226; 65). He says nothing of why it was cold—the climate itself, the wind, the sea air?—or the weather's effect on him. This absence of commentary typifies Pechorin's observations of natural phenomena: "The full moon shone on the thatched roof" (4: 226; 66); "The sea breeze kept blowing through the broken windowpane" (4: 227; 67); "The moon shone in the window and one beam played on the earthen floor of the shanty" (4: 227; 67); "Having concealed myself behind a protruding cliff on the rocky coast . . . " (4: 228; 68); "I lay down in the grass on the brink of the steep shore" (4: 234; 78). Barely an adjective, much less an emotion, accompanies his references to these elements of nature. The grass and cliffs merely afford concealment; the moon is simply a source of illumination. These are mere ambient facts, not sources of exaltation or inspiration.

Even on the occasions when he observes more than mere facts of nature and describes scenes with colorful detail, Pechorin appears emotionally detached from his own words. In describing the seashore, for instance, he says that "the dark-blue waves splashed" and "the moon quietly surveyed the seas, which were restless but submissive to her" (4: 226; 66), but then he moves on. A bit later, he finds an apt metaphor for a moment when he notes that "the moon had begun to clothe herself in clouds" (4: 227; 68), but he lets the moment pass, as he continues, "above the sea a mist had risen; through it, a lantern barely glimmered" (4: 227; 68). And on another night, he observes, "The moon had not yet risen, and only two little stars, like two guiding beacons, sparkled in the dark-blue vault" (4: 233; 77). A nice observation—but he remains unmoved. On still another occasion, when Pechorin actually pauses to appreciate a scene, he waxes almost poetic, but then abruptly drops the subject: "After having admired for a while through the window the blue sky strewn with torn cloudlets, and the distant shore of the Crimea, which extended in a lilac strip and ended at a rock on the summit of which a lighthouse shone white, I set off for Phanagoria Fort" (4: 229; 70). These lines may suggest a sharp eye and a poetic bent, but they end with sheer indifference. Unlike William Wordsworth, who gave "a moral life" to "every natural form" and "saw them feel, / Or linked them to some feeling" charged with "inward meaning" (*The Prelude* [1850 version], 3.130–35), Pechorin reacts to scenes and elements of nature with virtually no emotion. The most he can muster is a cool "admiration."

Pechorin even turns an opportunity for a reverie on the sublime in nature into a swift dismissal of the scene and recourse to self-absorption. Frustrated at his inability to figure out the "riddle" of the smugglers' seaside meeting that he witnessed the night before, Pechorin reports, "I wrapped myself in my cloak and sat down on a stone beside the fence, looking into the distance. In front of me spread out the sea, stirred up by last night's storm, and its monotonous sound, like the murmur of a city settling down to sleep, reminded me of past years, and carried my thoughts northward, to our cold capital. I was troubled by memories and lost myself in them" (4: 230; 71–72). Here the "sea stirred up by last night's storm" does not inspire a rhapsody on nature's vast majesty. Pechorin reduces this sea to a "monotonous sound" that reminds him of an urban environment and his troubled

times in the capital. By contrast to Romanticists who found themselves exulting in nature's magnificence, enthralled by its dark and turbulent allure,
and freed from the pressures of urban society by communion with natural
beauty, Pechorin casually dismisses nature and turns back toward society
and himself. In "Taman," Pechorin is largely indifferent to nature because
he is so wrapped up in his "adventure." And although he can rise to a few
Romanticized descriptions of natural scenes, he can neither idealize nature
like a Romanticist (nor, for that matter, de-idealize it like a Realist). He fundamentally drifts away from nature in the anomie of post-Romanticism.

After Pechorin leaves Taman, however, he tries to use nature to escape
from anomie. In the next section of his journal, "Princess Mary," we find
Pechorin voicing more admiration, and even affection, for nature. And it is
these expressions in particular that have led critics to emphasize Pechorin's
"abiding love of nature," as Mersereau puts it (*Lermontov*, 145). But Freeborn insightfully suggests that Pechorin is promoting an elevated image
of himself through these expressions, because "the scenery connives with
Pechorin's superiority in its grandeur and remoteness" (64). This rings true,
but I would reverse the order and say that Pechorin is "conniving with"
the scenery in order to elevate himself. For Pechorin articulates admiration
and affection for nature so self-consciously in this portion of his journal
that he seems to be affecting the kind of Romantic attitudes he thinks he
should have. And yet, despite his affectations, he displays the same underlying emotional detachment from nature that he had displayed in "Taman."
He continues to find no genuine source of inspiration in nature, no values,
no model of organic integrity, no possibility of transcendence.

In "Princess Mary" Pechorin often barely notices striking natural settings of events, limning them without emotion. For example, shortly after
expressing his preference for nature over a "female gaze" (4: 253; 106), he
describes riding along a road around which rose the Caucasian mountains
as "an amphitheater of blue masses." But instead of steeping himself in the
experience of this massive vista, he merely lists the names of the mountains and then says, "I stopped to water my horse," after which he notes
that "a noisy and resplendent cavalcade" of other riders came by (4: 254;
107). Later on, out walking with Mary, Pechorin observes "an extinct cra-
ter" situated on the rim of a mountain reachable only by "a narrow trail,
among bushes and cliffs" (4: 267; 126). And yet neither his curiosity nor
his imagination is aroused. Similarly, after a fraught conversation with
Mary about their relationship, Pechorin spends hours outside of town—

"till evening, I roamed on foot around the outskirts of Mount Mashuk"—but he offers no hint that he obtained any emotional succor or spiritual uplift from proximity to its heights. To the contrary, he simply records, "I got terribly tired and, on coming home, threw myself on my bed in utter exhaustion" (4: 275; 138). The same pattern recurs after the duel with Grushnitskii when, despite spending hours riding through the mountains in solitude as an escape from his mortal contest, he is not uplifted and renewed. He only comments that he had reached a place "unknown" to him and then had gone home, remarking that "the sun was already setting when I reached Kislovodsk, exhausted, on an exhausted horse" (4: 299; 172). This is not a character for whom nature has any powers of redemption or inspiration. Rather, it is just a prop on his life's stage.

We continue to see this pattern when, at several points, Pechorin gives far more extended descriptions of natural surroundings than he had in "Taman." For instance, after delineating the atmospherically "dense canopies of linden-lined paths," the torrential waterfall between "the verdant mountains," the gorges "filled with mist and silence," "the freshness of the aromatic air," and the "constant, sweetly soporific babble of cool brooks" in the region around Kislovodsk, Pechorin concludes not with some moving reflections on these beauties, but with a little fantasy prompted by a "dusty road" that "meanders" through a glen. "I keep imagining that a closed carriage is proceeding" on that road, he says, "and from the window of the carriage a rosy little face is peering out"—presumably the face of Princess Mary, whose affections Pechorin is attempting to engage (4: 276–77; 139–40). The lush sights and sounds of nature cannot stir his soul, but a "dusty road" can evoke the image of a "closed carriage" driving along while bearing the young woman central to his current schemes. Pechorin's self-absorbed activities easily eclipse nature in his mind.

This happens even when Pechorin explicitly intends to admire a natural wonder. Having joined a group of visitors beside a cliff forming an arch or gateway through which "the setting sun throws its last flaming glance on the world," in order to "view the sunset through that window of stone," Pechorin claims that "none of us," including himself, "was thinking of sunsets" (4: 279; 143). Cynically projecting his self-absorption onto others, he is contemplating his next steps in conquering Mary's affections without returning them. Preoccupied with this most un-Romantic and selfish plan, Pechorin is all but blind to the Romantic vision of nature. He may see the sunset, but his soul remains unmoved.[39]

There are, to be sure, a few moments in which Pechorin seems to display a more truly Romantic feeling for nature. One of these comes in the very opening passage of "Princess Mary," where Pechorin describes the view of Mount Mashuk out his window in the Caucasian spa town of Piatigorsk: "The view on three sides is marvelous," he effuses, identifying the surrounding mountain peaks and the town lying at their feet, then continuing,

> and there, further on, mountains pile up like an amphitheater, ever bluer and mistier, while on the edge of the horizon there stretches a silver chain of snowy summits, beginning with Mount Kazbek, and ending with the two-headed Mount Elbruz. It's delightful to live in such a region! A kind of joyful feeling permeates all my veins. The air is pure and fresh, like the kiss of a child; the sun is bright, and the sky is blue—what more, it seems, could one want? What need is there for passions, desires, or regrets here? (4: 236; 81–82)

This is an almost Wordsworthian reaction. His "joyful feeling" inspires him to acknowledge the value of escaping into nature's splendors and communing with its organic harmony. Yet several features of this incident as reported by Pechorin raise questions about the authenticity and depth of that reaction.

The first feature is that these comments come at the very beginning of the "mature" portion of Pechorin's journal, after he has lost his psychological innocence in Taman and decided to assert an identity as a superior individual. The prominent placement of a paean to nature therefore raises the suspicion that, in his capacity as author, Pechorin has decided to present an image of himself as a devotee of nature in order to establish his status as a true Romanticist. This suspicion grows stronger if we accept Cynthia Marsh's claim that Pechorin's description of this scene resembles all the other descriptions of nature in the novel.[40] In "Bela," for instance, the traveler exclaims about one stop during his journey through the Caucasian mountains, "What a glorious place this valley is!" and at another stop, he extols "dark-blue mountain tops, furrowed with wrinkles, covered with layers of snow" that were "silhouetted against the pale horizon, which still retained the last reflection of the sunset" (4: 186; 3). This rhetorical resemblance suggests that Pechorin had adopted typical Romantic perceptions of nature as his own, and just further Romanticized them as he saw fit. That is part of his post-Romantic style—adopting Romantic forms without the content, embracing the images without the passion, espousing the ideals without the convictions.

Another questionable feature of this incident lies in the fact that Pechorin follows his celebration of nature and his rhetorical question, "What
more . . . could one want? What need is there for passions, desires, or regrets here?" by announcing, "However, it's time. I'll go to the Elizabeth
spring: they say that the entire spa society gathers there in the morning"
(4: 236; 82). This abrupt reversal bespeaks the insincerity of Pechorin's professed "joyful feeling" in nature that "permeates" all his veins. Evidently
he needs much more than nature can give him—including the "passions,
regrets, and desires" of social life, where he feels at home thanks to his sense
of superiority over everyone else.

The next time Pechorin expresses what may at first appear to be a genuine feeling for nature comes after he has unexpectedly met his former lover,
Vera. After rekindling their affair, he goes for a ride on horseback across the
steppe, noting in his diary entry of the day that

> whatever sorrow may oppress my heart, whatever worry may burden my
> thoughts, everything is dispelled in a moment: my soul feels easy, my body's
> fatigue conquers my mind's distress. There is no female gaze that I would
> not forget at the sight of mountains covered with curly vegetation, illumi-
> nated by the southern sun, at the sight of the blue sky, or at the sound of a
> waterfall that descends from rock to rock. (4: 253; 106)

Pechorin here claims that he can forget his cares, he can lose himself in
awe amid the sorts of mountainous sights and sounds that thrilled countless Romanticists. However—as Todd astutely observes—Pechorin's out-
pouring of Romantic affection for nature promptly gives way to reflections
concerning "the Cossacks yawning on their watchtowers" nearby and what
they might be thinking of him (*Fiction and Society*, 158). Forgetting about
nature altogether, he fantasizes happily that, "seeing me galloping without any need or goal . . . surely they must have taken me for a Circassian because of my attire" (4: 253; 106–7). He relishes this image, since he
has dressed precisely as a native warrior would dress—"I am an absolute
dandy," he boasts—and then he affirms, "I have studied the mountain
peoples' style of riding for a long time." He has done these things not from
any Romantic fondness for the indigenous peoples of the region and their
customs, but because, he confesses, "nothing flatters my vanity better than
to acknowledge my skill in horseback riding in the Caucasian fashion" (4:
254; 107). Once again, Pechorin's enthusiasm for nature lasts only a moment, immediately succumbing to another bout of self-absorption—this

time in his role as a Circassian rider—for his own glorification. Nature is only the backdrop.

The moment when Pechorin voices his deepest and apparently most heartfelt attachment to nature occurs shortly before he faces Grushnitskii in their duel. But this, too, trails off into nothing. As he was riding with his second, Dr. Werner, toward the designated dueling site, he recalls,

> The sun had just appeared from behind the green summits, and the mingling of the first warmth of its rays with the waning coolness of the night pervaded all one's senses with a kind of delicious languor. The cheery beam of the young day had not yet penetrated the gorge; it gilded only the tops of the cliffs that hung on both sides of us. The densely leafy bushes, growing in the deep crevices, showered us with a silver rain at the least breath of wind. (4: 291–92; 161–62)

And he concludes by declaring, "I remember that on this occasion, more than ever before, I loved nature. How curiously I examined every dewdrop that trembled upon a broad vine leaf and reflected a million iridescent rays! How avidly my gaze tried to peer into the hazy distance!" A stirring account. And yet where does it lead but to another dead end. And this one is literal.

Peering into "the hazy distance," Pechorin does not perceive an enchanting vista or a sense of nature's infinite mysteries. Instead, he sees that "the road was becoming ever narrower, the cliffs ever bluer and more frightening, and finally, they seemed to merge into an impenetrable wall." Sublimely "frightening" as these blue mountains may be, they create an "impenetrable wall." And this is an exceptionally apt metaphor for the post-Romantic experience of nature. For here Romantic images of the sublime in nature do not inspire excitement or transcendence, but instead come to an impasse, inspiring nothing. And so, Pechorin reports, he and Dr. Werner "rode on in silence" (4: 292; 162). This is a silence betokening not wordless awe at nature's grandeur but rather a dull speechlessness in the face of nature's impervious facade. Detached from nature in all but rhetoric and borrowed images, Pechorin is more tantalized and taunted than inspired by nature to find there a means of overcoming the anomie that leaves him aimless. His silence at the "impenetrable wall" is as post-Romantic as his anomie.

A poignant and highly significant alternative to this silence and the "impenetrable wall" that inspired it comes in the last part of Pechorin's journal, "The Fatalist." Nature appears here only once, except for a few scattered remarks. It appears not as a dead end but as the infinite nighttime sky. And

Pechorin's reaction is not silence. This time he engages in a philosophical meditation. Yet the meditation is revealingly earthbound—and also highly post-Romantic. Gazing up at the "full and red" moon and the stars that "shone calmly upon that dark blue vault," Pechorin contemplates those human beings of the past "who thought that the heavenly bodies took part in our trivial conflicts over a piece of land or some imaginary rights." They might have been wrong, he goes on, but "what strength of will they derived from the certitude that the entire sky with its countless inhabitants was looking down upon them with mute but constant sympathy!" This is exactly what Pechorin now recognizes that he and his times lack:

> We, their miserable descendants, who roam the earth without convictions or pride, without hope or fear (except for that instinctive dread that compresses our hearts at the thought of the inevitable end), we are no longer capable of great sacrifice, neither for the good of mankind nor even for our own happiness, because we know its impossibility, and pass indifferently from doubt to doubt, just as our ancestors rushed from one delusion to another. But we, however, do not have either their hope or even that indefinite, albeit sincere, delight that the soul encounters in any struggle with men or with fate. (4: 309–10; 187–88)

How fitting that nature should remind Pechorin of the inspiration it had once provided humans but can provide no more. This is a moment of post-Romantic anomie if ever there was one.

It is worth noting that Lermontov also presents another notable character in *A Hero of Our Time* who experiences nature the same way Pechorin does, albeit not to quite the same effect: the anonymous traveler who narrates "Bela" and "Maksim Maksimich." Although he might appreciate nature more genuinely than Pechorin does, the traveler too remains peculiarly detached from it, and he thereby further demonstrates that merely intoning Romantic images cannot bring the sense of wholeness and exaltation that nature had brought to truly Romantic spirits.

The novel opens with the traveler's highly Romantic description of the Caucasian mountains he is traversing: "On all sides rise inaccessible mountains, reddish cliffs, overhung with green ivy and crowned with clumps of plane trees; tawny precipices streaked with gullies, and, far above, the golden fringe of the snows; below, the Aragva river, enfolding another nameless river that noisily bursts out from a black gorge full of mist, stretches out in a silver thread and glistens like the scales of a snake" (4: 184–85; 3).

The traveler's awe at the enormous expanse of height and depth, the array of colors, and the varieties of natural phenomena all convey a Romantic sensibility. However, rather than being spiritually exalted by the scene, the traveler merely grumbles that "it was already autumn and there was ice on the roads," and curses the "damned mountain" for making his passage by carriage difficult (4: 185; 4). His lofty Romantic images of nature give way to mundane complaints about a mountain journey—the traveler can describe nature with Romantic flair, but he cannot sustain Romantic ecstasy.

The same pattern appears when the traveler depicts nightfall in the mountains. He observes in apparent awe that "a dense fog, flowing out in waves from a cave, completely covered [the valley] and not one sound reached our ears from there." He subsequently adds that "stars were beginning to twinkle in the dark sky, and strange to say, they seemed to me to be much higher than at home." But then the traveler concludes his awed observations of his situation with the banal remark that he felt comforted at hearing, "amid the dead sleep of nature, the snorting of the three tired post horses and the irregular jangling of the Russian shaft bell" (4: 186; 5, 6). He might know how to describe the natural beauties surrounding him, yet he responds emotionally only to the sounds of domesticated animals and man-made artifacts, for these matter more to him than the wilds of nature do, despite his rhetorical tribute to them. Like Pechorin, the traveler has the Romantic vocabulary to describe nature, but his post-Romantic personality does not respond to his descriptions. Hence the glories, the majesty, the mysteries of nature inspire no lasting awe, prompt no profound introspection, and suggest no transcendent purpose to live for.[41]

A different version of this pattern of attraction to nature and yet detachment from it occurs when the traveler and Maksim Maksimich, who had been driving along with him, exchange words on a mountain summit during a storm. With his tendency to Romantic imagery, the traveler addresses the storm raging amid the mountains around them: "You too are an exile," he empathizes. "You mourn for your wide spacious steppes! There you had room to unfurl your cold wings, while here you are stifled and cramped like an eagle that shrieks as it beats against the bars of its iron cage." Proud of this poetic evocation of the storm, he then hears Maksim Maksimich's interpretation: "This is bad!" Maksim Maksimich cries. "Look, you can't see anything around us, only fog and snow; at any moment, we might expect to fall into a chasm or get stuck in the brushwood, and further down, the Baydara river has swollen so much, I gather, that it can't possibly be crossed"

(4: 205; 33, 34). As the traveler had done earlier, Maksim Maksimich has reduced a transcendent scene to immediate obstacles. And although the traveler had remarked that Maksim Maksimich, like all individuals with "simple hearts," enjoyed "a sense of the beauty and grandeur of nature that is a hundred times stronger and more vivid" than in "enthusiastic tellers of tales, oral or written," Maksim Maksimich does not show that here. He is worried and wants to go home. The post-Romantic spirit can admire nature from time to time, but it finds no restorative haven there.

The traveler provides an explicit instance of this post-Romantic pattern in comments he makes on the name of Chertova Valley, into which he descends the next day. "What a romantic name!" he exclaims. "You immediately envision the nest of an evil spirit among forbidding cliffs, but this is not how it was: the name of Chertova Valley comes from the word 'border' [черта] and not 'devil' [черт], because the boundary of Georgia was once here" (4: 204; 32). The traveler punctures a Romantic expectation with a prosaic, utterly un-Romantic explanation. He dispenses Romantic images of the spectacular and the supernatural, but, with post-Romantic predictability, he fails to sustain them—as though Lermontov was alerting attentive readers not to trust allusions to the Romanticism that they might find in the remainder of *A Hero of Our Time*.

Pechorin's relation to nature (as well as that of the traveler and Maksim Maksimich) thus strikingly illustrates the post-Romantic frame of mind, which contains numerous vestiges of Romantic images and ideas. But these are mere vestiges, no longer serving the genuine purposes that Romantic ideals once served. Lermontov could evoke nature beautifully, but he declined to make Pechorin—or any other character—feel at one with it. Consequently, nature gets a good deal of lip service in *A Hero of Our Time*, but it does not inspire. Pechorin acknowledges as much when he looks into that majestic nighttime sky and mourns the loss of a sense of purpose in life. Romantic images of nature alone cannot save Pechorin from post-Romantic anomie. And, with his dis-integrated personality, he cannot save himself. This is the psychological quandary of cultural *transitions out*.

SEVEN

Post-Romantic Anomie II

The "Post-" Scripts of A Hero of Our Time

UNREWARDED IDEALISM

Pechorin is a thoroughgoing post-Romantic personality suffering from cultural anomie. The six characters with whom he has significant encounters after he leaves Taman, three females—Bela, Princess Mary, and Vera—and three males—Maksim Maksimich, Dr. Werner, and Grushnitskii—exemplify some variations on this malaise of Pechorin's post-Romantic times. They do this by initially possessing quite genuine Romantic ideals, which give them more consistent identities than Pechorin has, but subsequently by discovering that these ideals do not avail, a discovery that leaves them bereft and dispirited. The ideals and virtues of these characters, which arguably elevate them above Pechorin emotionally and morally, do not suffice to sustain them in a culture that does not reinforce such ideals and virtues. Hence they all come to "post-Romantic ends"—disillusionment, frustration, dejection, or unromantic death—as though following invariant scripts that their post-Romantic times would write for them.[1] Although often dismissed as mere foils for Pechorin by critics, who highlight his superior intellect and manipulative facility (certainly each of these characters is flawed or enfeebled in some way, and it is tellingly Pechorin who serves as the focus of their ideals as well as a catalyst for their loss of those ideals), these six characters actually make a significant contribution to Lermontov's depiction of the times for which Pechorin was a hero.[2]

The three female characters with whom Pechorin has some relationship share the Romantic ideal of love as a transcendent union.[3] Although different in age, background, and life experience, Bela, Princess Mary, and Vera all place love at the center of their lives, as so many Romantic heroines had done before them. All three choose Pechorin as the object of their love, at least in part because he cultivates the image of a Romantic hero and thus becomes a screen onto which their imaginations can project a Romantic vision of love.[4] And all three have the will to sacrifice other sources of satisfaction in their lives in favor of this love. When Pechorin then fails to live up to his image, they are left in despair, their ideal destroyed. None holds out hope for a reunion with Pechorin either in this world or the next. To be sure, Pechorin plays the central role in the loss of their ideals—had he been the Romantic hero they imagined him to be, they might not have been so badly disillusioned.[5] Yet all three appear to experience disillusionment not only about Pechorin but about their existence in general—a variation on post-Romantic anomie. This broader disillusionment betrays a recognition not simply of the failure of an ideal of love in particular but of the fruitlessness of idealism overall. However, the despair accompanying their loss of idealism—as opposed to a "realistic" acceptance of this loss—conveys the value that these characters still place on ideals. They physically die or spiritually despair rather than resignedly adapt to a reality devoid of ideals—the reality of post-Romanticism.

In Bela, the daughter of a Circassian chieftain who is kidnapped and seduced by Pechorin, idealism is instinctive; her all-consuming love for Pechorin is a natural outgrowth of her spirit. Akin to Chateaubriand's eponymous character in *Atala* (1801), the adopted Christian daughter of a Muskogee Indian chief who falls in love with a non-Christian member of another tribe, Bela falls passionately in love with Pechorin despite his alien race and religion.[6] Bela confesses, according to Maksim Maksimich, that "ever since the day she first saw Pechorin, he often appeared to her in dreams, and that no man had ever made such an impression on her" (4: 201; 27). He fires her imagination as someone special, singular, powerful—a Romantic hero who proclaims his willingness to die if deprived of her love. Although initially resistant, she eventually becomes his lover and chief source of entertainment as well, singing and dancing to bring him pleasure—his happiness is her sole delight. When she is told that her father had died, she cries "for a couple of days" (4: 206; 35) and then forgets about the loss. Pechorin has become the center of her universe, and living with him is her ideal existence.

Consequently, as Pechorin gradually becomes bored with her, Bela grows "pale and so sad" (4: 207; 36), and, Maksim Maksimich observes, "she began to wilt noticeably; her little face became thinner, her big eyes lost their luster. You would ask her: 'What are you sighing about, Bela? Are you sad?' 'No.' 'Is there anything you'd like?' 'No.' 'Do you miss your family?' 'I have no family.' Sometimes for days on end, you could not get anything but 'yes' or 'no' out of her" (4: 209; 39). Bela virtually stops eating, she nearly stops speaking, and she withdraws from interactions with the outer world as her inner world collapses into a void.

Moreover, Bela has no other resources to draw upon. Although she retains the pride and will to declare, "If he doesn't love me, who prevents him from sending me home? I don't force him. But if things go on like this, I'll go away myself—I'm not his slave, I'm the daughter of a prince!" (4: 207; 36–37), she actually has nowhere to go, nothing to live for. She is too inexperienced to live in glorious solitude amid the mountains while cherishing the memory of a failed love, nor can she return to a loving family since, as Pechorin notes, she would likely be killed or sold as chattel for consorting with an infidel. Once she is certain that Pechorin does not love her, Bela pursues the only course left to her. She leaves the fort, ostensibly to feel the coolness of a nearby river on a hot day, despite Pechorin's warning that she risks being captured by her Chechen suitor Kazbich. She ventures forth nonetheless—the love she feels for Pechorin has metamorphosed into a despondent loss of the will to live. But whereas a Romantic heroine with a broken heart or a futile love might actively seek death, like Atala, who poisons herself, Bela merely wanders into harm's way, an image of anomie.

After the worst does indeed occur—Kazbich seizes and stabs her—Pechorin remains by her bedside as she lies dying, and Bela's love resurfaces as a concern for Pechorin's lack of sleep while he keeps the vigil.[7] And yet her feelings do not give her hope for a revival of their love together in the next world. Religion is one reason. By contrast to Atala, who on her deathbed beseeches her beloved Chactas to "learn the lessons of the Christian faith" because "it will prepare our reunion" (69), Bela neither attempts to convert Pechorin to Islam nor agrees to convert to Christianity herself. Despite the fact that, as Maksim Maksimich further reports, "she began to grieve that she was not a Christian, and that in the next world her soul would never meet Pechorin's soul, and that some other woman would be his sweetheart in heaven," Bela refuses Maksim Maksimich's offer to arrange for her baptism into Christianity before her death. She decides that "she would die in the same faith into which she had been born" (4: 213; 46). No deathbed conversion for Bela—while believing in heaven, she does not have a Romantic faith in spiritual reunification and reconciliation of loving souls. Bela is thus a Romantic lover who accedes to the post-Romantic impossibility of a transcendent love fulfilled either on earth or in heaven—her script promises no sequel.

Although different from Bela in many ways, Princess Mary Ligovskaia, the daughter of a wealthy Moscow nobleman, shares with Bela the Romantic ideal of having a lover to whom she can wholly surrender herself—and, like Bela, Mary finds that ideal shattered. Mary reacts with a similar loss of the will to live, but instead of wandering to her death like Bela, she sinks into a cold lifeless loathing of the man she had loved.

It is true that we see Mary's character and condition, her words and actions, only through the prism of Pechorin's mind, as recorded in his journal—unlike Bela, whom we observe through the sympathetic Maksim Maksimich. In his journal, Pechorin depicts Mary as a creature of society, a flirt callously accustomed to breaking the hearts of admirers, and a foolish young woman predictably drawn to the image of a Byronic hero.

Pechorin lays the groundwork for his treatment of Mary as a society belle in his initial description of her as "dressed according to the strict rules of the best taste" (4: 239; 86). She dresses this way, so he thinks, because she is vain and loves toying with men for her amusement. As he tells Grushnitskii: "The young princess, it seems, is one of those women who want to be amused: if she is bored in your presence for two minutes in a row, you are irretrievably lost. . . . Unless you gain some power over her, even her first kiss will not entitle you to a second; she will have had her fill of flirting with you" (4: 250; 101–2). Pechorin thereby justifies his heartless treatment of her as he sets out to elicit her love by cultivating a Byronic aura in her presence, first pretending utter indifference to her, then professing love, and finally rejecting her love once he has won it. Pechorin treats Mary rather the way he accuses her of treating men, although he is much more calculating and cruel.

However, at times Pechorin inadvertently reveals aspects of Mary's character and behavior that betoken a more noble spirit committed to an ideal of love, like that of Lucy Ashton in Walter Scott's *Bride of Lammermoor* (1819) or the title character of Germaine de Staël's *Delphine* (1802)—young women from socially established families with good educations—although he fails to acknowledge this spirit directly.[8] Pechorin unintentionally shows Mary diverging from his harsh portrait when he describes her at a ball: "Her pretty face bloomed," he observes, "she joked very charmingly, her conversation was witty without any pretension to wit, it was lively and free." And, he adds, "her observations were sometimes profound." Pechorin makes no further comment on these qualities, but he reports: "I gave her to understand, by means of a very involved sentence, that I had long been attracted to her," to which he says she responded, "You're a strange person!" (4: 260; 115). Mary's humor and charm, her perceptiveness and candor—qualities in her response that utterly pass him by—fail to alter Pechorin's general view of her as a stereotypically mindless creature of society.

In fact, as Dr. Werner suggests, Mary may be something of a social outsider, owing to her independence of mind and spirit. He informs Pechorin that Mary spent a winter in Petersburg and disliked the society there, possibly because she had been "given a cool reception" by it, since she preferred "discussing sentiments, passions, and so forth" (4: 247, 246; 97, 96), rather than society matters. Despite Pechorin's criticism, Mary appears to favor the honest discussion of genuine emotions over the performance of empty social rituals. But Pechorin cannot see that.

Thus Mary's belief in their shared social alienation, rather than the superficial gullibility that Pechorin attributes to her, may inspire her nascent compassion for Pechorin.[9] In any case, the compassion rapidly converts to love, just as Pechorin had predicted. But it is a love tinged with doubts and searching perceptions about this "strange person." After exclaiming, "Either you despise me, or you love me very much!" Mary astutely speculates, "Perhaps you want to laugh at me, to trouble my soul, and then to leave me." She here intuits almost exactly what Pechorin intends. And she goes on: "Perhaps you want me to be the first to say that I love you. Do you want that?" Pechorin does not reply, but only comments, "In the determination of her gaze and voice, there was something frightening" (4: 279–80; 144). Pechorin never specifies what he finds "frightening" about her "determination." But he is quite conceivably frightened by the very intensity of her feelings, the perceptiveness of her mind, the strength of her will, and the force of her honesty. Mary is more of a true Romantic than Pechorin had bargained for.

Mary's "determination" and strength lead her to further bold declarations—that neither the objections of her family nor Pechorin's lack of high social standing would prevent her from marrying him, since, she tells him, "I can sacrifice everything for the one I love" (4: 282; 148). But Pechorin, incapable of such sacrifice, denies any love for her and rejects the possibility of the union between them that she has dreamed of. He then describes in his journal her reaction to him during their final meeting: "Her large eyes . . . seemed to be seeking in mine something resembling hope" and "it seemed to me that tears glistened in them" (4: 304; 179). And as the irrevocable loss of her ideal love engulfs Mary's soul, even "something resembling hope" dies. "She turned to me as pale as marble," he states, "only her eyes glittered marvelously. 'I hate you,' she said" (4: 304; 180). These are Mary's final words. Facing a future deprived of her ideal love, she becomes as lifeless as a statue on the outside, cold with hatred.

And although we could view the cold hatred Mary now feels for Pechorin as a simple inversion of her love, her icy immobility more likely betrays the abandonment of her animating ideal altogether. Pechorin has conclusively demonstrated that her images of love and of him as her lover have been figments of her imagination—his feelings for her were no more real than those of "the hero of a novel" (4: 245–46; 95), just as Mary had at first regarded Pechorin, according to Dr. Werner. Now she sees that a loving union with the likes of Pechorin is no more possible in reality than a union with such a fictional hero could be—her "post-" script is in essence a non-script. In accordance with that script, her trust in love and in her own feelings and judgment undermined, Mary ends up frozen with disillusionment and hate. This hate indicates that Mary will not later kill herself, as Lucy Ashton does when forced to marry a man she does not love, or die of grief like Delphine because her beloved is already married. Mary will likely survive, but without love.[10] Hers is a post-Romantic fate of one who loved a hero for her times.

To Bela with her will-less de facto suicide and Mary with her disillusioned hatred Lermontov adds Vera, a third victim of Pechorin's wayward emotional life and post-Romantic culture. Vera is a former mistress whom Pechorin encounters anew in Piatigorsk and seduces into reviving their affair. She, too, loves Pechorin profoundly, even though she is well aware of his flaws and knows that loving him will cause her difficulty, married as she is to an older general. And like Bela and Mary, she follows a sad script to a sad end. Her end is not as dramatic as theirs, but it is just as symptomatic, when she gives up hope and unresistingly rides off with a hostile husband into an uncertain future of gradual physical decline—she is dying of consumption—leaving her Romantic ideal of love behind.

Pechorin recurrently permits Vera her own voice in his journal, quoting her directly more often than any other female characters, and reproducing her parting letter to him rather than paraphrasing her words. All her words of love show her to be a woman of intense feelings and boundless devotion. "You know that I am your slave," she declares, "I was never able to resist you. . . . You men don't understand the delights of a glance, of a handshake . . . when listening to your voice, I experience such deep, strange bliss that the most ardent kisses could not replace it." Even when she reveals that she is dying, she tells him, "in spite of that, I can't think about a future life, I only think about you" (4: 262; 119). And as she tells him in her final letter, "You can be sure that I'll never love anyone else; my soul has spent all its treasures, its tears and hopes, on you," concluding that "for you I have forsaken everything in the world" (4: 300; 173, 174). She has given herself to him entirely, exhausting the capacities of her soul through her devotion and sacrificing her reputation and her once comfortable marriage on the altar of her love for him.

In her abject submission to Pechorin, Vera noticeably resembles Ellenore in Constant's *Adolphe* (1816).[11] As Adolphe admits, Ellenore "had given up everything for me, her fortune, her children, her good name, and she asked for nothing in return but to wait for me like a humble slave, spend a few minutes with me each day, enjoy the moments I could spare her" (Constant, 78). A few minutes, a glance, a handshake—the most fleeting interaction brings joy to one who truly loves. At the same time, also like Ellenore, Vera knows that her beloved does not return her feelings due to his own emotional inadequacies. In her letter to Pechorin, Vera acknowledges that she "can't look at other men without a certain contempt," but "not because you are better than they—oh, no!" (4: 299; 173). For as she reminds Pechorin, "You've treated me as any other man would have done; you loved me as your property, as a source of joys, agitations, and sorrows that alternated with one another, without which life would have been boring and monotonous. I understood this from the beginning" (4: 299; 172–73). Vera thus concedes that she allowed herself to be objectified and exploited—but she has not been able to forsake her love for him.

Instead, she confesses, "I sacrificed myself, hoping that some day you would appreciate my sacrifice, that some day you would understand my deep tenderness regardless of the circumstances. Since then . . . I have penetrated all the secrets of your soul . . . and have become convinced that my hope was a vain one. This was bitter to me! But my love has conjoined with my soul; it has become darker, but it hasn't been extinguished" (4: 299; 173). Vera recognizes that their love affair would never be anything other than a self-indulgent, self-centered adventure to Pechorin, but that it had nonetheless entered into the very core of her being and could not be eradicated. This was true Romantic love, at least in its consuming power, if not its unworthy beloved. Vera could have told Pechorin what Ellenore tells Adolphe: "Love was my whole life but it could not be yours" (Constant, 115). For Vera, that love has become her sustenance, even though in becoming "darker," it has also cast a pall over her entire existence.

As Romantic as her love for Pechorin is, Vera comes to a post-Romantic end. When she concludes that there can be no future for her and Pechorin—even by forsaking her marriage—she passively allows her reproachful and unloved husband to lead her away into obscurity. In her farewell letter to Pechorin she laments, "I perish," and adds the pathetic plaint, "If I could be sure that you'll always remember me—I don't even say love me—no, only remember. . . . Goodbye" (4: 300; 174).[12] These words express a sad longing, not even for love any more, only for faint remembrance, differing dramatically from the parting words of Ellenore to Adolphe: "You will miss the heart that was yours, that lived on your affection and would have braved a thousand perils in your defense" (Constant, 122). Vera does not know that as she leaves, Pechorin suffers a bout of regret—to the point of riding his horse to death and then throwing himself on the ground and weeping. But, as she fears, he recovers quickly and dismisses this reaction as an aberration, returning home to bed, where he "slept the sleep of Napoleon after Waterloo" (4: 302; 176). Although Vera takes remnants of her Romantic love for Pechorin with her, like Bela and Mary she has given up on her ideal and her life, resigned to the variety of post-Romantic anomie to which her post-Romantic script has consigned her.

Like the subordinate female characters in *A Hero of Our Time*, the subordinate male characters—Maksim Maksimich, Dr. Werner, and Grushnitskii—also all embrace some ideal, whether explicitly or implicitly, and all of them follow their own post-Romantic scripts to post-Romantic ends, courtesy of Pechorin and his times. For Maksim Maksimich and Dr. Werner, that ideal is friendship. For Grushnitskii, it is both friendship and love. To Romanticists, of course, friendship was nearly as precious a commodity as love, and was even a form of Romantic love, since friendship represented to them not mere social acquaintance for the purpose of diversion or advantage, but a deep bond between kindred spirits and a source of high human fulfillment—think, for instance, of the devotion to Coleridge expressed by Wordsworth in *The Prelude* or the fictional bond of Julius to Antonio in Schlegel's *Lucinde*.[13] Both Maksim Maksimich and Dr. Werner try to establish a true friendship with Pechorin, and each believes that he succeeds. But Pechorin ultimately frustrates them both. As a result, although Lermontov suggests that Romantic friendship should be prized, he also suggests that the post-Romantic climate, with its exemplary "hero," does not serve deep and lasting friendship well. "What is friendship in our time?" he will have the disappointed and frustrated Maksim Maksimich ask, evoking the silent answer that friendship has gone the way of Romantic heroism and love.

Maksim Maksimich comes to question the nature and value of friendship for good reason.[14] His friendship for the much younger Pechorin shifts from companionship and tempered admiration to heartfelt attachment, only to culminate in baffled rejection. While narrating the story of Pechorin and Bela in the segment "Bela," Maksim Maksimich depicts his relationship with Pechorin largely in terms of comradeship—they attend parties together, hunt together, and nurse Bela through her final hours together. Although he describes Pechorin as "a fine fellow," and the type of individual "to whom it is assigned at birth to have various unusual things happen to them," Maksim Maksimich does not dwell on any feeling of special connection to Pechorin in "Bela," and he remarks at one point that the younger officer is "a little strange." But Maksim Maksimich is apparently intrigued by Pechorin's puzzling character from the outset, telling the traveler, "If a shutter banged, he'd start and grow pale, but I saw him tackle a wild boar all by himself," and "there were times when you couldn't get a word out of him for hours, but at other times he would start telling stories and you'd split your sides laughing" (4: 189; 10–11). Maksim Maksimich considers Pechorin fascinating in his impulsiveness and unpredictability. Therefore, although Maksim Maksimich reproaches Pechorin for kidnapping Bela, he goes along, explaining to the traveler, "What would you want me to do? There are some people with whom you simply have to agree" (4: 199; 24). To Maksim Maksimich, Pechorin comes to possess an irresistible personal magnetism or charisma that eclipses Pechorin's failings and sways Maksim Maksimich against his own moral convictions.

This view of Pechorin evidently sparks in Maksim Maksimich a desire for genuine friendship. And he believes that he achieves it, as we learn in the chapter "Maksim Maksimich." There, several years after the events of "Bela," Maksim Maksimich reencounters the anonymous traveler in the Caucasian town of Vladikavkaz. The traveler reports that Maksim Maksimich represents his relationship to Pechorin not only as that of "close acquaintances" [приятели] but of "bosom friends" [друзья закадычные] who "had lived together." And when Maksim Maksimich learns that Pechorin has also arrived in town, he becomes excited at the prospect of seeing this "bosom friend" after years of separate adventures, assuming that Pechorin will feel the same: "He'll come running right away!" Maksim Maksimich assures the traveler (4: 218; 53).

When Pechorin does not come running, the traveler notes, "It was clear that the old man was hurt by Pechorin's neglect, the more so as he had been telling me recently about their friendship, and only an hour before, had been sure that [Pechorin] would come running the moment he heard [Maksim Maksimich's] name" (4: 219; 54). But Maksim Maksimich is still enough of a friend to forgive that neglect. And so he himself runs to see Pechorin the following day, "as fast as he could," the traveler notes, until "he could hardly breathe; sweat was trickling down his face; wet clumps of gray hair, escaping from under his cap, had glued themselves to his forehead; his knees were shaking." Then, as "he was about to fall on Pechorin's neck" in an expression of affection, the traveler continues, Pechorin "rather coolly, although with a friendly smile, stretched out his hand"—greeting Maksim Maksimich with a formal gesture of detachment rather than a warm embrace of friendship. Taken aback, Maksim Maksimich becomes unsure of his true relation to Pechorin and switches from the familiar form of "you" [ты] to the formal form of "you" [вы], stammering in response to Pechorin's formal, "Well, how are you?" [Ну, как вы поживаете?]: "And . . . you [ты] . . . and you [вы]?" (4: 221; 58). The first ellipsis signals both an uncertainty about the best way to address Pechorin—as an intimate or a formal acquaintance—and a desire to *be* intimate. The second ellipsis and what follows betray Maksim Maksimich's regretful conclusion: since Pechorin has not greeted him as an intimate, they cannot, by definition, be intimate after all.

But Maksim Maksimich still harbors affection for Pechorin and is disappointed to hear that Pechorin is departing immediately for Persia. "Not right now?" Maksim Maksimich exclaims in disbelief. He then begs Pechorin to stay for a while so that they can trade news about the course of their lives over the past four years, and he reaffirms his devotion to Pechorin as "my dearest man," inviting him to "a splendid dinner" that he will cook in Pechorin's honor. This effusive appeal has no effect, however, as Pechorin merely thanks Maksim Maksimich for not "having forgotten" him and shakes hands in farewell. Responding that he has not forgotten anything, Maksim Maksimich then becomes "somehow constrained" and "cold" (4: 223; 61), according to the traveler, as though the memories of what he took to be friendship with Pechorin have become illusions and will now be solely a source of sorrow and pain, since Pechorin seems never to have partaken of that friendship.

Once Pechorin has gone, Maksim Maksimich grows reflective and a bit melancholy about what has happened. "Of course, we used to be friends," he sighs, "but what is friendship in our time?" Clearly it is not what it used to be in the Romantic era, when friendship was a powerful bond of affinity. At least not for Pechorin. And Maksim Maksimich knows it, to his sorrow. "A tear of vexation still sparkled on his eyelashes from time to time" as he thinks of this disappointment, the traveler observes. Maksim Maksimich also bitterly predicts that Pechorin will come to "a bad end," because "there's no good in someone who forgets his old friends!" (4: 222–23; 60). Maksim Maksimich wants to believe in the value of friendship even "in our time," but, the traveler sympathizes, he is forced to abandon "his fondest hopes and dreams" of a friendship with Pechorin, who seems indifferent to it, as a hero of that time. Maksim Maksimich is too old, the traveler finds, to "replace his old delusions with new ones." So he will live with his sorrows—that is his "post-" script. "Involuntarily," the traveler concludes, "the heart atrophies and the soul closes itself off." The traveler then winds up this segment as if pronouncing an epitaph for the emotional victims of post-Romanticism by observing simply, "I drove away alone" (4: 224; 60), just as Pechorin has done, and just as Maksim Maksimich will eventually do as well while mourning the loss of his ideal. Solitude, estrangement, emptiness—these are symptoms of a post-Romantic world that, among other things, has lost the value of Romantic friendship.

A similar consequence results from the friendship between Dr. Werner and Pechorin, although this friendship was much closer and its apparent end—all recorded by Pechorin in the "Princess Mary" segment of his journal—more ambiguous. Werner is clearly devoted to Pechorin, warning him of plots against him, serving as Pechorin's second at the duel with Grushnitskii, and helping to hush up its aftermath. And Pechorin voices seemingly genuine admiration for Werner, stressing their strong affinities as if finding a source of identification and ego gratification in their relationship. Nonetheless, Pechorin turns against Werner after perceiving that Werner faults him for the cold-blooded killing of Grushnitskii. Although in the end, according to Pechorin, Werner expects their friendship to continue, Pechorin will not have it, turning out to be no true friend to Werner. He was only using their companionship for his own egoistic purposes.

Pechorin at first describes Werner in generally appreciative terms. Pechorin says that Werner is "a poet in all his actions, and frequently in his utterances, although he has never written two lines of verse in his whole life." With admiration Pechorin reports that "ordinarily, Werner made unobtrusive fun of his patients, but I once saw him cry over a dying soldier." And he detects in Werner's "irregular features the imprint of a dependable and lofty soul" (4: 242–43; 91). Pechorin further describes Werner as resembling Byron in having one leg shorter than the other and a skull shape indicating a "strange interplay of contradictory inclinations," along with "small black eyes" that "tried to penetrate your thoughts." Pechorin also notes that some younger men had nicknamed Werner Mephistopheles, which "flattered his vanity" (4: 243; 92). A poetic nature, a "dependable and lofty" soul, a resemblance to Byron, penetrating vision, an aura of evil—the qualities that Pechorin sees in Werner match those Pechorin sees in himself.[15]

No wonder Pechorin stresses several times that he and Werner are kindred spirits. As he tells Werner one evening,

> We know almost all of one another's secret thoughts; one word is a whole story for us; we see the kernel of our every emotion through a triple shell. Something sad seems funny to us, something funny seems grim, and we are generally, if the truth be told, rather indifferent to everything except our own selves. Therefore between us there can be no exchange of feelings and thoughts: we know everything about one another that we want to know, and we don't want to know anything more. (4: 244; 93)

And when Werner demonstrates that he does in fact know what Pechorin was thinking at that moment, Pechorin exclaims, "Doctor! It is definitely impossible for us to converse; we read each other's souls" (4: 245; 94). Pechorin's identification with Werner clearly gives Pechorin much pleasure, and possibly serves to justify Pechorin's own peccadilloes, since he can share them with the doctor.

For his part, Werner apparently values Pechorin's friendship. He repeatedly seeks Pechorin's company and conversation, and he tries to protect Pechorin from harm. Thus, for instance, Werner cautions Pechorin, "as a close acquaintance" [как приятель] (4: 276; 138), not to get trapped into an official engagement with Mary. Subsequently, when Pechorin asks him to serve as a second during the duel with Grushnitskii, Werner instantly agrees. Later he warns Pechorin of his antagonists' plot to give him an unloaded gun, then urges him to expose this plot and call off the duel. Pechorin nevertheless insists on proceeding with the duel as planned, and as it turns out, that duel brings their friendship to an end.

Werner appears in the morning to escort Pechorin as his second with a face that was "completely unwarlike," Pechorin remarks, and looking "so sad" that Pechorin chides him for displaying uncharacteristic sentimentality, pointing out that Werner had "seen people off to the next world with the greatest indifference a hundred times before." Although Pechorin says that Werner "cheered up" somewhat in response to Pechorin's flippant sang-froid, Werner has come to the duel with the devotion and concern of a committed friend, and he wants to dissuade Pechorin from proceeding in a rigged contest (4: 291; 161). "What's the reason for this?" Werner asks. "They'll shoot you down like a bird" (4: 294; 164). Finally Werner decides to act. "If you don't say anything," he tells Pechorin, "then I myself . . . " (4: 296; 168). But he relents when Pechorin reminds him of his promise not to interfere and insists on continuing. Even after Grushnitskii only superficially grazes Pechorin's leg with a bullet, Werner turns "paler than Grushnitskii" in fear for his friend's safety (4: 297; 170).

But then comes the turning point. When Pechorin calmly shoots Grushnitskii and watches him fall off the cliff on which the duel had been fought, Werner is appalled. While Pechorin merely exclaims, "*Finita la commedia!*" as though Grushnitskii's death were the final stunt in a theatrical performance, Werner "turned away in horror." However unfair Grushnitskii's original plot against Pechorin might have been, Werner is horrified by Pechorin's callous act—this was not a duel, it was murder. Although Pechorin reports that when he himself catches sight of Grushnitskii's bloody body, "involuntarily, I shut my eyes" (4: 298; 171), this is not likely from true regret or remorse, but from unease at the untheatrical reality. He does not have Werner's conscience.

In the ensuing days, Werner nonetheless continues to serve Pechorin's interests as a friend, reassuring Pechorin that he will not be held responsible for Grushnitskii's death, and coming to warn Pechorin when rumors start circulating about the duel. But Werner also betrays a new ambivalence toward Pechorin. He first intimates this in a note to Pechorin with the subtle dig: "You should sleep peacefully . . . *if you can*" (4: 299; 172; emphasis Lermontov's). And then, in what would prove to be his last visit with Pechorin—because Pechorin will be transferred to another military post for participating in the duel—"contrary to custom," Pechorin observes, Werner does not shake Pechorin's hand. We do not learn the particulars, but Pechorin takes this as an unforgivable affront. And he gets swift revenge. As Werner prepares to leave, Pechorin later recalls, "on the threshold he stopped. He would have liked to shake my hand, and had I displayed to him the slightest desire for it, he would have thrown his arms around my neck; but I remained as cold as stone—and he left" (4: 302; 177). We have only Pechorin's word for what Werner was feeling, but we know how Pechorin wants to feel—triumphant. Friendship be damned. He now even scorns Werner for being insufficiently devoted to him and claims he was "the one who had the courage to take upon himself the entire burden of responsibility" for the outcome of the duel—a blatant misrepresentation of the facts (4: 302; 177).

In the end, Pechorin lets his friendship with Werner die because Pechorin is too self-centered to sustain it. From his side, it was not a true friendship, only a mirror of his self-image, where there was no place for the demands of friendship. We might also surmise that Werner goes off disillusioned with his former friend, who wanted loyalty but could not tolerate implicit criticism. Perhaps Werner still thought some friendship between himself and Pechorin could continue. But Werner's departure in silence—the conclusion to *his* "post-" script—yearning for a gesture from Pechorin, while Pechorin stands "as cold as stone," is another instance of how Pechorin treats the individuals he encounters. "I am not capable of true friendship," he had noted in his journal (4: 302; 92). Quite so. Pechorin is a hero for a time when friendships die.

There is one other subordinate character in the novel who also comes to an unhappy end because Romantic ideals do not survive around Pechorin in a post-Romantic climate: Grushnitskii. Pechorin never really likes Grushnitskii, whom Pechorin denounces as a hypocritical, self-dramatizing, self-important Romantic epigone. Grushnitskii is, Pechorin asserts, "one of those people who, for every occasion in life, have ready-made pompous phrases, whom unadorned beauty does not move, and who solemnly drape themselves in extraordinary emotions, exalted passions, and exceptional sufferings. . . . So often has he tried to convince others that he is a being not made for this world and is doomed to some sort of secret sufferings that he has almost convinced himself of it" (4: 238; 84–85). In essence, Pechorin portrays Grushnitskii as a mannerist version of a Romanticist who self-consciously projects the aura of a transcendent spirit purely as a means of ego gratification. His goal in life, Pechorin sneers, "is to become the hero of a novel." And he sums up his judgment of Grushnitskii by calling him a product of "Romantic fanaticism" (4: 238; 85). Critics have tended more or less to agree with Pechorin's view of Grushnitskii, although many also find in him something of an imitation of Pechorin himself.[16] But there is more to Grushnitskii than that.

For all of his faults, Grushnitskii does have some virtues—and yet these lead directly to his death. For one, he seems to feel genuine love for Princess Mary, idealized though it may be. For another, he appears to have a sincere appreciation for what he believes to be Pechorin's friendship, wrong though he is, and notwithstanding Pechorin's claim that "he dislikes me, although outwardly we are on the friendliest of terms" (4: 238; 85). And for yet another, he manifests an integrity at the duel that reflects a fundamental nobility of spirit, although this nobility virtually ensures his death. So Pechorin's derogatory depiction of Grushnitskii is not altogether fair, reflecting Pechorin's dislike of *him*, and possibly Pechorin's subconscious recognition of qualities in Grushnitskii that Pechorin dislikes in himself.

Grushnitskii attaches his Romantic ideal of love to Mary immediately after she takes pity on him for his wounded leg and picks up a glass that he has dropped. She is "simply an angel," he promptly affirms to Pechorin, and asks him, as a witness to her kindness, "You didn't feel at all touched looking at her at the moment when her soul shone in her face?" (4: 241, 242; 89). Shortly thereafter, Grushnitskii confesses to Pechorin that he loves Mary "madly" (4: 261; 117), avowing to her that "whoever has seen you will carry your divine image within him forever" (4: 272; 133). Thus, when Pechorin suggests that Mary is merely toying with him, Grushnitskii responds sharply, "I pity you, Pechorin!" (4: 267; 126). Grushnitskii idealizes both his beloved and love itself as enrapturing, divine, and pure. At the same time, his pity for Pechorin's cynicism bespeaks more genuine insight than Grushnitskii is generally given credit for.

Grushnitskii likewise apparently idealizes the friendship he believes he shares with Pechorin. He greets Pechorin as though they were "old close acquaintances" [старые приятели], and joyously embraces Pechorin after

being promoted to the rank of officer (4: 239; 85). He also confides to Pechorin his hopes and dreams of a future with Mary, and he thanks Pechorin for
defending Mary from the advances of a drunken soldier at a ball as though
Pechorin had intervened for friendship's sake. But Grushnitskii is deceiving
himself. Pechorin is no friend: he has been manipulating the younger man
in his plot to hurt Mary. And when Grushnitskii realizes that Mary is no
longer interested in him because she has become enamored of Pechorin, he
loses his ideals of love and friendship at once—and subsequently, he loses
his life.

Deeply hurt and angry, Grushnitskii decides to embarrass Pechorin in a
trumped-up duel using unloaded pistols. However, at the start of this duel,
Grushnitskii allows only his gun to be loaded, as Pechorin is aware. When
Pechorin threatens to kill him if he does not kill Pechorin with the first
shot, Grushnitskii "blushed," Pechorin notes, interpreting that to mean
"he was ashamed to kill an unarmed man" (4: 296; 167). Pechorin then
reports that, moments later, lowering the pistol aimed at Pechorin's forehead, Grushnitskii "turned toward his second. 'I can't,' he said in a hollow
voice." The unfairness, the baseness, the cruelty of killing an unarmed man
take hold of Grushnitskii—his elemental morality rises to overshadow his
poseur's persona and his rage at Pechorin.

Still, when his second responds by hurling the reproach, "Coward!" at
Grushnitskii, he does fire, grazing Pechorin's knee (4: 296; 168). Then it
is Pechorin's turn to fire and, knowing of the plot, Pechorin tells Werner
to "reload" his pistol because it was not loaded "properly" at the outset.
Grushnitskii's second immediately protests, but Grushnitskii insists, "You
yourself know very well that they're right" (4: 297, 298; 170). Conceding the
legitimacy of Pechorin's request, Grushnitskii displays both genuine honesty and bravery. Even when Pechorin offers Grushnitskii one final opportunity to recant, appealing to Grushnitskii's illusion that "we were friends
once," Grushnitskii does not yield. Disillusioned in love and friendship,
Grushnitskii is willing, with courageous despair, to let Pechorin take his
life. "Shoot!" Grushnitskii cries. "I despise myself and I hate you." And he
threatens to kill Pechorin later if Pechorin does not kill him, because "there
isn't room for both of us in this world" (4: 298; 171). Pechorin proceeds to
shoot Grushnitskii, who falls from the cliff to his death.

Golstein interprets Grushnitskii's final remark and Pechorin's shot to
mean there is no room for Grushnitskii, the posturing, pseudo-Romantic,
pale imitation of Pechorin, in Lermontov's fictional universe.[17] But in light

of the honesty and insight Grushnitskii displays in the last scene of his life, unflinchingly facing death amid his crushing disillusionment, Lermontov may be indicating that there is no appropriate place in a post-Romantic world for someone with Romantic ideals, whether exaggerated or not. Grushnitskii's post-Romantic script must remove him from the scene. Like Werner, Maksim Maksimich, Vera, Mary, and Bela, Grushnitskii has suffered because those ideals do not hold in a time for which Pechorin is the hero. And such a hero is no better off than the individuals he injures or destroys. Indeed, he may even be worse off. For they all had something to believe in at least at one time, whereas Pechorin has never had a genuine belief in anyone or anything. He may boast, "I am not capable of true friendship," because "one of the two friends is always the slave of the other" (4: 243; 92), and he may declare, "I have never become the slave of the woman I loved; on the contrary, I have always gained unconquerable power over their will and heart" (4: 252; 105). But this leaves Pechorin with nothing but a vaunted image of himself that he has to keep trying to confirm over and over, to the detriment of everyone he has some relationship with, until finally post-Romantic anomie engulfs them, along with this hero of his time and his world.

This brings us to the end, or rather, to the endings of *A Hero of Our Time*. And these endings give the novel the fitting post-Romantic finale to which it leads.

THE INCONCLUSIVE CONCLUSIONS OF
A HERO OF OUR TIME

The structural fragmentation and psychological and moral symptoms of cultural anomie in *A Hero of Our Time* strikingly shape the novel's conclusion, or conclusions, since Lermontov gives each chapter—the five narrative chapters and two nonnarrative sections—its own distinctive, not to say peculiar, ending. They tend to trail off inconclusively with last lines that bring no clear or even implicit closure, and they do not firmly tie the sections of the novel together. They rather leave us wondering, even puzzled. In these last lines, questions go unanswered; images hang suspended; uncertainties remain unresolved. As a result, these inconclusive conclusions confirm the chapters of Lermontov's novel not as Romantic fragments that can be completed and unified by an exercise of Romantic imagination, but rather as post-Romantic fragments that no act of imagination could confidently complete or unite. They therefore underscore the absence in *A Hero of Our Time* of a coherent vision of life and a set of defining ideals and norms, an absence that typifies a transition out of a historical period. These lines constitute another type of "post-" script—they are lines conveying the denouements that encapsulate a post-period's sense of anomie.

The first narrative chapter of the novel, "Bela," comes to a modestly inconclusive end with these words, addressed to the reader by the traveler:

> At Kobi, Maksim Maksimich and I parted ways; I continued with the post horses, whereas he, because of his heavy load, couldn't follow me. We didn't expect to meet ever again, and yet we did meet, and if you like, I'll tell you about it; it's quite a story. . . . Do you admit, however, that Maksim Maksimich is someone worthy of respect? If you admit that, I'll be fully rewarded for my perhaps overly long story. (4: 215; 49; ellipsis Lermontov's)

Cast in interrogative and conditional rather than declarative sentences, these last lines dangle. By rhetorically asking readers whether they consider Maksim Maksimich "someone worthy of respect," rather than asserting that he *is* worthy, the traveler introduces some odd uncertainties. In the first place, why should Maksim Maksimich's character become an issue at all, since his story—the bulk of the chapter—has not focused on him, but on Pechorin and Bela? In the second place, although we are led to believe that the traveler himself respects Maksim Maksimich, the traveler puts Maksim Maksimich's character and the import of his story in some doubt by raising the question—should we "respect" and trust Maksim Maksimich or not? In the third place, by in effect employing an "if-then" construction—"*if* you admit" Maksim Maksimich is "worthy of respect," *then* "I'll be fully rewarded"—the traveler adds further uncertainty about his purpose in repeating Maksim Maksimich's story at all. Was his purpose simply to win respect for Maksim Maksimich? And if so, why? Because Maksim Maksimich is a good storyteller? Or was the traveler's purpose to gain satisfaction for himself as a good scribe and secondhand storyteller? Yet by suggesting that his presentation of Maksim Maksimich's story was "perhaps overly long," the traveler interjects an element of doubt about his own storytelling competence. Nonetheless, the traveler promises the reader that "if you like," he will tell "quite a story" about a later encounter with Maksim Maksimich. This phrasing betrays that he is not sure that the reader would like that at all. And in fact, the story about this encounter that he goes on to tell in the next chapter, "Maksim Maksimich," turns out to be brief and anticlimactic, leaving his promise unfulfilled.

Hence the final lines of "Bela" serve not to draw its narrative to a close, or even to link it well to the narrative that follows, but rather to raise questions without answers and to elicit expectations that will not be satisfied. Indeed, the chatty and familiar tone of these lines may draw readers in, but what they are subtly drawn toward are uncertainties about the purpose, the meaning, and the value of the characters portrayed and the narratives that portray them throughout *A Hero of Our Time*. And these uncertainties will linger.

In the next narrative chapter, "Maksim Maksimich," the traveler reports firsthand an encounter between himself, Maksim Maksimich, and Pechorin, but it is an encounter that amounts to almost nothing. After Pechorin has tersely rebuffed Maksim Maksimich's warm reception and ridden off in his carriage, the traveler remarks: "It's sad to see a youth lose his fondest hopes and dreams, when the rose-colored veil through which he had regarded human actions and emotions is pulled aside in front of him, although there is hope that he will replace his old delusions with new ones that are no less transitory but no less sweet. . . . But what can they be replaced with at Maksim Maksimich's age? The heart involuntarily atrophies and the soul closes itself off . . . " The last paragraph then consists of the single line, "I drove away alone" (4: 224; 62; ellipses Lermontov's).

Beginning with an image of lost "hopes and dreams" as "delusions" that might be replaced in youth by new delusions, which will be just as "transitory," the traveler does not see even this prospect for an older man like Maksim Maksimich, who has lost his delusion of a friendship with Pechorin. Losses like these lead the traveler to reflect on the inevitability of disappointments so great that the "heart atrophies" and the soul "closes itself off." He lets his thought trail off into an ellipsis, and then he departs alone. Hopelessness, lost ideals, atrophy, the soul closing itself off, lonely isolation—these create an exemplary scene from a perfect "post-" script of disintegration and anomie. Everything falls apart or trails off in the traveler's description of human existence, articulated with regret. The traveler's conclusion does not provide the closure that comes with a definitive assertion of beliefs or a definite destination for his travels. We do not know where he is going or why he is going there. And we should not expect to find out.

"Taman" ends with a similar scene, or "post-" script, of disintegration and anomie. But here Pechorin makes a boast of it. After reporting on his misadventure and disillusionment at the hands of the smugglers, Pechorin winds up: "Thank God, in the morning the opportunity to move on presented itself, and I left Taman. What happened to the old woman and the poor blind boy—I don't know. And anyway, what do human joys and sufferings matter to me, me, a traveling military officer, and moreover, one with a road-pass for official obligations! . . . " (4: 235; 80; ellipsis Lermontov's). Defiantly, Pechorin proclaims his indifference to "human joys" in general, going off with his official pass, attached to no military base, but rather in transit—and, like the traveler, with no specified destination.

Although obviously intending to assert his own importance and superiority in relation to other human beings, Pechorin sounds more like he is rationalizing his indifference, disillusionment, and isolation. He has detached himself from those whose lives he upended, physically and emotionally, but to do so he must cloak himself in the impersonal—indeed, depersonalized—guise of a soldier. He expects this detachment to help him overcome the lack of a strong, autonomous identity that he has discovered in Taman. But the ellipsis following his final exclamation—revealingly phrased, however, as a rhetorical question—implies that Pechorin's underlying self-doubt and uncertainty about his identity, along with the appropriate emotions to accompany it, will prevent this expectation from being fulfilled. And that ellipsis causes the chapter to fade out rather than to close with emphasis, signaling that Pechorin has nothing affirmative to emphasize. He has only determined what does *not* matter to him; he does not know what does. Another inconclusive conclusion.

"Princess Mary," meanwhile, ends with the image of an isolated Pechorin, also in his own words. But here Pechorin soars off in a poetic reverie:

And now here, in this boring fort, reviewing the past in my mind, I often ask myself why I didn't want to follow the path opened up to me by fate, where quiet joys and spiritual peace awaited me. . . . No! I would not have reconciled myself to that lot in life! I'm like a sailor who was born and bred on the deck of a pirate ship. His spirit has grown accustomed to storms and battles, and if cast onto the shore, he is bored and he languishes, however the shady groves beckon to him, however the tranquil sun shines on him. He walks alone all day on the sand of the shore, as he listens to the monotonous splashing of the incoming waves and peers into the mist-shrouded distance. Won't the desired sail gleam out there on the pale horizon line separating the dark blue depths from the small gray clouds, appearing at first like the wing of a sea gull, but gradually separating itself from the foam of the breakers and in a smooth glide approaching the deserted pier . . . (4: 305; 181; ellipses Lermontov's)

These last lines artfully capture Pechorin's anomic and fragmentary perception of his own mature experience. At the outset, Pechorin explicitly presents himself once more as a Romantic hero, along the lines of Tieck's Christian or of Byron's Corsair, a unique soul not meant for a conventional, uneventful mere existence but born to carve out a life of adventure on his own. And yet uncertainties run through his words down to this final ellipsis. He "often" asks himself why he did not want a more conventional life, as though he is not sure of his own decisions. And even when he insists with an emphatic "No! I would not have become reconciled to such a lot in life!" he uses a reflexive verb—ужился, "become reconciled"—as if sensing that he would have reacted more passively than actively to such a fate.

Pechorin then invokes an extended simile comparing himself to a sailor unsatisfied with a life on shore. But he distances himself from this image by using not first-person but third-person singular pronouns and possessive adjectives: "his spirit has grown accustomed," "he is bored," "he languishes," "the shady groves beckon to him," "the sun shines on him," "he walks alone," "he listens" to the splashing waves, and he "peers into the distance." Although identifying himself with this figure, Pechorin appears to be lapsing into another one of his performances, elaborately describing a role in which he wants to cast himself, until he seems to get lost in his own vision and drifts off into ellipses. Once again he is writing his own script.

But this is another "post-" script. For once again the last lines culminate in an ellipsis, here showing that Pechorin cannot bring this scene to a close. He can imagine the sail approaching the shore, but he cannot imagine its *arrival*. And in Pechorin's mind the pier it approaches is deserted—neither he nor his sailor will be waiting. The sail as a symbol of the Romantic, unconstrained life is not welcomed and sent forth anew in Pechorin's mind. Its promise goes unfulfilled. The ellipsis at the end of these final lines consequently betokens a failed imagination, thwarted yearnings, and uncertain prospects. This is a post-Romantic ellipsis, like the many others that mark Lermontov's works.

The ending of "The Fatalist," which also concludes *A Hero of Our Time* as Lermontov has structured his complex narrative, reveals that Pechorin's uncertainties extend beyond himself to color his perception of his times. And the last lines themselves are very peculiar indeed. They arise in the aftermath of events that occurred when Pechorin was still treating Maksim Maksimich as a friend, events that revolve around the issue of whether or not fate exists. As noted in Chapter 6, toward the end of "The Fatalist," Pechorin expresses envy of ancient peoples for their belief in fate as executed by a pantheon of gods who were thought to guide human actions and destinies. "What strength of will [the ancients] derived from the certainty that the entire sky with its countless inhabitants was looking down on them with mute but unwavering sympathy!" he exclaims. He then opposes that "certainty" to the condition of his times, inhabited by the ancients' "miserable descendants" who lack "convictions or pride" and "are no longer capable of great sacrifice, neither for the good of mankind" nor for their own happiness. These descendents merely "pass indifferently from doubt to doubt," without any hope, or even "that indefinite, albeit sincere rapture that the soul encounters in any struggle with men or with fate" (4: 309–10; 187–88).

Here Pechorin voices the lament of someone who longs for comforting beliefs, even delusions, that would lend order and purpose to life. It is a lament of disillusioned belatedness—a quintessentially post-period lament. Pechorin wants to believe in fate as a source of order and purpose, but he cannot quite do so, and so he vacillates. He has a premonition that a fellow army officer, Vulich, is destined to die one particular day, but when Vulich openly defies fate by playing Russian roulette and survives, Pechorin muses, "I really don't know whether I believe in predestination now or not" (4: 310; 189). Then after Vulich ends up being murdered by a drunken Cossack later that night, Pechorin wonders, "After all this, how could one seemingly fail to become a fatalist?" And yet, he adds, "But how can anyone know for certain whether he is convinced of anything or not? . . . And how often we accept as conviction what is the deception of our senses or an error in judgment! . . . " (4: 313; 193). These words and the ellipses that separate and follow them reflect Pechorin's post-Romantic, wavering, inconclusive thoughts on the very nature of human experience.

But later, as he is wont to do, Pechorin reverses himself and sets out to test his own fate by attempting to subdue the Cossack who killed Vulich, and when he succeeds unscathed, he takes that as evidence against fate. At this point he declares, "I love to doubt everything. This disposition of mind does not undermine the resoluteness of my character. On the contrary, as far as I am concerned, I always proceed more bravely when I don't know what awaits me. For nothing worse than death can happen—and you can't avoid death!" (4: 313; 193–94). Now Pechorin commends doubts and uncertainties as invitingly challenging and inspiring, responding with a Romanticist's eagerness to engage the unknown. Had the novel ended there, these words would have stood as a willful assertion of Pechorin's autonomy amid his post-Romantic times.

But the novel does not end there. Instead, Pechorin reports that he quickly turned to Maksim Maksimich and asked his opinion about fate. Maksim Maksimich responds by observing that fate probably had nothing to do with Vulich surviving the game of Russian roulette, because "these Asiatic triggers often fail to fire if they are poorly oiled or if you don't pull hard enough with your finger." Then, upon further reflection, he decides that perhaps fate *does* govern lives, and that Vulich had died after all because "evidently this is what was already inscribed for him at birth." Pechorin follows this remark with the last words in his journal, bringing an end to the novel: "I couldn't get anything more out of him; he generally doesn't like metaphysical debates" (4: 313, 314; 194).

These last words, which Golstein sums up as a "brilliant statement of ambiguity" (125), are an epitome of inconclusiveness. They draw no conclusions about anything: not about the existence of fate in general; not about personal fate in particular; not about the conception of fate played out in the repeated references to it throughout the novel; not even about Pechorin himself and his view of the world or the future. Nor does this last line appear to shed any light on the import of the book and its title. The last words do not even take Pechorin as their subject, focusing instead on a subordinate character and his disinclination to talk about subjects such as those this entire chapter has revolved around. Pechorin's last words come as an aside. They are about as anticlimactic and forgettable as last words could possibly be.

And yet it is their very anticlimactic inconclusiveness that makes these last words an appropriate ending for the novel. For these words capture Pechorin's ultimate vacuity, revealing how devoid Pechorin is of fundamental beliefs, defining values, and an autonomous identity. Lacking such beliefs, values, and identity, Pechorin can have no conclusive, concluding statement of his own to make; he has nothing more to say for himself. Accordingly, his narrative ends when he "can't get anything more" out of Maksim Maksimich, his devoted older comrade, whom he will later spurn for no clear reason. The discussion of fate, Pechorin's journal, and the novel itself all end, or rather fall off, here with a final fragment. The rest is silence, as Hamlet said in his memorable last words. But unlike Hamlet's silence, signifying the decisive end that his death brings, Pechorin's silence reflects a mere absence of continuity, and the aimlessness of Pechorin's anomie.

One additional set of last lines in *A Hero of Our Time* conveys the fragmentary, anomic nature both of Pechorin's character and of the novel portraying that character. These lines come at the end of one of the novel's two nonnarrative sections—the traveler's "Introduction to Pechorin's Journal" (I address the other section and its ending in Chapter 8). In his "Introduction to Pechorin's Journal," the traveler explains that he is publishing portions of this journal to disclose "the history of a human soul" for the edification of readers. Then he concludes with the words: "Perhaps some readers will want to know my opinion of Pechorin's character? My answer is the title of this book. 'But this is evil irony!' they will say. I don't know" (4: 225; 68).

Chronologically, these are the last words in the events of *A Hero of Our Time*, since they follow everything recorded in Pechorin's journal and the two chapters leading up to the time when Maksim Maksimich hands over the journal, which Pechorin has dismissively left with him, for the traveler to dispose of as he wishes. And these are very curious last words on several counts. First, the traveler here surprisingly indicates that the title he has in mind is not *Pechorin's Journal* but *A Hero of Our Time* itself. And that means he is referring to the whole book we are reading, which comprises not only Pechorin's journal but the previous two chapters—a reference only compounding the formal complexity and shifting perspectives that make the novel so disrupted. What is more, the traveler tells us that his title signals his "opinion of Pechorin's character," and that this might appear as "evil irony," but that he does not know for certain. Not only is this strangely inconclusive, but it tantalizingly puts the whole import of the novel in question—is it all "evil irony"?[18]

Andrew Barratt and A. D. P. Briggs, who translate "evil irony" [злая ирония] as "wicked irony" and take the phrase as the title of their study of Lermontov's novel as a whole, concede that Lermontov "offers little to suggest precisely where the irony resides or how it is to be discerned." But they plausibly conclude that this irony causes readers "to contemplate a world in which no certain truths are granted" (124). And I would say that this is post-Romantic irony. As noted in Chapter 2, this type of irony differs both from traditional irony, which signifies a clash of truth and falsehood, and from Romantic irony, which embraces conflicting viewpoints as equally true. Post-Romantic irony cannot balance truth against falsehood or reconcile conflicting viewpoints because it arises from a sense that no clear norms or ideals exist for making such judgments. At the same time, it reflects a sincere desire for such norms and ideals—hence the frustration of post-Romantic characters whose quest for ideals is thwarted by the transitional state of their culture.

The traveler's very uncertainty about whether his title is ironic or not is itself an emblematic instance of post-Romantic irony. The traveler might have responded to his hypothetical readers' exclamation by saying, "Not at all," or, "Of course it is." But he says, "I don't know," because he actually does not know—he cannot know—whether Pechorin is a hero or not, or what kind of hero Pechorin is, only that, ironic as it may be, he is "a hero of our time." The traveler's uncertainty therefore bespeaks not some modest self-deprecation. It expresses the irony of the post-Romantic condition, when no authoritative cultural standards, values, and ideals by which to gauge someone's character or behavior exist, yet a sense of their loss remains, along with a yearning not to restore former, Romantic standards, values, and ideals, but to find new ones. In consequence, the post-Romantic irony of the traveler's final remark, "I don't know," leaves all questions about the novel open, all careful readers without conclusions. Their expectations of closure, like the secondary characters' expectations of fulfillment of their ideals, are dashed. And yet, by contrast to Golstein, who claims that Lermontov sought to demonstrate the futility and danger of all expectations, I would maintain that Lermontov found value in some expectations, hopes, and ideals.[19]

For, in the end, if the traveler cannot draw any firm conclusions about Pechorin as a hero of his time *or* as an ironic version of a hero, readers can do better. Lermontov saw to that, however unintentionally. In his own post-Romantic way, he recognized that he had created in Pechorin a hero for post-Romantic times alongside characters whose lingering Romantic idealism and integrity held out against that hero and his times as well as they could. He thus implies that readers might search for new ideals that would serve them better, bringing a new integrity to their culture. The post-Romantic anomie of *A Hero of Our Time* did not necessarily have to be theirs.

EIGHT

Conclusion

Lermontov's Last Words

CULTURAL DISEASE

The very last words that Lermontov wrote in *A Hero of Our Time* are actually not part of the novel but come in the author's preface that Lermontov added to the second edition, published in 1841, after the novel's initial publication in 1840 had provoked negative critical reactions. Lermontov says at its outset that this preface, like any other, is the "last thing," as well as the first, in a novel, since it "serves as an explanation of the aim of the composition, or as a correction and response to criticism" (4: 183; 1). His preface serves both ends, underscoring the post-Romantic implications of the novel specifically for a post-Romantic public in Russia, but also for readers in the West.

Lacing his preface with sarcasm, Lermontov reproaches the reading public for clinging to illusions and expectations that no longer fit the times and that—like Pechorin—they do not truly believe in. People have been "badly brought up," he says, in a culture that has nurtured false assumptions about themselves and the world they live in. Lazily relying on bankrupt values, dependent on familiar conventions, and oblivious to irony, they fail to understand life or literature. As evidence, Lermontov remarks that because "this book has recently evoked the unfortunate faith of certain readers and even journals [i.e., reviewers] in the literal meaning of words" (4: 183; 1), those readers and reviewers have been "horribly offended" that "such an immoral individual as the Hero of Our Time" has purportedly been "set forth to them as an example" to follow, or as a portrait of Lermontov himself. They have not gotten the point. Expecting more uplifting heroes, "tragic and romantic villains," and comforting fantasies (as Dostoevsky's Underground Man would also complain over two decades later), they have failed to recognize the truth that *A Hero of Our Time* is "a portrait composed of the vices of our entire generation."[1] Addressing his public directly, Lermontov asks rhetorically whether they also are blind to this portrait "because there is more truth in it than you would wish?"—just as Pechorin could not see himself as he truly was. That blindness befits a post-Romantic public seeking reassurances about its tired Romantic expectations and shunning unsettling questions about its illusions. But this public, Lermontov says, needs to be unsettled. "People have been fed enough with sweet treats," he declares. "Their stomachs have been ruined by this; they need bitter medicine, caustic truths." *A Hero of Our Time* offers some of these medicinal truths, Lermontov suggests, since he as author chose not to compose a work of romantic fantasy but "to draw a contemporary individual such as he understands him and, to his and your misfortune, has too often encountered him" (4: 184; 2).

And yet Lermontov does not presume that his "bitter medicine" will cure the public. As he insists to his readers: "Do not think after all this, however, that the author of this book ever entertained the proud dream of becoming a corrector of human vices. God save him from such foolishness!" This disclaimer leads to Lermontov's last and most memorable post-Romantic words: "Suffice it that the disease has been pointed out, but how to cure it—God only knows!" [Будет и того, что болезнь указана, а как ее излечить—это уж бог знает!] (4: 184; 2).

It is telling that in an early draft of the preface, Lermontov had used the word *evil* [зло] rather than *disease* [болезнь] in this last line. This revision reflected his perception that the troubled conditions of his time came not so much from immorality as from an illness, a cultural malaise.[2] And in *A Hero of Our Time* he explicitly—after doing this implicitly throughout his brief career—demonstrated and diagnosed that illness of his time, which I have labeled post-Romantic anomie. But because he very much belonged to those times, he could not see beyond them to prescribe an efficacious cure. At that moment of history, no one could have. The concluding phrase, "how to cure it—God only knows," thus expresses not a belief that God actually would have a remedy, but rather Lermontov's sense of his own transitional uncertainty.

A FINAL OBEISANCE

As it happens, on the reverse side of the notebook page upon which he wrote the author's preface to *A Hero of Our Time*, Lermontov wrote the initial outline for his last work of fiction, the short story "Shtoss" ["Штосс"]. Therefore it seems likely that some logical—or psychological—connection exists between the two works, as well as perhaps some hint in fictionalized form of Lermontov's cure for the "disease" of his times (his professions of ignorance notwithstanding). And we would reasonably expect that hint to take the form of "bitter medicine" or "caustic truths" in a searching exploration of contemporary cultural ills. But, in fact, "Shtoss" overtly contains no salutary medicine or painful truths about culture at large. Indeed, Lermontov first presented this short story to a small group of acquaintances as a joke, locking them in a room for the purpose, he said, of reading aloud a lengthy new novel requiring four hours of their attention; he then read them his story instead, concluding abruptly after about fifteen minutes.

What Lermontov read to his audience on that occasion is a narrative (which was left untitled and was only published posthumously in 1845) ambiguously treating either supernatural phenomena or an individual's delusional perception of them. It depicts an artist named Lugin who hears voices telling him to rent an apartment in the home of a government official named Shtoss [Штосс]. Lugin does so, discovering in one of the apartment's rooms a portrait of a middle-aged man with a surprisingly lifelike face. At midnight Lugin observes a mysterious man—who remarkably resembles the portrait—enter the apartment, despite its locked doors, and offer to play a card game called "shtoss" [штосс] with him. The man offers as his gambling stake a ghostly whitish form fluttering near him, against which Lugin puts up a sum of money that he promptly loses. They agree to play again the next night, at which point Lugin asks the man his name. The man merely responds, "Shto-s?" [что-с?] (4: 331), which is an elided expression meaning "What, sir?" but is pronounced exactly like the names of both the official who owns the home and the card game. Without ever learning the man's actual name, Lugin loses to him every night thereafter. But he persists in the game because he has fallen in love with the whitish form, which from the second night onward he perceives as a divinely beautiful woman. After weeks of losses, the story's narrator remarks, "[Lugin] foresaw that the moment would soon come when he would have nothing left to bet on the cards. It was necessary to make up his mind to do something. He made up his mind" (4: 332).[3]

With those words the story ends. What Lugin decided remains a mystery—Lermontov added nothing more to the story before he was killed a few months later. But this cliffhanger is just one of the mysteries about Lermontov's last work. For we must wonder: How seriously should readers take this story, when Lermontov presented it so jocularly and so pointedly toyed with a triple pun on forms of *s-h-t-o-s*? Did he intend but fail to add more to the story, or did he decide to leave it unfinished, or did he bring it to the conclusion he wanted? Was he seeking to create a Romantic tale of uncanny coincidences and supernatural apparitions, or was he trying to produce a proto-Realist depiction of an individual's gradual descent into insanity? And what relation, if any, can be found between "Shtoss" and the author's preface to *A Hero of Our Time*?

The few Lermontov critics who have written about "Shtoss" agree on some answers to these questions, but they strongly disagree on others.[4] They do agree by and large that, despite its initial mode of presentation by Lermontov, "Shtoss" was not merely a frivolous exercise for him. Vatsuro, for instance, maintains that "Shtoss" is "a work of serious literature and not a simple friendly joke" (252), and Mersereau goes so far as to call it an expression of Lermontov's ultimate "literary credo," as opposed to a mere "hoax" (*Shtoss*, 280). Critics also tend to concur that "Shtoss" is unfinished, typically viewing it as "a witty, skillfully written fragment" (Passage, 192) that Lermontov either did not have the time or the desire to complete—although Vatsuro provocatively suggests that Lermontov *intended* to leave it unfinished when he read it aloud in order to "mystify" his initial audience, but that he planned to finish it later (252).

However, critics significantly diverge on what kind of a story or fragment "Shtoss" is and how it fits into Lermontov's body of works. Appropriately enough, these disagreements mirror the critical divisions over his earlier major works and, for that matter, his literary career as a whole: some critics view "Shtoss" as an "organic whole" that constitutes a typical "Romantic tale" (Morozov, 191, 196); others consider it an "amalgam" of Romantic and realistic elements (Vatsuro, 245); and still others see it as another of Lermontov's steps on the road toward Realism.[5] Mersereau is most emphatic on this last point, arguing that "Shtoss" is "in essence an antiromantic work," in which Lermontov was "picking up the banner once carried by Pushkin in his battle against romantic clichés" by "parodistically" combining "traditional elements of the romantic supernatural tale" in ways that render those elements "absurd, pale, and anticlimactic," even "a burlesque" (*Shtoss*, 293, 294, 292, 288). Mersereau does concede that "the dominant manner of narration is straightforward, unembellished, outwardly objective," not humorously satirical or hyperbolic.[6] Nonetheless, he contends that "Shtoss" signals Lermontov's rejection of Romanticism in favor of Realism, on the grounds that "it would be unlikely that in 1841 Lermontov could have or would have seriously committed himself to writing a manifestly imitative work containing some romantic elements that he had apparently long since discarded" (*Shtoss*, 293).

I agree with elements of all these interpretations of "Shtoss." The story combines tendencies at once Romantic and proto-Realist, in its way summarizing Lermontov's artistic endeavors throughout his career. But I would say that this story does not confirm Lermontov as a Romanticist, or reveal Lermontov as a Romanticist-cum-Realist, or expose Lermontov as an anti-Romanticist. Instead it points to what he has been all along: a remarkable post-Romanticist. "Shtoss" does echo the Romantic tale of the supernatural, and it does contain numerous references and allusions to the works of European Romantic authors (most conspicuously, E. T. A. Hoffmann, Maturin, and writers belonging to *l'école frénétique*), as well as to Romantically inclined Russian authors like Vladimir Odoevskii and the early Nikolai Gogol (especially Gogol's story "The Portrait").[7] Yet these echoes, references, and allusions do not of themselves render "Shtoss" either elementally Romantic or parodistically anti-Romantic. Instead, in essence they tell us that for Lermontov, no less at the end of his brief literary career than at the beginning, Romanticism was a fallen idol that was still a god. That is, in "Shtoss" Lermontov did not embark intentionally on a new path toward Realism or elsewhere. Instead, he once again turned back toward Romantic ideas, images, and ideals for artistic inspiration as, even if unintentionally, he sought a "cure" for the "illness" of his times that he had remarked in the author's preface to *A Hero of Our Time*, written on the other side of the page where he outlined "Shtoss." And yet he could not confidently proceed along the old road of Romanticism either. Hence he produced still one more post-Romantic fragment made up of Romantic images undercut by post-Romantic ambiguity and ending in post-Romantic uncertainty and irony.

In turning one more time to his "idol," Lermontov filled "Shtoss" with a compendium of Romantic themes and motifs: the foreboding atmosphere limned by the narrator; Lugin's desire for earthly love and his enamoration of an unearthly creature; the extraordinary coincidences that lead Lugin to rent the apartment; the portrait that seems to come alive; Lugin's compulsion to gamble; the unnamed opponent who utters only a question; and so forth.[8] And the description of Lugin's "marvelous and heavenly vision" of the creature with whom he falls in love exudes a Romantic exaltation of his beloved reminiscent of Tieck's Christian for the Woodswoman:

> Life had never produced anything so delicately celestial, death had never taken from the world anything so full of ardent life: this was not an earthly being—it had colors and light instead of a form and a body, warm breath instead of blood, and an idea instead of a sensation; nor was this an empty and false phantom . . . because its indistinct features exuded a burning and greedy passion, desire, sadness, love, fear, hope. It was one of those marvelous beauties that a youthful imagination draws for us, before which in the throes of ardent dreams we fall to our knees and cry, and pray, and rejoice, God knows why—one of those heavenly products of a young spirit when, in an excess of strength, it creates for itself a new natural condition, better and fuller than the one to which it had been chained. (4: 331)[9]

Lugin unreservedly gives himself over to a quest to win this creature by winning at cards, a Romantic hero á la Byron who will sacrifice everything for the woman he adores.

But "Shtoss" also reveals that Lermontov as an artist could not wholeheartedly give himself over to the allure of Romanticism. For here we see his post-Romantic sensibilities at work—the same sensibilities that kept his aesthetic attachment to Byron ambivalent, that led him to becloud the image of his Demon with moral ambiguity, that caused him to expose Arbenin as an ideologue rather than a true Romanticist, and that inspired him to afflict Pechorin with anomie. These post-Romantic sensibilities would not allow Lermontov simply to create—or re-create—a Romantic supernatural tale. He undermined the story's Romantically supernatural trappings and emotional intensity not with parody, as Mersereau claims—I agree with Helena Goscilo that "not even a vestige of parody is detectable" in "Shtoss"

(344)[10]—but with post-Romantic uncertainty, casting doubts on the meaning and value of Lugin's Romantic tendencies and experiences.

I would distinguish this post-Romantic uncertainty from the Romantic uncertainty a Romanticist like E. T. A. Hoffmann, for instance, instills in his works. For Hoffmann intended readers to remain uncertain about the nature and significance of the potentially supernatural events he portrayed in order to expand those readers' conception of reality—an exercise in true Romantic irony. Thus, for instance, in "The Sandman" ["Der Sandman"] (1816), the main protagonist, Nathaniel, leaps off a tower to his death, possibly destroyed by a shape-shifting satanic evil force beyond human control, possibly the victim of psychotic hallucinations. As Leonard Kent and Elizabeth Knight note in the introduction to their translation of Hoffmann's tales, because of "the question marks imbedded in the fabric of the story," it "precludes a clear determination as to how much is happening and how much is imagined." As a result, such obscurity "enriches the range of potential interpretations but does not exhaust them" (xxx, xxxi). Interpretations are left to readers' imaginations. In "Shtoss," by contrast, the uncertainty tends not to encourage an expansive view of reality and enrich interpretation, but rather mainly to undermine each of two opposing interpretations (the supernatural and the psychological) without pointing toward others—hence it constitutes the post-Romantic uncertainty that underlies post-Romantic irony.

This uncertainty permeates the story through the narrator, who, on the one hand, dispassionately sets forth the story's seemingly supernatural events without comment, and yet, on the other hand, makes frequent references to Lugin's precarious physical and emotional state. He observes, for instance, that Lugin suffered from "a permanent mysterious ailment" (4: 321), that "traces of deep-seated exhaustion showed on his contorted face" (4: 323), and that "his thoughts were confused" (4: 329). On the first night Lugin spends in the apartment prior to the appearance of the old man, the narrator reports that Lugin "tried to read—his gaze slid across the lines and he read something completely different from what was written; he had bouts of chills and fever; his head ached; he heard ringing in his ears" (4: 328). In addition to observing such symptoms of Lugin's physical and intellectual deterioration, the narrator remarks that Lugin "deceived himself daily with the naiveté of a child" (4: 327), suggesting that Lugin's supernatural visitors might be no more than products of his own deficient and wayward imagination. Indeed, the narrator indirectly attributes the subsequent events that he represents to this faulty imagination, which, he says, amounts to a "disposition of soul" that had bred in Lugin "a fantastical love for a heavenly ideal." This kind of fantasy, the narrator warns, can be "most dangerous for a man of imagination" (4: 328).

Here Lermontov introduces a note of doubt about the capacities of the post-Romantic imagination, by contrast to the inspirational and life-serving power of the Romantic imagination. Lugin's imaginative quest for the "heavenly ideal" of a self-fulfilling Romantic love can be dangerous, the narrator implies, not because such ideals are damaging in themselves, but because, if the imagination that envisions them is deficient—that is, incapable of autonomously fashioning ideals into an integrated identity and an invigorating and expansive model for life—the fruits of that imagination will be at best uninspired, at worst self-destructive. And Lugin's imagination is surely deficient.

As an artist, Lugin cannot express any original vision. One unfinished portrait he is working on, for instance, shows "the same little head," which Lugin had redrawn "several times in different views" because he "had been unable to satisfy himself," as though he were "trying to realize his ideal on canvas" but lacked sufficient inspiration to give that ideal definite shape (4: 327). To his finished works he glumly imparts "some sort of indistinct, but morose feeling," stemming from his pallid and inadequate imagination (4: 321). Even his encounters with the "apparitions" that animate him seem secondhand—the old man that Lugin sees enter his apartment is a portrait come to life, just as portraits have done in works by Maturin, Gogol, and others; and the ephemeral young woman that he perceives at every card game as the incarnation of his ideal is a generic replica of a Romantic dream, reducing Lugin, so the narrator says, to a copy of all "our young poets who sigh over a non-existent beautiful woman" (4: 327). Whether these apparitions are real or not is ultimately beside the point. Lugin does not confront ghosts of his own—his deficient imagination can only envision imitations.

Why is Lugin uninspired and imitative? I would say it is because he is a product of his—and his author's—times. As Lermontov has the narrator further remark about Lugin's paintings: "They bore the stamp of that bitter poetry that our impoverished age [наш бедный век] has wrung from the hearts of its high priests" (4: 321). What is this "impoverished age" but post-Romanticism, weakened and ailing from the ambiguity, ambivalence, ideological distortion, and anomie that Lermontov had depicted in his previous works, in need of the "bitter medicine" and "caustic truths," as he puts in his author's preface to *A Hero of Our Time*, in order to distinguish original, authentic, integrated images and ideals from their imitations? We might therefore say that the "high priests" of this post-Romantic age are individuals like Lugin who aspire to originality, authenticity, and integrity, but cannot achieve them, and who thus face the transitional quandary of seeking to create art in a time of insufficient imaginative inspiration. Through Lugin, then, Lermontov provides in his last work one more variation on the quandaries of cultural transition that he had previously represented through the likes of his corsair, Izmail-Bei, the Demon, Arbenin, and Pechorin, all of whom are at once exemplars and victims of their post-Romantic "impoverished age."

In this light we can view "Shtoss" as Lermontov's final post-Romantic fragment, reminiscent of the individual chapters of *A Hero of Our Time*. Although the last words of "Shtoss"—"he made up his mind" [он решился] (4: 332)—are more emphatic than any of the chapter endings in that novel, these last words nonetheless leave the reader utterly uncertain of what will follow.[11] They hang in the air, making us wonder, as Lermontov himself might have wondered, what will come next. Has Lugin truly decided on a course of action that will end the game, either in ultimate victory or loss? Will Lugin abandon the game altogether in pursuit of a "real" life? Or is his declared decision just another one of Lugin's self-deceptions, to be followed by interminable participation in the game? Lermontov gives no clue. I suspect that he had none.

In consequence, by contrast to those critics who assume that Lermontov would have continued "Shtoss" and who speculate on which of the possible denouements Lermontov would have chosen (thereby, incidentally, responding imaginatively to "Shtoss" as though it were a Romantic fragment), I would suggest that Lermontov *did* finish "Shtoss." He finished it in the sense that he took it—and the Romanticism that it incorporates—as far as he could go. He sensed that the well of Romanticism had finally run dry for him, if not for Lugin, and that it could not supply him with the creative inspiration and ideals he required in order to continue writing this narrative. Since "God only knows" whence new inspiration and new ideals would come, "Shtoss" remains a post-Romantic fragment, at once pointing beyond itself and yet pointing to nothing, a last gesture of post-Romantic uncertainty and irony.

With its inconclusive conclusion, "Shtoss" thus provides a final example of Lermontov's post-Romantic sensibilities, enhanced across the 1830s (a bookend, as it were, to Lermontov's early unfinished narrative poems and his first endeavor in prose, the Romantically overwrought and unfinished *Vadim*). And yet the fact that he wrote such a work as "Shtoss" at all after having just written the author's preface to *A Hero of Our Time*, in which he reproaches those who succumb to Romantic illusions, indicates just how strong the attraction of Romanticism still was for Lermontov—he apparently sought to make an act of obeisance at its altar one more time, albeit with his own unorthodox devotion. And the enduring strength of this attraction not only for Lermontov but for others of his generation, who shared the post-Romantic longing for ideals and norms as certain as those of Romanticism amid the sense of an aimless future, can be seen on a wider scale through a brief comparison between post-Romanticism and another post-period: the period of postmodernism.

POST-ROMANTICISM IN POSTMODERN PERSPECTIVE

As a self-conscious, self-described post-period, postmodernism (which, like modernism, is generally written without capital letters) displays attributes of modernism and relations to it that set post-Romanticism and its relations to Romanticism, as well as Lermontov's relation to both, in a final, enlightening perspective. First I should note that postmodernism today—if it is still with us—is not quite a post-period as I have defined this concept. For beginning possibly as early as the 1950s and extending across at least two generations, postmodernism cannot be viewed simply as a transitional time out of the cultural period of modernism, when its values went into decline and no replacements had appeared. As diverse and disputed as it is, postmodernism has nonetheless broadly and avowedly embraced a set of postmodern values that render it a cultural period in its own right. As always, time will tell.

That said, postmodernism clearly possesses some qualities typical of transitions out of a previous period. For one, a sense of lost cultural integrity and dis-integration pervades postmodernism. Fragmentation is everywhere—in disjointed novels and films, in hybrid artworks, in "decentered" selves. This sense of disintegration also characterizes distinctive postmodernist irony, which encourages detached disillusionment, arch cynicism, and amused resignation to the loss of cultural integrity under the standardless standard that says "anything goes." Highly self-conscious and irreverent, postmodernist irony also both reflects and promotes a loss of faith in transcendence or any transcendent values. Consequently, postmodernism undermines the capacity to feel anything sincerely or to believe in anything unironically. Furthermore, postmodernism has brought a deliberate shift away from artistic originality toward various forms of imitation, including self-conscious parody and whimsical pastiche. As a result, Jorge Luis Borges can imagine writing the classic *Don Quixote* word for word anew; historical architectural features like cupolas and pediments get attached to new buildings; and pop culture and commercial images invade the arts. Finally, postmodernism, like other post-periods, evinces a sense of belatedness. But whereas post-Romanticists, for instance, felt they had come too late to the preceding period of Romanticism, postmodernists feel they have come too late not only to modernism but to Western civilization overall.

These general similarities of postmodernism to other post-periods notwithstanding, postmodernism differs particularly from post-Romanticism in significant ways, most of which arise from their divergent attitudes toward the past. Culturally sensitive post-Romanticists mourned the loss of the ideals, integrity, and integration of Romanticism, and they were haunted by a recognition of their cultural belatedness, at times bemoaning the imitative epigonism of many post-Romantic artists; their irony is tinged with regret for the uncertainty it instills. Culturally conscious postmodernists, by contrast, typically revel in disintegration and imitation, and bow to their belatedness with unregretful ironic acceptance of its inevitability. Although some literary and cultural critics like Irving Howe and Harry Levin might have lamented the passage of modernism even in the late 1950s, self-proclaimed postmodernists since then have generally rejected modernism, with its deeply serious quest for an architectonic culture and individual authenticity. And postmodern critics have affirmed the "breaking up of the grand Narratives," as the philosopher Jean-François Lyotard put it (15), that is, the futility of broad, integrative theories of human existence, history, and human nature such as Western culture has known for centuries.

Thus, instead of valuing coherence, unity, and integrity, as did post-Romanticists who regretted their loss, postmodernists, Ihab Hassan points out, celebrate "discontinuity, heterodoxy, pluralism, randomness," and related phenomena that allow for "deconstruction, decenterment, displacement," and so on (*Postmodern Turn*, 92). Jauntily embracing "whimsical experiment, eclectic forms, and a pop consumer style (amounting to a mirror image of the 'postmodern critique' of some of the same practices)" (J. S.

Allen, 313), postmodernists playfully produce works of "hybridity, promiscuous genres, recombinant culture, intertextuality, pastiche."[12] Originality becomes unimportant, virtually irrelevant. Contemporary historical and cultural and aesthetic self-consciousness is everything. In fact, according to literary historian Charles Newman, "what is unique about Post-Modernism is not its ambivalent quarrel with predecessors, which all movements share, but its refusal to resurrect and emulate a former 'golden age'" (57).

In addition to such marked differences between post-Romanticism and postmodernism regarding the past, these two cultural moments also distinctly differ in their sense of the future. Whereas post-Romanticists felt, however dimly and uncertainly, that a future cultural movement would eventually arrive, postmodernists tend to believe that everything in all of Western culture, from art to philosophy to history itself, has essentially worn out and come to an end. Therefore no original future is possible, only endless self-conscious repetitions of the past.

These differences between post-Romanticism and postmodernism cast a concluding ray of light on Lermontov, his relation to Romanticism, and his own post-Romantic times. The fact that Lermontov and others in his post-Romantic period retained an admiration for Romanticism's heroes and ideals, its originality and transcendence, its integrity and integration, even when these cultural values were in decline, indicates how profound the appeal of Romanticism was at the time—an appeal evidently far more profound than that of modernism today, since so many postmodernists have explicitly rejected modernism. Granted, once the new cultural period of Realism, along with Victorianism, had ascended in the middle decades of the nineteenth century, Romanticism in retrospect looked to some to have been immature and excessive, founded on illusions or, worse, delusions about the individual self and its vast capacities for action, emotion, and imagination. But before then, especially in the 1830s while the transition out of Romanticism was still occurring, Romantic energy and enthusiasm, its outsized passions—even dark passions—its imagination of life's possibilities, its faith in human beings to realize those possibilities, its exaltation of cultural integrity, its "Everlasting Yea," were nothing short of enthralling. Indeed, so enthralling was Romanticism that the diminution of its energy, the decline of its inspiriting ideals of self, morality, love, nature, imagination, and so forth, and the dis-integration of its integrity led the most culturally attuned artists and intellectuals to portray these developments as a dangerous cultural malaise, the "disease" Lermontov laments in the author's preface to *A Hero of Our Time*, for which he, like his contemporaries, saw no cure at the time. And without one, they could not help but feel that their cultural "life was going out like the last candles in windows before dawn" (135), as Herzen would say of a similar time later on. How different is their sorrow amid the last flickers of Romanticism from the gleeful, often cynical celebration of modernism's demise by postmodernists.

And yet I would say in conclusion that although Lermontov could not see a remedy for the "disease" of post-Romanticism, he did imply the *type* of remedy needed: the affirmation of new cultural ideals and values to replace those of Romanticism—a new deity to replace the fallen idol that to him was still a god. Sensing the passing of old ideals and values, and recognizing the need for new ones but being unable to prescribe what they should be, was Lermontov's greatest quandary as a culturally sensitive individual living in a time of transition. It is also the singular greatness of Lermontov as a transitional author.

From the beginning of his brief literary career to the end, Lermontov perceived the malaise of his transitional times with remarkable acuity. He subtly delineated that malaise and its ramifications, implicitly and explicitly, in a variety of ways. And while he could not see beyond the malaise of his times, he compellingly alerted us to the truths that he could see of all cultural *transitions out*.

Had Lermontov lived long enough to have completed the full course of a literary career, he might, as some critics assume, have become a committed Realist in the vein of either Flaubert or Dostoevsky. But it is not unreasonable to speculate that he might instead have charted a different course, helping to shape a culture that would find its integrity in values and beliefs closer to those of Romanticism. That integrity would encompass a spirit of wholeness, idealism, and noble selfhood that could impart more uplifting meaning to life than did Flaubert's brand of Realism, with its cult of fact and cynical pride in disillusionment and social criticism, or Dostoevsky's variant, with its pathology of the antihero (emerging full-blown only after midcentury in the Underground Man).[13] Hopes and ideals, values and norms, inspired by Romanticism but not beholden to it, integrated into a new cultural life, could have shaped a future that Lermontov might well have embraced.

Of course, we can only speculate. And we would not be alone. Vissarion Belinskii did so tellingly, at least regarding a future for Pechorin. Although an idiosyncratic and often unreliable nineteenth-century critic, Belinskii may have been onto something when he commented in a review of the newly published *A Hero of Our Time* on the prospect that Lermontov might write a sequel to the novel, as he had hinted in the anonymous traveler's "Introduction to Pechorin's Journal": "We thank the author for this pleasant promise," Belinskii remarks, "but we doubt whether he will fulfill it; we are strongly convinced that he has parted forever with his Pechorin." However, Belinskii goes on, "If Mr. Lermontov will fulfill his promise, then we are sure that he will present not the old and familiar Pechorin, about whom he has already said everything there is to say, but a completely new Pechorin, about whom it is still possible to say a great deal." This "new Pechorin," Belinskii muses, might be reformed but emotionally empty, or he might come to believe in life for others but not for himself. Or, Belinskii concludes, perhaps Lermontov would have depicted the "new Pechorin" as "one who partakes of the joys of life" (122–23).

Belinskii's is an amusing and suggestive critical exercise. I would add that if Lermontov had gone on to portray such a joyful "new Pechorin," it would have meant that he had found a hero for a new time. This would be a Pechorin who had the integrity of character to form an authentic identity, to experience true love, and to be worthy of the genuine friendship he had desired but never been able to find. However, Lermontov could probably have created this joyful "new Pechorin" only if he had been able to feel that he himself had reached the end of his period of cultural transition and had left its quandaries behind, or at least had seen a way out, a "cure" for his "impoverished age."

Unfortunately, Lermontov would never get that far. Killed in a duel in 1841, he remained confined to his transitional era with no end in sight. And this very confinement distinguishes Lermontov from even his contemporary post-Romantic artists and intellectuals. For it directed his youthfully keen cultural consciousness and exploratory artistry toward the transitional quandaries of the years given to him. Lermontov thus may have belonged to an "impoverished age" and a "fruitless" generation, as he wrote in his poem "Meditation," but he rose above them both to become the emblematic transitional author of his elementally transitional time.

Reference Matter

Notes

Preface

1. All quotations of Lermontov's works come from the four-volume Nauka [Soviet Academy of Sciences] edition and are cited by volume and page number. Lermontov employed the final couplet of this poem to much lesser effect in an eight-line lyric of the preceding year, "I do not love you" ["Я не люблю тебя"] (1: 235).

Iurii Lotman offers an elaborate analysis of the "semantic structure" of "We have parted" in his article on this poem. He finds it relying on sets of oppositions that derive from the "Romantic concept of the individual," which is rooted in "an assumption of his solitariness, his isolation, his uprooting from all earthly ties" (164). Lotman thus views this poem strictly through a Romantic prism.

Chapter 1: Cultural Transition and Its Quandaries

1. The highly influential nineteenth-century Russian literary critic Vissarion Belinskii singled out "Meditation" for particular praise as a protest against the deficiencies of contemporary Russian society, exclaiming, "These verses were written in blood . . . [they are] the lament of an individual for whom the lack of an inner life is an evil a thousand times worse than physical death!" (quoted in Lermontov, *Собрание сочинений* [Collected Works], 1: 599). However, Lermontov's hostility clearly extends beyond his immediate society.

2. Pitirim Sorokin even more dramatically declares that "all the theories [of cultural change] which take one factor or system and try to explain through its variation the variation of all the other social and cultural factors . . . of a given culture are hopelessly dead" (4: 153). However, Sorokin himself offers his own theory of cultural change, metaphorically describing the challenge of comprehending such change as that of attending a performance of the "music of the Concert Hall of History," where "simultaneously several orchestras were each playing its own symphony. The task of the audience becomes to single out the music of the main orchestras, and then that of the "main among the main" orchestras, in order

to grasp "the dominant principles that give shape to the performances of all the others" (4: 153, 154).

3. British Marxist Christopher Caudwell explicitly attributes every change in twentieth-century Western culture to "the lie which is killing it"—the bourgeois "illusion . . . that man is naturally free"—and advocates instead "the truth which will transform and revitalize culture"—the truth of communism (xxiii, xx). Today, Caudwell's embrace of communist ideology almost ironically supports Sorokin's dismissal of single-cause theories of change as "hopelessly dead."

4. See, among others by Mary Douglas, *Purity and Danger: An Analysis of Concepts of Pollution and Taboo* (London: Routledge and Kegan Paul, 1966); *Natural Symbols: Explorations in Cosmology* (New York: Vintage Books, 1973); and *Implicit Meanings: Essays in Anthropology* (London: Routledge and Kegan Paul, 1975). Salient works by Clifford Geertz include *The Interpretation of Cultures: Selected Essays* (New York: Basic Books, 1973), and *Local Knowledge: Further Essays in Interpretive Anthropology* (New York: Basic Books, 1983).

5. See most notably Marvin Harris, *Cows, Pigs, Wars, and Witches: The Riddles of Culture* (New York: Random House, 1974), and its more theoretical counterpart, *Cultural Materialism: The Struggle for a Science of Culture* (New York: Random House, 1979).

6. See Trygve Tholfsen, *Historical Thinking: An Introduction* (New York: Harper and Row, 1967), for a useful survey of historical modes of conceptualization and historiographical methodology.

7. As Spengler explains, "Civilizations are the most external and artificial states of which a species of developed humanity is capable. They are a conclusion, the thing-become succeeding the thing-becoming, death following life, rigidity following expansion, intellectual age and the stone-built, petrifying world-city following mother-earth and the spiritual childhood" (31).

8. Among this "revolutionary" group, Wellek particularly criticizes Russian Formalist theoreticians and critics for failing to see literature "not only [as] a structure to be analyzed" but as "a totality of values which do not adhere to the structure but constitute its very nature. All attempts to drain value from literature have failed," Wellek thus concludes, "and will fail because [literature's] very essence is value" (52).

9. Sociologist Don Martindale, who subscribes to what he labels "social behaviorism," takes a stance parallel to Wellek's when he asserts, "Only the individual creates or destroys social forms. When communities arise and are destroyed, certain persons play a central role in the process. These include the intellectuals of the community" (ix).

In his study *Social Life and Cultural Change* (1962), Martindale plausibly divides theories of sociocultural changes into four types: the first type assumes that "all social and cultural changes are either nonexistent or of little general significance"; the second type finds that such changes do occur, "but primarily for the worse"; the third type maintains that these changes "were or are progressive"; and the fourth type holds that these changes are "cyclical" (1–2). Martindale himself perceives what he calls a "semi-cyclical pattern" (3), as cultures undergo "creative epochs" of "community and civilization formation," which are succeeded by "conservative" periods of "maturity." He finds that intellectuals, "as a special stratum of individuals," play a leading role in the movement between these periods.

In addition to Martindale, see Robert Lauer, *Perspectives on Social Change* (Boston: Ally and Bacon, 1973), for a useful summary of theories of sociocultural change.

10. Kuhn's theory of scientific revolutions is in some ways presaged by C. S. Lewis in *The Discarded Image*. Devoting the majority of this work to a description of what Lewis terms the "Medieval Model" of how the universe is structured, Lewis concludes that he is "only suggesting considerations that may induce us to regard all Models in the right way, respecting each and idolizing none." For "we can no longer dismiss the change of Models as a simple progress from error to truth. No Model is a catalogue of ultimate realities, and none is a mere fantasy. Each is a serious attempt to get in all the phenomena known at a given period, and each succeeds in getting in a great many. But also, no less surely, each reflects the prevalent psychology of an age almost as much as it reflects the state of that age's knowledge" (222). I am indebted to my colleague Peter Briggs for this reference.

11. For an illuminating extension of Kuhn's ideas to a sociocultural context, see Anthony Wallace's "Paradigmatic Processes in Cultural Change." Wallace "attempts to embrace a far wider range of cultural change processes" than Kuhn's strictly scientific paradigm shift by tracing a model of "change sequences" with "five essential components: innovation, paradigmatic core development, exploitation, functional consequences, and rationalization," and then illustrating that change sequence through a "case study" of a Pennsylvania mill town during the Industrial Revolution (468, 472). I am indebted to my colleague James C. Wright for this reference.

12. Northrop Frye in effect derides such reductive and anachronistic thinking when he observes, for instance, that "not only did the 'pre-romantics' not know that the Romantic movement was going to succeed them, but there has probably never been a case on record of a poet's having regarded a later poet's work as the fulfillment of his own" (144).

13. Partaking of Coleridge's view, contemporaneous readers and critics of Byron found particular fault with the lack of transitions in his poems. William Hazlitt, for instance, found *Don Juan* "as disturbed, as confused, as disjointed" as a dream; a review of *The Giaour* laments "abrupt and perplexing transitions" (quoted in Stabler, 315).

14. Kermode further suggests that the modernist conception of transition in the twentieth century allows for the rejection of the past entirely: "Transition, decadence-and-renovation, have perhaps become the dominant aspects of apocalypse in the arts . . . and in consequence we have all grown more interested in the possibilities of a break with the past; of considering the present in relation to the end without calculations based on history" (114). In essence, this conception reduces all transition to *transition in*. For a wide-ranging and provocative study of apocalyptic thought in nineteenth- and twentieth-century Russian literature, see

David Bethea, *The Shape of Apocalypse in Modern Russian Fiction* (Princeton, NJ: Princeton University Press, 1989).

15. Even Kuhn refers to a "pre-paradigm period" but not to a "post-paradigm" period (84). To cite one recent example of this tendency, Marshall Brown's study of transitional moments in cultural history, *Turning Points*, focuses on "significant works" that are "beyond their moment, underway toward a new age." Thus, for example, he considers how a Mozart composition "becomes the vessel of a new sensibility through which new concepts and cultural shapes arise" (vii, viii).

16. *The Autumn of the Middle Ages*, trans. Rodney J. Payton and Ulrich Mammitzsch (Chicago: University of Chicago Press, 1996).

17. Bate subsequently argues that Romanticism, coming after the Enlightenment, could flower only when it found ways of "opening up of new subject matters where the challenge of the past was less oppressive: simple life . . . children, the poor and socially slighted; landscape and scenery; such inward experiences as revery, dream, and mysticism . . . the 'strange,' the past itself in periods and ways not previously exploited . . . the geographically remote or unusual" (116–17).

18. Bate attributes this sense of exhausted creative possibilities to an idealization of the past produced by "the treacheries of nostalgia," which distorts judgment" through "foreshortening and selectivity" (47, 67). See Svetlana Boym, *The Future of Nostalgia* (New York: Basic Books, 2001), for a more positive exploration of nostalgia, at least in the modern age.

19. This essay is included in the collection *С того берега* [From the Other Shore] (1847–50). I am indebted to Gary Saul Morson for this reference, as well as for several others discussed in this introduction.

Chapter 2: Romanticism and Its Twilight in Western Europe and Russia

1. For comprehensive reviews of the history of the terms *Romanticism, Romantic,* and so on, see René Wellek's well-known essays "The Concept of Romanticism in Literary History" and "Romanticism Re-examined," in Wellek's *Concepts of Criticism,* 128–98 and 199–221. See also *"Romantic" and Its Cognates: The European History of a Word,* ed. Hans Eichner (Toronto: University of Toronto Press, 1972), in which individual chapters are devoted to the use of these terms in individual countries.

2. In this essay Lovejoy archly remarks it would be fair to conclude that "Romanticism was 'born in the Garden of Eden' and that 'the Serpent was the first Romantic'" (229). Although Wellek's essays (see previous note) most famously reject Lovejoy's contentions, Lilian Furst offers an even more thorough disputation of Lovejoy's ideas in *Contours,* 1–15.

3. Berlin precedes this passage with over two pages of a glorious compendium mentioning virtually all of the often-opposing features associated with Romanticism, including innocence and decadence, rebelliousness and pastoral tranquility, exoticism and exaltation of rural life, the Gothic and antiquity, the natural and the supernatural, historicism and the cult of novelty, alienation and social cooper-

ation, Satanism and renewed Christianity, "the Toryism of Scott and Southey and Wordsworth" and "the radicalism of Shelley, Buchner and Stendhal," "Carlyle's worship of authority, and Hugo's hatred of authority," and so forth (16–18).

4. W. T. Jones defines this "syndrome" as "a pattern of preferences" or "biases" that appeared in European culture toward the end of the eighteenth century favoring the dynamic over the static, disorder over order, continuity over discreteness, softness over sharpness, the inner over the outer, and "Other-world" over "This-world" (120). Within the scope of these "preferences," however, variety and contradictions can still be found, as Jones's supporting evidence reveals.

5. Commentators on "The Runenberg" tend to offer negative interpretations of it, arguing that Christian indeed goes mad, the victim of his own selfish abandonment of domesticity and responsibility. Ralph Tymms, for instance, criticizes Christian on the grounds that "base greed depraves him, reducing him to moral impotence," and that he consequently ends up "overwhelmed by elemental forces which he has himself first released, or to which at any rate he too easily succumbs" (92, 97). Among the commentators who read the story less judgmentally, Oskar Walzel suggests that Tieck at least did not intend this *type* of story to be read didactically or negatively, noting that the author "did reveal to romanticism that marvel which is not mere illusion but which is inner experience, which rests not upon conscious misperception but upon mood." Christian's vision of the gems inside the dirty rocks would thus perfectly exemplify "the spirit of romanticism" that "ever sought to penetrate through the mass of sense impressions to the ultimate secret which lay buried behind those myriad perceptions and, dreamily presentient, to grasp the truth not in the trite and obvious every-day things but in the realm of the super-sensual" (243).

6. Some historians and critics, of course, see Romanticism fundamentally characterized not by integration but by its emphasis on particularity, individuality, and originality. Lovejoy, for instance, even when he does treat Romanticism as a distinct cultural period, claims that the period was distinguished by a turn from "uniformitarianism," typical of the Enlightenment, to "diversitarianism," which became "the most significant and distinctive feature of the Romantic revolution." M. H. Abrams counters this claim, however, by arguing that "this is true, but it is not the whole truth; one must add that what was most distinctive in Romantic thought was the normative emphasis not on plenitude as such, but on an organized unity in which all individuation and diversity survive, in Coleridge's terms, as distinctions without division" (both quotations in Abrams, *Natural Supernaturalism*, 185).

7. For an illuminating account of this emblematic incident, see Penelope Hughes-Hallett, *The Immortal Dinner: A Famous Evening of Genius and Laughter in Literary London, 1817* (London: Viking Press, 2000).

8. On the distinctive quality of the Enlightenment intellect, see Peter Gay, *The Enlightenment: An Interpretation*, vol. 2, *The Science of Freedom* (New York: Alfred A. Knopf, 1969).

9. As we might expect, this desire for integrity manifested itself in various and even contradictory ways. For instance, it underlies the love of many Romanticists

for the Middle Ages, which they idealized as "a Golden Age" in which social, psychological, and aesthetic experiences were intimately integrated, by contrast to "the alienated and divisive atmosphere of an increasingly urbanized and industrialized society" (Chandler, 3). Yet the same desire informed the admiration of other Romanticists for the Classical era, a "naïve" time, as Friedrich Schiller depicted it in *On Naïve and Sentimental Poetry*, operating "according to its own laws, its inner necessity, its eternal unity with itself" (quoted in Abrams, *Natural Supernaturalism*, 213).

The Romantic quest for integrity is described in different terms by other critics. For instance, Abrams calls "the great commonplace of the [Romantic] age" the idea that "unity with himself and his world [is] the primal and normative state of man" (*Natural Supernaturalism*, 278). Along similar lines, Michael Cooke asserts that Romanticism "takes the form, characteristically, of an act of inclusion" that "works as an avoidance of still and dusty compartmentalization of the honeycomb of experience" (*Acts*, xv, xvii). And Virgil Nemoianu finds "more agreement among the best critics than one would expect" that "the romantic paradigm is wholeness recaptured in its purity" (26).

10. Letter to John Thewall, 14 October 1797, *Collected Letters*, 1: 349; emphasis Coleridge's.

11. Abrams maintains that this organic conception of existence is "the root-principle" informing all of Coleridge's thought: "It is in this way that Coleridge conceives, for example, the process of cosmogony ('the eternal act of creation in the infinite I Am,' or 'absolute self'), of epistemology (the 'repetition' of this creation in 'the primary Imagination,' or act of perceiving in each individual mind), and of the poetic creation effected by 'the secondary Imagination' (an 'echo' of the primary imagination which, like that faculty, is a 'synthetic . . . power' that 'reveals itself in the balance or reconciliation of opposite or discordant qualities')" (*Natural Supernaturalism*, 268).

12. Eugene Stelzig is therefore correct when he insists that Romantic writers diverge "fundamentally from . . . postmodern and dispersive sensibility in their root assumption that there is a core self, no matter how mysterious or elusive, and their most telling experiences are intimately bound up with and often indeed are experiences *of* it" (11–12).

13. *On Naïve and Sentimental Poetry* (1795), quoted in Abrams, *Natural Supernaturalism*, 214, 215.

14. *Anima Poetae*, in *Notebooks* (published in 1895), quoted in Abrams, *Natural Supernaturalism*, 267.

15. *Religious Musings* (1794), in *Collected Works*, 16: 181.

16. Abrams makes a similar point when he claims that "what is called 'the problem of evil' . . . was precisely the central and pervasive concern of the major Romantic philosophers" (*Natural Supernaturalism*, 444).

17. In *De l'Allemagne* [On Germany] (1813), which introduced German Romantic thought to readers in France and England, de Staël attributes a unifying moral force to enthusiasm: "It would be no mistake to say that enthusiasm makes people

tend toward systematic theories . . . enthusiasm has nothing to do with fanaticism, and cannot lead people astray. Enthusiasm is tolerant—not out of indifference, but because it makes us feel the interest and beauty of everything . . . enthusiasm finds in the heart's reverie and the mind's whole range of thought what fanaticism and passion concentrate in a single idea, a single object. The universality of [enthusiasm] is precisely what makes it favorable to thought and imagination" (323). De Staël thus envisions enthusiasm as an animating, ameliorating, and integrating force.

18. See Richard Holmes, "Scrope's Last Throw," *Harper's*, April 1997, 77–85, for a delightful description of Davies' relationship to Byron—and the correct pronunciation of Davies' first name.

19. Passages like this lead cultural historian Peter Gay to label *Lucinde* "the canonical text of romantic love" (92). See the extended bibliographical essay provided for chapter 1, "Two Currents of Love," in Gay's *Bourgeois Experience: Victoria to Freud*, vol. 2, *The Tender Passion*, 425–31, for a broad range of sources on Romantic love in general and on depictions of that love in representative Romantic works.

20. In *On Love* (entitled *Love* in translation), Stendhal presents the image of a Romantic lover driven to distraction through the psychological "crystallization" of his beloved, defining crystallization as "a mental process which draws from everything that happens new proof of that perfection of the loved one," a parallel to the physical transformation that occurs when a bare branch is thrown into a pool of salt water and then extracted several months later, "studded with a galaxy of scintillating diamonds" (45). After undergoing such a process upon falling in love, an individual can experience "an incipient madness" as a physical disorder causing irrational behaviors and absurd ideas. In this condition, Stendhal informs his readers, "you observe some hardly distinguishable object as white, and interpret this as favourable to your love. A moment later you realize that the object is really black, and you now regard this as a good omen for your love" (60).

21. In addition to Abrams's *Natural Supernaturalism*, see Robert J. Richards, *The Romantic Conception of Life: Science and Philosophy in the Age of Goethe* (Chicago: University of Chicago Press, 2002), for an extensive exploration of Romantic views of nature.

22. Barker Fairley emphasizes the significance of this "discovery" for Goethe: "If, as he believed, he had elucidated the 'laws of transformation' whereby nature produces one part by means of another and reaches the utmost variety of form by modifying a single member . . . then the wholeness of organic life, which was coming to mean so much to him, was vindicated beyond his wildest dreams" (197–98).

23. *Die Lehrlinge zu Sais* [The Novices of Sais] (1802), quoted in Riasanovsky, 74.

24. *Biographia Literaria* (1817), *Works*, vol. 7, pt. 2, 16. Coleridge perceives this blending of "opposite or discordant" qualities, for instance, in a reconciliation "of sameness with difference; of the general, with the concrete; the idea, with the image; the individual, with the representative; the sense of novelty and freshness, with old and familiar objects; a more than usual state of emotion, with more than

usual order; judgment ever awake and steady self-possession, with enthusiasm and feeling profound or vehement" (*Works*, 7, 2, 16–17).

25. See Charles Rosen and Henri Zerner, "The Fingerprint: A Vignette," in their *Romanticism and Realism: The Mythology of Nineteenth-Century Art* (New York: Viking Press, 1984), 1–5, for an erudite introduction to the Romantic conception of fragments. See also Monika Greenleaf, *Pushkin and Romantic Fashion*, esp. 19–49, for some astute observations on the Romantic predilection for fragments, which she associates with Romanticists' appreciation for the eighteenth-century novels of Richardson and Sterne, as well as a taste for ancient artifacts.

26. See, for example, Furst, *Contours*.

27. In *The Romantic Agony* Mario Praz detects nothing much else but such excesses, which he deems the products of a Romantic "erotic sensibility," in Romanticism from the beginning. Yet he grants that his study of such excesses, proceeds by "isolating . . . one particular aspect, fundamental though it may be, of Romantic literature," and he therefore calls *The Romantic Agony* "a monograph," not "a synthesis" (xi).

28. Peckham defines "Negative Romanticism" as "period of doubt, of despair, of religious and social isolation, of the separation of reason and creative power. It was a period during which [Romantic sufferers] saw neither beauty nor goodness in the universe, nor any significance, nor any rationality, nor indeed any order at all, not even an evil order" (22).

29. Carlyle described an initial "state of crisis" besetting Teufelsdröch (122), who reports, while in this state, feeling himself to be "a feeble unit in the middle of a threatening Infinitude," so that, he despairs, "I seemed to have nothing given me but eyes, whereby to discern my own wretchedness," and, "To me the Universe was void of Life, of Purpose, of Volition, even of Hostility" (126). As a result, he finds, "thus had the EVERLASTING NO (*das ewige Nein*) pealed authoritatively through all the recesses of my Being, of my ME."

Immediately, however, Teufelsdröch defies the "EVERLASTING NO": "Then it was that my whole ME stood up, in native God-created majesty, and with emphasis recorded its Protest" (128). Undergoing a "Spiritual New-birth" after a period of "Indignation and Defiance" (129), he subsequently uncovers "the Knot that had been strangling him"—the desire for personal happiness—which he "straightaway could unfasten" and be "free," for "there is in man a HIGHER than Love of Happiness" (143, 145). This "higher" is "an Infinite" or "Godlike that is in Man," the development of which imparts surpassing "Strength and Freedom" (144, 146). Transformed by this conviction, he now affirms God as "the EVERLASTING YEA, wherein all contradiction is solved: wherein whoso walks and works, it is well with him" (146). The "Everlasting No" actually reigns only briefly; the "Everlasting Yea" will endure for all eternity.

30. Useful studies treating the beginnings of Romanticism include Leslie Brisman, *Romantic Origins* (Ithaca, NY: Cornell University Press, 1978); Morse Peckham, *The Birth of Romanticism* (Greenwood, FL: Penkeville, 1986); Marshall Brown, *Preromanticism* (Stanford, CA: Stanford University Press, 1991);

Riasanovsky; and Berlin. See also Brian Hepworth, comp., *The Rise of Romanticism: Essential Texts* (Manchester, UK: Carcanet New Press, 1978).

31. It should be noted that Lucas finds periods of Romanticism throughout Western history, labeling the Middle Ages a "Golden Age" of Romanticism, by contrast to which the nineteenth-century version appears to be more the product of "an artificial intoxicant, less of a national day-dream" (135, 136).

32. Lucas does envision a somewhat different demise for Romanticism in England, saying that there it "died finally of old age rather than of its own excesses, as abroad" (128). This "death" was likely more comfortable there than on the Continent in large part because the rapid ascendancy of English Victorian culture in the late 1830s quickly provided a new set of values and norms to replace those of Romanticism.

Like Lucas, Jacques Barzun generally attributes the decline of Romanticism to excess, although he unconventionally argues that Romanticism did not end in the middle decades of the nineteenth century, but evolved over the course of that century into three different "movements": Realism, symbolism, and naturalism. He nonetheless describes these subsequent "movements" as endeavors to correct some perceived failures of Romanticism and therefore at least in some ways as reactions against it. He singles out Realism, which blossomed in the middle decades of the nineteenth century, as adversarial to Romanticism, asserting that it "prided itself on correcting the errors and 'extravagances' of the romanticists" and sought to "amend" its excesses: "overexpressiveness; unsuccessful attempts at new forms; and exuberance of animal spirits; . . . a too zestful appetite for dramatic contrast, intensity, and distortion" (*Classic*, 103, 104). Thus Barzun shares Lucas's view that the end of Romanticism came about because it went too far, both psychologically and aesthetically.

33. Nemoianu subsumes this period under the established heading of the Biedermeier era, which was named after a fictitious author popularized in a Munich journal in the mid-nineteenth century who favored easy moralism, domesticity, cozy intimacy, conservatism, and resignation; the label Biedermeier was subsequently applied to the pretty paintings, heavy furniture, and quaint dress styles of the time. Nemoianu effectively contrasts what he terms "high romanticism" to the Biedermeier era, observing, for instance, that when the latter assumed cultural dominance, "the grand tour of the Alps ceased to be the property of the intense, lonely, and sublime poet and became the object of organized tourism. . . . Experimental balloon flights were symptomatic not only of the search for knowledge and communication but also of the search for controlled adventure" (11), and "the titans, the overwhelming personalities, disappeared and were replaced by the crotchety" (16). See pages 1–40 for his insightful overview of the European cultural climate during those years.

34. I should note that some historians and literary critics use the terms *post-Romanticism* and *post-Romantic* to refer to *any* cultural time or event occurring after Romanticism declined, and this can make for some odd assemblages. Edward Engelberg, for example, groups Lermontov, Ivan Turgenev, and Emily

Brontë together because, he claims, they wrote novels that "share certain common post-Romantic preoccupations." These preoccupations are revealed by their creation, respectively, of protagonists in *A Hero of Our Time, Fathers and Sons,* and *Wuthering Heights,* who all have "enormous energy," "display a destructive and self-destructive power," and arrive at "a state of lassitude leading to early death," as a result of which each "does not and cannot muster sufficient conviction for any cause—even the cause of nihilism itself—to sustain life" (57, 58). I would argue that any such similarities are far outweighed by differences among these characters and the narratives that portray them. In any event, I have a much more precise concept of post-Romanticism in mind.

35. Nemoianu does notably extend the chronological compass of "late Romanticism" from 1815 to 1840, thereby excluding from mature Romanticism numerous works and artists typically considered to participate in this movement during the 1820s. It is also worth noting that various literary critics and historians have placed artists and thinkers working well beyond the 1820s (and also well before the 1800s, as Lovejoy sardonically observed—see note 2) under the Romantic banner. Despite affinities with Romanticism that such individuals might have, however, they were working outside the time when this movement enjoyed its cultural dominance.

36. See Fuerst for an overview of German post-Romantic culture. See Enid Starkie, *Petrus Borel the Lycanthrope: His Life and Times* (Norfolk, CT: New Directions, 1954), and Joanna Richardson, *La Vie de Bohème in Paris, 1830–1914* (South Brunswick, NJ: A. S. Barnes, 1971), for vivid descriptions of Jeunes France and the literary culture of France in the 1830s.

37. Aleksandr N. Sokolov exemplifies this tendency in *От романтизма к реализму* [From Romanticism to Realism], where he reduces Romanticism in Russia to the years 1814–25, although he later expanded this compass to the first three decades of the nineteenth century. See Leighton, "Debate," for a review of the more open-minded treatment of Romanticism during the post-Stalinist years 1957–64. Even after this "thaw," which gave Soviet critics the opportunity to acknowledge and explore Romanticism in Russia more thoroughly, the need to connect Romanticism to Realism was still palpable. So, for example, I. F. Volkov would declare in 1974 that "such an essential feature of romanticism as the striving of the self-affirming individual toward a better life was assimilated by the literature of critical realism, and then also by the literature of socialist realism." Hence "romanticism was at the foundation of realist artistic creativity" (36).

38. Compare the "Sovietized" treatment of Russian Romanticism in the collection of essays in *Русский романтизм: Сборник статей* [Russian Romanticism: Collected Articles], ed. A. I. Beletskii (Leningrad: Akademiia, 1927), for example, with the far less ideologically influenced discussions of this subject by Evgenii A. Maimin in *О русском романтизме* [About Russian Romanticism] (Moscow: Prosveshchenie, 1975), or by Iurii Mann.

39. According to McLaughlin, "until far into the nineteenth century *roman* was associated with such unfavourable features as exaggerated feelings, exotic locations and names, bizarre events, complicated plots, and endless love adventures

always crowned with good fortune." Therefore, "it was inevitable that the adjective *romanicheskii* [*романический*], when it appeared in 1791, much later than *roman* [*роман*], carried these connotations along with imported meanings such as 'picturesque' and 'sentimental'" (464).

40. McLaughlin holds "the state of Russian literary criticism" in the 1810s and 1820s largely responsible for the semantic confusion over the meaning of Romanticism, on the grounds that, in those decades, "literary criticism was not a profession, and the best critics were themselves poets. Such criticism as there was consisted chiefly of subjective, impressionistic remarks about new literary works, of discussions of their patriotic qualities and their proper or improper subject matter, of biographical and bibliographical information, of listings of typographical errors and of statements about the quality of the paper on which the works were printed. . . . Literary polemics often deteriorated into undignified, vicious personal attacks. Views were presented arrogantly and naively. A writer's social class could be cause enough to despise his views" (467–68). In sum, critical precision, consistency, and objectivity were in short supply in early nineteenth-century Russia, McLaughlin affirms, precluding the use of clear, reliable terminology.

41. In his wide-ranging and perceptive study *Alexander Bestuzhev-Marlinsky and Russian Byronism*, Bagby specifically identifies "the theatricality of the Byronic prose and the techniques of *l'École frénétique* associated with the early Victor Hugo" (5) as the predominant models for the Russian author's writings. For an extended discussion of Bestuzhev-Marlinskii's relation to Romanticism, see especially chapter 2, "Bestuzhev and Romantic Praxis," 41–57.

42. Picchio in fact suggests that "to be a Romantic, or at least a romantically oriented person, became almost a social duty in Russia during and after the antinapoleonic war" (26). Here again he identifies Romanticism simply with an attitude, especially the attitude of nationalistic pride and resistance.

43. As Mersereau points out, Pushkin was "vitally concerned" with Romanticism in the 1820s and "actively followed and took part in the discussions centering around romanticism and its relationship to the latest developments in Russian literature," about which there was no consensus ("Pushkin's Romanticism," 28). For additional analyses of Pushkin's relationship to Romanticism, see V. V. Sipovskii, "Пушкин и романтизм" [Pushkin and Romanticism], in *Пушкин и его современники* [Pushkin and His Contemporaries] (Petrograd: n.p., 1916); Boris S. Meilakh, *Пушкин и русский романтизм* [Pushkin and Russian Romanticism] (Leningrad: Nauka, 1937); Grigorii A. Gukovskii, *Пушкин и русские романтики* [Pushkin and Russian Romanticists] (Moscow: Khudozhestvennaia literatura, 1965); Viktor M. Zhirmunskii, *Пушкин и Байрон; Пушкин и западные литературы* [Pushkin and Byron; Pushkin and Western Literatures] (Leningrad: Nauka, 1978); John Bayley, *Pushkin: A Comparative Commentary* (London: Cambridge University Press, 1971); Sandler; and Greenleaf, *Romantic Fashion*.

44. Letter to Aleksandr A. Bestuzhev, 30 November 1825.

45. Stephanie Sandler offers provocative reasons to view Pushkin's relation to

Romanticism as somewhat more lasting than I do in her analysis of his poem "К морю" [To the Sea] of 1824, where Pushkin bids farewell to both Byron and Napoleon. In so doing, Sandler argues, Pushkin also bids farewell to "the period of [his] life that was infused with Romantic circumstances." At the same time, "the poem's subject matter, its passionate diction and tone, its very interest in the contradictions involved in what it is trying to do—these are signals to the reader that, as it is being written, 'To the Sea' participates in the romantic movement it wants to leave behind" (68; 227, n. 51). In the same vein, Monika Greenleaf more broadly holds that, "far from 'overcoming Romanticism,' in the stock phrase of Soviet criticism, Pushkin may have played out [its] last scenes" (*Romantic Fashion*, 18).

46. For a useful survey of Gogol's affinities to German Romantic philosophy, see John Kopper, "The 'Thing-in-Itself' in Gogol's Aesthetics: A Reading of The *Dikanka* Stories," in *Essays on Gogol: Logos and the Russian Word*, ed. Susanne Fusso and Priscilla Meyer (Evanston, IL: Northwestern University Press, 1992), 40–62.

47. Proffer surmises that Gogol did not include his definition of Romanticism in the final draft of "Petersburg Notes of 1836" because, by the time Gogol was ready to publish the notes, "romanticism was moribund as the dominant, topical literary issue in Russia" (127).

48. Although Grigor'ian plants Lermontov firmly in the Romantic camp, he does distinguish Lermontov from other Romanticists by noting that although "the earth was alien to" Lermontov, "he had no faith in heaven" either (127), since he did not believe in "another reality" (128). Hence, while Lermontov hated life, Grigor'ian argues, he feared death. This fear betokened a lack of the faith in transcendence or a spiritual existence beyond the physical realm that was a hallmark stance of Romanticists. Coupled with his emphasis on Lermontov's consistent engagement with reality despite recurring disappointment in it, Grigor'ian in effect characterizes Lermontov as a sort of "realistic Romanticist"—one who confronts the ugliness of reality and opposes it without hoping for a better form of existence elsewhere.

49. In fact, Golstein declares, given the repressive tsarist regime and rigid censorship of the times, "Lermontov's own independence, his depiction of proud, autonomous, and self-reliant characters, is in itself heroic" (26).

50. Substantive critical works placing Lermontov in the Romantic camp, in addition to those mentioned in the chapter text, include Janko Lavrin, "Some Notes on Lermontov's Romanticism," *Slavonic and East European Review* 36 (1957–58): 69–80; Andrei V. Fedorov, *Лермонтов и литература его времени* [Lermontov and the Literature of His Time] (Leningrad: Khudozhestvennaia literatura, 1967); Margarita M. Umanskaia, *Лермонтов и романтизм его времени* [Lermontov and the Romanticism of His Time] (Iaroslavl': Verkhne-Volzhskoe knizhnoe izdatel'stvo, 1971); Iurii Mann, "Завершение романтической традиции" [The Completion of the Romantic Tradition], in *Лермонтов в литературе Советского Союза* [Lermontov in the Literature of the Soviet Union], by Iurii Mann (Moscow: n.p., 1974), 32–73; E. M. Pulkhritudova, "Романтизм в русской литературе

30-x гг.: Лермонтов" [Romanticism in Russian Literature of the 1830s: Lermontov], in *История романтизма в русской литературе, 1825–1840* [The History of Romanticism in Russian Literature, 1825–1840], ed. S. E. Shatalov (Moscow: n.p., 1979); and Powelstock, *Becoming Lermontov.*

51. Critical discussions acknowledging Lermontov's early connection to Romanticism but emphasizing Lermontov's anticipation of and affinities with Realism include S. N. Durylin, "На путях к реализму" [On the Path Toward Realism], in *Жизнь и творчество Лермонтова* [Lermontov's Life and Artistic Works], ed. N. L. Brodskii (Moscow: Khudozhestvennaia literatura, 1941), 163–250; Ginzburg; Mersereau, *Lermontov*; Viktor A. Manuilov, *Летопись жизни и творчества М. Ю. Лермонтова* [A Chronicle of Lermontov's Life and Artistic Works] (Leningrad: Nauka, 1964); and Fokht. Sokolov reflects this view of Lermontov by claiming that "in Lermontov's artistic works the process of maturation of realistic tendencies clearly reveals itself." He continues: "For Russian literature it was essential to assimilate the realistic achievements of the Pushkinian verse novel into the genre of the prose novel. It was Lermontov who achieved this" (89).

52. Golstein makes an ingenious effort in this regard, arguing that Pechorin adheres to a "peculiar morality" incorporating a "code of honor and chivalry" that at least affiliates Pechorin with noble Romantic forebears while bestowing upon him a "heroic combination of thorough skepticism and decisive action" (118, 124). However, in defending this view, Golstein has to downplay or dismiss the extent to which Pechorin is self-deceived about his own motives and actions, as well as the many instances in which Pechorin is far from either chivalrous or heroic. See Chapter 6 for discussion of ways in which Lermontov's novel has nonetheless been tied to Romanticism.

53. For a summary of these artists' assessments of Lermontov, see Eikhenbaum, *Lermontov*, 15–18.

54. Note that in her dissertation, "From Dissolution to Synthesis: The Use of Genre in Lermontov's Prose," Helena Goscilo also labels Lermontov transitional, affirming that a large portion of Lermontov's "significance lies in his role as a transitional figure." For "he represents the bridge between the Pushkinian era of Russian letters and the heyday of the Russian novel" (2). Along the same lines as Eikhenbaum, Goscilo maintains that Lermontov is transitional in extracting from the "fruitful disorder" of diverse prose genres—for example, travelogue, novella, historical novel, physiological sketch, society tale, and artist story—original and compelling narratives as he "fused seemingly incompatible genres into a single work, at first clumsily, but finally with such mastery that he converted the dissolution of genres into a literary strength" (46, 50). As he did so, Goscilo concludes, Lermontov "evolved from an imitator into an original and independent writer" (49). However, I will take the opposite view of Lermontov's works overall, arguing that what Goscilo perceives as a synthesizing tendency in those works more often entails dissolution of Romantic aesthetic, psychological, and ethical principles.

55. Susanne Fusso shares this view, at least in regard to *A Hero of Our Time*, which she deems to be engaged, along with Pushkin's *Eugene Onegin*, "in a strug-

gle with Romanticism that, in its intensity and explicitness, goes well beyond the self-conscious play known as 'Romantic irony'" (171).

56. In the introduction to her translation of *Vadim*, Goscilo pulls no punches in summing up this work as "a hybrid wherein the Gothic, the historical, and the Romantic narrative poem are primitively combined." As such, "the final impression is one of uncontrolled confusion." She thus concludes that "Lermontov's failure to complete the novel may have been a tacit recognition of his inability to reconcile the incompatible ingredients of his fictional hash" (27).

57. Regrettably, this study appeared too late for extended consideration in this book. In an article along the same lines, Powelstock suggests that Lermontov sought "a unitary self without hope of final discovery" (324), but Powelstock attributes that lack of hope to Lermontov's complex psychological make-up and ambiguous social status.

58. Golstein also observes some sense of disintegration in Lermontov and interestingly claims that Lermontov's response was to portray artistic creativity as having the power to redeem characters otherwise torn apart by psychological conflicts and existential crises. However, the examples of personal redemption he points to—the eponymous Mtsyri, Dr. Werner in *A Hero of Our Time*, and Tamara in *The Demon*—do not in fact *create* art at all. Mtsyri and Dr. Werner only voice appreciation of the artistic creations of others, and Tamara is primarily, as it were, a performing artist—she sings and dances, undoubtedly obtaining her inspiration from her native customs. In fact, Golstein exposes the *absence* of images of true artistic creativity in Lermontov—yet another indication of Lermontov's sense of the creative impasse at which his literary culture had arrived.

59. See especially the recollections of contemporaries such as Akim P. Shan-Gerei, Ekaterina A. Sushkova, Varvara I. Annenkova, and others who encountered him in society, in Grigorenko et al.

60. In his reminiscence of Lermontov, the sensitive and astute Russian author Ivan Turgenev declares after encountering the younger writer at a ball, "There was no doubt that he, following the mode of that time, had taken upon himself the well-known form of the Byronic genre, along with an admixture of other, still worse, caprices and eccentricities" (Grigorenko et al., 237). And Powelstock acknowledges that Lermontov actively sought to exploit "the Romantic mythologies of his age" by "projecting the image of the poet into the contemporary cultural mythology as an active hero"—an image established by Byron—and by placing himself in that role ("Language," 313, 311).

61. Note that Frederick W. Shilstone attributes this ironic Kierkegaardian "transitional consciousness" even to Byron (xiii).

62. In his article "Lermontov in the Negative," A. D. P. Briggs provides indirect support for my contention that Lermontov did not embrace a new set of values associated with Realism, as Briggs documents the extent to which Lermontov used negative rather than affirmative terms. Briggs argues that "Lermontov's use of negatives is out of the ordinary," so that "when compared to Pushkin, for example, [Lermontov] may be seen to have produced considerably more poems

which actually begin with *ne*, *net*, or *nikto* ['not,' 'no,' or 'no one'], even though the body of his shorter poems is only half the size" (12). And Briggs concludes that "there are no noticeable peaks and troughs in the incidence of his negatives. His affinity begins early, continues steadily, and ends late—just as . . . [his use of negatives] extends over all the genres which he employed" (21). Whereas Briggs attributes this prevalence of negation simply to a "habit of mind" (13) Lermontov possessed, I would attribute it more to Lermontov's inability to find a constellation of values to affirm.

Chapter 3: The Ambivalence of Influence

1. The Russian text of this poem reads:

Нет, я не Байрон, я другой
Еще неведомый избранник,
Как он, гонимый миром странник,
Но только с русскою душой.
Я раньше начал, кончу ране,
Мой ум не много совершит;
В душе моей, как в океане,
Надежд разбитых груз лежит.
Кто может, океан угрюмый,
Твои изведать тайны? кто
Толпе мои расскажет думы?
Я – или бог – или никто!

2. Lermontov based this identification in part on what he took to be a direct connection between himself and Byron through an apparent reference to Lermontov's paternal great grandfather, Vasilii Vasilievich Arsenev, in stanza 9, canto 8, of Byron's *Don Juan* (1819–24): "The columns were in movement one and all, / But of the portion which attack'd by water, / Thicker than leaves the lives began to fall, / Though led by Arseniew, that great son of slaughter, / As brave as ever faced both bomb and ball" (754).

3. Dostoevsky, for one, took the identification for granted, asserting that, "of course, Lermontov was a Byronist," although Dostoevsky qualifies the assertion somewhat by adding, "but by virtue of his great, unique poetic strength, a special sort of Byronist—[Lermontov's was] some sort of jocular, capricious, and petulant Byronism, eternally doubting even its own inspiration, in its own Byronism" ("Пушкин, Лермонтов и Некрасов" [Pushkin, Lermontov, and Nekrasov], in *Дневник писателя за 1877* [Diary of a Writer for 1877] [December], chap. 2, sec 2, in *Полное собрание сочинений* [Complete Works], 26: 417).

In addition to the studies mentioned in the text, significant critical discussions of Lermontov's Byronism include: V. Spasovich, "Байронизм у Лермонтова" [Byronism in Lermontov], *Вестник европы* [The European Herald] 4 (1888): 500–548;

Eikhenbaum, *Lermontov*; Ginzburg; M. Nol'man, "Лермонтов и Байрон" [Lermontov and Byron], in *Жизнь и творчество М. Ю. Лермонтова* [The Life and Artistic Works of M. Iu. Lermontov], ed. Nikolai L. Brodskii (Moscow: Gosudarstvennoe izdatel'stvo khudozhestvennoi literatury, 1941), 466–515; J. Thomas Shaw, "Byron, the Byronic Tradition of the Romantic Verse Tale in Russia, and Lermontov's *Mtsyri*," *Indiana Slavic Studies* 1 (1956): 165–90; Andrei V. Fedorov, "Лермонтов и Байрон" [Lermontov and Byron], in *Лермонтов и литература его времени* [Lermontov and the Literature of His Time] (Leningrad: Khudozhestvennaia literatura, 1967), 312–35; Kelly; and Diakonova. The section entitled "Лермонтов и Байрон" [Lermontov and Byron], in A. Pozov, *Метафизика Лермонтова* [Lermontov's Metaphysics] (Madrid, 1975), 130–36, presents a tidy summary of the areas most critics think the two authors had in common.

4. The other European authors most frequently mentioned by critics as influencing Lermontov include Shakespeare, Lessing, Scott, Hugo, and Schiller. See S. Shuvalov, "Влияния на творчество Лермонтова русской и европейской поэзии" [The Influences of Russian and European Poetry on Lermontov's Artistic Works], in *Венок М. Ю. Лермонтову: Юбилейный сборник* [A Tribute to M. Iu. Lermontov: An Anniversary Collection] (Moscow: Izdatel'stvo V. V. Dumnov, 1914), 290–342, esp. 311–42, for a survey of these and other often-perceived European influences on Lermontov.

5. Like Duchèsne, Diakonova argues that Byron's influence on Lermontov diminished over time, and yet she makes a compelling case for Byron's *Letters and Journals* as a model for Pechorin's journal in *A Hero of Our Time*, in "Byron and Lermontov."

6. David Powelstock provocatively treats Lermontov's relation to Pushkin as a product of such anxiety in "Living into Language." On Lermontov's manner of "overcoming" Byron, see, for example, Vadim Vatsuro, "Поэмы М. Ю. Лермонтова" [The Narrative Poems of M. Iu. Lermontov], in Lermontov, *Собрание сочинений* [Collected Works], 2: 525.

7. This feeling of profound personal kinship with Byron arguably extended into Lermontov's adulthood, due to what Lermontov gathered from Byron's reputation was, in Grigor'ian's words, their shared "dissatisfaction with life, protest against every form of oppression (personal and social), restless spiritual condition, violent passions, intense sufferings, incurable grief [and] torturous despair" (54). Eikhenbaum goes further, claiming that "the reason for Lermontov's special fascination with Byron lay outside literature: for him Byron was the ideal of 'the great man'" (*Lermontov*, 28).

8. Certainly Lermontov also knew many of Byron's lyrics, translating a number of them and using lines from many others in his own lyric poetry. For example, see Eikhenbaum, *Lermontov*, 49–52, 140–41; Diakonova, 90–95. But the expanded canvas of narrative poems affords a better opportunity to consider which elements of Byron's works Lermontov explores.

9. Biographer Richard Friedenthal notes that Goethe was evidently deeply touched by Byron's dedication of the closet drama *Sardanapalus* (1822) to Goethe

as Byron's "liege lord, the first of existing writers, who has created the literature of his own country, and illustrated that of Europe" (Byron, 453). Goethe saved the original draft of the dedication, sent to him by Byron's executors, in a special folder. For an extended discussion of the connections between the two authors, see Eliza M. Butler, *Byron and Goethe: Analysis of a Passion* (London: Bowes and Bowes, 1956).

10. As Bertrand Russell sums up Byron's public image: "Like many other prominent men, he was more important as a myth than as he really was. As a myth, his importance, especially on the Continent, was enormous" (752). On the conflation of Byron's private, public, and literary personas, see especially Gilbert Phelps, "The Byronic Byron," in *Byron: A Symposium*, ed. John D. Jump (London: Macmillan, 1975), 52–75; and Philip W. Martin, *Byron: A Poet Before His Public* (Cambridge: Cambridge University Press, 1984). Jacques Barzun strongly emphasizes the difference between Byron and his heroes in "Byron and the Byronic in History," in *The Energies of Art*, by Jacques Barzun (New York: Random House, 1956), 51–82.

11. The eponymous characters Manfred and Cain later added elements of misery and rage to the image of the type. In an unsigned review in the *Edinburgh Review* of February 1817, Byron's contemporary and frequent reviewer Francis Jeffrey offers a compelling description of the Byronic hero as a character "full of pride and revenge and obduracy—disdaining life and death and mankind and himself—and trampling, in his scorn, not only upon the falsehood and formality of polished life, but upon its tame virtues and slavish devotion" (Rutherford, 100).

12. This is the central thesis of Robert F. Gleckner's *Byron and the Ruins of Paradise* (Baltimore: Johns Hopkins University Press, 1967).

13. In his insightful study of Byron, Michael G. Cooke reports the ever-provocative Swinburne describing Byron as a "poet of the third class who now and then rises into the second" (*Blind Man*, viii). Bertrand Russell echoes Swinburne's notion that Byronic gloom was exaggerated when he maintains that "the world insisted on . . . omitting the element of pose in his cosmic despair and professed contempt for mankind" (752).

14. Monika Greenleaf persuasively suggests that Byron's image in Russia, which Lermontov would have encountered along with his contemporaries, was "strongly skewed" because "his works were preceded by anecdotes told by diplomats with political interests; his career was somewhat foreshortened by the time lag . . . ; his poetry was read in French prose translation, which had the effect of heightening plot, character, melodramatic action, and particularly political rhetoric." In addition, although Byron's devotion to the cause of Greek independence led the Russian censorship to control and even prohibit the dissemination of Byron's works, "the more persistently the censorship and police attempted to block Byron's infiltration into Russia, the more passionately the Russian public watched Byron's every move in the Greek movement and read and responded to his poetry in its light." This resulted in that public's "further romanticizing a Romantic persona" ("Apprenticeship," 387).

15. Lermontov's idea of Byron was undoubtedly also influenced by the so-called Russian Byronists, including, albeit to varying degrees, Vasilii Zhukovskii, Ivan Kozlov, Kondraty Ryleev, Aleksandr Odoevskii, Petr Viazemskii, the brothers Bestuzhev, and others, all of whom wrote works inspired by Byron and several of whom translated some of his works into Russian. But the fact that Lermontov knew English well enough to read and to translate Byron himself (Lermontov did a quite respectable prose version of Byron's "Darkness" [1: 515–16], for instance) would have tempered their influence on him. See, in addition to Diakonova and Vatsuro, the classic study by Viktor M. Zhirmunskii, *Байрон и Пушкин* [Byron and Pushkin], for a comprehensive discussion of Russian Byronism. See also G. R. V. Barratt, "Somov, Kozlov, and Byron's Russian Triumph," *Canadian Review of Comparative Literature* 1 (1974): 104–22. Lewis Bagby's "Bestuzhev's Byron: Cross-Cultural Transformation," *Canadian-American Slavic Studies* 29, nos. 3–4 (1995): 271–84, presents an insightful discussion of Byron's influence on Aleksandr Bestuzhev-Marlinskii, the most popular Russian Byronist of the 1820s and 1830s.

16. Greenleaf points to "many areas of Pushkin's behavior" that "received the impress of Byronism," including Pushkin's "elaborate etiquette for keeping his roles as gentleman and poet distinct," "his insistence on the gentlemanly negligence of his compositional practice," "the fusion of Orientalism with the theme of personal and civic freedom," "the well-publicized high-society love life," "the game of literary 'kiss and tell,'" and "the shimmering ambiguity of the boundary between real life and verbal construct" ("Apprenticeship," 394–95).

17. Acknowledging this dismissal, Greenleaf plausibly lists its advantages to Pushkin as "an important step in Pushkin's promotion of a different, contrapuntal image of his own writer's career: not a wild-eyed individualist and political incendiary, but a politically responsible national writer; not a deracinated, familyless cosmopolitan, but a mature family man rooted in the traditions of his nation and class; not a repetitive, melodramatic Romantic, but a writer developing in namable, Horatian stages" ("Apprenticeship," 384).

18. On Lermontov's relationship to Pushkin, see, in addition to Powelstock's study *Becoming Lermontov*, Boris V. Neiman, *Влияние Пушкина в творчестве Лермонтова* [Pushkin's Influence on Lermontov's Artistic Works] (Kiev: n.p., 1914); Duchèsne, 185–201; Dmitrii Blagoi, "Лермонтов и Пушкин (проблема историко-литературной преемственности)" [Lermontov and Pushkin (a Problem of Historical-Literary Influence)], in *Жизнь и творчество М. Ю. Лермонтов: исследования и материалы* [The Life and Artistic Works of M. Iu. Lermontov: Analyses and Materials], vol. 1 (Moscow: Goslitizdat, 1941), 363–421; Boris V. Neiman, "Пушкин и Лермонтов" [Pushkin and Lermontov], in *Пушкин: Сборник статей* [Pushkin: A Collection of Articles], ed. Aleksandr Egolin (Moscow: Gosudarstvennoe izdatel'stvo khudozhestennoi literatury, 1941), 315–48; Vladimir L. Markovich, *Пушкин и Лермонтов в истории русской литературе* [Pushkin and Lermontov in the History of Russian Literature] (St. Petersburg: Izdatel'stvo St. Peterburgskogo universiteta, 1997); and Makogonenko.

Michael Wachtel particularly points to Lermontov's experiments with the poetic form Pushkin employed in *Eugene Onegin*, the so-called Onegin stanza, to demonstrate the youthful Lermontov's overall attraction to Pushkin's artistry (134–37). However, Wachtel does observe that Lermontov's endeavors "lack the ironic layering so central to *Onegin* and offer nothing to compensate for it except a traditional atmosphere of Romantic melancholy" (137). This observation supports my contention that Lermontov remained more closely attached to Romanticism than Pushkin. At the same time, Wachtel also notes, "it appears that Lermontov himself recognized the shortcomings of these experiments [with the Onegin stanza], breaking [them] off after a few stanzas" (137). Here Wachtel suggestively points to Lermontov's dissatisfaction with "traditional" Romantic atmospherics as well.

19. These differences can be seen, for example, by comparing Lermontov's *Кавказский пленник* [The Prisoner of the Caucasus] of 1828 to Pushkin's narrative poem of the same name, written in 1821, both of which most notably combine elements of Byron's *The Prisoner of Chillon* and *The Bride of Abydos*. Similarities between Lermontov's and Pushkin's poems include basic characters and plot: a Russian soldier is captured by Circassians and then freed by a young Circassian woman who has become enamored of the captive and then commits suicide when her love is rejected; the two poems also share descriptions of the natural setting and local customs. However, Lermontov introduces more dramatic and in some ways decisive characters, and an emotionally engaged narrator more reminiscent of Byron's than Pushkin's. Furthermore, Lermontov ends on a far more psychologically and morally ambiguous note than either of them. Rather than echoing Byron's mournful or meditative perorations, and in striking contrast to Pushkin's final tribute to Russia's military might in *The Prisoner of the Caucasus*, Lermontov concludes with the despairing cry of the young woman's tormented father, "Where is my daughter?" followed by the echo, "Where?" The father does not know that his daughter has committed suicide because he has killed her beloved prisoner and thus, according to the narrator, can be deemed her "murderer" as well (Pushkin introduced no such complicating ambiguities—his male protagonist survives). Lermontov therefore leaves a final unanswered question hanging in the air, its inconclusiveness distinctly and distinctively distancing Lermontov from both of his renowned older contemporaries. See Sandler, 145–65, for highly insightful commentary on Pushkin's *Prisoner*, which she labels his "most Byronic poem" (157).

20. At least one other critic, John Garrard, shares this view, flatly declaring that Lermontov "did not come to Byron through a Pushkinian filter, but directly through French literature" ("Old Wine," 42–43), and, of course, in the original versions that Lermontov knew English well enough to read.

21. Lermontov cites *The Corsair* in an unfinished narrative poem of 1832 whose title, *Моряк*, would normally be translated as *The Sailor* but could also be translated as *The Corsair*; the latter actually seems preferable in light of the fact that Lermontov took its epigraph from Byron's poem. *The Sailor* is only one-third the length of *Korsar*, however, so it affords far fewer points of comparison. In *Korsar* Lermontov also borrowed six lines from Kozlov's translation of Byron's *The Bride of Abydos* (1813), as well as a couple of lines each from Pushkin's *Кавказский*

пленник [The Prisoner of the Caucasus] (1822) and *Братъя разбойники* [The Robber Brothers] (1825), and Kozlov's *Княгиня Наталья Борисовна Долгорукая* [Princess Natal'ia Borisovna Dolgorukaia] (1826).

22. These are the lines Lermontov chose for the epigraph to *The Sailor*. The first number of the citation refers to the page in Byron's *Poetical Works*.

23. See Sokolov, 34–38, for a discussion of the historical basis of *Izmail-Bei*; Ginzburg suggests that the Decembrist uprising provides this work with an additional historical subtext (55). Some commentators emphasize the historical roots of *Izmail-Bei* as a major difference between it and Byron's narrative poems, but this emphasis is misplaced, since Byron used history as a point of departure in several of his narratives as well (e.g., *The Siege of Corinth*, *The Prisoner of Chillon*, *Mazeppa*). See Peter Scotto, "Prisoners of the Caucasus: Ideologies of Imperialism in Lermontov's 'Bela,'" in *PMLA* 107, no. 2 (March 1992): 246–60, for a provocative discussion of Lermontov's treatment of the Caucasus in *A Hero of Our Time*; see also Susan Layton, *Russian Literature and Empire: The Conquest of the Caucasus from Pushkin to Tolstoy* (Cambridge: Cambridge University Press, 1994), for a comprehensive survey of this region's nineteenth-century literary depictions.

24. The epigraph for part 2 is taken from Walter Scott's narrative poem *Marmion* (1808), which tells the tale of the Scottish lord Marmion, who heroically dies in battle against the English.

25. Pushkin's influence on Lermontov can arguably be seen in this facet of *Izmail-Bei*, in that Pushkin notably employed quotidian descriptions in each of his Southern tales.

26. These include references to Allah (2: 136, 160), to Mohammad (2: 160,186), and to a mullah and a Moslem holiday (2: 159).

27. Of course, these participles could represent the first narrator's Russian translation of Circassian equivalents, but the employment of some of Russian's most complex linguistic forms more likely reveals that these delicate images proceed from the mind of the first narrator.

28. In fact, disruptive shifts of subject without transition repeatedly occur over the course of the dozen stanzas portraying this battle. For example, a stanza reporting on how Izmail and his followers plunge into the fighting is succeeded by a stanza that begins "Far from the conflict" [Далеко от сраженья] (2: 186) and goes on to depict a perfectly civilized conversation between Zara and a Circassian warrior resting his horse. Two stanzas later, the narrative abruptly returns to the battlefield, only to begin by focusing on a figure who literally appears out of nowhere: "Who is this Russian?" [Кто этот русский?] (2: 187). Until Izmail confronts him, this Russian's identity and role in the narrative are wholly obscure. We might see Pushkin's influence here too, in light of the renowned narrative digressions in Pushkin's *Eugene Onegin*. However, Pushkin's narrator tends to integrate his digressions more artfully, and to be far more playful when he digresses. Of course, narrative digression was such a staple of eighteenth-century European literature, most notably in Laurence Sterne's *Tristram Shandy* (1759–66), that Lermontov, like Pushkin, might have been inspired by such sources as well.

29. Izmail's characterization therefore calls into question the assertion of some critics that Lermontov's heroes are, in effect, *more* Byronic than Byron's. John Garrard, for one, claims, "If there is a difference between Lermontov's poems and Byron's, it is that Lermontov's heroes are more dynamic and active, his poems more violent and narrated on a more strident, less elegiac level. In other words, he is more extreme than Byron, 'plus royaliste que le roi même' " (*Lermontov*, 38–39).

30. Although Lermontov does imply an affinity by having Roslambek apostrophize Izmail as a "damned giaour" [джяур проклятый] (2: 195).

31. Eugene Onegin makes the same claim in rejecting the youthful Tatiana's espoused love for him (*Евгений Онегин* [Eugene Onegin], chap. 4, stanzas 13–14), but his words sound much more like an invented excuse than a disillusioned belief.

32. Rozanov, for one, argues that the young Lermontov went *too far* in emulating Byron (352). And even as eminent a critic as Lidiia Ginzburg describes Lermontov's early narrative poems as Byronic in all but name: "This is poetry about tragic exile and the struggle for freedom, about individuals of great passions and quests" (69).

Chapter 4: The Attenuation of Romantic Evil

1. Lermontov also placed demonic figures at the center of other works in every genre: lyric poems (notably two entitled "Мой демон" [My Demon] [1829 and 1831]), narrative poems (including one called *The Angel of Death* [Ангел смерти] [1831]), dramas, and prose—he even considered writing a satire treating "the adventures of a demon." But if demons were something of an *idée fixe* in Lermontov's life and his art, then *The Demon* was his obsession.

2. See Udodov, 213–450, for an exhaustive review of Lermontov's progress through the various revisions of this poem.

3. Examples of autobiographical interpretations can be found, for example, in Duchèsne; N. A. Kotliarevskii, *М. Ю. Лермонтов: Личность поэта и его произведений* [M. Iu. Lermontov: The Identity of a Poet and His Works] (Petrograd: n.p., 1915); and Kelly. More social and historical views of the work are presented in many Soviet studies, including Ginzburg; Iraklii A. Andronikov, *Лермонтов: Исследования и находки* [Lermontov: Analyses and Discoveries] (Moscow: Khudozhestvennaia literatura, 1977), and Viktor A. Manuilov, *Летопись жизни и творчества М. Ю. Лермонтова* [A Chronicle of M. Iu. Lermontov's Life and Artistic Works] (Leningrad: Nauka, 1964). The ethical and philosophical dimensions of the work are emphasized by, among others: Dmitrii S. Merezhkovskii, *М. Ю. Лермонтов: Поэт сверхчеловечества* [M. Iu. Lermontov: Poet of the superhuman] (St. Petersburg: Panteon, 1909); Pul'khritudova; Mann; and Reid, "Identity and Axiology." Eikhenbaum strenuously rejected any moral interpretation on the grounds that "there were not sufficiently strong traditions in Russian poetry" at the time Lermontov wrote *The Demon* to allow him to create "an abstract metaphysical poem" (*Lermontov*, 113).

An excellent summary of critical views of *The Demon*, at least prior to 1982, is provided by Reid in his "Lermontov's *Demon*: A Question of Identity."

4. Reid in fact suggests that "anthropomorphic interpretations of the poem have in general prevailed" ("Identity and Axiology," 235). This line of thought can be found, for instance, in I. I. Zamotin: "The poet humanizes [the Demon] and reduces him to a quite ordinary representative of human grief" (quoted in Reid, "Question of Identity," 196). Connolly carries on in this vein, arguing that in the course of revising *The Demon*, "Lermontov managed to complete Pushkin's initiative of 'humanizing' the demonic" (136), although Connolly also finds that Lermontov rendered the figure of the Demon "more majestic and awesome" in the process (135). Golstein too describes *The Demon* as a study in "the problem of human choice" (29), although he does not explicitly treat the Demon as human. Valentin Boss observes the possible influence of Milton's *Paradise Lost* on *The Demon* but concludes that "the titanic adversary of God and man in *Paradise Lost* is reduced in *Demon* to the scale of a fugitive lover, pleading that God will neither care nor notice" (113).

Pamela Davidson provides a provocative variation on this "anthropomorphizing" critical trend by proposing that the Demon be viewed as "a figure of the artist" whose "act of erotic seduction therefore becomes a mirror image of the act of artistic creation." "Both derive from an initial yearning for purity and wholeness," Davidson suggests, "but suffer from the concomitant danger of embracing a false, illusory form of embodiment, which could eventually lead to the corruption or destruction of the original impulse" and of the muse that inspired this impulse (181). Critics of this persuasion often point to the subtitle of *The Demon*, *An Eastern Tale* [*Восточная повесть*], as an indicator of the work's nonmetaphysical concerns, but situating the work in the East would hardly preclude such concerns.

By contrast to this critical line of interpretation, I agree with Reid that "Lermontov was moving towards, rather than away from, a supernatural definition of his hero's identity" ("Question of Identity," 197) as he put *The Demon* through its multiple redactions, and that this supernatural definition necessitates an understanding of the nature of evil that the Demon represents. However, I disagree with Reid's subsequent assertion that the Demon's attraction to Tamara reveals him to be "not so much a good person as one capable of great aesthetic experience," as a result of which "morality as such lies outside the scope of the poem, however much the reader's moral preconceptions are brought to bear on a reading of it" ("Question of Identity," 209). I would say that morality is central to *The Demon* but is rendered ambiguous, rather than irrelevant, by the Demon's reaction to Tamara.

5. Other European works most often mentioned by critics as possible sources of inspiration for *The Demon* are Milton's *Paradise Lost* (1667) (see previous note); Thomas Moore's *The Loves of the Angels* (1823) and *Lalla Rookh* (1817); Friedrich Klopstock's *Messias* (1748–73); and Byron's *Heaven and Earth* (1823). A number of Pushkin's works, especially the lyric poems "Ангел" [Angel] (1827) and "Демон" [Demon] (1823), are also viewed as direct antecedents, with Pushkin's narrative poems *Кавказский пленник* [The Caucasian Captive] (1821) and *Цыганы* [The Gyp-

sies] (1824) as indirect influences. In *Becoming Lermontov*, Powelstock persuasively delves into the connections between Pushkin and Lermontov in regard to *The Demon*—my goal in this chapter is to place *The Demon* in relation to European Romantic conceptions of evil.

6. Critics' sense of a close connection of *The Demon* to Romanticism can only have been furthered by highly romanticized depictions of Lermontov's Demon by the Russian painter Mikhail Vrubel in the late nineteenth century.

7. This conclusion causes me to differ strongly with Mann, who claims that "the Demon is the full and chief representative of evil" (217).

8. In surveying Western conceptions of evil, I have found the following sources particularly helpful: Paul Carus, *The History of the Devil and the Idea of Evil from the Earliest Times to the Present Day* (La Salle, IL: Open Court Publishing, 1900); Ruth Anshen, *Anatomy of Evil* (Mt. Kisco, NY: Moyer Bell, 1972); Frederic T. Hall, *The Pedigree of the Devil* (New York: Arno Press, 1979); Christopher Nugent, *Masks of Satan: The Demonic in History* (London: Sheed and Ward, 1983); and Andrew Delbanco, *The Death of Satan: How America Lost the Sense of Evil* (New York: Farrar, Straus and Giroux, 1995). Above all, Jeffrey Burton Russell's thoroughgoing review of the changing images of the Devil in the West across three volumes, *Satan: The Early Christian Tradition* (Ithaca, NY: Cornell University Press, 1981), *Lucifer: The Devil in the Middle Ages* (Ithaca, NY: Cornell University Press, 1984), and *Mephistopheles*, have been invaluable resources.

9. It is historically interesting to note that, in pursuing questions of theodicy, Augustine rejected the proposition that an evil will, displayed in the turn to "the lower," could arise from God, or from "a good nature created by God, the unchangeable good" (386). Augustine therefore concluded that an evil will is the product of "a defect. For defection from that which supremely is, to that which has less of being—this is to begin to have an evil will." But, he continues, "to seek to discover the causes of these defections . . . is as if someone sought to see darkness or hear silence. Yet both of these are known by us, . . . not by their positive actuality, but by their want of it. Let no one then seek to know from me what I know that I do not know" (387).

Thus Augustine does not blame the devil for these "defections," although he wholly accepted the existence and action of the devil as part of God's world. Augustine instead attributed the same deficiency of will to the devil as to human beings. "Hence," he declares, "not even the nature of the devil himself is evil, in so far as it is nature, but it was made evil by being perverted" (691), that is, by defecting from the good.

10. For a valuable overview of Romantic conceptions of morality, in addition to Russell's *Mephistopheles*, I particularly recommend Laurence Lockridge's *The Ethics of Romanticism*.

11. See Otzoupe for an extensive discussion of common influences on the two works and the similarities between them, which Otzoupe finds by far to outweigh the differences. Indeed, he claims that "the resemblances between *Eloa* and *The Demon* are among the most striking phenomena in the romantic poetry of the

early 19th century" (314). Parallels between the two works are also probed by Duchèsne, 315–18; and Reid declares *Eloa* to be one of *The Demon's* two "true antecedents" ("Question of Identity," 199), the other being, in his view, Moore's *Loves of the Angels*.

12. André von Gronicka gives a learned overview of Lermontov's artistic relationship to Goethe in an effort to dispel what he labels "the theory that Lermontov's debt to Goethe is negligible" (567), affirming in particular the influence of *Faust* on *The Demon*: "Nor can there be any doubt that Goethe's Mephistopheles . . . also stood as an archetypal figure behind Lermontov's creation," for the "traits of nihilistic doubt, of cynicism, of hatred and disdain" that are "the most typical of Lermontov's demon" are "quite as typical of Goethe's Mephisto, and underscore the fact that in creating his demonic figure, Lermontov found 'support and help' in Goethe's prototype" (578, 579). Although I would not go as far as von Gronicka in finding psychological affinities between the two figures, I concur with his view that Lermontov did contemplate Goethe's image of Mephistopheles as he developed the character of the Demon. And we know that Lermontov was sufficiently familiar with Goethe's works to place references to *Wilhelm Meister's Apprenticeship* and *Faust* in *A Hero of Our Time*. See also Viktor M. Zhirmunskii, *Гёте в русской литературе* [Goethe in Russian Literature] (Leningrad: Nauka, 1981), esp. chapters 2 and 3, for further discussion of Lermontov's relationship to Goethe.

13. Citations refer to Kaufmann's admirable translation of *Faust*, but I have modified that translation occasionally to enhance comprehensibility.

14. Pul'khritudova is one of several critics who suggest that the Demon is actually more like the character Faust than Mephistopheles, because "the Demon's skepticism does not resemble the corrosive, cold skepticism of Mephistopheles. Lermontov's hero is much closer in his internal world to Faust than to his fellow evil spirit of Goethe's tragedy," since, she claims, the Demon engages in "eternal struggle" (81). She subsequently acknowledges that when the Demon visits Tamara's cell, "interminable exhaustion, exhaustion with power, knowledge, struggle and endless motion, can be heard in his voice" (101)—but this would distinguish the Demon from Faust as well.

15. In regard to the Demon's attraction to beauty, I am reminded of Robert Louis Jackson's insightful analysis of Miltonic imagery in Pushkin's "little tragedy" *Моцарт и Сальери* [Mozart and Salieri] (1830), in which Jackson observes that "the commingling of good and evil, of the sense of beauty and the craving to destroy that arises from it" is "most typical" of a "Russian Satan" (269). It remains unclear, however, whether Lermontov's Demon truly experiences a "craving" to destroy beauty.

16. Virtually every critic commenting on *The Demon* makes reference to the influence of *Cain* on *The Demon*, no doubt themselves influenced by Lermontov's personal predilection for Byron (see Chapter 3). See, for example, Shuvalov's discussion of Lermontov's narrative poems *The Demon* and *The Novice*; and Shaw, 165–67. Shuvalov maintains that Lermontov employed the "general form of the Byronic

narrative poem," and "in various ways combined its intellectual-psychological and formal-stylistic elements," hence "to a greater or lesser extent departing from the fundamental model." Shuvalov also claims that Lermontov's departure from this Byronic model results in a "symbolic (allegorical) narrative poem" (95, 96), yet he never fully specifies precisely what is allegorized, focusing instead on stylistic elements of *The Demon*.

17. This absence is striking in comparison to the early redactions of the poem, especially the fourth and fifth ones, in which Lermontov specifies that the Demon is explicitly motivated by vanity and a proud antagonism toward both God and the angel representing God, and that he seeks revenge for sufferings, along with the preservation of his sinful autonomy, by deliberately killing Tamara. See Udodov, especially 294–320, for discussion of the more overtly rebellious image of *The Demon* in the early redactions. Amanda Ewington also fruitfully explores facets of the early redactions of *The Demon* in her comparison of this poem and Lermontov's play *Masquerade*.

18. Honoré de Balzac also vastly admired Maturin, and tellingly groups Melmoth with Molière's Don Juan, Goethe's Faust, and Byron's Manfred as "the great characters drawn by the greatest geniuses of Europe" (quoted in Rudwin, 213). The most extensive comparison of Lermontov's *The Demon* to Maturin's *Melmoth the Wanderer* to date has been provided by Simpson, who identifies a "close relation" between the two by virtue of "identical basic themes, worked out against similar exotic landscapes," "heroines of similar disposition," "an identical impact of the heroine upon a demon," "identical religious points of view," "a significant psychological element," and "similarities in description and phraseology" (285). Simpson is more concerned to establish these similarities than to analyze them; moreover, he does not account for differences between the two works either amid the similarities he discerns or in other aspects of those works.

19. In further contrast, I would note that Miller finds beneath the "successive layers of narrative" in *Melmoth* "a metaphysical dialogue between a dextrous spokesman for the devil and an innocent, less experienced defendant of faith in goodness and in God, whose primary role is that of listener rather than of speaker" (105). Although Lermontov similarly characterizes his main protagonists, the Demon does not so much participate in a dialogue as deliver several monologues, and these monologues are not buried under layers of narrative but rather dominate the dramatic foreground.

20. I would suggest that the complex narrative structures of Mary Shelley's *Frankenstein* (1816) and Emily Brontë's *Wuthering Heights* (1847) could be attributed to the same impulse to mitigate the impact of characters with evil propensities. Without drawing this conclusion, Walter Reed also observes similarities of narrative structure in *Wuthering Heights*, *Frankenstein*, and *Melmoth the Wanderer* in "Brontë and Lermontov: The Hero In and Out of Time," in *Meditations on the Hero: A Study of the Romantic Hero in Nineteenth-Century Fiction*, by Walter Reed (New Haven, CT: Yale University Press, 1974), 85–137. Miller explores similar topics in *The Brothers Karamazov* in "The Metaphysical Novel" (see preceding note).

21. For example, in describing Tamara's corpse, he cries, "No! Nothing has the strength to tear away now / The eternal mark of death!" [Нет! Смерти вечную печать / Ничто не в силах уж сорвать!] (2: 399); he laments, "Flowers of her native valley / (Thus the ancient rites require) / Waft their aroma above her / And, clasped by her dead hand, / They seem to be saying farewell to the earth!" [Цветы родимого ущелья / (Так древний требует обряд) / Над нею льют свой аромат / И, сжаты мертвою рукою, / Как бы прощаются с землею!] (2: 399). Later, he exclaims regarding a snake near her gravesite that "it gleams like a steel sword / Forgotten on the field of ancient battles / Unneeded by a fallen hero!" [И блещет, как булатный меч, / Забытый в поле давних сеч, / Ненужный падшему герою!], and he bewails the fact that the "hand of centuries" [рука веков] has erased the past, so that there is "nothing to remind anyone / Of the glorious name of Gudal, / Of his sweet daughter!" [И не напомнит ничего / О славном имени Гудала, / О милой дочери его!] (2: 403). These exclamations burst out only sporadically, almost as if the narrator himself suddenly recalls how he *ought* to feel about the images he is depicting. Thus this is more of his inconsistency.

22. Morson applies this concept to Bazarov in Ivan Turgenev's *Отцы и дети* [Fathers and Sons] (1861), as an example of a character who "lives in the wrong genre." According to Morson, Bazarov "is a hero from a [literary] utopia" where "absolute truths are possible," and even "explicitly recommended as a solution to all social problems." Thus "not typhus but the genre [of the novel] kills Bazarov," because of this genre's "intolerance of absolutes" ("Genre," 356, 355, 356).

Chapter 5: Ideals to Ideology

1. For a range of Romantic statements extolling Shakespeare, see the lectures of August Wilhelm von Schlegel and of S. T. Coleridge on Shakespeare, collected, respectively, in *Vorlesungen über dramatische Kunst und Literatur* [A Course of Lectures on Dramatic Art and Literature] (1809–11)], rev. ed., trans. John Black (London: G. Bell, 1976); and *Coleridge's Shakespearean Criticism*, 2 vols., ed. Thomas M. Raysor (London: Everyman's Library, 1960). See also Johann Wolfgang von Goethe, "Shakespeare ad infinitum," in *Goethe's Literary Essays*, ed. Joel E. Spingarn (New York: Harcourt, Brace, 1921), 174–89; and Stendhal, "Racine et Shakspeare." In this essay Stendhal flatly asserts that "Shakespeare was a romantic" (27). For critical discussions of Romantic views of Shakespeare, see, among others, Yurii Levin, "Russian Shakespeare Translations in the Romantic Era," in *European Shakespeares: Translating Shakespeare in the Romantic Age*, ed. Dirk Delabastita and Lieven D'hulst (Amsterdam: Benjamins, 1993), 75–90; Lilian Furst, "Shakespeare and the Formation of Romantic Drama in Germany and France," in *Romantic Drama*, ed. Gerald Gillespie (Amsterdam: Benjamins, 1994), 3–15; F. E. Pointner, "Bardolatry and Biography: Romantic Readings of Shakespeare's Sonnets," in *British Romantics as Readers: Intertextualities, Maps of Misreading, Reinterpretations*, ed. Michael Gassenmeier et al. (Heidelberg: Carl Winter Universitätsverlag, 1998),

117–36; and Peter Davidhazi, *The Romantic Cult of Shakespeare* (New York: Macmillan, 1998).

2. For further discussion of Lermontov's relation to Shakespeare, see in particular Yurii D. Levin, "Лермонтов и Шекспир" [Lermontov and Shakespeare], in *Шекспир и русская культура* [Shakespeare and Russian Culture], ed. Mikhail P. Alekseev (Leningrad: Nauka, 1965), 241–45.

3. Lermontov's direct knowledge of *Othello* is indicated by the quotation in English of Iago's hypocritical warning to Othello, "Beware, my lord, of jealousy" (3.3.165), as the epigraph for Lermontov's brief narrative poem of 1830 *Две невольницы* [Two Captives].

4. Compare, for example, S. N. Durylin, "Лермонтов и романтический театр" [Lermontov and Romantic Theater], and K. Lomunov, "*Маскарад* Лермонтова как социальная трагедия" [Lermontov's *Masquerade* as a Social Tragedy], both in *Маскарад Лермонтова: Сборник статей* [Lermontov's *Masquerade*: A Collection of Essays], ed. Pavel I. Novitskii (Moscow: VTO, 1941). See also, for readings of *Masquerade* as a Romantic drama, Z. S. Efimova, "Из истории русской романтической драмы: *Маскарад* М. Ю. Лермонтова" [From the History of Russian Romantic Drama: M. Iu. Lermontov's *Masquerade*], in *Русский романтизм: Сборник статей* [Russian Romanticism: A Collection of Essays], ed. Aleksandr I. Beletskii (Leningrad: Akademiia, 1927), 26–50; T. I. Khudokhina, "*Маскарад*" М. Ю. Лермонтова [M. Iu. Lermontov's *Masquerade*] (Tomsk: n.p., 1969); S. G. Kaplenko, "Трагическое в пьесе М. Ю. Лермонтова *Маскарад*" [The Tragic in M. Iu. Lermontov's Play *Masquerade*], in *Вопросы историзма и художественного мастерства* [Questions of Historicism and Artistic Mastery] (Leningrad: n.p., 1976), 88–116; and M. Iu. Karusheva, "К идее рока в драме М. Ю. Лермонтова *Маскарад*" [On the Idea of Fate in M. Iu. Lermontov's Drama *Masquerade*], *Русская литература* [Russian Literature] 3 (1989): 161–66. For readings of *Masquerade* as realistic, or proto-Realist, social criticism, see also N. S. Ashukin, "Историко-бытовые комментарии к драме Лермонтова *Маскарад*" [Historical-Popular Commentaries on Lermontov's Drama *Masquerade*], in *Маскарад Лермонтова: Сборник статей* [Lermontov's *Masquerade*: A Collection of Essays], ed. P. I. Novitskii (Moscow: VTO, 1941), 211–48; Viktor A. Manuilov, *М. Ю. Лермонтов* [M. Iu. Lermontov] (Moscow: n.p., 1950), 102–36; V. K. Bogomolets, "*Маскарад*" М. Ю. Лермонтова [M. Iu. Lermontov's *Masquerade*] (Leningrad: n.p., 1954); and Korovin. Korovin goes so far as to claim that "society is guilty" of Nina's murder and that Arbenin merely "plays the role of executioner" (206). N. M. Vladimirskaia offers a kind of compromise between these two interpretive positions in "О взаимодействии романтического и реалистического в драмах М. Ю. Лермонтова" [On the Interaction of the Romantic and the Realistic in M. Iu. Lermontov's Dramas], *Ученные записки Псковского педагогического института* [Scholarly Notes of the Pskov Pedagogical Institute] (1967): 51–59, but she essentially summarizes points for each side, rather than conceptually reconciling the two.

Ian Helfant further subdivides *Masquerade* criticism into studies that (1) connect this play to Lermontov's earlier dramatic works or to contemporaneous ones such as Griboedov's *Горе от ума* [Woe from Wit] (1833), (2) explore the play's autobiographical or social bases; (3) examine Pushkin's influence on the play; and (4) compare *Masquerade* to Lermontov's nondramatic works (127–28). However, these categories pertain more to the assessments of the play as a social critique.

5. Ewington does not explicitly label Arbenin a Romanticist, but she does repeatedly distance *Masquerade* from Realism. She further suggestively describes *Masquerade* as an "intermediate stage" (95) between early and late versions of Lermontov's *Демон* [The Demon], which, she argues, provides a "cosmic subtext" (124) for the play. Thus *Masquerade* combines elements of social satire with "otherworldly philosophy," as a result of which the play "teeters precariously between the social and the metaphysical, the realistic and the fantastic" (99). Ewington points to some striking similarities between *Masquerade* and *The Demon* in their language, plot, and characterizations, but she underestimates one key difference that, in my view, radically undermines these similarities: the fact that Arbenin intentionally kills his wife, whereas the motives behind the Demon's fatal kiss of his beloved remain highly ambiguous. This difference, at least in retrospect, renders Arbenin's elevated language more overtly self-conscious, his pivotal actions more expressly self-serving, and his depth of character more palpably suspect, than the Demon's.

6. Historian Eric Bentley maintains that in essence, to Carlyle, "the hero is the new God" who unites others in reverence and progressively leads them to a better life (67).

7. Furst therefore concludes that "even though the Romantic period still wanted a grandiose hero, what it actually produced was a hybrid half-way between the [traditional] hero and the [modern] anti-hero" (*Contours*, 42). Taking a strongly opposed view, James Wilson holds that "in the last analysis the Romantic hero is far more traditional than he is modern" (17), because he believes in a heroic ideal that "involved first an annihilation of self and assimilation of a transcendental consciousness, then a commitment to one's fellows" (22), which leads him to struggle "on behalf of his fellows to inaugurate a new culture" (65–66). Both these critics arguably go too far: Furst makes the Romantic hero a virtual nihilist and Wilson turns him into a selfless martyr.

8. There are some Romantic protagonists, of course, who combine lofty heroic aspirations and lowly unheroic traits that they are unable to integrate. For example, Mary Shelley's Frankenstein embarks on a grandiose quest to generate human life that is heroic in its visionary scope and egotism—and yet he responds with unheroic cowardice to the hideous creature born of this quest. A scientist turned alchemist, Frankenstein is "animated by an almost supernatural enthusiasm" that, after innumerable "days and nights of incredible labour and fatigue," led him to discover "the cause of generation and life" (50, 51). Possessing the secret of life, Frankenstein envisions himself as a divinity, thinking that "a new species would bless me as its creator. . . . No father could claim the gratitude of his child so completely as I should deserve theirs" (52). Moreover, he muses, "If I could bestow animation upon lifeless matter, I might in process of time . . . renew life where death had apparently devoted the body to corruption" (53).

However, Frankenstein cannot reconcile his heroic vision with what he takes to be the appalling reality of his creation, which he instantly abhors and at first flees, then determines to annihilate. Failing to do so and finding himself on his death-bed aboard a ship exploring the Arctic, he delivers an ambiguous message about the value of heroic endeavors, on the one hand exhorting the ship's sailors to "be men or be more than men," and not to "return to your families with the stigma of disgrace marked on your brows. Return as heroes who have fought and conquered and who know not what it is to turn their backs on the foe" (204). On the other hand, his last words to the ship's captain reject heroic enterprises: "Seek happiness in tranquility and avoid ambition, even if it be only the apparently innocent one of distinguishing yourself in science and discoveries." He then ends ambivalently with the words, "Yet why do I say this? I have myself been blasted in these hopes, yet another may succeed" (206). Whatever his influence on others, Frankenstein himself dies without achieving either the psychological or moral integrity charac-teristic of true Romantic heroes, despite his heroic intentions.

9. The subject of Romanticism as an ideology in itself has engendered some critical debate. At one end of the spectrum, Jacques Barzun avers that "Romanti-cism was never an ideology. If it had been, it would long ago have been classi-fied, put away, and forgotten" (*Classic*, xxii). See, by contrast, Jerome McGann, *Romanticist Ideology*, and Morse Peckham, *Romanticism and Ideology* (Hanover, NH: Wesleyan University Press, 1995), both of which treat Romanticism as an inherently biased ideological construct, the product, in McGann's words, of "the broad social and cultural determinations which are involved in the assumption of an intellectual position" (10). In *Art and Social Responsibility*, Alex Comfort assumes the "intellectual position" that Romanticism entails a worldview ac-cording to which human beings are always at war with forces larger than them-selves—from social and political power structures to the entire universe. In Aers, Cook, and Punter, eds., *Romanticism and Ideology*, Romanticism's "ideology" is defined more neutrally, as a distinctive, but not politically or socially biased, mode of perception and interpretation. Todd provides a succinct review of di-verse conceptions of ideology and then persuasively develops his own notion of the "ideology of [Russian] polite society" (*Fiction and Society*, 44) in the early decades of the nineteenth century (see esp. *Fiction and Society*, 10–44). In none of these studies, however, is ideology specifically defined and employed as it is here.

10. See George Lichtheim for a useful history of the term. Lichtheim eluci-dates how the positive meaning of "ideology" has been subverted over time, point-ing out that the original French *idéologues* advocated "the power of Reason to see through the veil of illusions to the enduring realities of human existence" (46) without determining a priori the nature of those realities. Lewis Feuer reviews this history as well, focusing on the influence of ideologies in Western social and political thought and concluding that ideology "assists in the irrationalization of political life" (191).

11. In "Prosaic Bakhtin," Gary Saul Morson discusses the collection of essays

entitled *Bexu* [translated as *Landmarks* or *Signposts*], published in 1909 by a notable group of Russian liberal thinkers, that insightfully exposes the self-aggrandizing inclinations of ideologues. Such inclinations were embodied for these thinkers in a Russian intelligentsia that, as Morson puts it, "tended to see itself as Russia's, and the world's, savior" (37). In this collection, for example, Mikhail Gershenzon observes in the intelligentsia "an unbridled tendency toward despotism and a total lack of respect for other people" (quoted in Shatz and Zimmerman, 58). And Sergei Bulgakov asserts that "anyone who has lived in intelligentsia circles is well aware of their arrogance and conceit, their sense of their own infallibility, their scorn for those who think differently, and the abstract dogmatism into which they fit all doctrines" (quoted in Shatz and Zimmerman, 29). This psychological state, Bulgakov maintains, engenders a "heroism of self-worship" as "the fundamental essence of the intelligentsia's world-view and ideal" (quoted in Shatz and Zimmerman, 26–27). And so emotionally invested does the intelligentsia become in its inflated heroic self-image, he concludes, that "no word is more unpopular with *intelligenty* [the intelligentsia] than humility" (quoted in Shatz and Zimmerman, 35).

Although viewing ideology and ideologues more neutrally, Parsons likewise acknowledges the self-exalting propensities of ideologues when he describes ideology as "the primary instrument of the modern secular intellectual classes in their bid to be considered generally important" (24).

12. Sowell deliberately employs religious terminology, suggesting that the possession of an ideological "vision" provides the psychic lift of a quasi-religious experience, a sense of being in "a special state of grace" (2). Individuals subscribing to such a vision "are deemed to be not merely factually correct but morally on a higher plane. Put differently, those who disagree with the prevailing vision are seen as being not merely in error, but in sin" (2–3).

To Feuer, ideologues deem themselves "elected," and everyone else "rejected" (193). He also points out that "ideologists in modern times have often been depicted as the successors of the Hebrew prophets, and as filled with the same moral passion and vision," and he suggests that "the linkage of ideologist with prophet is a real one." But, he continues, "what, perhaps, is not realized . . . is that the prophetic personalities were a blight on the life of the ancient Hebrews . . . they were fanatics who reveled in the idea of the destruction of their own society" (197).

13. Mannheim, for one, argues that this self-deception is not deliberate, quoting in this regard Francis Bacon's theory of *idola* presented in *Novum Organum*: "The idols and false notions which have already preoccupied the human understanding and are deeply rooted in it, not only so beset men's minds that they become difficult of access, but even when access is obtained will again meet, and trouble us . . . unless mankind when forewarned guard themselves with all possible care against them" (62). Bacon's theory effectively exculpates ideologues when they deceive themselves or others, since, as Mannheim notes, it does not hold "individuals personally responsible for the deceptions we detect in their utterances" (61), instead locating the source of such deceptions in "society and tradition" (62). However,

this theory ignores the enjoyment of psychological rewards that morally implicates individuals in the embrace, whether conscious or subconscious, of an ideology.

14. Although Cooke quotes liberally from Schopenhauer's *Die Welt als Wille und Vorstellung* [The World as Will and Idea] (1818–20) and "Über die Freiheit des Willens" [Essay on the Freedom of Will] (1839), he gives somewhat short shrift to Schopenhauer's view of the will as a source of ceaseless turbulence that must be conquered and transcended in order to achieve spiritual tranquility, focusing on more positive Romantic evocations of will.

15. Arbenin even calls himself a "coward" [трус] after his failure to murder the prince (3: 325). Later, in one more morally positive, although arguably still conformist, moment, notwithstanding his alleged disdain for the members of his society, he acknowledges and acts on the possibility that one of them may also inadvertently be hurt when he poisons his wife. After observing her consume her tainted ice cream, he muses to himself, "The fatal step is taken, it is far to go back, / But let no one else perish because of her" [Шаг сделан роковой, назад идти далеко, / Но пусть никто не гибнет за нее] (3: 353), and he smashes the ice cream dish on the floor. This act requires no real courage, however.

16. Indeed, Helfant concludes that "ultimately, Arbenin is only a standard-bearer among the hordes of gamblers who swarmed through the pages of Russian literature in Lermontov's day" (143). See Helfant's expanded discussion of this subject in his *The High Stakes of Identity: Gambling in the Life and Literature of Nineteenth-Century Russia* (Evanston, IL: Northwestern University Press, 2002).

17. Golstein insightfully explores Arbenin's fear of anything unknown and therefore uncertain (74–79), and he astutely notes that Arbenin goes mad after being confronted with his fatal error by a character usually called simply "A Stranger" in English translation, but whose Russian name, "Неизвестный," literally means "Unknown" (79). Golstein does not connect this fear, however, to Arbenin's adherence to an ideologically derived self-image. Several critics have noted Arbenin's resemblance to Pushkin's Germann in "The Queen of Spades" in the shared desire for certitude. See, for example, Makogonenko, "Пушкинское начало в драме Лермонтова Маскарада" [The Pushkinian Core of Lermontov's Drama *Masquerade*], in *Лермонтов и Пушкин* [Lermontov and Pushkin], 103–72.

18. Karlinsky finds evidence of what he terms "Lermontov's strongly sadistic attitude toward women" throughout Lermontov's dramatic works, claiming that the extended torture of the female protagonist Vera in *Два брата* [Two Brothers] "is a form of spiritual rape, as are the tormenting of Emiliya by the Jesuit villain in *Испанцы* [The Spaniards] and the slow, cruel poisoning of Nina in *Masquerade*" (171). Karlinsky attributes this attitude to Lermontov's personal difficulties with women—yet one more example of the lengthy critical line interpreting Lermontov's works fundamentally in terms of his biography.

19. See Chapter 2, note 20, for a description of Stendhal's concept of "crystallization."

20. He thus exemplifies the tendency of ideologues, as observed by Mannheim, to "avow allegiance to ideals" while pursuing interests they seek to conceal (96).

21. Edmund Kostka notes that "apart from *Die Rauber* [The Robbers], *Kabale und Liebe* seems to have exercised considerable influence upon the drama" of Lermontov (79)—Lermontov apparently saw a production of the latter in St. Petersburg. Kostka does not remark the specific plot parallels between *Politics and Passion* and *Masquerade*, but he does claim that Arbenin's monologues elevate *Masquerade* "to the dignity of a sublime lyrical tragedy, comparable to the philosophical tragedies of Schiller" (84)—a claim bespeaking Kostka's reading of Lermontov's work as a Romantic play.

22. Sowell also connects ideology to rhetoric, although he goes too far in the end, when he virtually reduces all ideology to mere rhetoric in describing ideologues as "'thinking people' who do remarkably little thinking about substance and a great deal of verbal expression" (260).

23. Lewis Feuer makes a similar claim, asserting that "ideology envelops [the ideologue] in intellectual ramparts which make him immune to criticism. He has a complete world-system with prefabricated answers to every question, and he is impervious to disconfirming evidence" (193).

24. As Helfant has astutely pointed out, Arbenin conjures up an entire narrative of infidelity, twisting Nina's own words to fit his prejudged explanation of them (136–38).

25. At this point his ideology is exposed to Arbenin as literally, in Sowell's words, "fatally independent of reality" (241).

26. Makogonenko, for instance, argues that, by the mid-1830s, Lermontov, having discovered "the distance and alienation of Romanticist ideals from reality," had begun to "overcome" Romanticism (123). Thus, in order to portray in *Masquerade* "the tragedy of a Romantic . . . individual unable to explain whence and why evil has appeared and triumphed," Lermontov followed in the path of Pushkin and turned to Realism because "only realism could fulfill this task," as it had already done for "Pushkin the realist" (138).

27. At the risk of engaging in a bit of backshadowing myself (see Chapter 1), I would note that by exposing the dangers of what might be termed a *cultural* ideology—that is, the rigid, exclusionary embrace of a set of reigning ideas and ideals of a culture during a particular era—*Masquerade* anticipates what Gary Saul Morson has labeled the later nineteenth-century "tradition" of the "negatively philosophical" Russian novel. Exemplified by such works as Turgenev's *Fathers and Sons*, Dostoevsky's *The Devils*, and Tolstoy's *War and Peace*, this tradition, Morson contends, assailed "the faith in abstract ideas and ideologies so common among the intelligentsia in pre-revolutionary Russia" ("Philosophy," 151). Although Morson stresses the blindness to the realities of Russian life wrought by political, social, and religious ideologies that these renowned Russian authors depicted, Lermontov's play arguably prefigures the tradition they established by illustrating how an ideology born of Romantic culture could be as pernicious as ideologies born of any other source.

Chapter 6: Post-Romantic Anomie I

1. Many critics have noted a resemblance between these two complex and compelling figures. See, for instance, Andrei V. Fedorov, "Влиял ли на Лермонтова французский романтизм?" [Did French Romanticism Influence Lermontov?], in *Лермонтов и литература его времени* [Lermontov and the Literature of His Time], by A. V. Fedorov (Leningrad: Khudozhestvennaia literatura, 1967), 336–57.

2. Erich Auerbach nonetheless tellingly describes Stendhal as "a man born too late who tries in vain to realize the life of a past period" (465).

3. For an extensive survey of Russian and Anglo-American critical commentary on *A Hero of Our Time* since its publication, see Natasha A. Reed's unpublished Harvard dissertation, "Reading Lermontov's *Geroj našego vremeni*," esp. 152–233 and 378–421.

4. Reed points out that, over a century after the novel's publication, the issue still remained contentious. As she notes, question number 3 on the agenda of the Fifth International Congress of Slavists in 1962 was: "What sort of composition should *A Hero of Our Time* be considered—realist or romantic?" (186).

5. Golstein elaborates by describing Pechorin as heroically skeptical, "a hero who refuses to be engaged in a vain search for convictions," so that Pechorin's "lack of ideological convictions is a source of strength rather than of weakness" (127). Golstein subsequently qualifies his assessment of Pechorin, however, when he notes that "Pechorin is an enigma: a hero whose heroism is both highlighted and undermined," attributing this paradox to Lermontov's desire "not to create new certainties and new illusions" for readers. Lermontov therefore "demythologizes the old Romantic hero but . . . refuses to remythologize" a new hero (150, 151). Yet Golstein does not make quite clear how this refusal nonetheless accommodates what he deems Pechorin's heroic "adherence to the aristocratic code of behavior, to the rules of honor and obligation" (116). The critic who insists most strongly that Romanticism lies at the core of *A Hero of Our Time* is Kamsar N. Grigor'ian, in *Лермонтов и его роман, "Герой нашего времени"* [Lermontov and His Novel *A Hero of Our Time*] (Leningrad: Nauka, 1975). In the same vein, Gary Rosenshield maintains that, on balance, "Lermontov's novel owes its power far more to its romantic aura than to the depth of its [realistic] psychological analysis," and thus that affiliating this novel with Realism does it a "disservice" (98).

6. Critical works most explicitly attaching *A Hero of Our Time* to Realism include Sergei N. Durylin, *Как работал Лермонтов* [How Lermontov Worked] (Moscow: MIR, 1934); Fokht; Viktor A. Manuilov, "*Герой нашего времени* Лермонтова как реалистический роман" [Lermontov's *A Hero of Our Time* as a Realistic Novel], in *М. Ю. Лермонтов: Вопросы жизни и творчества* [M. Iu. Lermontov: Questions of His Life and Artistic Works], ed. Aleksandr N. Sokolov (Ordzhonikidze: Severo-osentinskoe knizhnoe izdatel'stvo, 1963), 25–35; and Manuilov, *Роман М. Ю. Лермонтова "Герой нашего времени": Комментарии* [M. Iu. Lermontov's Novel *A Hero of Our Time*: Commentaries] (Moscow: Prosveshchenie, 1966); Maksimov; and Emma G. Gershtein, *"Герой нашего времени"*

М. Ю. Лермонтова [Lermontov's *A Hero of Our Time*] (Moscow: Khudozhest-vennaia literatura, 1976). Additionally, in the West, for example, Marie Gilroy asserts that Lermontov's "acid cynicism does not permit a Romantic yearning for an ideal" to enter the novel (50). And Barratt and Briggs suggest that *A Hero of Our Time* "recommends itself as a reaction against a Romanticism which was previously the author's own" (129).

7. Vissarion Belinskii's writings on Lermontov have usefully been collected in *М. Ю. Лермонтов: Статьи и рецензии* [M. Iu. Lermontov: Articles and Reviews].

8. For instance, Mersereau points to the chapter "Taman" as "a tale which is typical of romanticism at full blossom. Yet in the context of the whole novel, the story assists in the further delineation of the hero's realistic portrait" (*Lermontov*, 110). Mersereau then emphasizes the Realism of the segment of Pechorin's diary entitled "Princess Mary," in which "the actual thought process of the hero is reproduced," and which "thus represents an important and original contribution to Russian realism" (*Lermontov*, 121, 122).

9. Heidi Faletti, for one, explicitly labels Lermontov's novel "transitional," on the grounds that it resembles "novels of 'romantic realism'" in their tendency "to project the mythic destiny of its figures within a realistic frame" (366). Other critics have viewed *A Hero of Our Time* as transitional in other terms. John Garrard, for one, finds the novel "a transitional work" in moving "Russian fiction from the short to the long form and from first-person narrative to multiple viewpoints" ("Old Wine," 47). H. Porter Abbott calls Lermontov's novel "a case of art in transition" because it "both contains and transcends the art out of which it grows," which Abbott takes to be "reflexive diary art" (70, 71). And Gilroy sees this novel "at a transitional point in literary history" because it "reflects the metamorphosis of irony from traditional, classical definitions, through Romantic irony," to "modern, unstable irony expressing a changing, disjointed world of shifting values" (47). See Chapter 7 for a discussion of irony in *A Hero of Our Time*.

10. Eugène Duchèsne, for one, declares that the novel's segments are "poorly connected to one another or are united by a singularly artificial connection" (90). Some of this disjointedness may have originated in the fact that Lermontov published several chapters of *A Hero of Our Time* separately before publishing the entire work. "Bela," "Taman," and "The Fatalist" appeared in 1839 in *Отечественный записки* [Notes of the Fatherland] as excerpts from *Записки Офицера о Кавказе* [An Officer's Notes Regarding the Caucasus]. However, this fact would not have obligated Lermontov to any particular ordering of the chapters of *A Hero of Our Time*—and so the order chosen bears close scrutiny.

11. C. J. G. Turner goes as far as any critic in this regard, calling Pechorin "the general cynosure" of *A Hero of Our Time* and describing the structure as "solipsistic, in that there is no counterweight to Pechorin" (66). At the same time, Turner does acknowledge "significant gaps," both chronological and psychological, that make for "multiple hypotheses" about Pechorin's true character (88). Richard Gregg also insists that the structure "cannot help but invite us to view Pechorin as an evolving rather than a static character" whose evolution binds the novel into a whole (388).

12. Meyer attributes to Lermontov the "advantage" over Pushkin of having "a greater awareness afforded by the accumulated models, Western European and Russian" (71), of the potential tragedies inherent in the plots Pushkin treats in a comic vein. I would suggest that this enhanced "awareness" contributes to Lermontov's post-Romantic vision.

13. Like Turner (see note 11), Debreczeny does acknowledge some structural disjointedness in *A Hero of Our Time*, although he explains it by suggesting that "the tendency of the lyrical verse tale to fragment the narrative and to leave parts of the plot sequence in the dark is at least partially responsible for the form Lermontov chose for *A Hero of Our Time*—the form of a "'chain of tales,' rather than a coherent novel" (96). Barratt and Briggs find the novel's disjointedness surmounted by the "uninterrupted existence" of a "line of self-conscious literariness," which provides "one of the strongest unifying forces" in the novel (24); in related fashion, Reid detects "a unity of theme in questioning the morality of the artistic process" throughout ("Eavesdropping," 20).

14. A comparison of *A Hero of Our Time* to Pushkin's *Eugene Onegin* would be particularly intriguing in light of the various forms of fragmentation both works demonstrably incorporate, but I have chosen to focus on Lermontov's relation to the broader European cultural context of Romanticism and I will not embark on such a comparison here. In passing, however, I would note Monika Greenleaf's provocative suggestion that *Eugene Onegin* as a whole is "a deliberately fabricated Romantic fragment" in which "Pushkin's ironic plot keeps all the balls in the air to the end," as he seeks "to prevent the reader from . . . giving in to the temptation of drawing a conclusion" (*Romantic Fashion*, 206, 207). This view of *Eugene Onegin* sets it in marked contrast to *A Hero of Our Time*, an assemblage of post-Romantic fragments that readers are prevented from completing for very different reasons. See Chapter 3, note 18, for comparative studies of Lermontov and Pushkin, in which the similarities and differences between the novels are addressed in a variety of ways. Todd's chapters on *Eugene Onegin* and *A Hero of Our Time* in *Fiction and Society* offer numerous insightful comparisons between these two seminal Russian novels.

15. As has become conventional, I will not quote the original Russian text in full; instead I will provide page references to Nabokov's excellent translation of *A Hero of Our Time*. However, I have occasionally modified this translation in light of the original in order to enhance the precision or smoothness of the English. Thus I cite first the original Russian text.

16. Here I disagree with Debreczeny, despite the number of examples of repetition in the language and imagery of *A Hero of Our Time* that he adduces to support his argument for one "lyric persona" as the narrator. In his article on "double-voicing" in Lermontov's novel, Bagby at least indirectly provides additional reason to disagree with Debreczeny's contention that the novel has a single narrator by persuasively revealing shifting modes of discourse *within* each narrator's speech that thereby further disrupt the narrative flow and distinguish one narrator from another.

17. Early reviewers were particularly confused regarding the work's generic classification; twentieth-century critics who typically possess a more flexible definition of "the novel" as a genre have been more accepting. For extended discussions of the genre of *A Hero of Our Time* and the genres employed within it, see Eagle; and Goscilo, 221–381 ff.

18. I would note that, in addition to its structural disjunctures, the novel is also rife with incidents and images of fragmentation and dis-integration. In fact, the main narrative of each chapter can be said to follow plotlines and characters that break down or trail off into obscurity. As W. W. Rowe has astutely observed, images of *falling down* frequently appear in *A Hero of Our Time*, and I would add that falling down suggests someone or something *falling apart*, losing a hold or, in a word, disintegrating, literally or figuratively. So we see objects, animals, individuals, plots, relationships, hopes, and expectations collapse, or dissolve, or come undone, or run aground, sometimes because they are merely worn out, other times because they are shattered, but always because they cannot persist or be completed. For instance, in "Taman" the smuggling operation that the story revolves around is uncovered and abandoned; the conspiracy to kill Pechorin in "Princess Mary" falls apart; hopes of romance vanish in "Bela" and "Princess Mary"; expectations of friendship are frustrated in "Maksim Maksimich"; a Cossack's escape attempt is foiled in "The Fatalist." In both "Bela" and "Princess Mary," as Rowe notes, characters "fall to the ground and sob" over the loss of something they loved (135)—in "Bela" a local warrior has lost a prized horse, and in "Princess Mary" Pechorin has lost the only woman he claims ever to have truly loved (and this after the horse he has ridden to try to catch up with her "crashed to the ground" in exhaustion [4: 301; 175])—as if suddenly deprived of a relationship that they had relied upon to hold themselves together. Todd also observes numerous instances of this motif of fragmentation in Lermontov's novel, pointing out "four fragmentary quotations" from *Eugene Onegin*, "fragments of tired worldly wisdom" repeated by Pechorin, and "a virtually unmitigated succession of destructive acts" that cause some sort of disjuncture (*Fiction and Society*, 143, 157, 147). Few things in *A Hero of Our Time* evade the forces of fragmentation.

19. Ripp also holds that, along with this lost confidence came a certain longing for norms, for ideals, for principles that give order to human experience. "What was once a naïve faith in the existence of a rational order," he maintains, "has given way to a desperate nostalgia for it." And Lermontov's novel, he declares, "emphatically acknowledges the desire to fit the fragmented aspects of life, the moments of experience, to a general pattern" (978, 985). In consequence, "the fragmentary nature of experience, including the potential disorganization of every work of art, is a topic the book examines." Nonetheless, Ripp concludes, the novel avoids "both the facile assertion of harmony and the accession to disharmony" (973). I agree with Ripp that the novel does not give way to complete disorder or "disharmony," but I disagree that the longing for a sense of order in *A Hero of Our Time* is "nostalgic," because nostalgia implies a desire for a return to the past that, throughout the novel, Lermontov suggests to be impossible.

20. Cooke points to Friedrich Schlegel's novel *Lucinde* as an exemplar of the Romantic conception of fragments, in that this novel virtually flaunts the fragmentariness of its seemingly arbitrarily assembled, often confusing and even incomprehensible, always somehow incomplete passages of poetry, drama, dithyramb, epistle, allegory, and fantasy. But, Cooke claims, Schlegel found that this was the only way he could mirror nature, that most fragmentary, profusely disordered, and yet profoundly ordered of all phenomena in human experience. Endlessly evolving, eternally incomplete, yet irrevocably organically unified, nature for Schegel, in Cooke's view, ideally exemplifies the combination of immanent integrity and ultimate wholeness to which Romantic art aspires. See Cooke, *Acts of Inclusion*, 171–77.

21. Taking an opposite view, Rosenshield asserts that "the very vagueness, the very indefiniteness of [Pechorin's] past is an essential element of his aura" of Byronic heroism (86), which Pechorin so assiduously cultivates. However, I would argue that Pechorin lacks the psychological integrity Byronic heroes possess, as shown through their personalities and behavior. Thus Pechorin projects less of an "aura" and more of an emptiness, both within and without.

22. A few critics go too far in their characterizations of Pechorin, in my view, by representing him as deeply psychologically diseased. Barratt and Briggs, for instance, call Pechorin's portrayal "a case study of mental illness" that they diagnose in Jungian terms (3). And Natasha Reed devotes her dissertation to the analysis of Pechorin as a victim of "imitative sickness," or "mimetic desire" as defined by René Girard, that is, the envy of satisfactions achieved by others that leads an individual first to imitate and ultimately to destroy and replace others in hopes of acquiring those same satisfactions. These analyses, while thought-provoking, actually attribute too much coherence to his character. On a different tangent, Barratt and Briggs find that Pechorin is fundamentally "a thinly veiled self-portrait" of Lermontov (5), but this interpretation fails to acknowledge Lermontov's artistic achievement and cultural sensibility.

23. Elena Mikhailova likewise connects the novel's structure with Pechorin's psychological makeup, declaring that "the compositional structure of the novel" with its "absence of narrative direction" mirrors "the aimlessness of Pechorin's personality" (211). She considers this mirroring a part of the work's attempts at Realism, however, whereas I see it as a reflection of Pechorin's post-Romantic dis-integration.

24. See Todd, *Fiction and Society*, esp. 33–44, 151.

25. The second sentence of this chapter—"I almost died of hunger there and, moreover, an attempt was made to drown me" (4: 225; 65)—reveals the retrospective nature of "Taman." Bagby astutely detects in this line a "mask" that Pechorin dons "for the sake of his own ego" in an effort to "conceal Pechorin's self-humiliation" during the events he proceeds to portray ("Double-Voicing," 273).

26. Nabokov revealingly dismisses this movement as a "rather sterile postromantic fad" (Lermontov, *Hero*, 204). Théophile Gautier, who participated in this movement with Petrus Borel, Philothée O'Neddy, and others, entitled a collection of autobiographical sketches *Les Jeunes France* (1833).

27. See, for example, Garrard, 136; Peace, 12; Turner, 23.

28. I thus agree with Peace's observation that in "Taman" Pechorin is "seeing himself from the outside" (28), precisely because there is so little that is distinctive "inside" to see. But I disagree with Peace's claim that Pechorin's final assertion of indifference to others "rings very false"; in my view, it follows both logically and psychologically from Pechorin's discovery of his own insignificance and emptiness.

29. Nabokov simply declares it "the worst story in the book" (xviii).

30. This strength, which he believes he has discovered after leaving Taman, manifests itself, according to Mersereau, in "courage, assurance, individuality, and aloofness" (*Lermontov*, 124–25), while Goscilo points to Pechorin's "higher consciousness, keener perceptions, resoluteness, and energy" (294)—these are the types of characteristics upon which Pechorin now apparently prides himself as the core of his mature identity. Tomashevskii simply declares, "Pechorin's superiority is affirmed on every page of the novel" (511).

31. His confidence in his own intellectual prowess and insight constitutes one of Pechorin's several marked similarities to Arbenin in *Masquerade* (see Chapter 5), although Pechorin is too inconsistent to be labeled an ideologue.

32. Natasha Reed too sees this emptiness, but she attributes it to "mimetic desire" (see note 22 above). I view it as a product of gaps in his personality mirroring the lack of integrating values in his culture.

33. Critics widely differ in their assessment of this event. Golstein expands at length on the heroic qualities Pechorin displays during this incident (110–32); Milner-Gulland shares his view, calling Pechorin's daring act a "selfless and courageous exploit" (133). By contrast to these critics, Rosenshield questions the heroism of this action, if not Pechorin's will per se, suggesting that "Pechorin must have recognized, at least subconsciously, that his experiment with fate was invalidated by the precautions he took and the calculations he made. Charging a dazed man with the assistance of troops, however risky, is after all not the same thing as pointing a loaded pistol at one's head and discharging it" (92). Gregg takes a middle position, declaring that Pechorin was "uncharacteristically beneficent" in subduing the Cossack, which might lead some to infer that he had "unaccountably turned over a new leaf." However, Gregg adds, "the inference would surely be false" (391), as Pechorin's ensuing treatment of Bela reveals.

34. Arguably no facet of Pechorin's character or behavior has received as much critical comment as Pechorin's acting. Todd offers a particularly insightful discussion of this subject, noting: "Theatricality and the idea of 'being on stage' are so much a part of Pechorin that when he is alone he must posit a conscious spectator for his actions and speech acts" (*Fiction and Society*, 160). See also, for example, Garrard, 140; Kesler, 492.

35. His decision to write a journal, even an ostensibly private one, calls to mind the assertion of Mikhail Bakhtin: "It is only when my life is set forth for another that I myself become its hero" (111).

36. These Romantic "confessors" include Charles Lamb (1813), Thomas de

Quincey (1822), James Hogg (1824), and Jules Janin (1830). See Susan M. Levin, *The Romantic Art of Confession: DeQuincey, Musset, Sand, Lamb, Hogg, Frémy, Soulié, Janin* (Columbia, SC: Camden House, 1998), for extended comparison and analysis of works in the confessional genre.

37. See Henri Peyre, *Literature and Sincerity* (New Haven, CT: Yale University Press, 1963); and Trilling, *Sincerity and Authenticity*, for the leading discussions of this subject.

38. See, for example, A. Angeloff and Pr. Klingenburg, "Lermontov's Uses of Nature in the Novel *Hero of Our Time*," *Russian Language Journal* 24 (July 1970): 3–12, for a representative discussion of Lermontov's treatment of nature and Pechorin's attitude toward it in the novel.

39. Pechorin even remains unmoved by nature's more ominous aspects. Before a tryst with Vera, for instance, he states without commenting, "It was pitch dark outside. Heavy, cold clouds lay on the summits of the surrounding mountains; only now and then a dying breeze rustled in the crests of the poplars around the restaurant." He then merely continues, "There was a crowd of people outside the windows" (4: 284; 150).

40. Marsh asserts: "The reader [of *A Hero of Our Time*] has heard a number of different voices as he moves from narrator to narrator, but one voice remains constant: it is the voice heard in the landscape description. The landscapes are a remnant of the travelogue form and they retain a predominantly Romantic voice. It is a voice shared between the fictional author [the implied author Lermontov creates in the novel] and Pechorin" (39).

41. Barratt and Briggs also detect inconsistencies in the traveler's treatment of nature, which they interpret as evidence of his narratorial unreliability. See especially 13–19.

Chapter 7: Post-Romantic Anomie II

1. See Todd, *Fiction and Society*, 152–61, for a discussion of "scripts" in *A Hero of Our Time* as social conventions.

2. Critics finding the minor characters of *A Hero Of Our Time* wholly inferior to Pechorin include Mersereau, who suggests that these minor characters merely fulfill the needs of the plot and serve as "mirrors reflecting the image of the hero" (*Lermontov*, 124); Grigorenko, who claims they are "depicted only to elucidate Pechorin" (237); Debreczeny, who sees those characters as "extensions" of Pechorin (104); and Freeborn, who dismisses them as "little more than projections of [Pechorin's] own dilemma" (63). Other critics simply perceive these characters as weak in themselves. Cox, for one, deems them inferior Romantic types "totally lacking in self-awareness" (168); Entwistle argues that they lack "character" and make Pechorin look more "alive" as a result (144). No wonder these characters have received so little thoughtful analysis either in Russian or Western criticism. Barratt and Briggs are an exception, finding independently redeeming features in

the secondary characters, many of whom, they assert, "possess greater strength of character and more courage" than Pechorin (124).

3. Despite Todd's suggestion that "*A Hero of Our Time* . . . would seem to be one of the rare subjects on which Vladimir Nabokov held no 'strong opinions'"—Todd does note that "Nabokov did, in fact, pay considerable attention to Lermontov" ("*A Hero of Our Time*," 178, 179)—Nabokov clearly finds little value in these female characters, derisively remarking that "Lermontov was singularly inept in his descriptions of women." Nabokov therefore dismisses Bela as "an Oriental beauty on the lid of a box of Turkish delight," Mary as "the generalized young thing of novelettes," and Vera as "a mere phantom" (Lermontov, *Hero*, xviii). Although I will show connections between these characters and some Romantic predecessors, I do not accept Nabokov's view of them as mere feeble imitations. He ignores the subtle signs of complexity that Lermontov introduces into the female characters, thereby demeaning not only the characters themselves, but also Lermontov's authorial skills. Nabokov also fails to take into account the extent to which these female characterizations might be affected by the perspectives of the male narrators transmitting them and thus serve as enhancements of their characterizations as well.

4. As Helena Goscilo provocatively suggests, Pechorin's "most outstanding asset is his capacity for stirring others' imaginations" (256). V. Fisher affirms the female characters' Romantic inclinations in a backhanded way, calling them "monotonously romantic" (quoted in Barratt and Briggs, 90).

5. Throughout her dissertation Natasha Reed insistently makes the case that Pechorin not only affects but "infects" the characters he encounters with "imitative sickness"—Girard's "mimetic desire"—through a "process of contamination" (49).

6. We have direct evidence that Lermontov knew *Atala*, in that he noted to himself in 1830 that "the subject of a tragedy" set in America could be drawn from "the French novel *Atala*" (4: 340). In characterizing Bela, however, he introduced some significant differences, the main one being that, unlike Atala, who resists her beloved Chactas and upholds a youthful vow of chastity by taking poison to avoid consummating their relationship, Bela does give herself to Pechorin.

7. Here Bela's worries echo those of Atala for Chactas, who reports that as she lay dying, "she now seemed concerned only with my sorrow and sought only to help me endure my loss" (67). Similarly, according to Maksim Maksimich, Bela "tried to make Pechorin think she felt better" and "tried to get him to go to bed" (4: 213; 59).

8. Lermontov mentions Walter Scott and his works in numerous contexts, and he depicts Pechorin reading a French translation of Scott's *The Tale of Old Mortality* (1816) the night before the duel. We have no direct evidence that Lermontov knew de Staël's works. However, they enjoyed broad popularity across Europe and Russia—Delphine was mentioned among heroines Pushkin's Tatiana knew (*Eugene Onegin*, chap. 3, stanza 10)—so it is highly likely that Lermontov knew of them and had even read portions either in translation or in the original. And we see more than a hint of Tatiana in Mary, as many critics have noted.

9. Marie Gilroy views Mary as a victim specifically of Romantic literary illusions, arguing that because she was "reared on Romantic novels, Mary imagines herself in the role of saviour who redeems the demonic anti-hero" (59). Gilroy here appears to be conflating Mary and Pushkin's Tatiana in *Eugene Onegin*, since we do not know precisely what Mary has read.

10. At the same time, Mary may not survive her disillusionment as well as Pushkin's Tatiana does, since Tatiana marries without love and yet finds the psychological resources to create a satisfactory existence for herself. See Olga Peters Hasty, *Pushkin's Tatiana* (Madison: University of Wisconsin Press, 1999), for an insightful analysis of Tatiana's character and role in Pushkin's narrative poem.

11. Although we have no direct evidence that Lermontov had read *Adolphe*, critics take his familiarity with Constant's novel for granted on the basis of temperamental similarities between Pechorin and Adolphe. However, it is the female protagonists who bear the greater resemblance, as Priscilla Meyer notes in her pithy comparison of the letters written by Ellenore and Vera (60–62).

12. Rosenshield provocatively suggests that Vera's letter is a product of Pechorin's fantasy, in that it resembles "many other romantic passages of Pechorin's diary" (96). He thereby denies the letter the authenticity most critics find it has, especially by contrast to many of Pechorin's self-consciously Romanticized remarks.

13. In *The Familiar Letter as a Literary Genre in the Age of Pushkin*, Todd thoroughly explores the early nineteenth-century view of friendship in Russia. Arguing that "friendship became one of the major themes of Russian literature" at this time, he observes that friendship "lent its name to two of the most popular [types of] letters of the time—familiar letters (*druzheskiye*, literally 'friendly') and familiar verse epistles (*druzheskiye stikhotvornye poslaniya*)" (40–41). Todd demonstrates that friendship assumed special importance for the members of the literary and social group known as Arzamas, in which Pushkin actively participated. Todd also tellingly suggests that Pushkin "kills off" the idealist poet Lensky in *Eugene Onegin* because of Lensky's "blind faith in the reality of this literary convention" of friendship (42). Lensky's fate might therefore be construed as post-Romantic.

14. Most critics consider Maksim Maksimich an avuncular figure, decent, kindly, and unpretentious. Barratt and Briggs offer an even more positive assessment, describing him as "resourceful and energetic" and "not especially humble or simple" (19).

15. Barratt and Briggs present a distinctly harsh view of Werner, contentiously labeling the connection between Pechorin and Werner "a collusive relationship" bolstering the egos of both characters. At the same time, they suggest that Werner, as a doctor, has "real potential to help" Pechorin resolve his psychological problems, but that Werner instead weakly succumbs to the force of Pechorin's pathology (90).

16. Golstein is notably hard on Grushnitskii, accusing him of what Golstein, among others, terms "marlinism," that is, being an imitator of the characters of Aleksandr Bestuzhev-Marlinskii, the highly popular, epigonal Russian author of

adventure tales in the 1820s and 1830s. Thus Golstein finds Grushnitskii "a nonentity who wears the mask of a heroic person" (148).

Golstein is certainly not alone in his derogatory view of Grushnitskii—Abbott derides the latter as "a shallow character, transparent, the opposite of a mystery, who makes the fatal mistake of pretending to be one" (65). Fokht makes the negative comparison: "Pechorin has the advantage over Grushnitskii not so much because Pechorin is a subtle psychologist, while Grushnitskii is uncouth and thickheaded, but because Pechorin comprehends his actions, whereas Grushnitskii is a hypocrite, even to himself, from the beginning to the end" (168). However, Barratt and Briggs insightfully notice that critical comments on Grushnitskii tend to "re-enact Pechorin's own hostility towards Grushnitskii," when "at heart he is a decent man drawn . . . into a sordid scheme which offends against his better nature" (78, 85).

17. Golstein dismisses Grushnitskii's concession of the unfairness of the duel, maintaining that "Grushnitskii persists in avoiding moral choices to the very end." However, Golstein does not explain why Grushnitskii "chooses to rebel against [his second] and allows Pechorin to recharge" his weapon (147).

18. Gilroy strongly reacts to this phrase, declaring it "infuriating" as a form of "suspensive irony" (37). At the same time, she acknowledges that it fits what she takes to be the novel's purpose by forcing the reader "to re-examine his understanding of the nature of knowledge and his right to pass judgements on anyone else" (37). That purpose, she claims, is to render a protoexistentialist portrayal of "our modern predicament," which, quoting Daniel O'Hara, she takes to be "the crumbling arch of western metaphysics" (74). In my view, it is Romantic culture, rather than Western metaphysics, that the novel exposes as having crumbled.

19. See especially in Golstein, 142–53.

Chapter 8: Lermontov's Last Words

1. See Chapter 5 for a summary of the Underground Man's complaints about Romanticism.

2. Lermontov additionally deleted from the final draft of his preface explicit comparisons of Pechorin to vampires and to Melmoth the Wanderer (on Melmoth, see Chapter 4), thereby—significantly, in my view—downplaying Pechorin's connection to Romanticism proper. And although he also toned town his complaints about what he took to be misinterpretations of his novel, this preface constitutes, according to Barratt and Briggs, "as angry a piece of writing as anything produced by his pen" (3).

3. For an excellent translation of this little-known narrative, see David Lowe's in *The Ardis Anthology of Russian Literature*, ed. Christine Rydel (Ann Arbor, MI: Ardis, 1984), 361–70.

4. In fact, very few critics have examined "Shtoss" at all: the story is often omitted or dismissed with a few sentences in both Russian and Western studies of Lermontov, and only a handful of articles have been devoted to it. This neglect

suggests that many critics deem "Shtoss" too slight—or too mysterious—to merit much comment.

5. See Udodov, 633–53, for a survey of the critical responses to "Shtoss."

6. Granted, Mersereau also notes a "strong undercurrent of subjective evaluation in the tone and choice of words" (*Shtoss*, 289), which he evidently takes to undermine the objective tone of "Shtoss," but most other critics would disagree with Mersereau, as they find that tone generally consistent and un-ironic.

7. Mersereau also emphasizes parallels between "Shtoss" and Pushkin's ambiguous story "Пиковая дама" [The Queen of Spades] (1833), which he takes to be explicitly anti-Romantic as well. Interpretations of Pushkin's story vary widely, however, as some critics find it highly Romantic. For a recent example of this interpretive stance, see, for example, Claire Whitehead, "The Fantastic in Russian Romantic Prose: Pushkin's *The Queen of Spades*," in *The Gothic-Fantastic in Nineteenth-Century Russian Literature*, ed. Neil Cornwell (Amsterdam: Rodopi, 1999), 103–25.

8. Goscilo specifically complains that "Shtoss" suffers aesthetically from Lermontov's "tendency to overstuff the narrative with motifs from Hoffmannesque *Künstlernovellen*" (344–45).

9. Several critics have remarked in particular the similarities of this image to that of Piskarev's fantasy in Gogol's short story "Невский проспект" [Nevsky Prospect] (1835). See, for instance, Mersereau, *Shtoss*, 292.

10. Vatsuro also would dispute Mersereau's contention that "Shtoss" is anti-Romantic, arguing that "the fantastic world . . . is more significant than the real world" (246), as a result of which the story cannot be excluded from the realm of Romanticism.

11. In fact, the precise final words of the story are not themselves certain, because the fair copy ends, "Lugin's heart painfully contracted—with despair" [у Лугина болезненно сжималось сердце—отчаянием] (4: 332). The last three sentences, which most critics accept as canonical, actually come from Lermontov's notebook. See the notes to "Shtoss," in Lermontov, *Собрание сочинений* [Collected Works], 4: 468–70.

12. Martin Irvine, "The Postmodern, Postmodernism, Postmodernity: Approaches to Po-Mo," quoted in Berger, 104).

13. In *Beyond Realism: Turgenev's Poetics of Secular Salvation*, I offer yet another view of Realism—one more congenial to George Eliot (see Chapter 5)—as rooted in an ethical ideal of integrity that requires integration into a true community "as the only way to redeem the individual from psychological incompletion and spiritual incarceration" (24). Despite Lermontov's desire for integrity and integration, however, I am not confident that he would have embraced this communal version of Realism either.

Selected Bibliography

Abbott, H. Porter. *Diary Fiction: Writing as Action*. Ithaca, NY: Cornell University Press, 1984.

Abrams, M. H. *The Mirror and the Lamp: Romantic Theory and the Critical Tradition*. New York: W. W. Norton, 1958.

———. *Natural Supernaturalism: Tradition and Revolution in Romantic Literature*. New York: W. W. Norton, 1971.

Aers, David, Jonathan Cook, and David Punter, eds. *Romanticism and Ideology*. London: Routledge and Kegan Paul, 1981.

Allen, Elizabeth Cheresh. *Beyond Realism: Turgenev's Poetics of Secular Salvation*. Stanford, CA: Stanford University Press, 1992.

Allen, James Sloan. *The Romantic of Commerce and Culture: Capitalism, Modernism, and the Chicago-Aspen Crusade for Cultural Reform*. Rev. ed. Boulder: University Press of Colorado, 2002.

Anshen, Ruth. *Anatomy of Evil*. Mt. Kisco, NY: Moyer Bell, 1972.

Auerbach, Erich. *Mimesis: The Representation of Reality in Western Literature*. Trans. Willard Trask. Princeton, NJ: Princeton University Press, 1953.

Augustine, St. *The City of God*. Trans. Marcus Dods. New York: Modern Library, 1950.

Babbitt, Irving. *Rousseau and Romanticism*. Boston: Houghton Mifflin, 1919.

Bagby, Lewis. *Alexander Bestuzhev-Marlinsky and Russian Byronism*. University Park: Pennsylvania State University Press, 1995.

———. "Narrative Double-Voicing in Lermontov's *A Hero of Our Time*." *Slavic and East European Journal* 22, no. 3 (1978): 265–86.

Bakhtin, Mikhail. *Art and Answerability: Early Philosophical Essays by M. M. Bakhtin*. Ed. Michael Holquist and Vadim Liapunov. Trans. Vadim Liapunov. Austin: University of Texas Press, 1990.

Barratt, Andrew, and A. D. P. Briggs. *A Wicked Irony: The Rhetoric of Lermontov's "A Hero of Our Time."* Bristol, UK: Bristol Classical Press, 1989.

Barzun, Jacques. *Classic, Romantic, and Modern*. Garden City, NY: Anchor Books, 1961.

———. *From Dawn to Decadence: Five Hundred Years of Western Cultural Life*. New York: HarperCollins, 2000.

Bate, W. Jackson. *The Burden of the Past and the English Poet.* New York: W. W. Norton, 1970.

Becker, Howard, and Harry Elmer Barnes. *Social Thought from Lore to Science.* 3rd ed. New York: Dover Publications, 1961.

Belinskii, Vissarion. *M. Iu. Lermontov: Статьи и Рецензии* [M. Iu. Lermontov: Articles and Reviews]. Leningrad: Khudozhestvennaia literatura, 1941.

Bentley, Eric. *A Century of Hero-Worship: A Study of the Idea of Heroism in Carlyle and Nietzsche, with Notes on Other Hero-Worshipers of Modern Times.* Philadelphia: J. B. Lippincott, 1944.

Berger, Arthur Asa. *The Portable Postmodernist.* Walnut Creek, CA: AltaMira Press, 2003.

Berlin, Isaiah. *The Roots of Romanticism.* Princeton, NJ: Princeton University Press, 1999.

Bertens, Hans. *The Idea of the Postmodern: A History.* New York: Routledge, 1995.

Bishop, Lloyd. *The Romantic Hero and His Heirs in French Literature.* New York: Peter Lang, 1984.

Blake, William. *The Complete Poetry and Prose of William Blake.* Rev. ed. Ed. David V. Erdman. Berkeley and Los Angeles: University of California Press, 1982.

Bloom, Harold. *The Anxiety of Influence: A Theory of Poetry.* New York: Oxford University Press, 1973.

Boss, Valentin. *Milton and the Rise of Russian Satanism.* Toronto: University of Toronto Press, 1991.

Bouwsma, William J. *The Waning of the Renaissance, 1550–1640.* New Haven, CT: Yale University Press, 2000.

Briggs, A. D. P. "Lermontov in the Negative." *New Zealand Slavonic Journal* (1986): 11–24.

Brontë, Emily. *Wuthering Heights.* London: Penguin Books, 1965.

Brown, Marshall. *Turning Points: Essays in the History of Cultural Expressions.* Stanford, CA: Stanford University Press, 1997.

Browning, Robert. *Robert Browning: The Poems.* Ed. John Pettigrew. 2 vols. New Haven, CT: Yale University Press, 1981.

Byron, George Gordon. *Poetical Works.* Oxford: Oxford University Press, 1970.

Carlyle, Thomas. *On Heroes, Hero-Worship, and the Heroic in History.* Ed. Mark K. Goldberg, Joel J. Brattin, and Mark Engel. Berkeley and Los Angeles: University of California Press, 1993.

———. *Sartor Resartus.* Philadelphia: John Wanamaker, n.d.

Caudwell, Christopher. *Studies and Further Studies in a Dying Culture.* New York: Monthly Review Press, 1971.

Chandler, Alice. *A Dream of Order: The Medieval Ideal in Nineteenth-Century English Literature.* Lincoln: University of Nebraska Press, 1970.

Chateaubriand, René. *Atala.* Trans. Irving Putter. Berkeley and Los Angeles: University of California Press, 1952.

Chesterton, G. K. "On the Optimism of Byron." In *Twelve Types,* by G. K. Chesterton, 31–44. London: Arthur L. Humphreys, 1902.

Clement, N. H. *Romanticism in France.* New York: Modern Language Association in America, 1939.

Coleridge, Samuel Taylor. *Coleridge's Poetry and Prose.* Ed. Nicholas Halmi, Paul Magnuson, and Raimondo Modiano. New York: W. W. Norton, 2004.

———. *Collected Letters of Samuel Taylor Coleridge.* 6 vols. Ed. Earl Leslie Griggs. Oxford: Clarendon Press, 1956.

———. *The Collected Works of Samuel Taylor Coleridge.* 16 vols. Ed. Kathleen Coburn. Princeton, NJ: Princeton University Press, 2001.

Comfort, Alex. *Art and Social Responsibility: Lectures on the Ideology of Romanticism.* London: Falcon Press, 1946.

Connolly, Julian W. *The Intimate Stranger: Meetings with the Devil in Nineteenth-Century Russian Literature.* New York: Peter Lang, 2001.

Constant, Benjamin. *Adolphe.* Trans. Leonard Tancock. Middlesex, UK: Penguin Books, 1980.

Cooke, Michael G. *Acts of Inclusion: Studies Bearing on an Elementary Theory of Romanticism.* New Haven, CT: Yale University Press, 1979.

———. *The Blind Man Traces the Circle: On the Patterns and Philosophy of Byron's Poetry.* Princeton, NJ: Princeton University Press, 1969.

———. *The Romantic Will.* New Haven, CT: Yale University Press, 1976.

Cox, Gary. "Dramatic Genre as a Tool of Characterization in Lermontov's *Hero of Our Time.*" *Russian Literature* 11 (1982): 163–72.

Davidson, Pamela. "The Muse and the Demon in the Poetry of Pushkin, Lermontov, and Blok." In *Russian Literature and Its Demons,* ed. Pamela Davidson, 167–213. New York: Berghahn Books, 2000.

Debreczeny, Paul. "Elements of the Lyrical Verse Tale in Lermontov's *A Hero of Our Time.*" In *American Contributions to the Seventh International Congress of Slavists,* ed. Victor Terras, 93–117. The Hague: Mouton, 1973.

Diakonova, Nina. "Byron and the Evolution of Lermontov's Poetry, 1814–1841." *Renaissance and Modern Studies* 32 (1988): 80–95.

———. "Byron and Lermontov: Notes on Pechorin's 'Journal.'" In *Lord Byron and His Contemporaries: Essays from the Sixth International Byron Seminar,* ed. C. E. Robinson, 144–65. London: Associated University Presses, 1982.

Diakonova, Nina, and Vadim E. Vatsuro. "Byron and Russia." In *Byron's Political and Cultural Influence in Nineteenth-Century Europe,* ed. Paul Trueblood, 143–59. London: Macmillan, 1981.

Dostoevsky, Fedor M. *Полное собрание сочинений в тридцати томах* [Complete Works in Thirty Volumes]. Leningrad: Nauka, 1972–90.

du Bos, Charles. *Byron and the Need of Fatality.* Trans. E. C. Mayne. London: n.p., 1932.

Duchèsne, Eugène [Diushen, E.]. "Лермонтов и английская литература" [Lermontov and English Literature]. In *Поэзия М. Ю. Лермонтова в отношений к русской и западноевропейским литературам* [The Poetry of M. Iu. Lermontov in Its Relation to Russian and European Literatures], 51–110. Kazan: Izdatel'stvo knizhnago magazina M. A. Goludeva, 1914.

————. *Michel Iourevitch Lermontoff: Sa vie et ses oeuvres*. Paris, 1910.

Durkheim, Emile. *Suicide: A Study in Sociology*. Trans. John A. Spaulding and George Simpson. Glencoe, IL: Free Press, 1951.

Eagle, Herbert. "Lermontov's 'Play' with Romantic Genre Expectations in *A Hero of Our Time*." *Russian Literary Triquarterly* 10 (Fall 1974): 299–315.

Eikhenbaum, Boris M. "Пять редакций Маскарада" [Five Redactions of *Masquerade*]. In *О поэзии* [On Poetry], by Boris M. Eikhenbaum, 215–33. Leningrad: Sovetskii pisatel', 1963.

————. *Lermontov: A Study in Literary-Historical Evaluation*. Trans. Ray Parrott and Harry Weber. 1924. Reprint, Ann Arbor, MI: Ardis, 1981.

Eliot, George. *Adam Bede*. New York: New American Library, 1961.

Engelberg, Edward. "Rebels Without Cause: Lermontov, Turgenev, Brontë." In *Elegiac Fictions: The Motif of the Unlived Life*, by Edward Engelberg. University Park, PA: Pennsylvania University Press, 1989.

Entwistle, W. J. "The Byronism of Lermontov's *A Hero of Our Time*." *Comparative Literature* 1 (1949): 140–46.

Erlich, Victor. *Gogol*. New Haven, CT: Yale University Press, 1969.

Ewington, Amanda. "A Demon in the Drawing Room: Echoes of *The Demon* in Lermontov's *Masquerade*." *Romantic Russia* 2 (1998): 95–124.

Fairley, Barker. *A Study of Goethe*. London: Oxford University Press, 1947.

Faletti, Heidi E. "Elements of the Demonic in the Character of Pechorin in Lermontov's *A Hero of Our Time*." *Forum for Modern Language Studies* 14 (1978): 365–77.

Fetzer, John Francis. "Romantic Irony." In *European Romanticism: Literary Cross-Currents, Modes, and Models*, ed. Gerhart Hoffmeister, 19–36. Detroit: Wayne State University Press, 1990.

Feuer, Lewis S. *Ideology and the Ideologists*. Oxford: Basil Blackwell, 1975.

Fokht, Ul'rikh R. *Лермонтов: Логика творчества* [Lermontov: The Logic of Artistic Creation]. Moscow: Nauka, 1975.

Freeborn, Richard. *The Rise of the Russian Novel: Studies in the Russian Novel from "Eugene Onegin" to "War and Peace."* Cambridge: Cambridge University Press, 1973.

Friedenthal, Richard. *Goethe: His Life and Times*. Cleveland: World Publishing, 1963.

Frye, Northrop. "Towards Defining an Age of Sensibility." *ELH: A Journal of English Literary History* (June 1956): 144–52.

Fuerst, Norbert. *The Victorian Age of German Literature: Eight Essays*. London: Dennis Dobson, 1966.

Furst, Lilian. *The Contours of Romanticism*. London: Macmillan, 1979.

————. *Romanticism in Perspective*. London: Macmillan, 1969.

Fusso, Susanne. "The Romantic Tradition." In *The Cambridge Companion to the Classic Russian Novel*, ed. Malcolm V. Jones and Robin Feuer Miller, 171–89. Cambridge: Cambridge University Press, 1998.

Garrard, John. *Mikhail Lermontov*. Boston: Twayne Publishers, 1982.

———. "Old Wine in New Bottles: The Legacy of Lermontov." In *Poetica Slavica: Studies in Honour of Zbigniew Folejewski*, ed. J. Douglas Clayton and Gunter Schaarschmidt, 41–52. Ottawa, ON: University of Ottawa Press, 1981.

Gay, Peter. *The Bourgeois Experience: Victoria to Freud*. Vol. 2, *The Naked Passion*. New York: Oxford University Press, 1987.

———. *The Bourgeois Experience: Victoria to Freud*. Vol. 4, *The Tender Heart*. New York: W. W. Norton, 1995.

Gellner, Ernest. *Thought and Change*. Chicago: University of Chicago Press, 1964.

Gibbon, Edward. *The Autobiography of Edward Gibbon*. New York: Meridian Books, 1961.

Gilroy, Marie. *The Ironic Vision in Lermontov's "A Hero of Our Time."* Birmingham, UK: Birmingham University Press, 1988.

Ginzburg, Lidiia. *Творческий путь Лермонтова* [Lermontov's Creative Path]. Leningrad: Khudozhestvennaia literatura, 1941.

Goethe, Johann Wolfgang von. *Faust*. Trans. Walter Kaufmann. New York: Anchor Books, 1963.

———. *The Sorrows of Young Werther and Selected Writings*. Trans. Catherine Hutter. New York: Signet Classics, 1962.

Gogol, Nikolai Vasilievich. *Полное собрание сочинений* [Complete Collected Works]. 10 vols. Moscow: Izdatel'stvo AN SSSR, 1937–52.

Golstein, Vladimir. *Lermontov's Narratives of Heroism*. Evanston, IL: Northwestern University Press, 1998.

Goscilo, Helena. "From Dissolution to Synthesis: The Use of Genre in Lermontov's Prose." Ph.D. diss., Department of Slavic Languages and Literatures, Indiana University, 1976.

Greenleaf, Monika. *Pushkin and Romantic Fashion: Fragment, Elegy, Orient, Irony*. Stanford, CA: Stanford University Press, 1994.

———. "Pushkin's Byronic Apprenticeship: A Problem in Cultural Syncretism." *Russian Review* 53 (July 1994): 382–98.

Gregg, Richard. "The Cooling of Pechorin: The Skull Beneath the Skin." *Slavic Review* 43, no. 3 (Fall 1984): 387–98.

Grigorenko, V. V., et al. *М. Ю. Лермонтов в воспоминаниях современников* [M. Iu. Lermontov in the Reminiscences of His Contemporaries]. Moscow: Khudozhestvennaia literatura, 1964.

Grigor'ian, Kamsar N. *Лермонтов и романтизм* [Lermontov and Romanticism]. Moscow: Nauka, 1964.

Hassan, Ihab. "Ideas of Cultural Change." In *Innovation/Renovation: New Perspectives on the Humanities*, ed. Ihab Hassan and Sally Hassan, 15–38. Madison: University of Wisconsin Press, 1983.

———. *The Postmodern Turn*. Columbus: Ohio State University Press, 1987.

Hazlitt, William. "Lord Byron." In *The Complete Works of William Hazlitt in Twenty-one Volumes*, ed. P. P. Howe, 11: 69–78. London: J. M. Dent and Sons, 1930–34.

Hegel, G. W. F. "From *The Philosophy of Fine Art*." In *The Hero in Literature*, ed. Victor Brombert, 186–201. Greenwich, CT: Fawcett Publications, 1969.

Heine, Heinrich. *Selected Works*. Ed. and trans. Helen M. Mustard. New York: Vintage Books, 1973.

Helfant, Ian. "Gambling Practices and the (Dis)honorable Acts of Lermontov's *Masquerade*." *Romantic Russia* 2 (1998): 125–43.

Herzen, Alexander. *From the Other Shore*. Trans. Moura Budberg. London: Weidenfeld and Nicolson, 1956.

Hesse, Herman. *Steppenwolf*. Trans. J. Mileck and H. Frenz. New York: Holt, Rinehart, and Winston, 1963.

Hobsbawm, E. J. *The Age of Revolution, 1789–1848*. New York: Mentor Books, 1962.

Huizinga, Johan. *The Waning of the Middle Ages: A Study of the Forms of Life, Thought, and Art in France and the Netherlands in the XIVth and XVth Centuries*. Trans. of *Herfsttij der Middeleeuwen* (no translator's name). 1949. Reprint, Garden City, NY: Doubleday Anchor Books, 1954.

Jackson, H. J. "Coleridge's Lessons in Transition: The 'Logic' of the 'Wildest Odes.'" In *The Lessons of Romanticism: A Critical Companion*, ed. Thomas Pfau and Robert F. Gleckner, 213–24. Durham, NC: Duke University Press, 1998.

Jackson, Robert Louis. "Miltonic Imagery and Design in Puškin's *Mozart and Salieri*: The Russian Satan." In *American Contributions to the Seventh International Congress of Slavists*, ed. Victor Terras, 261–70. The Hague: Mouton, 1973.

Jones, W. T. *The Romantic Syndrome: Toward a New Method in Cultural Anthropology and History of Ideas*. The Hague: Martinus Nijhoff, 1961.

Karlinsky, Simon. "Misanthropy and Sadism in Lermontov's Plays." In *Studies in Russian Literature in Honor of Vsevolod Setchkarev*, ed. Julian W. Connolly and Sonia I. Ketchian, 166–74. Columbus, OH: Slavica, 1986.

Kelly, Laurence. *Lermontov: Tragedy in the Caucasus*. New York: George Braziller, 1977.

Kent, Leonard J., and Elizabeth C. Knight. Introduction to *Tales of E. T. A. Hoffman*, ed. and trans. Leonard J. Kent and Elizabeth C. Knight. Chicago: University of Chicago Press, 1969.

Kermode, Frank. *The Sense of an Ending: Studies in the Theory of Fiction*. New York: Oxford University Press, 1966.

Kesler, R. L. "Fate and Narrative Structure in Lermontov's *A Hero of Our Time*." *Texas Studies in Literature and Language* 32, no. 4 (Winter 1990): 485–505.

Kierkegaard, Søren. *The Concept of Irony: With Constant Reference to Socrates*. Trans. Lee Capel. Bloomington: Indiana University Press, 1965.

———. *Either/Or*. Vol. 2. Trans. Walter Lowrie. Garden City, NY: Anchor Books, 1959.

Korovin, Valentin I. "Драма *Маскарад*" [The Drama *Masquerade*]. In *Творческий путь Лермонтова* [Lermontov's Creative Path], by Valentin I. Korovin, 203–16. Moscow: Prosveshchenie, 1973.

Kostka, Edmund. "Lermontov's Debt to Schiller." *Revue de Littérature Comparée* 37 (1963): 68–88.

Kuhn, Thomas S. *The Structure of Scientific Revolutions.* Chicago: University of Chicago Press, 1962.

Leighton, Lauren G. "On a Discrimination of Russian Romanticism." In *Russian Romanticism: Two Essays*, by Lauren G. Leighton, 1–39. The Hague: Mouton, 1975.

———. "The Great Soviet Debate over Romanticism, 1957–1964." *Studies in Romanticism* 22, no. 1 (Spring 1983): 41–65.

———. "Romanticism." In *Handbook of Russian Literature*, ed. Victor Terras, 372–76. New Haven, CT: Yale University Press, 1985.

———. "Russian Romantic Criticism: An Introduction." In *Russian Romantic Criticism: An Anthology*, ed. and trans. Lauren G. Leighton, v–xxii. New York: Greenwood Press, 1987.

Lermontov, Mikhail Iu. *Собрание сочинений в четырех томах* [Collected Works in Four Volumes]. 2nd rev. ed. Ed. V. A. Manuilov et al. Leningrad: Nauka, 1979–81.

———. *A Hero of Our Time.* Trans. Vladimir Nabokov. New York: Anchor Books, 1958.

———. *Vadim.* Trans. and ed. Helena Goscilo. Ann Arbor, MI. Ardis, 1984.

Levin, Jonathan. *The Poetics of Transition: Emerson, Pragmatism, and American Literary Modernism.* Durham, NC: Duke University Press, 1999.

Lewis, C. S. *The Discarded Image: An Introduction to Medieval and Renaissance Literature.* Cambridge: Cambridge University Press, 1964.

Lichtheim, George. "The Concept of Ideology." In *The Concept of Ideology and Other Essays*, by George Lichtheim, 3–46. New York: Vintage Books, 1967.

Lockridge, Laurence S. *The Ethics of Romanticism.* Cambridge: Cambridge University Press, 1989.

Lotman, Iurii M. "М. Ю. Лермонтов: Расстались мы, но твой портрет" [M. Iu. Lermontov: We Have Parted, but Your Portrait]. In *О поэтах и поэзии* [On Poets and Poetry], by Iu. M. Lotman, 163–72. St. Petersburg: Iskusstvo-SPB, 1996.

Lovejoy, Arthur O. "On the Discrimination of Romanticisms." In *Essays in the History of Ideas*, by Arthur O. Lovejoy, 228–53. New York: Capricorn Books, 1948.

Lucas, F. L. *The Decline and Fall of the Romantic Ideal.* New York: Macmillan, 1937.

Lyotard, Jean-François. *The Post-Modern Condition: A Report on Knowledge.* Trans. Geoff Bennington and Brian Massumi. Minneapolis: University of Minnesota Press, 1984.

Maguire, Robert. *Exploring Gogol.* Stanford, CA: Stanford University Press, 1994.

Maikov, V. A. *М. Ю. Лермонтов: Разборъ главнейших произведений.* [M. Iu. Lermontov: Selected Major Works]. St. Petersburg: Razbor", 1913.

Makogonenko, Georgii P. *Лермонтов и Пушкин: Проблемы преемственного развития литературы* [Lermontov and Pushkin: Problems of the Continued Development of Literature]. Leningrad: Sovremennyi pisatel', 1987.

Maksimov, Dmitrii E. *Поэзия Лермонтова* [Lermontov's Poetry]. Leningrad: Nauka, 1964.

Malinowski, Bronislaw. *The Dynamics of Culture Change: An Inquiry into Race Relations in Africa.* New Haven, CT: Yale University Press, 1945.

Mann, Iurii. "Завершение традиции 'Мцыри' и 'Демон' Лермонтова" [The Completion of the Tradition of Lermontov's "Mtsyri" and "The Demon"]. In *Поэтика русского романтизма* [The Poetics of Russian Romanticism], by Iurii Mann, 197–232. Moscow: Nauka, 1976.

Mannheim, Karl. *Ideology and Utopia.* Trans. Louis Wirth and Edward Shils. New York: Harcourt, Brace, 1936.

Marchand, Leslie. *Byron: A Biography.* New York: Alfred A. Knopf, 1957.

Marsh, Cynthia. "Lermontov and the Romantic Tradition: The Function of Landscape in *A Hero of Our Time.*" *Slavic and East European Review* 66, no. 1 (1988): 35–46.

Martindale, Don. *Social Life and Cultural Change.* Princeton, NJ: D. Van Nostrand, 1962.

Maturin, Charles. *Melmoth the Wanderer.* Oxford: Oxford University Press, 1968.

McGann, Jerome J. *The Romantic Ideology: A Critical Investigation.* Chicago: University of Chicago Press, 1983.

McLaughlin, Sarah. "Russia/Romanicheskij—Romanticheskij—Romantizm." In *"Romantic" and Its Cognates: The European History of a Word,* ed. Hans Eichner, 418–74. Toronto: University of Toronto Press, 1972.

Mersereau, John, Jr. "Lermontov's *Shtoss*: Hoax or Literary Credo?" *Slavic Review* 21, no. 2 (1969): 280–95.

———. *Mikhail Lermontov.* Carbondale: Southern Illinois University Press, 1962.

———. "Pushkin's Conception of Romanticism." *Studies in Romanticism* 3, no. 1 (Autumn 1963): 24–41.

———. "Romanticism or Rubbish?" *Romantic Russia* 1 (1997): 5–16.

———. *Russian Romantic Fiction.* Ann Arbor, MI: Ardis, 1983.

———. "Yes, Virginia, There Was a Russian Romantic Movement." In *The Ardis Anthology of Russian Romanticism,* ed. Christine Rydel, 511–17. Ann Arbor, MI: Ardis, 1984.

Meyer, Priscilla. "Lermontov's Reading of Pushkin: *The Tales of Belkin* and *A Hero of Our Time.*" In *The Golden Age of Russian Literature and Thought,* ed. Derek Offord, 58–75. New York: St. Martin's Press, 1992.

Mikhailova, Elena. *Проза Лермонтова* [Lermontov's Prose]. Moscow: Goslitizdat, 1957.

Miller, Robin Feuer. "The Metaphysical Novel and the Evocation of Anxiety: *Melmoth the Wanderer* and *The Brothers Karamazov,* A Case Study." In *Russianness: Studies on a Nation's Identity,* ed. Robert Belknap, 94–112. Ann Arbor, MI: Ardis, 1990.

Milner-Gulland, Robin. "Heroes of Their Time? Form and Idea in Büchner's *Danton's Death* and Lermontov's *Hero of Our Time*." In *The Idea of Freedom: Essays in Honour of Isaiah Berlin*, ed. Alan Ryan, 115–37. Oxford: Oxford University Press, 1979.

Morozov, A. A. "Загадка Лермонтовского 'Штосса'" [The Riddle of Lermontov's "Shtoss"]. *Russkaia literatura* 26, no. 1 (1983): 189–96.

Morson, Gary Saul. "Genre and Hero/*Fathers and Sons*: Inter-generic Dialogues, Generic Refugees, and the Hidden Prosaic." In "Literature, Culture, and Society in the Modern Age: In Honor of Joseph Frank," pt. 1. *Stanford Slavic Studies* 4, no. 1 (1991): 336–81.

———. *Narrative and Freedom: The Shadows of Time*. New Haven, CT: Yale University Press, 1994.

———. "Philosophy in the Nineteenth-Century Novel." In *The Cambridge Companion to the Classic Russian Novel*, ed. Malcolm V. Jones and Robin Feuer Miller, 150–68. Cambridge: Cambridge University Press, 1998.

———. "Prosaic Bakhtin: *Landmarks*, Anti-Intelligentsialism, and the Russian Counter-Tradition." *Common Knowledge* 2 (Spring 1993): 35–74.

Musset, Alfred de. *Le Confession d'un enfant du siècle* [The Confession of a Child of the Century]. Paris: Garnier Frères, 1968.

Nabokov, Vladimir. Foreword to *A Hero of Our Time*, by Mikhail Lermontov, trans. Vladimir Nabokov, v–xix. New York: Anchor Books, 1958.

Nemoianu, Virgil. *The Taming of Romanticism: European Literature and the Age of Biedermeier*. Cambridge, MA: Harvard University Press, 1984.

Neuhäuser, Rudolf. *The Romantic Age in Russian Literature: Poetic and Esthetic Norms. An Anthology of Original Texts (1800–1850)*. Munich: Sagner, 1975.

Newman, Charles. *The Post-Modern Aura: The Art of Fiction in an Age of Inflation*. Evanston, IL: Northwestern University Press, 1985.

Otzoupe, N. "Vigny's *Eloa* and Lermontov's *Demon*." *Slavic and East European Review* 34 (1955–56): 311–37.

Parsons, Talcott. "'The Intellectual': A Social Role Category." In *On Intellectuals*, ed. Philip Rieff, 3–26. New York: Doubleday, 1969.

Passage, Charles. *The Russian Hoffmannists*. The Hague: Mouton, 1963.

Peace, R. A. "The Role of *Taman'* in Lermontov's *Geroy nashego vremeni*." *Slavonic and East European Review* 45 (1967): 12–29.

Peckham, Morse. *The Triumph of Romanticism*. Columbia: University of South Carolina Press, 1970.

Picchio, Riccardo. "On Russian Romantic Poetry of Pushkin's Era." *Slavic and East European Studies* 15 (1970): 16–30.

Powelstock, David. *Becoming Mikhail Lermontov: The Ironies of Romantic Individualism in Nicholas I's Russia*. Evanston, IL: Northwestern University Press, 2005.

———. "Living into Language: Mikhail Lermontov and the Manufacturing of Intimacy." In *Russian Subjects: Empire, Nation, and the Culture of the Golden*

Age, ed. Monika Greenleaf and Stephen Moeller-Sally, 297–324. Stanford, CA: Stanford University Press, 1998.

Pratt, Sarah. *Russian Metaphysical Romanticism: The Poetry of Tiutchev and Boratynskii*. Stanford, CA: Stanford University Press, 1984.

Praz, Mario. *The Romantic Agony*. Trans. Angus Davidson. Cleveland: Meridian Books, 1956.

Proffer, Carl. "Gogol's Definition of Romanticism." *Studies in Romanticism* 6, no. 2 (Winter 1967): 120–27.

Pul'khritudova, E. "'Демон' как философская поэма" ["The Demon" as a Philosophical Narrative Poem]. In *Творчество М. Ю. Лермонтова: 150 лет со дня рождения, 1814–1964* [The Creative Works of M. Iu. Lermontov: 150 Years After His Birth, 1814–1964], 76–105. Moscow: Nauka, 1964.

Pushkin, Aleksandr Sergeevich. *Полное собрание сочинений в десяти томах* [Complete Collected Works in Ten Volumes]. 4th ed. Leningrad: Nauka, 1979.

Reed, Natasha A. "Reading Lermontov's *Geroj našego vremenni*: Problems of Poetics and Reception." Ph.D. diss., Department of Slavic Languages and Literatures, Harvard University, 1994.

Reid, Robert. "Eavesdropping in *A Hero of Our Time*." *New Zealand Slavonic Journal*, no. 1 (1997): 13–22.

———. "Lermontov's *The Demon*: Identity and Axiology." In *Russian Literature and Its Demons*, ed. Pamela Davidson, 215–39. New York: Berghahn Books, 2000.

———. "Lermontov's *Demon*: A Question of Identity." *Slavic and East European Review* 60, no. 2 (1982): 189–210.

Riasanovsky, Nicholas. *The Emergence of Romanticism*. New York: Oxford University Press, 1992.

Ridenour, George. *The Style of "Don Juan."* New Haven, CT: Yale University Press, 1960.

Ripp, Victor. "*A Hero of Our Time* and the Historicism of the 1830s: The Problem of the Whole and the Parts." *Modern Language Notes* 92 (1977): 969–86.

Rosenshield, Gary. "Fatalism in *A Hero of Our Time*: Cause or Commonplace?" In *The Supernatural in Slavic and Baltic Literature: Essays in Honor of Victor Terras*, ed. Amy Mandelker and Roberta Reeder, 83–101. Columbus, OH: Slavica Publishers, 1988.

Rowe, W. W. *Patterns in Russian Literature II: Notes on Classics*. Ann Arbor, MI: Ardis, 1988.

Rozanov, Mikhail. "Байронические мотивы в творчестве Лермонтова" [Byronic Motifs in Lermontov's Creative Works]. In *Венок М. Ю. Лермонтову* [A Garland for M. Iu. Lermontov], 343–84. Moscow: Izdatel'stvo V. V. Dumnov, 1914.

Rudwin, Maximilian. *The Devil in Legend and Literature*. 1931. Reprint, New York: AMS Press, 1970.

Russell, Bertrand. *A History of Western Philosophy, and Its Connection with Political and Social Circumstances from the Earliest Times to the Present Day.* New York: Simon and Schuster, 1945.

Russell, Jeffrey Burton. *Mephistopheles: The Devil in the Modern World.* Ithaca, NY: Cornell University Press, 1986.

Rutherford, Andrew, ed. *Byron: The Critical Heritage.* Vol. 1. London: Routledge and Kegan Paul, 1970.

Ryals, Clyde. *A World of Possibilities: Romantic Irony in Victorian Literature.* Columbus: Ohio State University Press, 1990.

Sandler, Stephanie. *Distant Pleasures: Alexander Pushkin and the Writing of Exile.* Stanford, CA: Stanford University Press, 1989.

Schiller, Friedrich. *Passion and Politics.* Translation of *Kabale und Liebe.* In *Five Plays,* trans. Robert D. MacDonald, 191–297. London: Oberon Books, 1998.

Schlegel, Friedrich von. *Lucinde and the Fragments.* Trans. Peter Firchow. Minneapolis: University of Minnesota Press, 1971.

Shatz, Marshall S., and Judith E. Zimmerman, eds. and trans. *Signposts: A Collection of Articles on the Russian Intelligentsia.* Irvine, CA: Charles Schlacks, 1986.

Shaw, Joseph T. "Lermontov's *Demon* and the Byronic Oriental Verse Tale." *Indiana Slavic Studies* 2 (1958): 165–80.

Shelley, Mary. *Frankenstein; or, The Modern Prometheus.* New York: Signet Classics, 1963.

Shelley, Percy Bysshe. *Selected Poems, Essays, and Letters.* Ed. Ellsworth Barnard. New York: Odyssey Press, 1944.

Shilstone, Frederick W. *Byron and the Myth of Tradition.* Lincoln: University of Nebraska Press, 1988.

Shuvalov, Sergei V. *М. Ю. Лермонтов: Жизнь и творчество* [M. Iu. Lermontov: Life and Artistic Works]. Moscow: Gosudarstvennoe izdatel'stvo, 1925.

Simpson, Mark S. "Lermontov's *The Demon* and Maturin's *Melmoth the Wanderer.*" *Russian Literature* 16 (1984): 275–88.

Sokolov, Aleksandr N. *Михаил Юрьевич Лермонтов* [Mikhail Iur'evich Lermontov]. 2nd ed. Moscow: Izdatel'stvo Moskovskogo Universiteta, 1957.

———. *От романтизма к реализму* [From Romanticism to Realism]. Moscow: Izdatel'stvo Moskovskogo Universiteta, 1957.

Sorokin, Pitirim A. *Social and Cultural Dynamics.* 4 vols. New York: American Book Company, 1937–41.

Sowell, Thomas. *The Vision of the Anointed: Self-Congratulation as a Basis for Social Policy.* New York: Basic Books, 1995.

Spengler, Oswald. *The Decline of the West: Form and Actuality.* Trans. Charles Francis Atkinson. New York: Alfred A. Knopf, 1926.

Stabler, Jane. "Transition in Byron and Wordsworth." *Essays in Criticism* 50, no. 4 (October 2000): 306–28.

Staël, Germaine de. *An Extraordinary Woman: Selected Writings of Germaine de Staël.* Trans. Vivian Folkenflik. New York: Columbia University Press, 1987.

Stelzig, Eugene L. *The Romantic Subject in Autobiography: Rousseau and Goethe.* Charlottesville: University Press of Virginia, 2000.

Stendhal. *Love* [*De l'amour*]. Trans. Gilbert Sale and Suzanne Sale. London: Penguin Books, 1975.

———. "Racine et Shakspeare." In *Oeuvres Complètes*, 25 vols., 16: 9–31. Paris: Pierre Larrive, 1951–54.

Terras, Victor, ed. *Handbook of Russian Literature*. New Haven, CT: Yale University Press, 1985.

Tieck, Ludwig. "The Runenberg." In *Tales by Musaeus, Tieck, Richter, in Two Volumes*, trans. Thomas Carlyle, 1: 214–35. London: Chapman and Hall, 1847.

Titov, A. A. "Khudozhestvennaia priroda obraza Pechorina" [The Artistic Nature of Pechorin's Image]. In *Проблемы реализма русской литературы XIX века* [Problems of Realism in Nineteenth-Century Russian Literature], ed. Boris I. Bursov and Il'ia Z. Serman, 76–101. Leningrad: Nauka, 1961.

Todd, William Mills III. *The Familiar Letter as a Literary Genre in the Age of Pushkin*. Princeton, NJ: Princeton University Press, 1976.

———. *Fiction and Society in the Age of Pushkin: Ideology, Institutions, and Narrative*. Cambridge, MA: Harvard University Press, 1986.

———. "A Hero of Our Time." In *The Garland Companion to Vladimir Nabokov*, ed. Vladimir Alexandrov, 178–83. New York: Garland Publishers, 1995.

Tomashevskii, Boris. "Проза Лермонтова и западно-европейская литературная традиция" [Lermontov's Prose and the Western European Literary Tradition]. *Литературное наследство* [Literary Legacy] 43–44 (1941): 469–516.

Toynbee, Arnold. *A Study of History*. London: Oxford University Press, 1945.

Trilling, Lionel. "The Meaning of a Literary Idea." In *The Liberal Imagination: Essays on Literature and Society*, by Lionel Trilling, 272–93. New York: Anchor Books, 1953.

———. *Sincerity and Authenticity*. Cambridge, MA: Harvard University Press, 1972.

Turner, C. J. G. *Pechorin: An Essay on Lermontov's "A Hero of Our Time."* Birmingham, UK: University of Birmingham, 1978.

Tymms, Ralph. *German Romantic Literature*. London: Methuen, 1955.

Udodov, Boris T. *М. Ю. Лермонтов: Художественная индивидуальность и творческие процессы* [M. Iu. Lermontov: Artistic Individualism and Artistic Creative Processes]. Voronezh: Izdatel'stvo Voronezhskogo Universiteta, 1973.

Vatsuro, Vadim E. "Последняя повесть Лермонтова" [Lermontov's Last Short Story]. In *М. Ю. Лермонтов: Исследования и материалы* [M. Iu. Lermontov: Analyses and Research Materials], ed. Mikhail P. Alekseev, A. Glasse, and Vadim E. Vatsuro, 223–52. Leningrad: Nauka, 1979.

Vigny, Alfred de. *Eloa*. In *Poèmes antiques et modernes; Les Destinées*, ed. André Jarry, 23–46. Paris: Gallimard, 1935.

Volkov, I. F. "Основные проблемы изучения романтизма" [Fundamental Problems in the Study of Romanticism]. In *К истории русского романтизма* [Toward the History of Russian Romanticism], ed. Iurii Mann et al., 5–36. Moscow: Nauka, 1973.

von Gronicka, André. "Lermontov's Debt to Goethe." *Revue de Littérature Comparée* 40 (1966): 567–84.

Wachtel, Michael. *The Development of Russian Verse: Meter and Its Meanings.* Cambridge: Cambridge University Press, 1998.

Wallace, Anthony F. C. "Paradigmatic Processes in Cultural Change." *American Anthropologist,* n.s., 74, no. 3 (June 1972): 467–78.

Walzel, Oskar. *German Romanticism.* Pt. 1, "Romantic Philosophy and Aesthetics." 1932. Reprint, New York: Capricorn Books, 1966.

Wellek, René. *Concepts of Criticism.* New Haven, CT: Yale University Press, 1963.

White, Leslie. *The Evolution of Culture: The Development of Civilization to the Fall of Rome.* New York: McGraw-Hill, 1959.

Whitehead, Alfred North. *Adventures of Ideas.* New York: Macmillan, 1933.

Wilson, James D. *The Romantic Heroic Ideal.* Baton Rouge: Louisiana State University Press, 1982.

Wordsworth, William. *The Poetical Works of Wordsworth.* Ed. Paul D. Sheats. Boston: Houghton Mifflin, 1982.

Zhirmunskii, Viktor M. *Байрон и Пушкин* [Byron and Pushkin]. Leningrad: Nauka, 1978.

Index